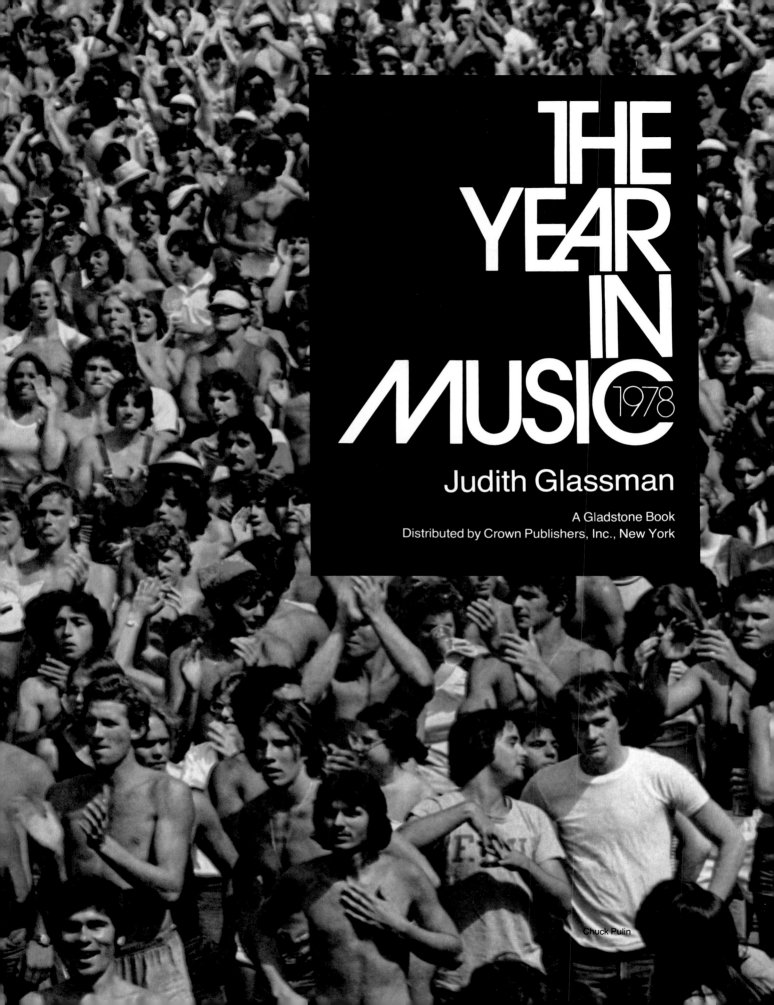

THE YEAR IN MUSIC 1978

Judith Glassman

A Gladstone Book
Distributed by Crown Publishers, Inc., New York

Chuck Pulin

ISBN 0-517-533464

Editorial Director: Ford Hovis
Designer: Allan Mogel
Photo Editor: Judith Glassman
Photo Research: Lester Glassner, Neal Peters
Contributing Editor: Toby Goldstein
Editorial Assistants: Grair Glassman, Jeanne McClow
Indexer: Lonnie Danchik

for Columbia House:
Paul A. Harris, *Vice President, Editorial Services*
Kathleen Nevils, *Manager, Editorial Services*
Joanne Loria, *Editorial Coordinator*
Frank Gesualdi, Robert J. Kasbar, *Production*

John Travolta and Olivia Newton-John in *Grease*

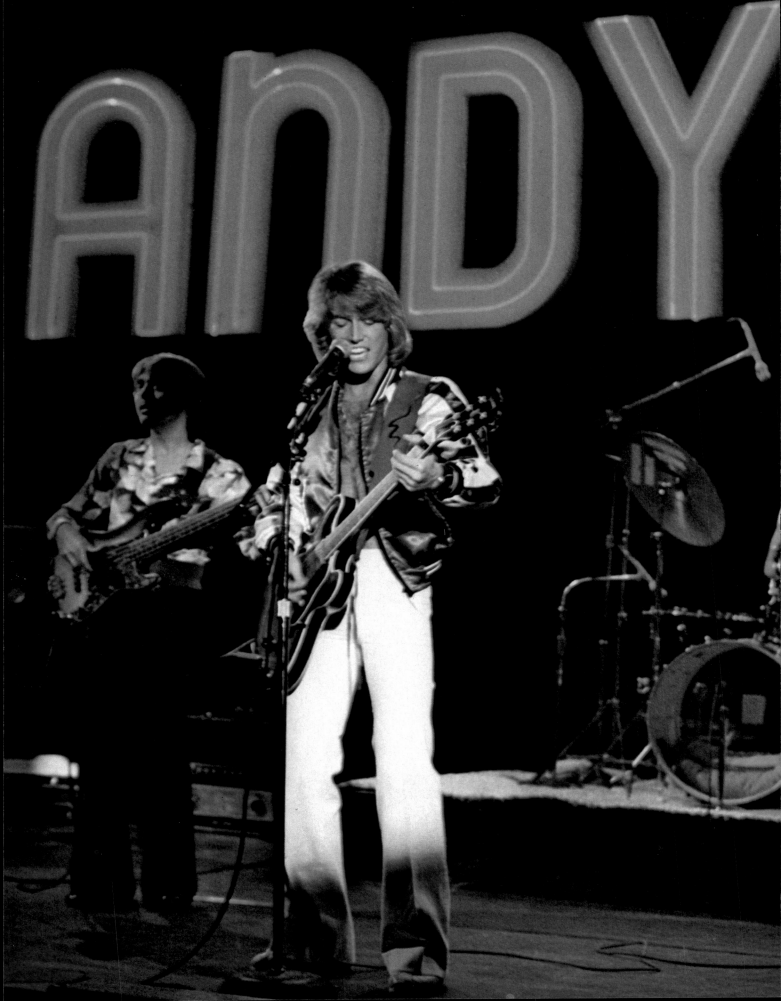

Contents

Andy Gibb
Tony Rizzo

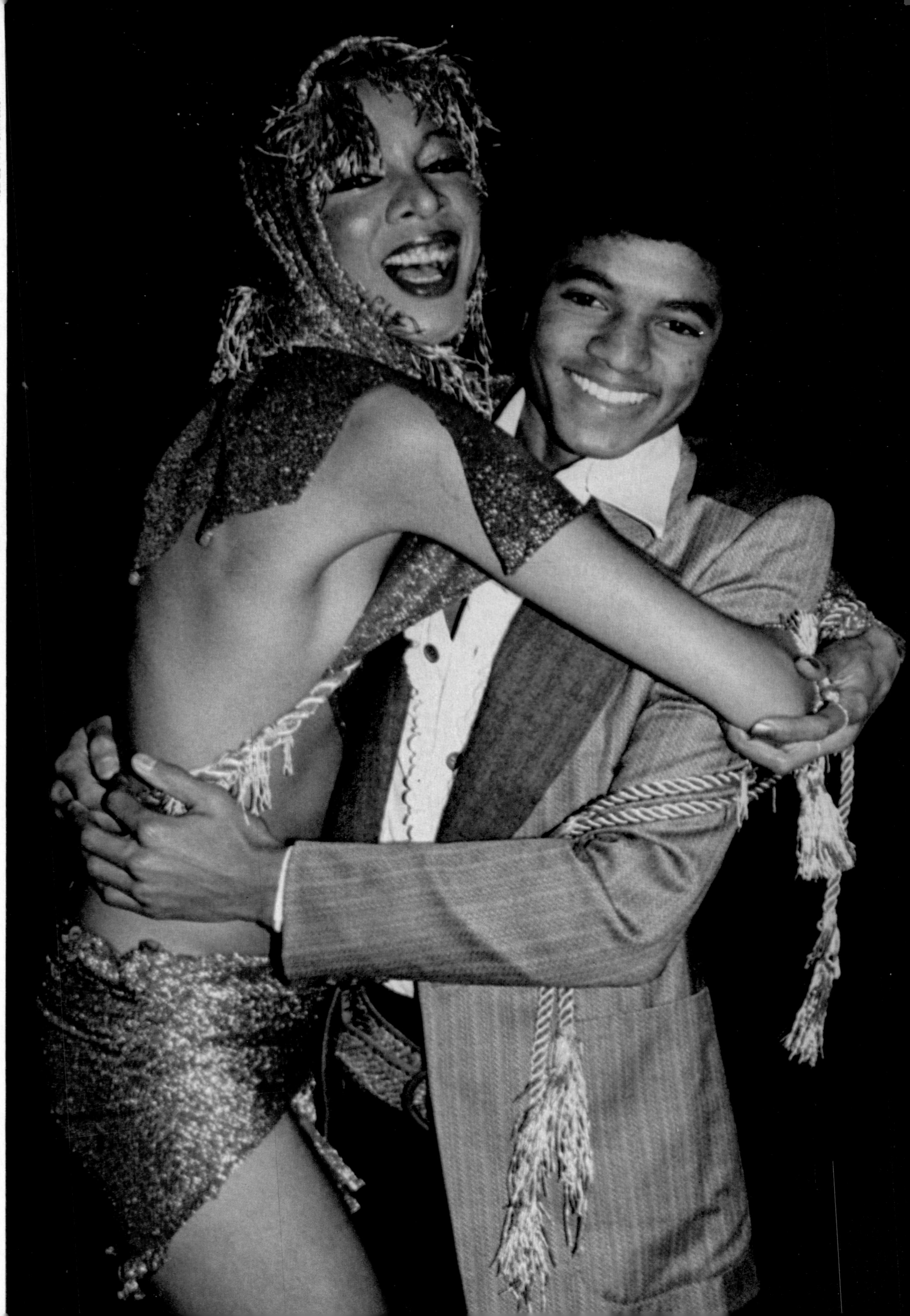

Roz Levin Perlmutter

INTRODUCTION

The year in music in 1978 was the sound of a multitude of voices on many different stages. It was Barry Gibb picking up a guitar on David Frost's "Headliners" and joining spontaneously with his brothers in the melancholy harmonies of "Massachusetts." It was President Jimmy Carter, Dizzy Gillespie, and Max Roach singing and playing a spirited "Salt Peanuts" on the south lawn of the White House. It was a no-longer-square Olivia Newton-John coolly tossing the opening lines of "You're the One that I Want" to a stunned John Travolta in *Grease*. It was Paul Simon cradling his guitar, softly playing and scat-singing phrases of his latest song-in-progress to Dick Cavett and his television viewers.

It was a radiant Vladimir Horowitz performing with an orchestra for the first time in twenty-five years, bathed in the warm adulation of a glittering Carnegie Hall audience. It was a spinning, dipping, fast-stepping crowd on the dance floor of Los Angeles's Dirty Sally's and thousands of other dance palaces across the country. It was eighty-two-year-old jazz singer Alberta Hunter at New York's Cookery, her voice clear, vital, and youthful. It was Bruce Springsteen leaping into a tightly coiled crouch to play his harmonica solo at the end of "Promised Land," dancing to his music with the ecstatic abandon of a Pan. It was Dolly Parton playing an acoustic guitar and singing her song "Coat of Many Colors" to Barbara Walters and an audience of millions. It was Mick Jagger strutting the stage with a fever of 103, slicing out the words to "Miss You" for 90,000 people in Philadelphia's JFK Stadium.

It was Rita Coolidge and Kris Kristofferson magnetized by each other's eyes, carried

Opposite: Ramona Saunders and Michael Jackson, both appearing in Motown's film version of the Broadway smash The Wiz, *share an exuberant hug at a party held during the filming.*

higher and higher on their waves of sound. It was the O'Jays' Sammy Strain heating up the women in the audience at Los Angeles's Greek Theatre. It was Willie and Waylon crooning sweetly together at the Nassau Coliseum.

It was Stevie Wonder bowing to standing bravos at the end of a magical show and then climbing into an empty box and being transformed into a cascade of flowers. It was Stevie Nicks leaping jubilantly in the air, tambourine crashing, arms waving, urging 250,000 people on a sunny California morning to join in her exultation.

Music in 1978 was a party in the house of pop, a vast celebration in which 1977's crossover trickle had become a flow. To reach the massive audience that increasingly hungered for music's captivating good time, the year's top performers sought to create sounds that were not limited by categories such as rock, rhythm and blues, country, or jazz. The top records of the year, with their heavy use of synthesizers, echoes, and layers of smoothly intertwined overdubs, all pulsing with a swingy, danceable beat, could not be categorized as anything but pop. It was music to enjoy, music that provided a snappy, breathless rush from beginning to end.

In the year 1978, music's high was pure—and it was costly, for only a few have the gift of music, and to reach the millions who craved it required the labors of many. Behind each singular performance, behind each blockbuster record, there was an army of managers, booking agents, music publishers, stagehands, road crews, record companies, sound technicians, producers, arrangers, record retailers, advertising agencies, theater-owners, promoters.

In the year 1978, that diligent army helped to raise all the numbers. Led by the record-breaking 25 million sales of the *Saturday Night Fever* album—almost double the previous high—record sales stabbed to new peaks. As the late Joel Friedman pointed out in his last speech as president of industry giant WEA, "Selling a gold album is no longer unusual." The year 1977 closed with the most explosive Christmas retail sales season ever, with retailers reporting sales increases ranging from 15 to 80 percent. Throughout 1977, record and tape dealers sold more than $3.5 billion worth of records and tapes, and continued healthy sales indicate that 1978 figures will be even higher. According to the Recording Industry Association of America, as many singles sold 2 million copies by August 1978 as had in 1976 and 1977 combined; by the end of August 1978, fifty-three albums had received platinum certification as opposed to twenty-nine during the same period in 1977.

At Columbia Records' July convention, Walter Yetnikoff, president of the CBS Records Group, projected disk sales of one billion dollars in 1978, a figure that Columbia had not expected to reach until 1980. This growth took place despite the inexorably rising costs of albums. The $6.98 list price was totally gone by 1978, and *Saturday Night Fever* was a double album with a list price of $12.98, as was the multimillion-selling *Grease*. The soundtrack album for *Sgt. Pepper's Lonely Hearts Club Band,* which shipped over a million copies to one account alone, was listed at $15.98.

In addition, sales of print music were up to $228 million in 1977, an increase of 8 percent over 1976. Musical movies and Broadway musicals did bonanza business in 1978; clubs flourished; and, except for some weakness in the very large stadiums because of a glut of

Clockwise from top: *David Frost, Robin Gibb, Robert Stigwood, Barry and Maurice Gibb meet to chat before the Gibb brothers' appearance on Frost's television show "Headliners" during the summer of 1978. Until the fall, when his 1978 album was released, Elton John enjoyed a quiet year, partying with such stars as lovely Olivia Newton-John. Debby Boone, whose "You Light Up My Life" was a record-breaking smash hit for her near the end of 1977, dances with Shaun Cassidy, whose Under Wraps was his third terrific album. For John Travolta, whose career has blossomed in the last few years, Saturday Night Fever was the spark that set off an explosion of recognition and adulation in 1978. Jimmy Carter's White House was the scene of a new musical diplomacy, including such events as Jazz at Jimmy's. Here the president greets pianist Eubie Blake.*

Waring Abbott

Paul A. Schmick, *Washington Star*

Robin Platzer, Images

Robin Platzer, Images

Robin Platzer, Images

11

major acts touring the country during the summer months, the concert scene was lively.

The best words to describe record retailers in 1978 were *more* and *bigger*. In the United States in 1978 there were some 35,000 outlets that sold records and tapes. And that number was growing. At the end of 1977, almost all major retail chains announced plans for new and larger outlets, including superstores and record supermarkets boasting 10,000 to 15,000 square feet of selling space.

In 1978, record merchandisers gleefully took advantage of new tools to lure customers in off the streets, make them stay longer, and encourage them to buy more. The most powerful of these promotional tools were videotape cassettes featuring top acts in performance. In addition, posters, mobiles, streamers, inventive displays of album covers, buttons, stand-up figures, neon signs, live deejays spinning customer requests, midnight-special sales, all caught the customers' eyes, pulled them into record stores, and urged them to buy.

Put simply, the growth of the music industry has been caused by an increase in the number of people who listen to music and buy records. In past years, record buying tapered off when customers passed out of their teens. Today, according to a survey sponsored by Warner Communications, Inc., people twenty-five and older buy 55 percent of all records and tapes; twenty to twenty-four-year-olds buy 22 percent; and teens buy 23 percent. What's more, as record buyers become more sophisticated, they are willing to listen to a wider variety of music

Ebet Roberts

Allan Tannenbaum

Lynn Goldsmith

Clockwise from upper right: *Stevie Nicks and Rod Stewart share a rare quiet moment. Vladimir Horowitz, Wanda Toscanini Horowitz, and close friend Sally Horwich greet the pianist's fans at an autographing session. Natalie Cole's shining command of the stage and records won her many new fans in 1978, driving her album* Thankful *to platinum and* Natalie Live *to gold. Opposite: A crackerjack publicist and owner Steve Rubell's personal attention guarantee that Studio 54 remains New York's hottest disco.*

Dagmar

Clockwise from top: *Andy Gibb, whose success in 1978 rivalled that of his older brothers, seen here in one of his dazzling performances. Powerhouse Rudy Isley is one reason that the Isley Brothers continually reach success, as they did in 1978 with their platinum album,* Showdown. *Bruce Springsteen opened many of his summer shows with a sizzling version of "Summertime Blues," as he did in his concert at Los Angeles's Roxy, seen here. Her steps beyond country music were shrewdly taken and in 1978 won for Dolly Parton a wide pop audience and her picture on the cover of* Playboy *magazine.*

and to explore areas that might not have appealed to them when they were younger. Several retailers point out that the deaths of Elvis Presley and Bing Crosby in 1977 drew older record customers back into stores. Because there is more mellow music to appeal to them, they often become steady customers once again.

As the numbers grow and the record buyer becomes older, music has become political in a new way. No longer does music support revolution, but in 1978 the political establishment supported music. Not only did Jimmy Carter host the White House Jazz Festival, but Vladimir Horowitz gave a full-length concert in the East Room, and the President honored the Country Music Association with a reception celebrating its twentieth birthday.

The music establishment also supports politicians, with Casablanca President Neil Bogart helping in the re-election campaign of California Governor Jerry Brown. Mike Curb, owner of Warner Brothers-distributed Curb Records, was the Republican nominee for lieutenant governor in California.

Music has also become a key to open international doors. Between late 1977 and early 1978, a number of record-company executives visited Cuba to observe its music scene. Columbia Records signed jazz fusion group Irakere, making them the first Cuban band since Castro's takeover to have a record released in the United States. Columbia Records also presented a free music festival in Havana in September at a 50,000-seat stadium. Although a scheduled Beach Boys, Santana, Joan Baez concert planned for Moscow on the Fourth of July was cancelled at the last minute, United Artists and the Soviet Union came to an agreement to exchange product, with UA selling Russian popular records in the United States and sending the Soviet Union American material to press and distribute. In addition, a group of music-business executives visited China in June and reported that the Chinese are eager to learn recording technology from the United States.

Record and tape piracy was also booming in 1978, but the illegal duplication of records and tapes was one activity about which the legitimate record industry was not happy. According to Jules Yarnell, counsel for the Recording Industry Association of America, sales of pirated material could amount to as much as $200 million a year. Not only do record companies lose sales to pirates (according to one anonymous industry executive quoted in the *New York Times,* pirated versions of *John Denver's Greatest Hits* may have sold as much as RCA's legal version), but performers and composers lose royalties, and governments lose tax revenues as well.

To deal with this global problem, representatives at 1978's International Music Industry Conference resolved to take stringent action against piracy around the world. Because duplication of records and tapes is relatively inexpensive and because there is a proven market for popular product, piracy is a difficult—but not impossible—problem to solve. In Hong Kong, where pirates once skimmed off almost half the revenue of the entire tape and record industry, a vigilant program of stepped-up enforcement has virtually halted the illicit sales.

Observing the explosive growth of popularity and revenues, some industry sources expressed fears of commercialism. Jazz impresario George Wein speaks witheringly of the rock

With a combination of the hulking yet magnetic presence of Meat Loaf, the powerful yet fragile voice of Karla Da Vito, and the grandiose rock schemes of composer Jim Steinman, Meat Loaf barreled up the charts with the platinum album Bat Out of Hell *and three singular hits: "Two Out of Three Ain't Bad," "Hot Summer Nights," and "Paradise by the Dashboard Light."*

"business" rather than of rock "music." United Artists president Artie Mogull gloomily observes in *Billboard,* "The guy in the record company who has the authority won't listen to the tape; and the guy who listens to the tape doesn't have any authority. That's a syndrome that's going to kill the record companies. The deal has become more important than music. Can you imagine? The biggest irrelevancy in a record company today is music." And in his keynote speech at *Billboard*'s eleventh annual International Programming Forum held in August, Warner Brothers Records Executive Vice President Stan Cornyn forcefully attacked the trend to pure commercialism, fearing that the drive to produce successful product will drive out experimentation.

But what all these doomsayers forget is the resiliency of the creative spirit. It is the task of the musician to create music, the task of the record company to sell it. If commercialism drives music to repetitive pap, there will arise, just as there has always arisen, an Elvis Presley with a new idea of how music should sound, a Dylan with a view of the world that no one has ever considered before, a group of young teen-agers who give themselves and neighborhood listeners the most outrageous high with musical constructions that have never occurred before.

And as sure as these sounds are born, there will be the record company executive who will somehow be coerced into hearing them, who will listen silently, and who will know that what he's hearing is inevitable, unfashionable though it may sound.

It will happen. It is happening now. It is music, and, in 1978, as always, it was ineffable and inexplicable, mere vibrations in the air with the power to cheer or sadden, to gladden and amaze, to move, to soothe, to awaken. It was the expression of an ancient art, wrapped in layers of myth, echoes of Prometheus who shares his fire anew on each fresh, darkened stage. It was glorious and inexhaustible.

THEYEAR IN M

USIC

Rock

Chuck Pulin

In the year 1978 rock was both bigger than ever, its beat the driving force behind most of the year's best-selling music, and more diluted than ever, its primal ferocity tamed by studio techniques and comprehensible lyrics. Mightiest of all the rockers, their shiny pop sound a diverting confection shrewdly blended of rock, disco, and soul, were the Bee Gees. At the end of 1977, the RSO label released "How Deep Is Your Love," the first single from *Saturday Night Fever,* and from then until August the upper stratosphere of the singles charts was dominated by the Bee Gees, their kin, their music. They ruled the airwaves with other songs from the film: "Night Fever" and the platinum monster "Stayin' Alive"; Yvonne Elliman's "If I Can't Have You"; and Tavares's treatment of "More Than a Woman." There was younger brother Andy excitedly projecting one smash after another: "Love Is Thicker than Water," the platinum "Shadow Dancing," and "An Everlasting Love." There was Samantha Sang doing their song "Emotion."

And, of course, there was the soundtrack album from *Fever* that screeched to the top of the charts in January and nested snugly there until July. With some twenty-five million copies sold, it is the biggest selling disk of all time.

The Bee Gees and their commercial bonanza can't be separated from Robert Stigwood, master manager/record company owner/film producer who rated a *Newsweek* cover story for his cool domination of the rock scene. When sales of *Saturday Night Fever* finally began to slow down in mid-1978, Stigwood was ready with the soundtrack album of *Grease,* the powerhouse film he produced. That disk also rocketed to the top of the charts, and the movie spawned one marvelous hit song after another: John Travolta and Olivia Newton-John's platinum-winner "You're the One that I Want" was followed by "Summer Nights," a second smash duet. There was also Olivia's solo, "Hopelessly Devoted to You," and Frankie Valli, in a stunning solo comeback, singing the Bee Gees' "Grease," specially written for the film.

Stigwood followed those winners with *Sgt. Pepper's Lonely Hearts Club Band,* another film and soundtrack package. Critics savaged the film, audiences stayed away, but Stigwood remained

Preceding pages: *They've had so much written about them that it's often difficult to separate the Rolling Stones' myth from the Rolling Stones' reality.* Above: *The leonine Barry Gibb, guitarist, chief songwriter, and falsetto voice of the Bee Gees, revealed to Crawdaddy reporter Greg Mitchell that it's sometimes hard for him to spend money.*

serene. The album shipped platinum, whisked to the top of the charts, and spawned three hit singles, continuing his winning streak.

Although it sometimes seemed that RSO was the only record company in existence and the Bee Gees the only band, their towering commercial success represented what was happening throughout the rock scene. Rock and roll, now a comfortable grandfather familiarly called rock, had sired disco, punk, new wave. That backbeat you can't lose was the basis for almost all the popular sounds heard during the year. A study of the top twenty-five markets made by New York's respected market research firm the McGavren-Guild showed that the rock radio audience had increased an astonishing 90 percent since 1973. Galvanized by the gigantic success of *Fever,* movie studios spewed out rock movies at breakneck speed, filling the country with the sounds and sights of *American Hot Wax, FM, I Wanna Hold Your Hand, The Last Waltz,* and *The Buddy Holly Story.* Television executives began to realize that the rock market was massive enough to rate prime-time programming. Although such an attempt as late 1977's "The *Rolling Stone* 10th Anniversary Special" was flawed, at least it was a first step, leading to Dick Clark's successful "Dick Clark's Live Wednesday."

Somehow the death of Elvis Presley on August 16, 1977, was the key to this acceleration. It was as if with his death, rock finally became totally acceptable. Suddenly a spate of advertisers began to raid the rock-and-roll coffers for commercial jingles, and such rock classics as the Beach Boys' "Fun, Fun, Fun," "California Girls," and even "Good Vibrations" were heard pushing commercial products by major manufacturers. Disco commercials based on the images from *Saturday Night Fever* were the summer's most common advertising spots. In May, the National Academy of Recording Arts and Sciences, long criticized for ignoring rock, set up a committee to study the possibility of establishing separate rock categories for the Grammy awards.

The top rock albums were almost all million-sellers. Closing out 1977 were the stupendous *Rumours* by Fleetwood Mac and the album that finally knocked Fleetwood's monster out of first place, *Simple Dreams* by Linda Ronstadt. Leading into 1978, there was *Aja* by Steely Dan, *Elvis in Concert* by Elvis Presley, and *Foot Loose and Fancy Free* by Rod Stewart. The last leaped to the number two spot on the record charts in its second week of release—but, like

The other two-thirds of the Bee Gees, Maurice (left) and Robin (above) can join Barry in recalling a career that began almost twenty-three years ago, when they were youngsters in Australia. Their first success in the United States was 1967's plaintive "New York Mining Disaster, 1941."

Lynn Goldsmith

Robin Platzer, Images

Waring Abbott

Opposite: *John Travolta added rock to his successes in 1978 thanks to two smash duets with Olivia Newton-John from* Grease. *Above: Linda Ronstadt scored in 1978 with Chuck Berry's "Back in the USA." Left: Andy Gibb.*

27

Opposite: *Queen's Freddie Mercury performs at Madison Square Garden at the end of 1977. Queen's American tour was climaxed by the platinum awards won by* News of the World *and "We Are the Champions." Above:* Rod Stewart *won platinum success in 1978 with* Foot Loose and Fancy Free.

so many others that banged up against the immovable Brothers Gibb, it could never make it to the top spot. There was Lynyrd Skynyrd's *Street Survivors, Out of the Blue* by ELO, *News of the World* by Queen, *The Stranger* by Billy Joel, *Running on Empty* by Jackson Browne, *Slowhand* by Eric Clapton, *The Grand Illusion* by Styx, *Point of Know Return* by Kansas, *Earth* by Jefferson Starship, *London Town* by Wings, *Showdown* by the Isley Brothers, and *City to City* by Gerry Rafferty, the album that finally knocked *Saturday Night Fever* from first place.

There was also the soundtrack album from *FM, Some Girls* by the Rolling Stones, *Stranger in Town* by Bob Seger and the Silver Bullet Band, *Darkness on the Edge of Town* by Bruce Springsteen, *Shadow Dancing* by Andy Gibb, *Double Vision* by Foreigner, *Bat Out of Hell* by Meat Loaf, *But Seriously, Folks* by Joe Walsh, and *The Album* by ABBA.

These albums were filled with dynamic music, but the real excitement of 1978 was in the growing tension between those top disks, with their overdubbing and creamy studio polish, and the raw, hungry voices of the new wave, inheritors of the punk mantle. And punk, for all its hype and subsequent disappointment, was very real, a continuation of the rebellious energy that radiated from the early Elvis Presley, the revolutionary fervor that has always been part of rock and roll.

The punk global media barrage began at the end

Lynn Goldsmith

Opposite: *Eric Clapton's onstage seriousness is an indication of the way he regards his music.* Top: *Billy Joel's 1978 platinum-winner,* The Stranger, *was a top-charted album for months.* Above: *Kansas has good reason to clown; in 1978,* Point of Know Return, *featuring the smash single "Dust in the Wind," became their second double platinum album.*

of 1977. Punk inspired an avalanche of publicity releases, newspaper articles, and television coverage of the British scene. Every record label rushed out to seize its own punk artists. In America, the most heavily hyped group was a British band, the Sex Pistols. For months before their American tour, the country was regaled with stories about how their single "God Save the Queen" was banned from radio play in England, how disgusting they were in person, how their concerts degenerated into rowdy riots. In London, a record shop manager was charged with four counts of displaying indecent printed matter for showing the Pistols' album *Never Mind the Bollocks, Here's the Sex Pistols* in his window. He was found not guilty.

Tension built when rumors began to surface that the band wouldn't be able to gain entry into the United States because three of the group had arrest records. After months of such preparation, when Johnny Rotten and his crew finally appeared in America for the first time at the Great Southeast Music Hall in Atlanta, Georgia, on January 5, the concert was something of an anticlimax. The Pistols performed a rousing if repetitive set for the enthusiasts who packed the club. Front row fans reported some spitting, but no deluge. Reaction here could only be called tepid, inspiring neither Britain's adoring frenzy nor the vehemence of Israel's radio listeners, who voted "God Save the Queen" the worst single of 1977. At the end of the tour, Johnny Rotten, undeniably the best performer of the Pistols, left the band, which then broke up. In October, Sid Vicious, former Pistols' bass player, was arrested for the alleged murder of his girlfriend.

When the Sex Pistols' tour fizzled, it seemed to be the end of punk. Despite the hype, there had been no hit record in America, and a January report from the music industry's Midem convention at Cannes indicated that punk's international disk sales were poor. A number of punk clubs throughout America ran into difficulties: On December 30, the New York Fire Department closed down a sold-out show at Hilly Kristal's CBGB Theatre because of overcrowding; on January 17, the Los Angeles Fire Department closed L.A.'s only all-punk club, the Masque, because it had no fire exits; on March 16, Philadelphia's Hot Club caught fire; on April 27 Chicago's La Mère Vipere, a punk disco, was destroyed by flames; and, in July, The Whiskey in Los Angeles changed its policy from booking punk groups to bringing in more popular acts.

But, of course, punk was not dead at all. The music in its pure form was very much alive in New York's East Village, and the Clash, now Britain's prime punk band, continued to jam halls throughout England. In addition, two of the seminal names of the rock rebellion, Lou Reed and Patti Smith, were very much in evidence. Both had new albums. Reed, who began his protests back in the late sixties with the Velvet Underground, had *Street Hassle,* arguably his best album, but largely unplayed because of its street language. Patti Smith, whose album *Easter* was a best-seller, faced the difficult problem of reconciling her underground anarchy with her aboveground success.

The word punk and its connotations—safety pins pushed through cheeks, spitting at concerts, green-dyed hair, and heavy dog collars—were repugnant to most. But the punks' attempts at firecracker crisp, live rock and roll were renamed new wave. And new wave effortlessly won the good press, enthusiastic reviews, and audience response that punk had failed to earn. New wave in 1978 was hard-edged, pared down, swift, and sturdy. It was the Ramones, Talking Heads, Mink de Ville, Elvis Costello, Nick Lowe, Graham Parker, Richard Hell. New wave expression was also passionate individualist exhortation, as in such songs as the Dictators' "Stand Tall," Elizabeth Barraclough's "Who Do You Think's the Fool," Tom Robinson's gay anthem "Sing If You're Glad to Be Gay."

Despite punk, new wave, and other variations, rock and roll in 1978 was still the Rolling Stones. Shrugging off all pretenders, they showed strong evidence that they still deserve to be called the greatest rock-and-roll band in the world. Their 1978 album, *Some Girls,* was their seventh LP to reach the top of the charts, tying them with Elton John for second place in the race for the most number-one LPs. (The Beatles, still far ahead, had fifteen top-charted albums between 1964 and 1973.)

They wouldn't be the Stones without some controversy. Soul stations dropped the title single when they heard its derogatory reference to black women. Some other women, notably Lucille Ball, objected so strenuously to the use of their faces on the cover of the album that a new cover was struck, making the original a collector's item.

If the album wasn't rock and roll enough, there was the tour, with concerts jamming in either 90,000 people at one of the larger events (on July 13 the Stones broke an indoor attendance record at the New Orleans Superdome when 80,173 people bought $12.50 to $15.00 tickets to see them there) or jamming in only a

Opposite: *1978's hottest star, John Travolta keeps developing his acting talents to ensure a long career. Films on tap for the star of* Saturday Night Fever *and* Grease *are* Moment by Moment, *with Lily Tomlin,* American Gigolo, *and* Conversations with the Vampire.

Robin Platzer, Images

Opposite: *Country star Mel Tillis triumphed again in 1978 with such hit songs as "What Did I Promise Her Last Night" and "I Believe in You." Far from being an impediment, Tillis's stutter serves only to endear him to fans.* Above: *Mick Jagger wails onstage at Philadelphia's JFK Stadium during the Rolling Stones' sometimes controversial but always successful 1978 American tour.*

Clockwise from right: *Teen heartthrob Shaun Cassidy claims he has no time for any one special relationship. Dynamic singer Rita Coolidge spent the year touring with husband Kris Kristofferson, cutting her new album* Love Me Again, *and enjoying her growing success. Released in England at the end of 1977, the song "Mull of Kintyre" by Paul McCartney became Britain's biggest single of all time. Opposite: Sizzling songstress Bette Midler knocked 'em in the aisles in night clubs from coast to coast. She also starred in the film* The Rose.

Their demonic onstage behavior often overshadows the dedication of Kiss, who strive to give their audiences an unforgettable experience at every show. Early in 1978, the band decided to take a break from touring and group recording, instead offering their fans solo albums and a television special, "Kiss Meets the Phantom."

Courtesy The Press Office

few thousand at the more intimate halls, such as Passaic, New Jersey's, Capitol Theatre or Washington D.C.'s Warner Theatre. In Washington, 2,000 lucky fans somehow heard it through the grapevine that the Stones were going to perform and waited on line from 4 A.M. Few who saw the Stones were disappointed, although fans at Rich Stadium in Buffalo and JFK Stadium in Philadelphia rushed the stage and threw bottles when an ailing Mick Jagger —who normally disdains encores anyway—refused to do any encores.

Because of such mayhem and other incidents, such as the hurling of cherry bombs and Roman candles at a Foghat concert in St. Paul, Minnesota, security searches of rock patrons before large concerts continued in 1978. In Hawaii at the end of 1977, Judge Arthur S. K. Fong ruled that such searches were illegal, but his decision was overturned in January by State Circuit Judge Yasukata Fukushima, who declared searches necessary for public safety, referring to a pre-concert search that had uncovered a loaded gun.

In many American rock venues patrons were asked to show the contents of purses and packages voluntarily. If they refused, they were frequently denied admission to the concert and their money was returned. The ACLU continued to battle against searches, the Indiana branch filing a class-action suit in Fort Wayne against the Allen County War Memorial Coliseum.

No violence marred the well-planned, beautifully executed mammoth musical extravaganza of 1978, Cal Jam II. On March 18, some quarter of a million people poured into the Ontario Speedway at Ontario, California, making the speedway the seventh-largest city in California. For fifteen hours fans soaked up the sunshine and the music of such top-name hard rockers as Bob Welch, Dave Mason, Santana, Heart, Ted Nugent, Foreigner, and Aerosmith, enjoying the world's biggest sound system (108,000-watt speakers, a total of forty-six tons of equipment). The day was a success from its beginning at 9:45 in the morning when Bob Welch was joined by a vivacious Stevie Nicks, who, despite the early hour, bounced enthusiastically around the stage, urging the audience awake.

The bands that followed obviously had an equally extraordinary time, picking up energy from the crowd and feeding it back to them in an escalating love affair between performers and audience. Ted Nugent, who grinningly told interviewers from Metromedia, "This is what rock and roll is designed to do. Pound city is the place to be," performed a ferocious set. Ann Wilson

prowled the stage in her seven-league boots, high-kicking and singing up a storm; Steven Tyler of Aerosmith flailed his microphone stand and electrified the audience; and Foreigner blasted its dynamic electronics.

No other United States festival was nearly so large; in England, however, on July 15, Bob Dylan attracted 250,000 Britons to an abandoned World War II airfield at Blackbushe, near London. His open-air concert, officially called "The Picnic" was a twelve-hour treat and grossed $2 million. Preceded by strong performances from Eric Clapton, Graham Parker and Rumour, and Joan Armatrading, Dylan performed such classics as "Blowin' in the Wind," "Don't Think Twice It's All Right," "Subterranean Homesick Blues," "Rolling Stone," "Masters of War," and "Gates of Eden" in a thrilling three-hour set. The event was part of Dylan's avidly welcomed international tour in 1978, the longest continuous series of performances in his career. He and a firecracker back-up band began in Japan on February 20, swung through Australia and New Zealand, touched down in California's Universal Amphitheatre for seven performances beginning June 1, appeared in London and throughout Europe during June and July, and ended with three months of concerts throughout the United States and Canada, beginning September 15 in Augusta, Maine, and ending December 16 in Miami, Florida.

His performances were greeted with pleased surprise by critics who were flabbergasted by his new friendly image and dazzled by brilliant reworkings of his old songs. The critics were less entranced by his new album, *Street Legal,* but despite mixed reviews the disk swiftly sold half a million copies.

Rock and roll in 1978 was the trimphant return of Bruce Springsteen. His juggernaut concert tour with the fabulous E Street Band was a sold-out exaltation that inspired a piece by Dave Marsh in the August 24 *Rolling Stone* that's perhaps the finest piece of writing about rock and roll ever done. You can almost dance to it. Springsteen's new album, *Darkness on the Edge of Town,* was a howl from the soul, effective if ponderous. It was a studio album, however, and anyone who has been to a Springsteen concert and heard the awesome power of his guitar (he, alone, is a wall of sound), knows that only a live recording can capture the stunning vitality and drive of his music.

Other rock-and-roll bands took to the road with shows of crackling electricity and visuals. Lasers knifed through every performance, and the Food and Drug

Opposite: *Earth, Wind and Fire's Maurice White belts out one of the band's energetic numbers in concert at Madison Square Garden. The Garden was but one stop on a fabulously successful nationwide tour to support their powerhouse album* All 'n All.

41

Dagmar

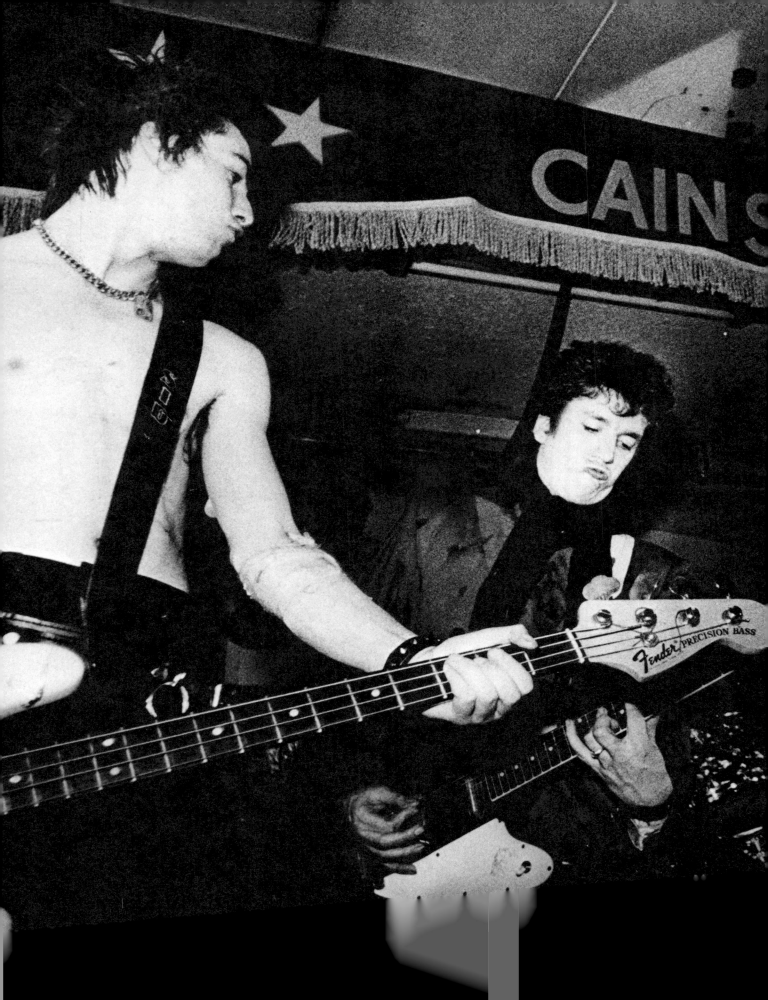

Preceding pages: *In the year 1978, the face of punk evolved into new wave. The Sex Pistols, hyped heavily by the media, could not possibly live up to expectations.* Opposite: *Patti Smith, one of the seminal voices of punk, saw her success reach new heights in 1978 with her album* Easter *and hit single "Because the Night."* Above: *Elvis Costello is one face of future rock.*

Administration nervously warned Blue Öyster Cult to tone down its beams. In the rock spectacle of the year, the Electric Light Orchestra provided space-age thrills with their very own flying saucer.

As the closed saucer lid lifted, flashes of laser light zipped through the audience. Onstage, ELO had no wires—new audio pickups enabled them to move freely. Other rockers who thrilled the nation were Shaun Cassidy—who began his show with brilliant lights flashing through a cloud of fog—Andy Gibb, Aerosmith, Fleetwood Mac, the Eagles, the Doobie Brothers, Crosby, Stills and Nash, the Grateful Dead, Genesis, Kansas, REO Speedwagon, Bob Seger, and, until Grace Slick became ill, the Jefferson Starship.

The big rock songs of the year included hard rockers, soft ballads, some R & B tunes, some disco-oriented pulsers. In addition to the Bee Gees' blitz, other hits were Rod Stewart's "You're In My Heart," Randy Newman's controversial "Short People," Player's "Baby Come Back," Paul Simon's "Slip Slidin' Away," Queen's "We Are the Champions," Eric Clapton's "Lay Down Sally," "Roberta Flack's "The Closer I Get to You," Kansas's "Dust in the Wind," Wings' "With a Little Luck," Gerry Rafferty's "Baker Street," Bonnie Tyler's "It's a Heartache," ABBA's "Take a Chance on Me," Carly Simon's "You Belong to Me," Sweet's "Love Is Like Oxygen," Bob Seger's "Still the Same," the Rolling Stones' "Miss You," and Foreigner's "Hot Blooded."

Rock's long history was showing in 1978, and the year was full of musical nostalgia. At the beginning of December 1977, at San Francisco's Boarding House, Roger McGuinn, Gene Clark, David Crosby, and Chris Hillman, four-fifths of the original Byrds, sang together, recreating their sweet 1960s sounds. Linda Ronstadt began the year singing Buddy Holly's "It's So Easy," and Holly's life and music were captured in the film, *The Buddy Holly Story. Grease* and *American Hot Wax* also looked back to the 1950s.

On April 15 and 16, America's first rock-and-roll convention was held at Philadelphia's Sheraton Hotel. Called Music Expo '78, the jam-packed event included a million-dollar collection of rock-and-roll memorabilia, a Rock 'n' Roll Video Room, an exhibit called Ten Years of Live Rock, prepared by Philadelphia's leading concert hall, the Electric Factory, and many seminars.

Neil Young released *Decade,* a collection of his greatest songs, including such classic mellow rockers as "After the Gold Rush," "Cinnamon Girl," "Southern Man," and some of his songs for the Buffalo

Opposite: *Elizabeth Barraclough, a passionate new voice on the rock scene, projects intensity as well as lyricism.* Above: *The Tom Robinson Band rocks hard, much of its music conveying fierce social and political messages.* Following pages: *The ever-chic David Bowie roused audiences in a 1978 tour of the United States.*

Robin Platzer, Images

Springfield, such as "Burned," "Mr. Soul," "Broken Arrow," and "Expecting to Fly." Peter, Paul and Mary reunited after a separation of eight years to record a new album called *Reunion.*

Lonnie Donegan, one of England's original skiffle rockers, created a new album called *Puttin' on the Style.* He was joined in the studio by such luminaries as Elton John, Ringo Starr, Ron Wood, Leo Sayer, Rory Gallagher, Albert Lee, Klaus Voorman, and Nicky Hopkins. Produced by Adam Faith, the album included updates of some of Donegan's early hits, such as "Rock Island Line" and "I Wanna Go Home."

Summing it all up, record producers Richard Perry and Mark Carline spent most of the year preparing a six-hour television special called "Solid Gold...the Birth of Rock 'n' Roll," shown on CBS-TV at the end of the year.

In August of 1978, millions of people around the nation observed the first anniversary of the death of Elvis Presley. Still grieved by his passing, his fans descended on Memphis to view his grave and attend a memorial concert, flocked to Las Vegas for the first "Always Elvis" festival, watched reruns of his films in theaters and on television, and listened to his songs on radio.

Chuck Pulin

51

Lynn Goldsmith

Preceding pages: *Some
ninety thousand fans saluted
the Big Beat when the Rolling
Stones performed at JFK Stadium
in Philadelphia on June 17.*
Opposite: *Heart's Ann
Wilson can command a
stage with sizzling
rock intensity.*
Left: *When some
critics accused* Darkness
on the Edge of Town *of being
sorrowful, Bruce Springsteen
responded with onstage
performances that
were pure joy.*

53

Above: *His combination of good looks, enthusiasm, and seasoned professionalism has helped Shaun Cassidy achieve at an early age the kind of success many older performers would envy. Despite the overwhelming response he has received, Shaun manages to keep everything in proper perspective, knowing that if he wants fame to last he must grow continually. On his 1978 album,* Under Wraps, *Shaun abandons the 1950s rock 'n' roll hits that first brought him fame, showing that he is more than simply a repackager. Opposite: Meat Loaf is a force of nature. His whirlwind of a voice and his cyclonic stage presence are at the heart of his band's 1978 success.*

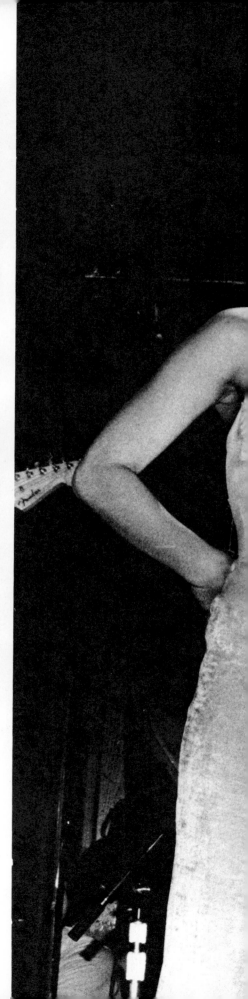

Rhythm and Blues

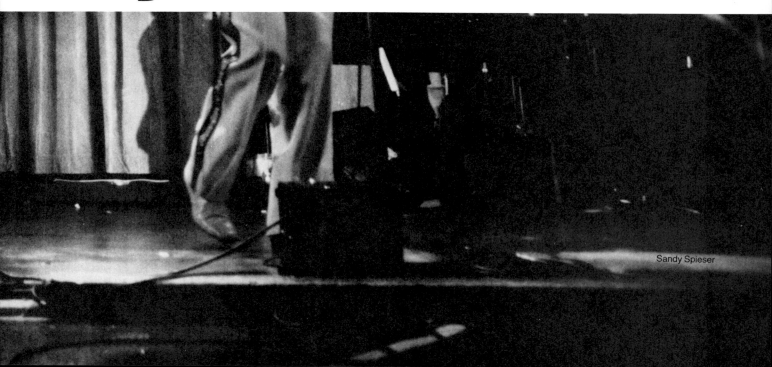

Sandy Spieser

The infectious bounce of rhythm and blues in 1978 was spearheaded by the dynamic success of such platinum-winning albums as the Commodores' *Natural High,* Teddy Pendergrass's *Life Is a Song Worth Singing,* Natalie Cole's *Thankful,* Earth, Wind and Fire's *All 'n All,* the Isley Brothers' *Showdown,* Johnny Mathis's *You Light Up My Life,* the O'Jays' *So Full of Love,* and Rose Royce's *In Full Bloom.* In 1978, the soul music scene flashed with abundant vitality.

Black concerts this year were dynamite. There was the suave Lou Rawls appearing at New York's Mark Hellinger Theatre for two weeks beginning November 23, 1977. While other artists might travel by limousine or arrive in space ships, Lou sailed in on the Anheuser-Busch beer wagon, drawn by its six Clydesdale horses. He maintained that old-fashioned elegance in concerts that included tributes to Nat King Cole, Duke Ellington, and Louis Armstrong. Earth, Wind and Fire brought their magical stage show to sold-out auditoriums and arenas all over the country. Patti LaBelle sizzled at New York's Radio City Music Hall on January 27. King of funk George Clinton and Parliament/Funkadelic, his hard-working princes of that realm, zapped their audiences with ray guns, bombarded them with a flashily inventive stage show, and blasted them with nonstop R & B energy of the funk variety. Eddie Kendricks was a class act as he zipped through his numbers at Los Angeles's Roxy on March 8.

R & B in 1978 was Rose Royce, the Bar-Kays, Con Funk Shun, and Stargard showing L.A.'s Forum what smooth and slick soul music was all about. Rufus and Chic were at New York's Felt Forum on April 22, where they belted out one flaming number after another. Rufus featured a more dynamic than ever Chaka Khan, who gracefully shared center stage with lead guitarist Tony Maiden. R & B queen Natalie Cole belted out songs with her inimitable command of the stage; Gladys Knight poured forth soulful gladness with dynamic energy. Stevie Wonder in one or two rare appearances, as always, provided magical, unforgettable performances of genius. Smokey Robinson packed New York's Felt Forum, along with Brass Construction, Brainstorm, and young, exciting, Evelyn "Champagne" King.

R & B included reggae, most notably the rhythmically potent music of Bob Marley and the Wailers. It also included the newly liberated Tina Turner, socking it to her audiences with a blistering song and dance show; the dynamite charge of the Commodores; and the O'Jays' complex yet simple, soaring yet regretful work of art "Use Ta Be My Girl."

But there were problems to be faced as well. Although many top soul recordings were also pop smashes, in 1978 the black community faced the growing need to attract white audiences to their performances. As Benjamin Ashburn, president of Commodore Entertainment Corporation, pointed out, "We're still playing to an 80 percent to 90 percent black audience, yet we sell records across the board." Some observers blamed the reluctance of white fans to attend black concerts on bad press. Any disturbances at black concerts are overemphasized by the media, and both whites and middle-class blacks are fearful of incidents. But in order for black music to take part in crossover, black concerts must attract a racially mixed audience.

In response to this need, black leaders of the music industry put their heads together and began organizing to promote black music. The most powerful of the new organizations is the Black Music Association, conceived by songwriter/producer Kenny Gamble and public relations expert Ed Wright.

Patterned after the Country Music Association, the Black Music Association is concerned with getting black music heard by more people than ever before. Executive Director Glenda Gracia feels that the best way to accomplish this, as she explained it to *Billboard* reporter Jean Williams, is "through the back door." The association's plans include image-building through a black music museum and a black music hall of fame, educational programs aimed at interesting black youngsters in the business side of the music industry, and television programming to show black music at its best.

The dynamic head of the new group is Jules Malamud, former director of the National Association of Record Merchandisers. Although many questioned the wisdom of choosing a white man to lead a black organization, the choice was evidently the right one, as Malamud speedily gathered supportive donations of $500,000 from record labels.

Preceding pages: *If any band symbolized the musical mood of 1978 it was the O'Jays, who traded in their faintly paranoid edge for the purely good-timey* So Full of Love. Right: *With a platinum album for* Life Is a Song Worth Singing, *Teddy Pendergrass was a hot R & B star in 1978.*

Dagmar

The National Progressive Communications Association is the brainchild of a group of southern disk jockeys. Originally called the Irresistible 14 after the fourteen deejays who formed it, this association is headed by Joe Medlin, vice-president of promotion for Brunswick Records. The major aim of this group is to be an information and service organization for the black music community, offering a credit union, an insurance plan, scholarships, and special workshops for young blacks entering the business.

Because of the need to grow, in 1978 the black music community began to become more conscious of black music's long history and rich tradition. Oldies concerts at Philadelphia's Shubert Theatre attracted a mixed audience of black and white, young and old, to hear groups like the Flamingos, the Drifters, Little Anthony, the Tymes, and Ben E. King. A company called Memory Lane Productions in Atlanta, Georgia, began production of a series of programs called "Souldie," featuring the best R & B hits of the past forty years. The Four Tops began work on a new album, persuading top Motown producers Holland-Dozier-Holland, who had not worked together for the past seven years, to produce them. John Lee Hooker released a new album of his classic songs,

recorded live at Palo Alto's Keynote club. The fabulous Aretha Franklin returned to Las Vegas after an absence of seven years and socked out a sizzling performance at the Aladdin Hotel on June 21. Aretha, who married actor Glynn Turman in April, was featured in an August segment of "Hot City," a television disco program. Unfortunately, Aretha's year was somewhat marred by cancellations and a sullen performance she gave at a special tribute to her held on July 9 at Reve Gibson's eighteenth annual Youth on Parade program at L.A.'s Good Shepherd Baptist Church. Surrounded by an impressive audience of friends and music-business luminaries and preceded by jubilant, spontaneous performances of spiritual music by such performers as Deniece Williams, Linda Hopkins, and Patti Williams, Aretha sang only when pushed to do so, and her performance was dull and lifeless.

Stevie Wonder, whose new album—tentatively called *The Secret Life of Plants*—not yet released at this writing, was represented by a limited-edition three-record set called *Looking Back,* which included many of his famous past hits and several never before available on record.

The black image suffered a small setback at this year's annual NAACP Awards. The presentations were

Roz Levin Perlmutter

Opposite: *When Rudy Isley tears into a song he brings to it an abundance of fresh energy as well as the polished professionalism of years of experience.* Above: *Funkster George Clinton in two of his guises: nomadic outer-space ace and slick-as-silk con man.*

Opposite: *George Duke brings together elements of jazz and R & B in his music.* Left: *One of the reasons for the success of the film* Thank God It's Friday *was the dynamic performance of one of 1978's hottest R & B bands, the Commodores.* Below: *Caught together backstage at the Grammy Awards are three of the year's hottest stars: Lou Rawls, Natalie Cole, and jazz/R & B fusion artist, the inimitable George Benson.*

Robin Platzer, Images

Roz Levin Perlmutter

ineptly handled and the show was so tedious that, despite performers of the caliber of Stevie Wonder, Deniece Williams, and Linda Hopkins and presenters of the stature of Donna Summer, Thelma Houston, Barbara McNair, Cicely Tyson, and Sidney Poitier, by the last act almost everyone had gone home. The NAACP announced that there would be no awards given in 1979.

Bootsy Collins and George Clinton received rather dubious awards on July 21 at a dinner sponsored by The Rod McGrew Scholarship Fund, Inc. Communicators with a Conscience gave them a slap on the wrist with the responsibility award, challenging the musicians to do something more ambitious with their popular music. Archie Ivy, managing director of Clinton's production company (called Thang, Inc.) disputes the award's contention that Clinton's message is superficial. He claims that in *Funkentelechy vs. the Placebo Syndrome* Clinton is conveying a deep message against complacency and lack of spirit. He also pledged to donate fifty cents for every ticket sold for August and September concerts in Dallas, Chicago, St. Louis, and L.A. to the United Negro College Fund.

One award that was unequivocally serious, and joyful, was the grand prize given to Al Green at the Seventh Tokyo Music Festival on June 17. Green won the $14,000 prize with his stirring version of "Belle," beating out fifteen other performers, including Debby Boone, who won the gold prize. It was a second triumph for Green following his fiery concert at Los Angeles's Dorothy Chandler Pavilion on February 13, which had been declared Al Green Day in L.A.

In addition to sizzling live action, the soul scene blossomed with extravagant albums, including such winners as *Barry White Sings for Someone You Love; Brick* by Brick; *Something to Love* and *Togetherness* by L.T.D.; *Too Hot to Handle* and the platinum-winning *Central Heating,* both by Heatwave; *Feelin' Bitchy* by Millie Jackson; *Reach for It* and *Don't Let Go* by George Duke; *Funkentelechy vs. the Placebo Syndrome* by Parliament; the reverse crossover of *Saturday Night Fever* by the Bee Gees; *Live at the Bijou* by jazz saxophonist Grover Washington, Jr.; *Weekend in L.A.* by George Benson; *Blue Lights in the Basement* by Roberta Flack; *Player of the Year* by Bootsy's Rubber Band; *Street Player* by Rufus and Chaka Khan; *Sounds* by Quincy Jones; *Come Get It* by Rick James & the Stone City Band; and *A Taste of Honey* by Taste of Honey.

Dagmar

Courtesy A & M Records

David Gahr

Courtesy Arista Records

Opposite: *Chaka Khan of Rufus shows the onstage energy that has made her a star.* Clockwise from upper left: *Roberta Flack had a 1978 winner with* Blue Lights in the Basement. *Quincy Jones scored the soundtrack for* The Wiz. *Ray Parker heads up the group Raydio.*

Waring Abbott

Top soul songs for the year included "Serpentine Fire" by Earth, Wind and Fire, "Back in Love Again" by L.T.D., "You Can't Turn Me Off (In the Middle of Turning Me On)" by High Inergy, "Dusic" by Brick, "It's Ecstasy When You Lay Down Next to Me" by Barry White, "If We're Not Back in Love by Monday," Millie Jackson's country crossover, "Ffun" by Con Funk Shun, "Reach for It" by George Duke, "Ooh Boy" by Rose Royce, "Our Love" by Natalie Cole, "Galaxy" by War, "Which Way Is Up" by Stargard, "Always and Forever" by Heatwave, "Too Hot ta Trot" by the Commodores, "Jack and Jill" by Raydio, "It's You that I Need" by Enchantment, "Flash Light" by Parliament, "Stayin' Alive " by the Bee Gees, "Bootzilla" by Bootsy's Rubber Band, "The Closer I Get to You" by Roberta Flack and Donny Hathaway, "Too Much, Too Little, Too Late" by Johnny Mathis and Deniece Williams, "Dance with Me" by Peter Brown, "On Broadway" by George Benson, "Take Me to the Next Phase" by the Isley Brothers, "Stay" by Rufus and Chaka Khan, "The Grooveline" by Heatwave, "Use ta Be My Girl" by the O'Jays, "Close the Door" by Teddy Pendergrass, "Runaway Love" by Linda Clifford, "Dukey Stick" by George Duke, "Annie Mae" by Natalie Cole, "Stuff Like That" by Quincy Jones, "You and I" by Rick James, "Boogie Oogie Oogie" by Taste of Honey, "Last Dance" by Donna Summer, and "Three Times a Lady" by the Commodores.

Above: *R & B star Eddie Kendricks displays the magnetism that won him fans when he was part of the smash group the Temptations.* Right: *For Bootsy Collins and his band of renown 1978 was a year of superior, flashy concerts in support of his gold-winning R & B chart-topper* Player of the Year.

Paul Cox/L.F.I.

Opposite: *Robin, Maurice, and Barry Gibb created music in 1978 that appealed to a wide range of listeners, winning the Bee Gees places on the pop, R & B, and disco charts. Above: For Bob Marley, with a new group of Wailers, 1978 was a year of bold musical attempts to unite the warring political factions within his country, as well as a year of love songs in his album, Kaya.*

Country
and Western

David Gahr

In April, Jimmy Carter hosted a party for the Country Music Association at the White House; as he introduced such country charmers as Loretta Lynn, Conway Twitty, Tom T. Hall, and Larry Gatlin, he announced, "When I come back to the White House from a long day at the oval office, I often put on country music. It reminds me of home and my roots."

Soaring country sales figures make it seem that the nation shares President Carter's love of country music. In 1976, Willie Nelson and Waylon Jennings earned the first country platinum album with their renegade disk *Wanted: The Outlaws*. In 1977, *Linda Ronstadt's Greatest Hits* and Jimmy Buffett's *Changes in Latitudes—Changes in Attitudes* were platinum-winners, and a million of Elvis Presley's fans bought *Elvis Sings "The Wonderful World of Christmas."* In 1978, twice as many albums by country artists won platinum. Dolly Parton took the prize with *Here You Come Again;* Willie Nelson and Waylon Jennings snapped it up with *Waylon and Willie;* the Statler Brothers smashed through with *Best of the Statler Brothers;* Jimmy Buffett's *Son of a Son of a Sailor* shipped platinum; Kenny Rogers' *Ten Years of Gold* sailed effortlessly through the gold mark to platinum; Linda Ronstadt's *Simple Dreams* added to her gleaming collection; and Crystal Gayle's *We Must Believe in Magic* soared to platinum. There were a handful of gold albums too: Willie Nelson's daringly old-fashioned collection of standards, *Stardust,* Emmylou Harris's *Elite Hotel,* and Ronnie Milsap's *It Was Almost Like a Song.*

But if you listen to those albums, you'll hear that they were not traditional country. They were country with a boogie beat, or country buffed to a high pop finish, or country with a smooth, pretty voice rather than a nasal or raspy one. The twang was still there, but it was seldom the most prominent feature. Pure country music, the sounds of the president's favorite artists—Loretta Lynn and Conway Twitty, for example—continued to sell as well as ever, but the audience for a pure country sound was not nearly as massive as the audience for those lively country variations. It was, after all, renegade Willie Nelson whose red hair gleamed from the cover of *Newsweek* and crossover queen Dolly Parton who laughed and flirted with audiences coast to coast during a television interview by Barbara Walters.

Nashville's twenty-year-old Country Music Association has campaigned long and hard to get country music heard around the world. Ironically, country music's greatest commercial success has not come from the purists. As Larry Baunach of ABC/Dot Records pointed out in *Billboard* magazine, "The hardcore country consumer market is not large enough for labels to realize immediate gold record sales, but gold sales are available through those country artists who appeal to a crossover audience." In 1978, there were a couple of unexpected country hybrids in the name of crossover: Country artist Bill Anderson's "I Can't Wait Any Longer" blazed up the country charts and was also popular in discos. Millie Jackson's version of Merle Haggard's "If We're Not Back in Love by Monday" was another surprising crossover, a winner on both country and soul charts.

As the Country Music Association celebrated its twentieth year, it looked with pride on many accomplishments. Back in 1959, the earliest Country Music Association meetings were held in a rented hotel room because the offices weren't big enough to hold the entire board of directors. The room was paid for by passing the hat. In those days there were only eighty-one country music stations in the United States and Canada. Today, largely because of the Association's promotional labors, there are more than a thousand.

The crossover phenomenon, however, has created some threats to Nashville's control of country. With growth has come change, including a new emphasis on the West Coast, home of the splinter Academy of Country Music. Both CBS and Capitol Records have shifted their country emphasis from Nashville to Los Angeles. ABC, whose Dot label has for years been synonymous with a country sound, dropped that label at the beginning of the year as part of their program to introduce more country acts as pop. Willie Nelson, always the renegade, started his own label, Lone Star, operating out of Austin, Texas. Although the Chappell and Intersong music publishing companies have announced decisions to expand their country music divisions, moving to larger quarters in Nashville, several other music publishers have moved in the opposite direction.

In 1978, the great success of their pop-oriented

72

Preceding pages and opposite: Dolly Parton and Willie Nelson, the blond bombshell and the red-headed stranger, were country music's two hottest stars in 1978. Each symbolized country's stretch, Dolly achieving pop success with Heartbreaker *and Willie singing an album of standards,* Stardust.

peers must have tempted many country stars to change their music. But crossover was not the route for everybody. Don Williams, a phenomenally successful country figure, added some strings to his band for a festival performance, but he was not eager to change his style to win a larger audience. Charley Pride, the Kendalls, Merle Haggard, the Oak Ridge Boys, and other country successes remained determined to sing and play what they consider pure country.

Although the modified country sounds were most successful in the United States, in the rest of the world, the purer the country sound, the more audiences loved it. The 1978 International Festival of Country Music at Wembley, England, celebrating its tenth anniversary, attracted some thirty-two thousand fans of American country. For three days audiences stomped and whooped, cheering Don Williams, Marty Robbins, Kenny Rogers, Larry Gatlin, Carl Perkins, and others. Merle Haggard, who closed the festival, was an enormous hit, winning a thunderous standing ovation at the end of a powerful set.

Haggard followed his Wembley triumph with two European dates and a tour of the United Kingdom. The size and enthusiasm of the British audience amazed and delighted him. A surprise birthday party for him on April 6 turned into a fine jam session, featuring Haggard and his band, the Strangers, and tourmates the Joe Ely Band.

Other country troupers spread the message around the world. Dr. Hook toured New Zealand, Australia, Thailand, and Japan in May and June. Crystal Gayle was Special International Guest Artist at Tokyo's ninth annual World Popular Song Festival on November 10 through 12. Don Williams appeared May 13 on British television's "The Val Doonican Music Show" and appeared on his own British show, "Don Williams in Concert," in the fall. Larry Gatlin wowed audiences in Sweden and England; Roy Clark and Loretta Lynn taped two different segments of "The Muppet Show" in England; and Loretta Lynn's best-selling autobiography, *Coal Miner's Daughter*, was published in the United Kingdom by Granada Publishing. The British Country Music Association proclaimed Hank Williams Month in January.

The Nashville sound flourished all around the United States as well in 1978. Regional country sounds, from the Austin outlaw country-rock of Waylon, Willie, and Kris Kristofferson to the raucous hoedowns of Texas swing to the biting Cajun fiddle to the rocking Memphis backbeat, added richness to the country mix.

74

Dagmar

Robin Platzer, Images

Opposite: *In the year 1978 Crystal Gayle earned a Grammy.* Above: *Ronnie Milsap enchanted Las Vegas audiences in 1978.* Right: *Kenny Rogers gathered a huge number of prestigious awards in 1977 and 1978.*

Ebet Roberts

New Yorkers welcomed country at Carnegie Hall on November 28, 1977, when Mel Tellis, Donna Fargo, the Oak Ridge Boys, and Alvin Crow and his Pleasant Valley Boys set the rafters ringing with country jive. Crystal Gayle brought her sweet country style to New York's sophisticated Bottom Line on April 11 and 12, and Johnny Paycheck, Freddy Fender, Billie Joe Shaver, and a host of other country artists whooped it up at the Lone Star Cafe to help New Yorkers celebrate March 2, Texas Independence Day. In Washington, D.C., a spate of bluegrass clubs featured the music of the popular Seldom Scene, the Country Gentlemen, Hickory Wind, and Grass Menagerie. Even Linda Ronstadt turned up at the Birchmere Club and sang with the Seldom Scene.

In Tulsa, Oklahoma, the Tulsa Opry celebrated its first birthday on April 22 with concerts by Merle Haggard. The successful venue holds shows at the Tulsa Performing Arts Center and has attracted capacity crowds with such artists as Haggard, Don Williams, the Oak Ridge Boys, and Minnie Pearl. Don Williams and Waylon Jennings toured the Southwest together in February; in Las Vegas, Larry Gatlin and his two brothers filled the Golden Nugget's Gold Strike Lounge to overflowing on February 11.

It was a year of mixed response to country music festivals. Some were fabulously successful. Fan Fair, Nashville's annual celebration that brings together fans and country stars in a down-home mix that includes autograph sessions, the Slow-Pitch Celebrity Softball Tournament, a square dance, and the Grand Master's Fiddling Championship, packed enough concerts into the week to satisfy any country fan.

Held between June 5 and June 11, the event drew more than thirteen thousand. The Municipal Auditorium, Opryland U.S.A., and the Grand Ole Opry House were filled to bursting when such country luminaries as Tammy Wynette and Charley Pride—who closed the international show with a duet—the Statler Brothers, Larry Gatlin, Jerry Reed, and Tommy Overstreet outdid themselves belting out songs and making fans feel welcome. The shows were so jammed that the Country Music Association's executive director considered adding an extra day to Fan Fair 1979.

The Fourth of July was the occasion of two major country celebrations; Willie Nelson's picnic, held at the Cotton Bowl, was part of a two-day Texas World Music Festival. The picnic, held on Sunday, was preceded by a hard-rock Texas Jam, starring Aerosmith, Heart, and Ted Nugent. The jam drew some seventy-five thousand

Above: *Emmylou Harris's hard work and dedication to her craft won her a gold album in 1978 for* Elite Hotel. *Right: In the year 1978, even dyed-in-the-wool country star Don Williams cast an eye towards reaching a larger market.*

76

Courtesy ABC Records

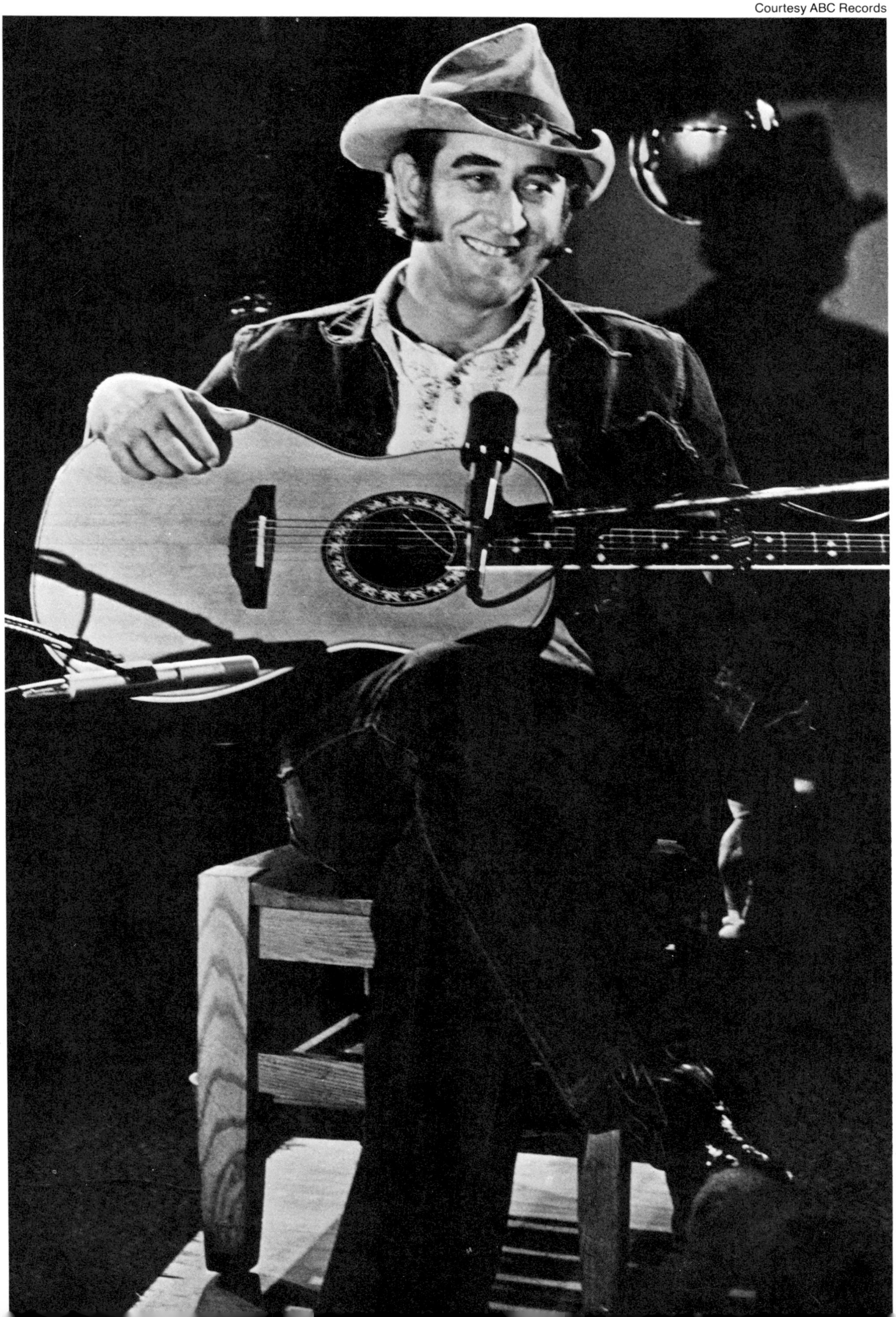

rock fans. Although the audience for Willie's picnic was not as large as those of previous years, thirty thousand people can still make a mighty roar, and this crowd hollered its approval of Willie's dazzling roster of country dynamos: Emmylou Harris, Kris Kristofferson and Rita Coolidge, the Charlie Daniels Band, Billy Swan, Waylon Jennings and Jessi Colter, and of course, Willie. Willie's past picnics have always been uncontrolled free-for-alls, held in the unconfined outdoors of the vast plains of Texas. And, although *Rolling Stone* reporter Joe Nick Patoski said that Willie was dubious about the setting when he began, by the end of the rave-up day he was grinning at the possibilities for July 4, 1979.

The Statler Brothers held their ninth annual "Happy Birthday USA" fest in their home town of Staunton, Virginia, where fifty-three thousand people gave the fabulously popular Statlers a standing ovation and cheered guest star Johnny Rodriguez. The evening concert capped a festive family day, during which children and adults played games, swam, strolled and chatted, soaked up the sun, and ate. The free event attracted Jody Powell, President Carter's press secretary, and Frank Moore, head of the White House Congressional Liaison Office.

Kool cigarettes, whose Kool Jazz Festival is well known, held the first Kool Country Music Shindigs in 1978. Comprising three dates, the festival began February 9 at the Louisville Convention Center. Despite blizzard conditions, some six thousand fans slogged through the snow to hear Crystal Gayle, Ronnie Milsap, and Jacky Ward. The second two concerts were held on April 16 at St. Louis's Keil Auditorium, featuring Ronnie Milsap and Ray Stevens, and on April 22 at Memphis's Mid South Coliseum, featuring Ronnie Milsap and Jerry Reed.

From July 2 to 4 in Columbia, Tennessee, the Nashville Music Festival's "Greatest Country Music Show on Earth" survived disgruntled ex-promoters, cantankerous country officials, and endless red tape, only to draw twenty thousand fans instead of the expected sixty to one hundred thousand. Featuring such top names as Kenny Rogers, Larry Gatlin, Eddie Rabbitt, Tammy Wynette, and Merle Haggard, the show was enjoyed by both artists and audience, and producer Tom Moon was confident that future events would be more successful.

Another festival that started with high hopes was the Giant Country Spring Festival, billed as the country counterpart of Cal Jam. Despite stellar headliners,

Opposite: *Top country singer Charley Pride scored in 1978 with the album* Someone Loves You Honey, *a top-ten country disk.* Above: *In addition to touring with wife Rita Coolidge and releasing the album* Easter Island, *Kris Kristofferson was a hit in Sam Peckinpah's movie* Convoy.

79

including Johnny Paycheck, Crystal Gayle, Hank Williams, Jr., Commander Cody, the Kendalls, Mickey Gilley, Molly Bee, Susie Allanson, and a host of other stars, the concert, held at the Riverside International Raceway, Riverside, California, attracted fewer than ten thousand people instead of the hoped-for sixty thousand. Those who were there enjoyed a superior show, but rueful first-time promoter Jess Jewett could salve his disappointment only with the thought that almost the entire concert had been videotaped.

Although Elvis Presley died in August of 1977, the urge to keep his memory alive continued to grow in 1978. Elvis may have given the world rock and roll, but his heart and soul were in the country, and after his death the country fans who loved him so fiercely continued to do so. His records dotted the country charts throughout the year; more than a million and a half mourners thronged to Memphis to view his grave. Delbert "Sonny" West, Elvis's long-time friend and bodyguard, presented an Elvis Memorial Fan Club concert on August 16, the anniversary of Elvis's death. Radio stations across the country also planned various special tributes and commemorations on that day, ranging from an increase in the number of his songs to such polished events as ABC radio's three-hour special called "Elvis: Memories," the first time in more than ten years that ABC Radio has programmed a network music show.

Some country stars had difficult moments in 1978. Olivia Newton-John tried to get out of her contract with MCA, claiming that they hadn't promoted her albums sufficiently. She was stopped from recording for any other company by a preliminary injunction in MCA's favor handed down by a Los Angeles Superior Court judge in July. George Jones was a no-show for the third time in a year in Tulsa, disappointing fans who had come to see him on New Year's Eve. Arrested for driving while drugged, Jerry Lee Lewis was fined $200, given a thirty-day suspended sentence, placed on a year's probation, and lectured by Criminal Court Judge William H. Williams about his responsibility to his talent. Donna Fargo, whose career had been barreling successfully along, suffered from a hard-to-diagnose nerve disorder. Doctors at the Sansom Medical Clinic in Santa Barbara, California, reported in July that her condition was improving.

But for the majority of country artists, 1978 was a successful year, marked by such winning albums as *Elvis in Concert, Heaven's Just a Sin Away* by the Kendalls, *Daytime Friends* by Kenny Rogers, *Take This*

Below: *Johnny Paycheck's long career has been filled with ups and downs. The year 1978, with the hit single "Take This Job and Shove It," was a major triumph for the singer. Opposite: A hot new country duo in 1978 was formed by the pairing of Kenny Rogers and Dottie West for the hit song "Every Time Two Fools Collide."*

Courtesy Epic Records

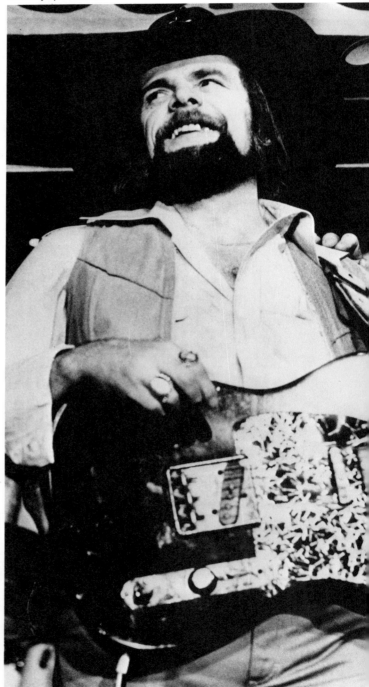

Job and Shove It by Johnny Paycheck, *Someone Loves You Honey* by Charley Pride, *Every Time Two Fools Collide* by Kenny Rogers and Dottie West, *It's a Heartache* by Bonnie Tyler, *Room Service* by the Oak Ridge Boys, *Only One Love in My Life* by Ronnie Milsap, *Entertainers... On and Off the Record* by the Statler Brothers, *When I Dream* by Crystal Gayle, and *Love or Something Like It* by Kenny Rogers.

Some of the year's most successful country singles were "I'm Just a Country Boy" by Don Williams, "More to Me" by Charley Pride, "Love Is Just a Game" by Larry Gatlin, "Roses for Mama" by C. W. McCall, "The Wurlitzer Prize (I Don't Want to Get Over You/Lookin' For a Feeling)" by Waylon Jennings, "Blue Bayou" by Linda Ronstadt, "From Graceland to the Promised Land" by Merle Haggard, "Here You Come Again," by Dolly Parton, "You Light Up My Life" by Debby Boone, "I'm Knee Deep in Loving You" by Dave & Sugar, "Georgia Keeps Pulling on My Ring" by Conway Twitty, "Take This Job and Shove It" by Johnny Paycheck, "Come a Little Bit Closer" by Johnny Duncan (with Janie Fricke), "What a Difference You Made in My Life" by Ronnie Milsap, "My Way" by Elvis Presley, "Do I Love You (Yes in Every Way)" by Donna Fargo, "Middle Age Crazy" by Jerry Lee Lewis, "Out of My Head and Back in My Bed" by Loretta Lynn, "You're the One" by the Oak Ridge Boys, "To Daddy" by Emmylou Harris, "I Just Wish You Were Someone I Love" by Larry Gatlin, "Don't Break the Heart That Loves You" by Margo Smith, "What Did I Promise Her Last Night" by Mel Tillis, "Mamas Don't Let Your Babies Grow Up to Be Cowboys" by Waylon and Willie, "Woman to Woman" by Barbara Mandrell, "Someone Loves You Honey" by Charley Pride, "It Don't Feel Like Sinnin' to Me," by the Kendalls, "A Lover's Question" by Jacky Ward, "I Cheated on a Good Woman's Love" by Billy "Crash" Craddock, "Ready for the Times to Get Better" by Crystal Gayle, "Every Time Two Fools Collide" by Kenny Rogers and Dottie West, "Hearts On Fire" by Eddie Rabbitt, "It's All Wrong, But It's Alright/Two Doors Down" by Dolly Parton, "She Can Put Her Shoes Under My Bed (Anytime)" by Johnny Duncan, "I'm Always on a Mountain When I Fall" by Merle Haggard, "Do You Know You Are My Sunshine" by the Statler Brothers, "If You Can Touch Her at All" and "Georgia on My Mind" by Willie Nelson, "Night Time Magic" by Larry Gatlin, "Gotta' Quit Lookin' at You Baby" by Dave & Sugar, "Two More Bottles of Wine" by Emmylou Harris, "I'll Be True to You" by the Oak Ridge Boys, "It Only Hurts For a Little While" by Margo Smith,

"I Can't Wait Any Longer" by Bill Anderson, "I Believe in You" by Mel Tillis, "There Ain't No Good Chain Gang" by Johnny Cash and Waylon Jennings, "Only One Love in My Life" by Ronnie Milsap, "Love or Something Like It" by Kenny Rogers, "You Don't Love Me Anymore" by Eddie Rabbitt, "Tonight" by Barbara Mandrell.

Robin Platzer, Images

Waring Abbott

Opposite: *Tanya Tucker campaigned in 1978 to save the seals.* Left: *The dynamic Billy "Crash" Craddock began 1978 with the country hit "I Cheated on a Good Woman's Love."* Below: *Guitar legends Les Paul (left) and Chet Atkins perform at New York's Bottom Line.*

Chuck Pulin

Jazz

Richard Creamer

Jazz in 1978 shimmered with a warm nostalgia, as several jazz titans celebrated memorable anniversaries. At the end of 1977, Dizzy Gillespie turned a youthful sixty; throughout 1978 Lionel Hampton sparkled at every concert, each of them another tribute to his fiftieth year as a musician; Benny Goodman celebrated his fortieth anniversary with a Carnegie Hall concert that featured inspired performances by guests Lionel Hampton, Martha Tilton, and Mary Lou Williams. Benny also won the First California Jazz Award presented by Governor Brown on June 20. In January, the historic Cotton Club in Harlem reopened, featuring a sizzling set by jazzman Cab Calloway; the University of Massachusetts at Amherst held a Duke Ellington Spring Music Festival on May 6. Dynamic eighty-two-year-old Alberta Hunter made a triumphant comeback after twenty-five years, sharing her sprightly wit on television talk shows, singing at New York's The Cookery, and writing the score for and singing in Robert Altman's film *Remember My Name.*

Warner Brothers Records issued a deluxe set of six Charlie Parker LPs; and a new record company, Signature Gramophone, Ltd., re-released a slew of recordings by such forties greats as Coleman Hawkins, Pee Wee Russell, James P. Johnson, Erroll Garner, Lester Young, and Anita O'Day.

Record sales, however, belonged to the young generation of jazz fusion artists. George Benson's *Weekend in L.A.* was a million-seller. Chuck Mangione's *Feels So Good* and Grover Washington, Jr.'s, *Live at the Bijou* earned them gold disks. Other jazz best-sellers were electric as well, including *Heads* by Bob James, *New Vintage* by Maynard Ferguson, *Magic* by Billy Cobham, *Sophisticated Giant* by Dexter Gordon, *Tequila Mockingbird* by Ramsey Lewis, *Inner Voices* by McCoy Tyner, *Hold On* by Noel Pointer, *Rainbow Seeker* by Joe Sample, *Say it with Silence* by Hubert Laws, *Casino* by Al Di Meola, *Modern Man* by Stanley Clarke, *Sounds* by Quincy Jones, *Arabesque* by John Klemmer, *Magic in Your Eyes* by Earl Klugh, *Sunlight* by Herbie Hancock, *Images* by the Crusaders, and the scintillating *Electric Guitarist* by John McLaughlin.

But there were rumblings of a return to less electric jazz. In January, George Butler, Columbia Records' vice-president of jazz and progressive music, predicted that authentic, non-fusion jazz sounds would be returning. Herbie Hancock, although experimenting with a vocoder that turns his speech into music, surprised audiences by performing several acoustic sets in the summer of 1977. He and Chick Corea played acoustic pianos during their early 1978 tour. Trumpeter Freddie Hubbard announced that he was abandoning electric instrumentation and returning to straight, old-fashioned acoustic jazz.

With this blending of old and new, the jazz scene jumped in 1978. It was a year of breathtaking festivals. In March, the scene began popping at the first Women's Jazz Festival. Held from March 17 through 19 in Kansas City, Missouri, and Kansas City, Kansas, the three-day event drew a collection of stunning musicians, both male and female, from all around the country. It featured a jazz mass by pianist/composer Mary Lou Williams and climaxed with a five-hour marathon concert that brought the cheering audience to its feet again and again. Toshiko Akiyoshi, the first woman to have composed an entire jazz library and to organize a big band to play it, emerged as an impressive conductor, urging her band to sizzling heights. From March 14 to March 18, prime jazz producer George Wein exhilarated Boston with the 1978 edition of the *Boston Globe* Jazz Festival, featuring a Lionel Hampton tribute, a Count Basie evening with the Sarah Vaughan Trio, and such treats as dixieland concerts for the kids, a Stan Getz performance, an impressive debut by a twelve-year-old drummer, Terri Lyne Carrington, who pounded out a tasty jazz beat with the best of them.

That was the first of a series of triumphs for Wein. His next success was the ninth annual New Orleans Jazz and Heritage Festival. Two hundred thousand jazz fans snapped and tapped and hummed their way through this ten-day musical extravaganza, enjoying a total of 250 acts at such sites as the New Orleans Fair Grounds Race Track, various music halls, and aboard the S.S. *Admiral.* Such jazz dynamos as Grover Washington, Jr., Hubert Laws, Count Basie, Dave Brubeck, Bobby Bland, and McCoy Tyner joined bluesmen Muddy Waters and B. B. King, singer Odetta, bluegrass star Doc Watson, and Cajun fiddler Doug Kershaw, all of whom flourished in the exuberant

Preceding pages: *George Benson.* Opposite: *Jazz, more vital than ever in 1978, celebrated with successful festivals all over the country, including Jazz at Jimmy's, an afternoon of jazz on the White House lawn that featured Dizzy Gillespie and Benson.*

Wide World Photos

Above: *Benny Goodman celebrates his fortieth year in show business at Carnegie Hall.* Opposite: *Linda Ronstadt, elegant in concert, sports roller skates and knee pads on the cover of her 1978 album,* Back in the USA. *Late in the year, Linda announced plans to move her base of operations from California to New York City.* Following pages: *The Rolling Stones' singular logo of open mouth and tongue dominated many of their 1978 concerts.*

mix of musical styles.

From May 26 to 29, Sacramento, California, hosted the fifth annual edition of The World's Greatest Jazz Festival. Featuring seventy-three bands, the festival drew one hundred thousand spectators who drank in the music from 10:30 A.M. to 2:00 A.M. every day.

The twelfth annual Berkeley Jazz Festival at the Greek Theatre on May 27 and 28 included such stars as Noel Pointer, Herbie Hancock with Tony Williams and Ron Carter, Freddie Hubbard, Ramsey Lewis, Flora Purim, and the Oscar Peterson Trio.

On June 18, President Jimmy Carter, aided by the producing genius of George Wein, opened the White House gates to the jazz world. An exclusive audience of 800 invitees sat on the south lawn and enjoyed the balmy weather, a southern-style buffet, and an awesome collection of jazz talent, opening with the irrepressible ninety-five-year-old ragtime pianist Eubie Blake and continuing with Benny Carter, Sonny Rollins and McCoy Tyner, Dizzy Gillespie accompanied by an all-star sextet, Ornette Coleman accompanied by his son Denardo Coleman, and Lionel Hampton leading Chick Corea, Ray Brown, Stan Getz, and Zoot Sims, and closing with one staggering climax after another. Lionel Hampton started to play "Flying Home"; Gerry Mulligan joined in; Pearl Bailey followed with "In the Good Old Summertime" and "St. Louis Blues." Finally, Dizzy Gillespie, backed by Max Roach, led fledgling jazz singer Jimmy Carter through a creditable version of "Salt Peanuts."

But the best was yet to come for jazz lovers: the twenty-fifth Newport Jazz Festival, about which founder and producer George Wein told *Billboard* magazine, "It's been euphoric this year." With an audience of a quarter million attending thirty-four concerts and events held in New York City and Saratoga, New York, the festival was the biggest ever, featuring memorable performances by Sarah Vaughan with the Thad Jones–Mel Lewis band; a glorious Ella Fitzgerald; an astonishing virtuoso concert with Ornette Coleman and Cecil Taylor; Count Basie; Sonny Rollins; Betty Carter with Dexter Gordon and Max Roach; Maynard Ferguson; Buddy Rich; and, together in some inspired moments, Mel Tormé, Stan Getz, and Dizzy Gillespie.

Other jazz festivals in 1978 included the third annual Vermont Jazz Festival and the Concord Summer Jazz Festival in California, July's five days of jazz in Lewiston, New York, twenty-one summertime

Lynn Goldsmith

Above: *Backed by the explosive Silver Bullet Band,
Bob Seger's husky growl drove fans to frenzies in another
hard-touring year. The Detroit rocker scored platinum with
the album* Stranger in Town *and had hit singles with "Still the
Same," "Feel Like a Number," and "Hollywood Nights." Right: Zubin
Mehta became executive director of the New York Philharmonic in the
fall of 1978. Following pages, left: Ferocious rocker Ted Nugent
looks almost mellow, but during 1978 Ted's heavy-metal
blitz won him a platinum disk for* Double Live Gonzo
*and captured fans at Cal Jam II. Right: The year
of the disco, 1978, saw dinner jackets and jeans
mingling at New York's glittery Studio 54.*

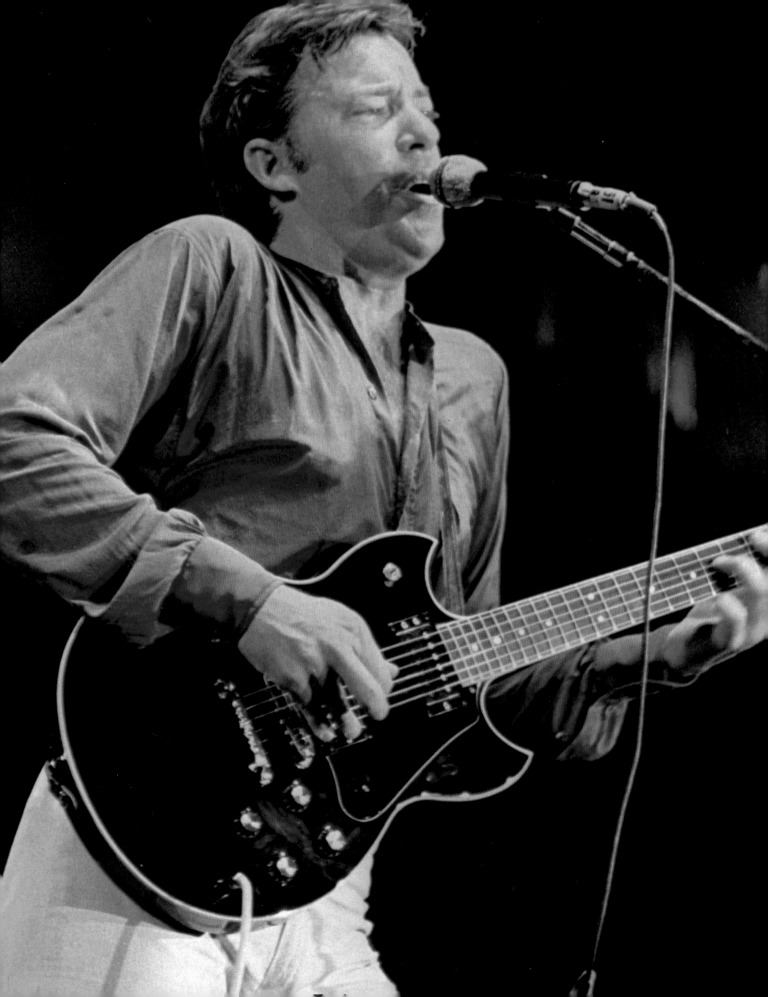

Kool Jazz Festivals, Colorado's second annual Telluride Jazz Festival and New York's first Harlem Jazz Festival, both toward the end of August, and the Monterey Jazz Festival in September.

Radio stations across the country picked up the "Jazz Album Countdown," a three-hour jazz program that featured cuts from the top-selling jazz albums according to *Billboard*'s charts. The show debuted February 10 on fifty-five stations and, by the end of June, had grown to include more than one hundred domestic radio stations and three hundred American Armed Forces Radio Network stations around the world. Hosted by Rod McGrew, the show ironically was not aired by any pure jazz stations. A special Labor Day Weekend edition of the Orcas Productions program featured a retrospective spotlighting all-time jazz greats and the biggest names of today.

During the year 1978 jazz was also a successful export. The indigenous American art form spread around the world, sizzling in such venues as London's Ronnie Scott's Club, Paris's the Riverbop, Munich's the Domicile, and Copenhagen's Montmartre. Switzerland's twelfth annual Montreux Jazz Festival was a sprawling event, its more than two weeks of July concerts crackling with an electric mix of European and American performers, ranging from the blues of Taj Mahal and Sonny Terry and Brownie McGhee to the pure jazz of Freddie Hubbard, Pharoah Sanders, Norman Connors, the Buddy Rich Band, Count Basie, and Oscar Peterson to the electric fusion sound of the Brecker Brothers. The festival featured an exclusive performance by the inimitable Ray Charles. The first annual Maseru Music Festival, held in January, drew ten thousand Africans to the open-air Lesotho National Stadium to hear Dizzy Gillespie, Al Wilson, the Rutgers-Livingston Jazz Professors, and two South African bands. George Benson took his fusion jazz sound around the world, beginning in Tokyo on March 2.

Opposite: *Boz Scaggs, who won platinum in 1978 with* Down Two, Then Left, *lost out on royalties when manager Irv Azoff turned down a request to use Scaggs' song "Lowdown" in a film. The movie?* Saturday Night Fever. *Boz's response? A shrug.* Above and top: *Lionel Hampton and Cab Calloway both celebrated fiftieth anniversaries in 1978. Each reaffirmed his youth in a year packed with concerts, and Cab recorded a disco version of his classic "Minnie the Moocher."*

Robin Platzer, Images

98

*Music and joy reigned
in the jazz world in 1978.
Opposite: Lou Rawls and Chuck
Mangione share laughs at the Grammy
festivities. Jazz singer Alberta
Hunter enjoyed a comeback
during the year.
Left: Herbie Hancock and
Chick Corea at Carnegie Hall.
Above: Grover Washington, Jr.*

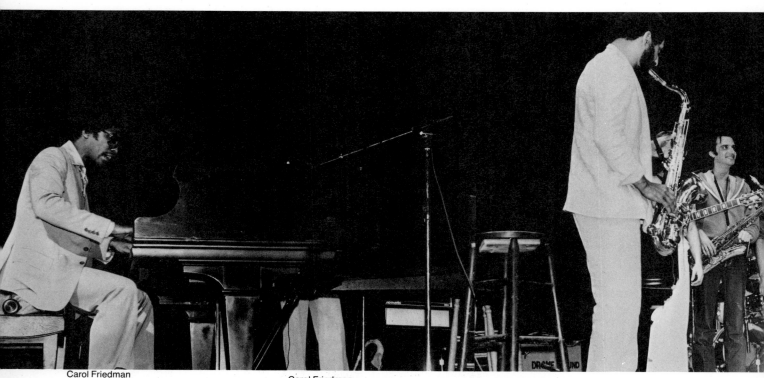

Carol Friedman

Carol Friedman

100

Top: *The Newport Jazz Festival at Saratoga: Herbie Hancock, Sonny Rollins, Larry Coryell, Mike Brecker, Randy Brecker, Dexter Gordon, Dizzy Gillespie, Al Jarreau, George Benson. Opposite: Ornette Coleman at Carnegie Hall during Newport. Above: Eubie Blake at his Concert for the Young at Heart.*

Classical

For classical music the year 1978 was one of unprecedented growth and dazzling achievements. Just as every other area of music sought to reach a larger audience, so classical performers, composers, conductors, record companies, and retailers sought to bring the joys of classical music to a larger number of listeners.

Perhaps the most exciting classical events triggering a crossover consciousness were the spectacular successes of the scores for *Star Wars* and *Close Encounters of the Third Kind* by John Williams. These dramatic pieces of music inspired a rush of concerts of the third kind, neither rock nor classical, but described as Music from Outer Space. The first of these Los Angeles Philharmonic concerts, held at the Hollywood Bowl, November 19, 1977, blitzed its audiences with a laser light show and sent them spinning into orbit with Williams's scores, Gustav Holst's *The Planets,* and Strauss's *Thus Spake Zarathustra.* The concert was such a smash that promoters Wolf-Rismiller took the show on the road. On April 1, the second Music from Outer Space concert was held at the Anaheim Stadium. This was the first time a symphony orchestra ever performed at a baseball stadium and was the largest paid event ever for the Los Angeles Philharmonic. Inspired by the Hollywood Bowl concert, the Houston Symphony performed its version of the show, called the Ultimate Musical Voyage, on January 25. On June 24, a similar concert, called Starship Encounters, featuring the American Symphony under the direction of Richard Hayman and lasers, synthesizers, and the whole arsenal of outer space effects, was performed in New York's Madison Square Garden.

In 1978, several composers fused classical music with other forms. Perhaps the most significant was the rock-classical piece *Missa Universale,* a pop mass based on themes by Anton Bruckner. This work was performed for the first time at the International Brucknerfest in Linz, Austria, on September 22. Another blend was the *Suite for Violin and Jazz Trio* by Claude Bolling, the French composer/pianist whose *Suite for Flute and Jazz Piano* was so remarkably successful in 1977 and 1978. In addition, composer Andrew Lloyd Webber composed a series of pop variations on the Twenty-Fourth Solo Caprice for Violin

by Paganini, a piece that has inspired an enormous number of variations.

Classical began to change its image in other ways as well. First, several record companies, including Columbia and London, mounted huge publicity campaigns for their classical artists, patterning these sales pushes after successful pop strategies. Several record labels with classical entries have also introduced low-price classical tape cassettes. Listing for $4.98, these tapes have sold extraordinarily well.

At a meeting of Concert Music Broadcasters Association, the organization received the happy news that classical music radio stations have 10 percent more listeners this year than they have had in the past. Since the general population is increasing by only 6 percent, broadcasters reasoned that the increase in listeners also meant the audience was getting younger, perhaps including rock fans.

But crossover events were just a small part of 1978's shining classical picture. For hundreds of thousands of music lovers, the most significant musical event of 1978 was the appearance of master-pianist Vladimir Horowitz at Carnegie Hall on January 8. On that date he celebrated the fiftieth anniversary of his American debut by performing with an orchestra for the first time in twenty-five years. The historic concert, a performance of the Rachmaninoff Third Piano Concerto with the New York Philharmonic conducted by Eugene Ormandy, was a transcendent event. Carnegie Hall was sold out for months in advance, with concert-goers waiting on line from the early morning hours of the day tickets went on sale. The concert was recorded, and the resulting album was a classical best-seller, the $8.98 list price no deterrent to record buyers who eagerly snapped up more than 100,000 copies in three weeks.

On February 26, Horowitz gave an afternoon recital at the White house, including works by Chopin and Schumann and themes from the opera *Carmen.* The concert was heard live on all National Public Radio stations and was broadcast later that same evening over PBS television stations.

Delighted by the response of record buyers to his performances and his new disks and amazed at the rush of autograph seekers who mobbed him every time he visited a record store in 1978, the charming

Preceding pages: *Zubin Mehta, new musical director for the New York Philharmonic, had a classical best-seller in 1978 with Stravinsky's* Rite of Spring. *Right: Jean-Pierre Rampal remained America's best-loved flutist in 1978 despite the sudden popularity of newcomer James Galway.*

piano virtuoso agreed to appear on commercial television. On September 24, NBC-TV telecast his memorable appearance with the New York Philharmonic, conducted by Zubin Mehta, performing the Rachmaninoff Third Piano Concerto.

Another major classical event was the capture by Americans of two first prizes in Russia's gruelling Tchaikovsky Competition. The gold medals were won by Nathaniel Rosen, a thirty-year-old Californian, currently a cellist with the Pittsburgh Symphony Orchestra, and by violinist Elmar Oliveira. The double victory was the first time any American had captured a gold medal in that competition since Van Cliburn won it for piano twenty years ago. It was also the first time American string instrument players had won the award, making Mr. Rosen's and Mr. Oliveira's triumphs doubly exciting.

The year 1978 also saw the rediscovery of phenomenal pianist Ervin Nyireghazi (pronounced Near'-itch-hazi). The seventy-five-year-old former prodigy retired from performing in the early 1930s because of bad management, and his own feeling that his style of playing was out of synch with the times.

A master of the nineteenth-century repertoire, his intense, fiery playing is most often compared to that of Liszt. The remarkable pianist—whose playing is described as almost superhuman by Michael Walsh, music critic for the *San Francisco Examiner*—was featured on the cover of *Stereo Review,* interviewed by NBC-TV's "Weekend," and profiled by *Time* magazine. An album he released through the International Piano Archives in the fall of 1977 led to a Ford Foundation subsidy and to his recording a two-record set for Columbia Records.

On August 25, 1978, one of America's greatest classical music figures, Leonard Bernstein, the first American to become director of a major orchestra, celebrated his sixtieth birthday. To honor that day, a special concert was given by the National Symphony at Wolf Trap Farm. Organized by Mstislav Rostropovich, the concert included such stars as Yehudi Menuhin, Claudio Arrau, Aaron Copland, Lukas Foss, William Schuman, Christa Ludwig, and Donald Gramm. Other Bernstein celebrations included Deutsche Grammophon's release of Bernstein's latest recording of his symphonies with the Israel Philharmonic. CBS reissued his recordings of the Mahler Symphonies, and the first Leonard Bernstein Festival of American Music, featuring Bernstein's works, was held at the University of Massachusetts

at Amherst from June 29 to July 23. Columbia Masterworks also produced a special radio program highlighting his career for broadcast on his birthday.

Another classical music titan, pianist Rudolf Serkin, celebrated a special birthday this year. Mr. Serkin's seventy-fifth birthday was marked by his first full-scale solo recital on television, a performance that opened the PBS series "Tonight at Carnegie Hall." In the fall he also appeared on "Live from Lincoln Center." On that broadcast he performed the Beethoven Emperor Concerto and became the first soloist to perform under Zubin Mehta in Mehta's new position as music director of the New York Philharmonic. Serkin was honored on March 4, twenty-four days before his birthday, by Mstislav Rostropovich and the National Symphony Orchestra in a Carnegie Hall Concert that was altered at the last minute to include a piece by Serkin's father-in-law and mentor, Adolph Busch.

In the year 1978, Zubin Mehta became Musical Director of the New York Philharmonic, opening the season September 14 with *Ambiguities (After Melville),* a new work by Samuel Barber. Michael Tilson Thomas announced his decision to resign as conductor of the Buffalo Philharmonic at the end of the 1978–79 season. At the end of 1977, Mstislav Rostropovich began his inaugural season as music director of the National Symphony. The overture *Slava* was composed by Leonard Bernstein for Rostropovich and was recorded with Rostropovich conducting. Conductor Carlos Kleiber made his debut with the Chicago Symphony on October 12.

The year 1978 was one of splendid advances for opera. On March 16, *Don Giovanni* was telecast by PBS. Starring Joan Sutherland, the performance was a treat for lovers of the Mozart opera. On April 21, *Danton and Robespierre,* a new opera composed by John Eaton, premiered at Indiana University's Musical Arts Center. In the modern work, Eaton used a new synthesizer especially developed for him by Robert Moog.

Fulfilling a long-talked-about promise, RCA began to reissue all the recordings of the legendary tenor Enrico Caruso. The series, which will contain fifteen or sixteen records, will be as complete as possible according to John Pfeiffer, the man in charge of the project. Pfeiffer is even searching for test pressings for which the masters were destroyed. The extraneous sounds that accompanied Caruso's early recordings because of the primitive state of the recording art

Courtesy Judd Concert Bureau

Opposite: *Cellist Nathaniel Rosen won first prize in Russia's Tchaikovsky Competition in 1978, the first time an American has won since Van Cliburn's piano triumph twenty years ago. Below: Pianist Vladimir Horowitz brought rapture to hundreds of thousands of fans with his performances of the Rachmaninoff Third Piano Concerto during the year.*

Lynn Goldsmith

have been largely removed from the records by an electronic process called Soundstream.

Luciano Pavarotti, the modern tenor whose fame equals that of Caruso, reached new heights of popularity in 1978, as his recordings of *La Favorita, Operatic Duets* with Joan Sutherland, *Bravo Pavarotti,* and *Hits from Lincoln Center* became classical best-sellers.

The opera world lost one of its foremost sopranos when Maria Callas died in 1977. On November 1, more than fifty-five hundred persons attended a memorial tribute to her at the Dallas Civic Opera House, the site of her American debut twenty-three years earlier. On January 21, Beverly Sills announced that she would retire from the stage in 1980 to codirect the New York City Opera. Miss Sills who will then be fifty, did promise to continue making records if it would not conflict with her new job.

Two interesting new ensembles made news. In Philadelphia a new all-black symphony was formed. Called the National Afro-American Philharmonic Orchestra, the 100-member group held its premiere performance at Philadelphia's Academy of Music on May 22. The concert included music by Shostakovitch, Schubert, and Beethoven. The orchestra's conductor is James Frazier, Jr., the first black conductor of the Philadelphia Orchestra. The New Koto ensemble of Tokyo, an eight-woman group of koto players, recorded Vivaldi's *Four Seasons,* Mozart's *Eine kleine Nachtmusik* and *Symphony No. 40* and, in the fall, toured America with their unique sound.

On March 4, a revolutionary new concert hall was inaugurated in Denver, Colorado. The glittering crowd that paid $100 per ticket to hear Van Cliburn playing the Tchaikovsky First Piano Concerto—accompanied by the Denver Symphony Orchestra, conducted by Brian Priestman—may have been disappointed by Cliburn's perfomance, but everyone was thrilled by the Boettcher Concert Hall. The first American concert auditorium to have its stage at the center, the 2,700-seat room boasts superb acoustics, excellent sight lines, and an intimate ambience. Rows of seats arranged in arches closely surround the stage, and no seat is more than eighty-five feet from the performers.

Although the 1977 *Schwann Record and Tape Guide* listed Mozart as today's favorite classical composer (he added more classical titles to the guide than any other classical composer, leading the pack with 145 titles, while Beethoven had 129 and Bach a mere 117), according to radio station KFAC in Los Angeles, Ludwig is still the favorite in that city. One of the station's unique features is a top-forty countdown of classical works. According to George Fritzinger, head of the AM-FM station, Beethoven easily won 1978's top two spots with his Ninth and Sixth symphonies. Brahms's First Symphony was third, Beethoven's Fifth Symphony was fourth, and Tchaikovsky's Sixth Symphony, fifth.

The best-selling classical albums of the year included Lazar Berman's interpretation of the Rachmaninoff Piano Concerto #3; Claude Bolling's *Suite for Flute and Jazz Piano,* performed by Bolling and Jean-Pierre Rampal; Richard Kapp's *Greatest Hits of 1720;* Verdi's *Il Trovatore,* performed by the National Philharmonic Orchestra under the direction of Richard Bonynge and featuring Joan Sutherland, Luciano Pavarotti, and Marilyn Horne; Pachelbel's *Canon* performed by the Paillard Chamber Orchestra; *Operatic Duets* by Sutherland and Pavarotti; Zubin Mehta and the London Philharmonic performing John Williams's suites for *Star Wars* and *Close Encounters; Rachmaninoff's Concerto #3,* performed by Vladimir Horowitz and the New York Philharmonic under Eugene Ormandy; *Horowitz's Golden Jubilee Recital; The Great Pavarotti;* and Donizetti's *La Favorita* and Mahler's *Symphony #9* performed by the Chicago Symphony Orchestra.

Hundreds of thousands of listeners were attracted to summer music festivals that ranged from the Berkshires' Tanglewood extravaganza to Gian Carlo Menotti's transplanted Spoleto Festival, flourishing in Charleston, South Carolina, and from performances by the Metropolitan Opera and the New York Philharmonic in New York City's parks to the Colorado Opera Festival.

Lorsbach

Christian Steiner, Courtesy ICM Artists, Ltd.

Top: *Composer/conductor Leonard Bernstein celebrated his sixtieth birthday in 1978.* Left: *Beloved tenor Luciano Pavarotti sold more records than ever before in 1978 as RCA, his record company, gave his albums the same kind of promotional push they would give pop disks.* Bottom: *For Itzhak Perlman, 1978 was a year of continued growth.*

Easy Listening

A s smooth as cream, the easy-listening songs of 1978 provided a breathing space among the aggressive powerhouses of rock, R & B, jazz, and country. And, in 1978, so-called middle of the road (MOR) music offered its mellow tranquility to a growing audience. During late 1977's Musexpo, one of the music industry's trade conventions, members of the radio and record panel pointed out that almost every radio station battles for the ear of the young audience, even though that group makes up only 15 percent of total radio listeners. MOR radio stations have already begun to feel the results of the World War II baby boom. Those babies, who form a large bulge in the population curve, are in their mid-thirties, and many of them who grew up with rock and roll now want a more serene music. The quieting down of rock and roll in the last few years is one indication of this desire. The gold-winning success of country star Willie Nelson's album of standards, including such classic easy-listening songs as "Georgia on My Mind" and "Stardust," the title song, was another indication.

In the year 1978 Irving Berlin, the creator of all-American standards from "White Christmas" to "Easter Parade," celebrated his ninetieth birthday in May. A *Billboard* company called Music in the Air offered to radio stations a special two-and-a-half hour tribute to Berlin for airing on July 4. The show featured such all-time great performers as Bing Crosby, Al Jolson, Judy Garland, Johnny Mathis, and Kate Smith. The venerated songwriter was also honored on television in an August 22 "Salute to Irving Berlin."

More easy-listening nostalgia was provided by Margaret Whiting, Rose Marie, Rosemary Clooney, and Helen O'Connell, who got together in a traveling show called 4 Girls 4 that included such classic songs as "It Might as Well Be Spring" and "Moonlight in Vermont," as well as contemporary songs performed by the popular thrushes.

Contemporary MOR acts also did well. Tony Orlando, a top easy-listening performer, made a triumphant return to the stage in November 1977 at the Circle Theater in San Carlos, California. His December performance dates at Las Vegas's Riviera Hotel included bantering byplay with Paul Anka and Wayne Newton. Anne Murray, another easy-listening favorite,

made her return to performing in November 1977 at Las Vegas's Aladdin Hotel. Her strong, sure voice easily handled a number of styles, from the gentle rock of "What About Me?" and "Dream Lover" to the country sounds of "Snowbird" and "He Thinks I Still Care," George Jones's song.

Las Vegas, home of easy-listening artists, did strong year-end business in 1977, offering a wide roster of stars for Thanksgiving and Christmas festivities: Engelbert Humperdinck sang at the Riviera, the Carpenters performed at the MGM Grand, Harry James and his orchestra played in the grand ballroom of the MGM, Caesars Palace offered Manhattan Transfer, and the Aladdin featured Loretta Lynn.

Atlantic City, America's newest gambling paradise, followed in the musical footsteps of Las Vegas, featuring the new Ziegfeld Follies and Si Zentner's big band at Resorts International Hotel. Frankie Valli was the first act to perform there.

Other signs of the strength of mellow music was the enormous pop success of many easy-listening winners. Debby Boone's recording of "You Light Up My Life," for example, was one of the biggest pop hits of the past twenty years, as was Andy Gibb's "Shadow Dancing."

Other easy-listening songs that were top pop hits in 1978 included "How Deep Is Your Love" by the Bee Gees, "Blue Bayou" by Linda Ronstadt, "Don't It Make My Brown Eyes Blue" by Crystal Gayle, "Baby, What a Big Surprise" by Chicago, "Nobody Does It Better" by Carly Simon, "Slip Slidin' Away" by Paul Simon, "Here You Come Again" by Dolly Parton, "Just the Way You Are" by Billy Joel, "Emotion" by Samantha Sang, "I Can't Smile Without You" and "Copacabana" by Barry Manilow, "We'll Never Have to Say Goodbye Again" by England Dan and John Ford Coley, "Too Much, Too Little, Too Late" by Johnny Mathis and Deniece Williams, "The Closer I Get to You" by Roberta Flack and Donny Hathaway, "You Belong to Me" by Carly Simon, "With a Little Luck" by Wings, and "Baker Street" by Gerry Rafferty.

Additional songs that captured the easy-listening market in 1978 were "Just Remember I Love You" by Firefall, "We're All Alone" and "You" by Rita Coolidge, "How Can I Leave You Again" by John Denver, "Desirée" by Neil Diamond, "(What a) Wonderful

Preceding pages: *Carly Simon and husband James Taylor had a huge easy-listening and a solid pop hit with their beautifully harmonized version of the Everly Brothers' "Devoted to You."* Right: *Barry Manilow kept turning out hits in 1978, including the danceable "Copacabana."*

Tony Korody

Couples abounded in 1978, in life as well as on disk.
Above: *John Denver and wife Ann celebrate at the Grammy awards gala party.* Opposite: *Richard and Karen Carpenter had an easy-listening hit with "Sweet Sweet Smile."*

World" by Art Garfunkel with Paul Simon and James Taylor, "Goodbye Girl" by David Gates, "Curious Minds (Um, Um, Um, Um, Um)" by Johnny Rivers, "Everybody Loves a Rain Song" by B. J. Thomas, "Lady Love" by Lou Rawls, "Before My Heart Finds Out" by Gene Cotton, "The Circle Is Small" by Gordon Lightfoot, "Feels So Good" by Chuck Mangione, "Ready for the Times to Get Better" by Crystal Gayle, "If Ever I See You Again" by Roberta Flack, "Songbird" by Barbra Streisand, "Bluer Than Blue" by Michael Johnson, "My Angel Baby" by Toby Beau, and "You Needed Me" by Anne Murray.

Courtesy A & M Records

Denny Laine and Paul McCartney, who along with Linda McCartney form the group Wings, scored during the year with the album London Town *and its title single.*

Robert Scott

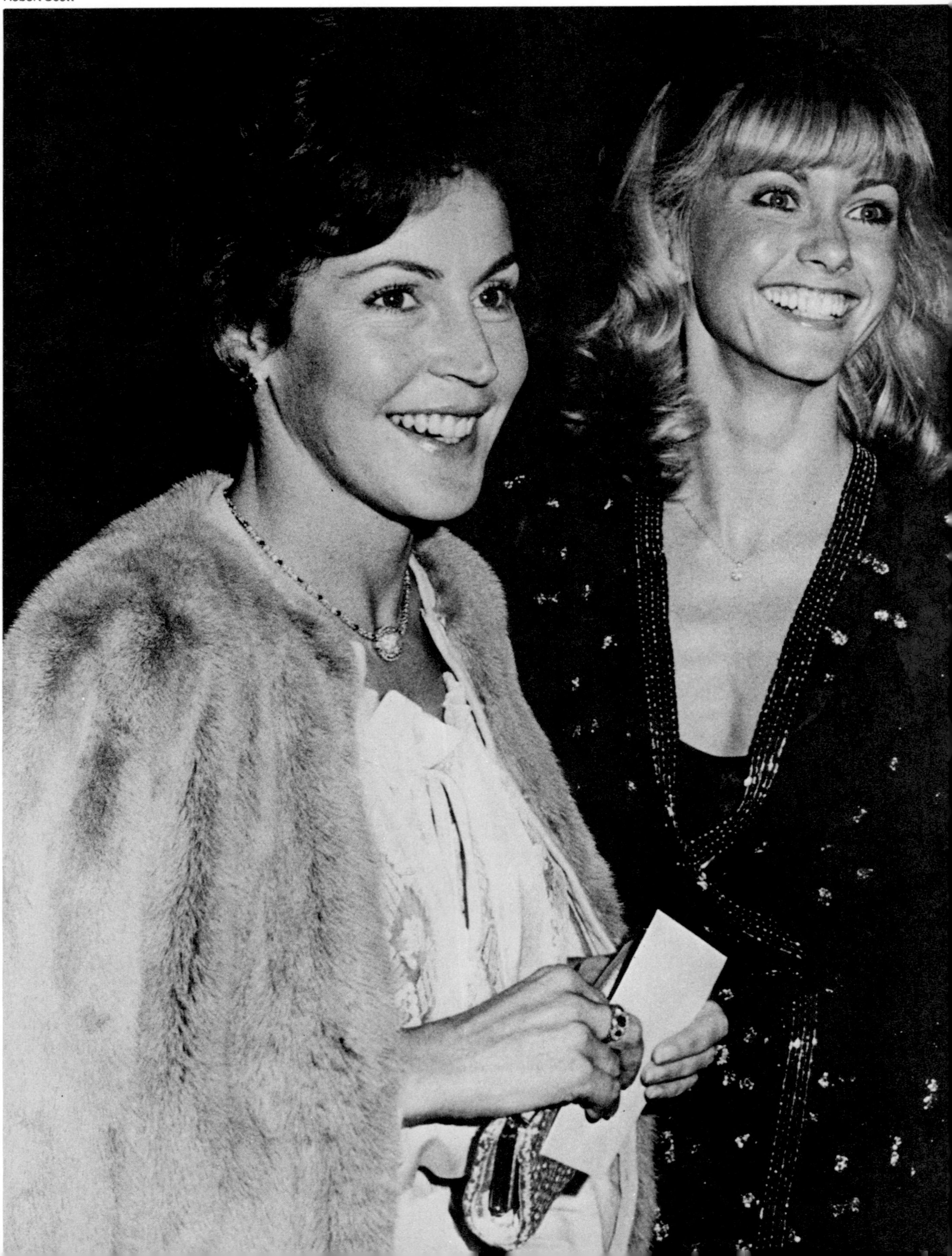

Waring Abbott

Opposite: *Two easy-listening stars,*
Helen Reddy and Olivia Newton-John, share
a smiling moment after a Hollywood
party. Left: *Art Garfunkel, whose version*
of "(What a) Wonderful World" was a big
easy-listening hit in 1978, views
an exhibit of Linda McCartney's photos
in New York's Bayard Gallery.

Disco

The year 1978 was the year of the flash, the pulse, the pounding beat of disco. Ignited by the incendiary success of *Saturday Night Fever,* the disco explosion rocked the world. High society may have done the twist in much-publicized embryonic discotheques in the 1960s, but it wasn't until the end of 1977, when a bigger-than-life John Travolta strutted across a strobe-lit dance floor, that disco suddenly had an irresistible image.

Sparked by the relentless rhythms of the Bee Gees, Travolta acted out everyone's dance floor fantasy, and more than 40 million Americans couldn't wait to strap on their dancing shoes and boogie to their favorite club, where, amid swirling clouds of smoke, banks of pulsing lights, stabbing lasers, and glittering mirrored balls, dancers could shed their problems (and, in some of the more sophisticated pleasure palaces, their clothes as well), and party. Blacks and whites, gays and straights, young and old mingled buoyantly on the dance floor, proudly showing off the latest dance steps, from the hustle to the freak.

Those potential kings and queens of the dance floor made disco a $4-billion business in 1978. They fought to gain admittance to New York's haughty Studio 54; they crowded Dirty Sally's, Los Angeles's sleek shipboard club; they jammed Chicago's Galaxy Disco, with its futuristic, underlit dance floor; they gave new life to New Orleans's revamped, elegant, seventy-four-year-old Civic Theatre; and they lined up for North Miami's California Club, Portland's Earthquake Ethel's, Washington, D.C.'s, Tramps, and San Francisco's mammoth new Trocadero Transfer.

They spun and whirled to such disco hits as Chic's "Dance, Dance, Dance," Odyssey's "Native New Yorker," Santa Esmeralda's "Don't Let Me Be Misunderstood," Donna Summer's album *Once Upon a Time,* and her "Last Dance," from the film *Thank God It's Friday,* Le Pamplemousse's "Le Spank," Cerrone's "Supernature," "Give Me Love," and "Love Is Here," the THP Orchestra's "Two Hot for Love," T-Connection's "On Fire," Bionic Boogie's "Bionic Boogie," Love Express's "Let's All Chant," the Bee Gees' "Stayin' Alive," Alec R. Costandinos and the Syncophonic Orchestra's "Romeo and Juliet," Peter Brown's "Dance with Me," Village People's "Macho

Man," Linda Clifford's "If My Friends Could See Me Now," the USA-European Connection's "Come Into My Heart," Marlin's "Voyage," the Saturday Night Band's "Come on Dance, Dance," Madleen Kane's "Rough Diamond," Taste of Honey's "Boogie Oogie Oogie," Karen Young's "Hot Shot," Rick James's "You and I," and Grace Jones's "Do or Die."

The record companies that dominated the field were TK, Casablanca, and Salsoul, but when disco hits began to display crossover activity into the vast pop market, other record labels began making forays into the disco field as well. Warner Brothers took a chance with Madleen Kane, as did Capitol with Taste of Honey—both were strikingly successful. Radio stations that initially resisted disco product were impressed by crossover hits from the Village People, Peter Brown, Donna Summer, Evelyn "Champagne" King, and Linda Clifford, as well as by the growing success of such disco radio stations as New York's WKTU-FM and WBLS-FM and Philadelphia's WCAU-FM.

Television also jumped on the bandwagon. Never-say-die Dick Clark introduced "Le Disco," a ninety-minute pilot shown on NBC on August 19. "Disco '77" reappeared as "Disco Magic" and was shown in sixty U.S. cities. Producer/director Kip Walton's "Hot City" was sold to Metromedia before the program had a host, staff, or name. Other television programs, such as "American Bandstand," "Midnight Special," and "Soul Train," regularly featured such disco artists as Donna Summer, KC & the Sunshine Band, and Peter Brown. Merv Griffin and Dinah Shore also featured disco artists.

As Neil Bogart, president of Casablanca Records, expressed it at *Billboard*'s overwhelmingly successful fourth annual Disco Forum (so successful that the event will now take place twice a year), disco is "a major influence in the world of fashion. It is a dynamic factor in contemporary advertising. It is a message from every consumer that there has been a rediscovery of America's greatest by-product—fun."

Bogart, whose company made the film *Thank God It's Friday,* a box-office smash with a platinum soundtrack, predicts that the disco wave has not yet crested. Judging from the momentum of disco growth, he's probably right.

Preceding pages: *Perhaps the person most responsible for 1978's disco craze was John Travolta, seen here with costar Karen Gorney in* Saturday Night Fever, *the disco film of the year.* Opposite: *Donna Summer began to grow beyond disco in 1978 with her shining version of "MacArthur Park."*

Robin Platzer, Images

In addition to the usual light and sound extravaganzas, clubs, in the fierce competition for the disco crowd, have adopted other attractions to lure customers. The trend to live performers in discos began in New York City when Bette Midler's January stint at the Copacabana drew heavy crowds. Hurrah's, another Manhattan club, opened with female impersonator Devine performing in *Neon Woman*. New York's Starship Discovery 1 featured such hot performers as the Crown Heights Affair and Andrea True, while Chicago's Happy Medium swelled its attendance with shows by B. T. Express and Pablo Cruise and San Francisco's The City had fabulous success featuring such stars as Grace Jones, Tuxedo Junction, and Silver Convention.

Some clubs used decorating novelties to attract customers. Club 747 in Buffalo, New York, was the flagship of a growing chain of discos designed to look like 747 planes, using actual 747 interior accessories for decoration. Other clubs flashed continuous slide shows on the walls, while still others offered animated films designed by computers. Roller rinks saw the disco phenomenon as a way to boost sagging patronage. They packed away their barrel organs, invested in some of the spiffiest new sound equipment (to drown out the sound of skates), and showed customers how easy it was to dance on wheels. In California, the Conejo Valley Ice Skating Center became the country's first icecotheque.

The disco craze also inspired a rush of dance contests and marathons. At the Hollywood Palladium on January 21, 415 dancers tripped the light fantastic in a twenty-four-hour dance marathon that netted seventy thousand dollars for the Los Angeles County Easter Seals Society. Janet Cutting and Alphonse Robles of Boston won grand prize in a contest sponsored by Casablanca Filmworks/Nightfall Magazine. Susan Cullen and Frank Andriolo danced off with the grand prize offered by Miami's California Club for its Wednesday Night Fever competitions, impressing such expert judges as disco stars Harry Wayne Casey and Vickie Sue Robinson and tennis sensation Ilie Nastase. On May 5, 42,000 spectators jammed Philadelphia's Veteran's Stadium to cheer on contestants in the *Philadelphia Daily News* Disco Fever Contest. And New Jersey hoofers got their chance to shine in July when Broadway Productions launched a Sunday Night Fever Dance Contest, with the big prize a vacation for two in the Bahamas.

Alas, all this hedonism had its price. Jill Carty,

Merry Alpern/Goldsmith Studios

Ebet Roberts

124

community medicine student at the University of Utah's College of Medicine—a part-time disco deejay herself—warned that the loud sounds of disco could cause permanent hearing loss. Proof of this clear and present danger was offered by the results of a hearing test given in July to disco deejays by the New York League for the Hard of Hearing. Forty percent of the twenty-five deejays tested showed hearing loss. Filling the need for protection, California's Norton Safety Products developed a filter to be worn in the ear, allowing users to hear the music clearly but eliminating the pain of high volume. The ever-vigilant Food and Drug Administration pointed out yet another disco hazard by warning that laser beams can burn the skin or damage the eyes if safety standards set by the FDA's Bureau of Radiological Health were not met.

Disco fans remained undaunted by such caveats, however, and continued to push the budding industry from one high to another.

Opposite page, top: *Heatwave sizzled in 1978 with their* Central Heating. Bottom: *Janice Johnson of* Taste of Honey, *who soared with "Boogie Oogie Oogie."* This page, top: *The Village People.* Bottom: *Boston Celtics' Kevin Stacom hustles.*

Movies

The movie world was ablaze in 1978, sizzling to the irresistible flame of Robert Stigwood's grand-slam winner *Saturday Night Fever*. Movie-goers cheered *Nur Samstag Nacht* in Germany, jammed theaters for *La Fièvre du Samedi Soir* in Paris, and queued up in London to hear the exotic accents of Bay Ridge, Brooklyn. The film that cost $3 million to produce and another $3 million to promote set new box-office records in Australia and Puerto Rico and by mid-July, according to *Variety,* had grossed more than $35 million in the United States alone.

It was more than a film; it was a phenomenon: posters, T-shirts, books, magazines, ten-foot tall record-store displays, all carried John Travolta's smoldering image. Sales campaigns for countless products suddenly caught fire, everything from Disco Fever and T-Shirt Fever to Wall-to-Wall Carpeting Fever. "Saturday Night Live" created a parody, "Samurai Night Fever"; *Mad* magazine frolicked with "Saturday Night Feeble"; New Yorkers were treated to a hilarious television ad by a benignly lunatic stereo dealer: Crazy Eddie Fever. And, in late July, Sesame Street Records announced *Sesame Street Fever,* a take-off album produced with the full cooperation of Robert Stigwood and featuring Andy Gibb, Cookie Monster, Oscar the Grouch, and Big Bird.

Beginning in November 1977 with the release of "How Deep Is My Love," the Bee Gees' sweet harmonies, propelled by an intense disco beat, were everywhere. The music from the film broadcast its vibrant message from radio stations, record stores, and chic boutiques. It was blasted incessantly on the streets and at every discotheque; no party was complete without the throb of "Stayin' Alive," "More Than a Woman," "If I Can't Have You," and "Night Fever."

Slick and glossy, the film was a stunning vehicle for John Travolta, who took the one-dimensional, macho character of disco king Tony Manero, shaped it, and gave it depth and meaning. The plot was overburdened with gratuitous violence: an unnecessary brawl, an "accidental" death, a gang rape, a fallen priest. But sensitive performances from Travolta, Karen Gorney, Donna Pescow, and the pulsing brilliance of the disco scenes gave the movie an unequalled sparkle.

Not only did the film itself set the stage for an eruption of rock movies, its promotion sparked new concepts in cinematic publicity style as well. As Paramount Pictures President Michael D. Eisner told *New York Times* reporter Aljean Harmetz, "The days of just opening a movie with no fanfare are over for Paramount. The trick is to get people to know about your movie before it reaches the theatres." Paramount introduced *Fever* with a $400,000 party that was filmed for television and shown across the country the week before the movie opened. Two other 1978 rock films distributed by Paramount, *Grease* and *American Hot Wax,* used the same technique. *Grease,* another Stigwood production, was a sensational box-office winner, while *American Hot Wax* brought in a comfortable but not substantial gross, proving that it's not promotion alone that sells movies.

Nor does Elizabeth Taylor alone sell movies. She once did, as September 1977's Elizabeth Taylor retrospective at the Deauville Film Festival amply displayed. *A Little Night Music,* a Roger Corman production starring Miss Taylor, was shown as the climax to that retrospective and opened in New York in March. The film, which won Jonathan Tunick an Academy Award for Best Original Score Adaptation followed a curious course, appearing first as a movie, then a musical play, then a musical movie. It had its cinematic beginnings as Ingmar Bergman's *Smiles of a Summer Night.* Set to brilliant music and lyrics by Stephen Sondheim, the work appeared on Broadway as the 1973 Tony-award-winning *A Little Night Music;* in 1978 it was back on the silver screen. In this film, which featured Diana Rigg, Len Cariou, Lesley-Anne Down, and Hermione Gingold, Taylor performed "Send in the Clowns." The film musical was labored and dull, particularly in comparison to the delicious frothiness of the earlier versions.

Although there was a big hole in the center of *American Hot Wax* where the real story of Alan Freed should have been, the movie, an April release, captured the slang, style, and music of 1959 so vividly that it was possible to forget the way the film blatantly ignored payola, which was Freed's real problem. Marvelously, Tim McIntyre as Freed managed to suggest a great depth of character. In the film's climactic scene, after anxious days of not knowing

Preceding pages: *John Travolta, and Eve Arden tear up the dance floor in* Grease. *Opposite, top: Karen Gorney and John Travolta in one of the disco scenes from* Saturday Night Fever, *the film that made America dance.* Bottom: *Elizabeth Taylor in* A Little Night Music.

whether he will be allowed to hold his first anniversary rock-and-roll show, Freed quietly but passionately tells a policeman backstage at the Brooklyn Paramount, "You can close the show, you can stop me, but you never can stop rock 'n' roll." The line invariably raises a heartfelt cheer from audiences already carried to a fever pitch by Jerry Lee Lewis, Screaming Jay Hawkins, and Chuck Berry.

The film was studded with sweet, memorable moments, such as Laraine Newman as teen-age Louise, a budding songwriter, corralling a black street-corner a cappella group and teaching them her song. There are wonderful scenes of would-be recording stars trouping through Freed's office, where he gives them either a fast yes or an equally fast no.

When the income tax people come swooping down on the box office just before the show begins and grab the receipts, Freed tells Chuck Berry, scheduled to go on next, that there will be no money to pay him. Berry grins. "It's okay," he says. "It's been good to me," and he goes on to duck walk across the stage, raising the screams of the crowd to even higher decibels. Produced by Art Vinson, who produced 1977's *Car Wash,* the movie was rich with a non-stop soundtrack of fifties greats, such as "Tutti Frutti," "Great Balls of Fire," and "Rave On."

Produced, written, directed, co-edited, distributed, and starred in by Bob Dylan, *Renaldo and Clara* was a nearly four-hour-long opus that left most of its viewers certain that they had seen a work of some import but rather uncertain as to what that import was. Featuring forty-seven songs, twenty-two written by Dylan, the concert shots taken from the Rolling Thunder Revue and the bicentennial tour were electrifying. The story, however, with its improvised scenes and multiple character changes was murky. Ronnie Hawkins played a character named Bob Dylan and Ronee Blakely played a character named Mrs. Dylan. The discernible plot concerned attempts of Renaldo (Dylan), Clara (Sara Dylan), and the Woman in White, a past lover of Dylan's (Joan Baez), to work out their emotional entanglements.

The film was indulgent yet somehow riveting, with Dylan's cinematic images often as powerful as his verbal ones. The cast featured Bob Neuwirth, Allen Ginsberg, Ramblin' Jack Elliott, Roger McGuinn, Mick Ronson, Joni Mitchell, and David Blue, who provided a slight narrative, the only cement the film had.

Dylan, who set up Circuit Films, headed by his brother David, to distribute the film, refused to sell the

Top: *Chuck Berry struts his stuff onstage in* American Hot Wax. Bottom: *Nancy Allen, Wendie Jo Sperber, Eddie Deezen, and Susan Kendall Newman play a group of New Jersey teens watching the Beatles in* I Wanna Hold Your Hand.

soundtrack rights to Columbia, although Columbia did send out 5000 promotional disks with songs from the film, including "People Get Ready," "Isis," and "It Ain't Me, Babe," all sung by Dylan, and a Johnny Ace song, "Never Let Me Go," sung by Dylan and Baez. The film did not do well, and at last report, Dylan was readying a slimmer, trimmer two-hour version for release.

Released in April, Motown's production of *Almost Summer* featured a score by Charles Lloyd and Ron Altback and a title song by Beach Boys Brian Wilson, Mike Love, and Al Jardine. The Beach Boys were originally slated to perform the song as well, but other commitments made it impossible for them to do so. The band that *did* perform the title song, a top-forty hit, was called Celebration, and included Mike Love and Charles Lloyd.

Although the real Beatles never appear in *I Wanna Hold Your Hand,* the low-budget, first full-length feature by Robert Zemeckis and Bob Gale, the Fab Four informed every moment of this charming April flop about six New Jersey high school students who travel to Manhattan in 1964, hoping to crash the Ed Sullivan Show on which the Beatles appeared. An endearing, innocent film, bursting with early Beatles music and capturing the fine frenzy that surrounded them, it featured Susan Kendall Newman, Paul Newman's daughter, as a folkie who hated the Beatles and who, with a schoolmate played by Bobby DeCicco, another Beatle hater, tried to sabotage the show. Murray the K, the disk jockey who called himself the fifth Beatle in those early days, played himself in the movie. Impressionist Will Jordan played Ed Sullivan.

While *I Wanna Hold Your Hand* concentrated on the audience, Martin Scorsese's masterful *The Last Waltz* focused on the performers. As Scorsese told *Daily News* reporter Susan Toepfer about his filmed document of the Band's Thanksgiving, 1976, farewell concert at Winterland in San Francisco, "I wanted to show the performers. But I was shocked at what we got. Their expressions, attitudes, the way they looked at each other. It was remarkable. I loved it."

The film was indeed a concert-goer's dream, offering sensational close-ups of a size and quality unobtainable in any other medium. It was an aural treat as well, an unforgettable concert captured on a twenty-four-track Dolby stereo soundtrack. At the beginning of the movie, the line "Play This Film Loud" flashes across the screen, and in theaters across the country, especially those among the growing number equipped to handle films with a Dolby soundtrack, they did just that.

The muted sepia tones of the print and the poignant melody of the waltz that opens and closes the film underline the movie's elegiac nature. The concert marked the end of the Band's sixteen years of touring together, and although the film contained upbeat performances by top musicians—Eric Clapton, Neil Diamond, Bob Dylan, Joni Mitchell, Neil Young, Emmylou Harris, Van Morrison, the Staples, Dr. John, Muddy Waters, Paul Butterfield, Ronnie Hawkins, Ringo Starr, and Ron Wood—it was a celebration tinged with sadness. It was also a box-office disappointment.

At the end of April the film *FM* premiered. Sparked by the tight performances of Jeff Dugan as the manager of top-rated Los Angeles radio station QSKY and Martin Mull, Eileen Brennan, and Cleavon Little as his three top jocks, the movie focused on the conflicts between the manager of the station, who wants to increase profits by selling advertising time to the army, and the staff, who insist on maintaining the image that has made them successful and on continuing to give their audience what it wants. But, as Andrew Sarris pointed out in the *Village Voice,* the film was a "fantasy on the crudest comic-strip level."

The film did not do well; what made its one-dimensional attitudes bearable was the music. Ignited by the fine live performances of Jimmy Buffett and Linda Ronstadt, the soundtrack album sold more than a million copies and contained the hit single "FM" by Steely Dan.

In May, Motown and Casablanca brought moviegoers thirty-two songs wrapped up in *Thank God It's Friday,* a flimsy construction taking place during one night at the Zoo, a Los Angeles discotheque. Produced in the fragmented style of *Car Wash,* the film featured Donna Summer as an aspiring singer and Chick Vennera as the Zoo's deejay. While the movie was roundly trounced by reviewers, it drew well, and the soundtrack was a top-ten album, selling more than a million copies.

On May 18, another low-budget movie, *The Buddy Holly Story,* opened in Lubbock, Texas, home of the legendary singer/songwriter. Holly, who was killed in a plane crash in 1959 at the age of twenty-two, left a legacy of seminal, diamond-hard rockers, such as "That'll Be the Day," "Peggy Sue," "Oh Boy," "Well, Alright, " "Maybe Baby," and others. He left his mark on the generation, and in this condensed, powerful

film, he is portrayed with electric excitement by actor Gary Busey, himself a drummer since junior high school. Under his musician's stage name, Teddy Jack Eddy, Busey has appeared on television and toured with Leon Russell. All the music in the movie, performed by Busey with Don Stroud and Charles Martin Smith as his back-up band, the Crickets, was recorded live, giving the film a crackling vitality.

If Ever I See You Again, May 1978's film from Joe Brooks, creator of *You Light Up My Life,* gave us the title song (a top-thirty hit for Roberta Flack), "California," "Come Share My Love," and "When It's Over." The low-key love story, critically beaten to death, starred Joe Brooks, Shelley Hack, and Jimmy Breslin and featured George Plimpton.

Other films released in May included American International's *Our Winning Season,* a high school love story with songs by Charles Fox and Dave Loggins. Music by Rod Stewart and Ted Nugent sparked *On the Air Live with Captain Midnight.* The original hard-rocking score by War for *Youngblood* added a great deal to that melodrama about street blacks. May also saw the reissue of *American Graffiti,* which did fine business in theaters around the country.

Nelson Riddle wrote the music for *Harper Valley PTA,* but the title song, on which the music was based, was written by Tom T. Hall and was sung by Jeannie C. Riley, who had a huge hit with it ten years ago. The movie tells the story of how Barbara Eden and her best friend (played by Nanette Fabray) take revenge on the Harper Valley hypocrites who try to run Eden out of town. Funny and low key, the movie was a box-office success.

Several classical films also made their appearance in May. Hans Conrad Fischer produced and directed three musical biographies—lives of Beethoven, Bruckner, and Mozart—designed to be shown in the mornings, when movie theaters are normally closed. Alban Berg's opera *Lulu,* a violent film, appeared under the production of Ronald Chase.

In June, moviegoers were treated to the zip of another Robert Stigwood bonanza, *Grease,* based on the long-running Broadway show (it passed the twenty-seven-hundred-performance mark in 1978). A refreshing fantasy of teen life in the 1950s, the film starred Olivia Newton-John and John Travolta and featured a sterling collection of personalities associated with the 1950s, including Eve Arden, Frankie Avalon, Joan Blondell, Edd Byrnes, Sid Caesar, and a guest appearance by those glorious

Clockwise from upper left:
Phil Adams plays a Tarzan-type waiter in Thank God It's Friday. *Two scenes from the Band's farewell concert, immortalized in Martin Scorsese's* The Last Waltz. *Martin Mull, Cassie Yates, Michael Brandon, and Jay Fenichel celebrate the victory of DJs over management in* FM.

133

greasers themselves, Sha Na Na.

Both the movie and the music did spectacularly. The soundtrack album, containing the original show music by Jim Jacobs and Warren Casey and beefed up with a batch of new songs by John Farrar and one by Barry Gibb, was a million-seller, and before the month of July was over, three songs from the movie had become winners. The first hit was the speedy number-one, two-million-selling Newton-John and Travolta duet "You're the One That I Want." That was followed by Frankie Valli's performance of Barry Gibb's song "Grease," and close on its heels came Olivia singing John Farrar's "Hopelessly Devoted to You."

Another film based on a song was *Convoy,* from the country hit by C. W. McCall. The Sam Peckinpah movie, starring Kris Kristofferson and Ali MacGraw, won no flowers from the critics, but audiences enjoyed it. It was a smash in Japan and grossed fairly well in the United States.

Corvette Summer, a June release from MGM, featured Dusty Springfield singing "Give Me the Night" in an enjoyable story about Mark Hamill's adventures as he tries to recover a stolen sports car.

The importance of good sound in a rock movie was amply demonstrated by the lack of it in *The Punk Rock Movie,* a murky, at times almost inaudible British import featuring a solidly punk lineup including the Sex Pistols, the Clash, the Slits, Siouxsie and the Banshees, Generation X, and Slaughter and the Dogs.

In July came the long-awaited, much-heralded release of Robert Stigwood's *Sgt. Pepper's Lonely Hearts Club Band,* the film based on the 1968 Beatles album of the same name. (The movie also included a couple of songs from other Beatles albums.)

How could a film be based on that album? Why should the Bee Gees undertake Beatles songs, so different from the Gibbs' current style, in arrangements very similar to the originals? Reviewers asked those questions repeatedly, because the film did not hold together. The Bee Gees and Peter Frampton, fine musicians, were lackluster thespians; the plot was ultimately silly, and the connection between songs and story line sometimes absurdly forced and awkward.

However, the film did not merit the viciousness of the critical attacks that were hurled against it. As *Billboard*'s Roman Kozak shrewdly pointed out when he described the negative atmosphere of the press screenings, *Sgt. Pepper* was not made for film critics or for rock reviewers but for Bee Gees and Frampton

fans too young to know the original Beatles album.

Despite its shortcomings, the film boasted rich, polished production values and moments that were quite marvelous. George Burns sang and soft-shoed his way through "Fixing a Hole," with a twinkle and cheerful warmth and agility; Stargard and newcomer Dianne Steinberg purred lusciously in an aggressively seductive "Lucy in the Sky with Diamonds"; Billy Preston, resplendent in yellow satin, pranced through a white-hot version of "Get Back"; Steve Martin leaped fiendishly about in a purely lunatic production number of "Maxwell's Silver Hammer"; the Bee Gees, in striking silhouette, sang "Nowhere Man" with breathtaking sweetness; and Aerosmith, standing atop stacks of mammoth coins, brought a sinister new meaning to "Come Together." Perhaps the film would have made more sense if it had been presented as a straight collection of acts performing the songs with no pretense of a story line.

At the end of October, Universal Pictures released *The Wiz,* a bountiful bonanza of a musical based on the Broadway smash *The Wiz,* which was based on L. Frank Baum's book *The Wonderful Wizard of Oz,* featuring exuberant performances by Diana Ross, Michael Jackson, Nipsey Russell, Ted Ross, Lena Horne, and Richard Pryor. Quincy Jones's adaptation of the rambunctious score and Albert Whitlock's audacious visual effects combined in an irresistible blockbuster movie.

Other autumnal musical confections included the Who's movie, *The Kids Are Alright,* and *Aloha Donny and Marie,* with the inimitable Osmond duo cavorting in a lush, tropical setting.

Top: *Barry, Robin, and Maurice Gibb and Peter Frampton play "Sgt. Pepper's Lonely Hearts Club Band" in the Robert Stigwood production.* Bottom: *Gary Busey stars in the title role of* The Buddy Holly Story, *based on Holly's life. Don Stroud and Charlie Martin Smith play the Crickets.*

Television

Courtesy CBS

Music in all its variety flowed abundantly from television sets in 1978. Classical, country, jazz, pop/rock, R & B, and easy listening were all represented in programs that captured, with varying degrees of success, the vitality of 1978's music scene. Such regularly programmed music series as "American Bandstand," "Soul Train," "Don Kirshner's Rock Concert," "Midnight Special," "Austin City Limits," "In Concert," "Lawrence Welk," and the music portions of such variety shows as "Saturday Night Live" continued to please viewers, and the following highlights of television's year in music were special treats.

On November 17, 1977, NBC aired Neil Diamond's special "I'm Glad You're Here with Me Tonight." Featuring live segments from concerts in England and Australia and some disarming patter from Neil, the show shimmered with fine music, performed with Neil's usual intense artistry. He sang the title song, a powerful "Desirée," "You Don't Bring Me Flowers," "Let Me Take You in My Arms Again," and "Skybird," from *Jonathan Livingston Seagull.*

On November 25, *Rolling Stone* brought its ambitious, expensive (more than a million dollars was spent by producer Steven Binder) "*Rolling Stone...* the 10th Anniversary" to CBS. Fans of the excellent magazine were disappointed by a program that was long on gimmicks but short on imaginative use of the medium. The pace was slow, the humor strained, and, except for the infectious drollery and explosive stage presence of Bette Midler and the unbeatable professionalism of Gladys Knight and the Pips, the show was a sluggish embarrassment.

On November 30, CBS hosted "The Johnny Cash Christmas Special." Joined by Jerry Lee Lewis, Carl Perkins, Roy Orbison, and Roy Clark, Johnny was his usual relaxed self, easily swinging the show from a reminiscence of Gene Autry songs to an Elvis tribute.

Tied together with a behind-the-scenes motif, December's "Paul Simon Special" on NBC was a less-than-successful ratings entry, but it was worth watching for songs like "Something So Right," "Loves Me Like a Rock," "Still Crazy After All These Years," The Boxer," and, with Art Garfunkel, "Old Friends."

"Benny Goodman In Concert at Wolf Trap" on December 26 was a PBS offering that went awry.

The show's sound was poor and Goodman's band sounded under-rehearsed.

On December 7, television got its first taste of disco fever when Paramount titillated moviegoers with scenes from *Saturday Night Fever* and presented a gala post-premiere party in a $76,000, specially built disco to promote the film.

NBC had the honor of presenting the "*Billboard* No. 1 Music Awards" on December 11. Featuring a clean-shaven Kris Kristofferson and the Bee Gees as hosts, the show included a warm tribute to Goddard Lieberson performed by Leonard Bernstein, Paul Simon, and Marvin Hamlisch. Other highlights were Patti Page, Frankie Laine, and Teresa Brewer singing their early fifties pre-rock-and-roll hits, and the Four Preps doing a parody of 1950s rock groups. Rod Stewart sang "Hot Legs" as he kicked soccer balls into the star-studded audience; George Benson and Glen Campbell performed "Nature Boy," and award presenters Donna Summer, Karen Carpenter, Peter Frampton, Rita Coolidge, Stevie Wonder, and Natalie Cole took their tasks seriously.

ABC's "Perry Como Christmas Show" on December 14 featured the smooth crooner along with Petula Clark and Leo Sayer in a tuneful hour. And New Year's Eve, although not the same without Guy Lombardo, did offer a sprightly Suzanne Somers hosting "Dick Clark's New Year's Rockin' Eve" on ABC. Crystal Gayle, K. C. & the Sunshine Band, Andy Gibb, and the Ohio Players provided festive music, and, at midnight, East-Coast viewers watching the frenzied Hollywood festivities could almost forget that when the televised revelers were shouting Happy New Year! it was really only 9 P.M. on the West Coast.

On January 8, 1978, NBC presented "Nashville Remembers Elvis on His Birthday," a tribute to the late singer featuring Jimmy Dean as host.

On January 9, Peter Frampton, Steve Martin, Barry Manilow, and Art Garfunkel appeared in "Variety '77—The Year in Entertainment," a CBS presentation that focused on 1977's biggest entertainment winners, featuring a performance by the entire cast of the smash Broadway musical *Annie.*

"Land of Hype and Glory," an Edwin Newman NBC report, presented on January 10, examined the various ways entertainment products are promoted.

Preceding pages: A galaxy of stars appeared on "Rolling Stone...the 10th Anniversary," among them such performers as Jerry Lee Lewis, Gladys Knight, Bette Midler, Richie Havens, Art Garfunkel, Sissy Spacek, and Steve Martin. Opposite: Neil Diamond in "I'm Glad You're Here with Me Tonight."

Courtesy NBC

The program featured books, movies, and music, using Kiss as the musical example, detailing the merchandising strategies that keep the world's most recognizable band in everyone's consciousness.

For two hours on January 16, ABC telecast Dick Clark's "The American Music Awards." America's favorite performers and records were chosen by a randomly selected group of 15,000 people across the country. The winners of this poll were honored in a show that featured such stars as Glen Campbell, Natalie Cole, Barry Manilow, David Soul, and Lou Rawls. Although the show was a noble attempt, it ran into many snags. None of the gaffes, however, could spoil the final moments, when Stevie Wonder sang "A-Tisket, A-Tasket" in tribute to a visibly moved Ella Fitzgerald.

January 22 offered two superior musical treats, particularly for Ray Charles fans, who got to see the master musician on two vastly different programs. He shared the spotlight with Gladys Knight and the Pips on a musical special produced for Home Box Office,

Opposite: *Leslie Uggams leads a male chorus on "The Kraft 75th Anniversary Special."* Top: *Singer Paul Simon took viewers backstage for his December 1977 special.* Bottom: *Carl Perkins, Roy Orbison, Johnny Cash, and Jerry Lee Lewis on "The Johnny Cash Christmas Special," on November 30, 1977, on CBS.*

the pay-cable television system. Filmed at Los Angeles's Greek Theatre, the polished, well-paced show featured top performances, offstage interviews, and rehearsal shots.

Charles also appeared on NBC's mammoth three-hour Big Event, "50 Years of Country Music." On that program, the stirring soul singer, whose songs are equally popular with country audiences, sang "I Can't Stop Loving You" and performed a duet with Glen Campbell on "Bye Bye Love." The show, cohosted by Campbell, Roy Acuff, and Dolly Parton, was a bountiful, authentically down-home extravaganza. Taped before a vigorously responsive live audience at Nashville's Grand Ole Opry House, the show featured performances by Country Music Hall of Fame members Roy Acuff and his Smoky Mountain Boys, Bill Monroe and his Blue Grass Boys, Ernest Tubb with the Texas Troubadours, Minnie Pearl, Kitty Wells, and Chet Atkins. Also appearing was a host of contemporary country greats, including Johnny Cash, Loretta Lynn, Merle Haggard, Charlie Rich, Mel Tillis, Larry Gatlin, Crystal Gayle, Doug Kershaw, the Oak Ridge Boys, the Statler Brothers, Tammy Wynette, and dazzling new country-rock star Carlene Carter, daughter of June Carter Cash and stepdaughter of Johnny Cash.

On January 24, CBS presented home viewers with "The Kraft 75th Anniversary Special," a look at forty-five years of radio and television broadcasting, featuring nostalgic moments from radio's "Kraft Music Hall" with the Paul Whiteman Orchestra, Al Jolson, long-time host Bing Crosby, and a look at "The Kraft Music Hall" on television, following hosts Perry Como, Andy Williams, John Davidson, and Alan King through the years.

In February, CBS displayed the dazzling Liberace in a special called "Leapin' Lizards, It's Liberace." Mr. Flash was his usual extravagant self, bringing on a sparkling Debbie Reynolds for a duet of "I Don't Need Anything But You," from *Annie.*

With his usual low-key ease, John Denver took ABC viewers on a relaxed, music-filled tour of Australia on "John Denver in Australia." Denver's songs were pleasant, Debby Boone did a shimmering job on "You Light Up My Life," and, although the attempts at humor were sophomoric, Denver's ingenuous manner made them all endearing rather than offensive.

Mary Tyler Moore, television's favorite sunshine girl, sparkled in "How to Survive the '70s and Maybe Even Bump Into Happiness," a CBS variety-music

Courtesy PBS

special on February 22.

On February 18, Eugene Ormandy led the Philadelphia Orchestra and the Mendelssohn Club Chorus in Gustav Holst's *The Planets.* No space-age lasers flashed from the home screen, but the performance was superior and the PBS telecast was enhanced by excellent audio, a rarity for television music shows.

"The 20th Annual Grammy Awards Show," telecast by CBS on February 23, ran for a crisp, smooth 135 minutes. The Pierre Cossette production featured John Denver as emcee and performances by Grammy-winners Count Basie, James Cleveland, and Crystal Gayle, as well as by nominees Shaun Cassidy, Ronnie Milsap, Joe Tex, and Igor Kipnis. Cab Calloway received a standing ovation when he appeared to present the Hall of Fame disks.

ABC presented "The Second Barry Manilow Special" on February 24, an inventive return for the award-winning singer. Featuring Ray Charles, it was a well-paced hour, which segued easily from sketches to straight songs.

On February 26, PBS telecast Vladimir Horowitz's historic White House concert, celebrating the fiftieth anniversary of the pianist's American debut. Horowitz

Courtesy NBC

Clockwise from upper left: *Singer Helen Humes on PBS's "Big Band Bash." The Rutles, Eric Idle's satirical view of the Beatles, starred in NBC's "All You Need Is Cash." The Jackson brothers competed in "The First Annual Rock 'n' Roll Sports Classic." Kenny Rogers and Dottie West hosted "The World's Largest Indoor Country Music Show."*

Robin Platzer, Images

Courtesy NBC

Above: *"Ringo" starred Ringo Starr as both a famous rock star and as his double, poverty-stricken Ognir Rrats.* Opposite: *Donna Summer surprised audiences with her fine performance in* Thank God It's Friday. *She toured the country with a varied stage show, singing a wide spectrum of songs, from ballads to rock as well as disco.*

charmed President Carter and guests with performances of Chopin, Mozart, and Schumann.

PBS's "Big Band Bash" was a noble three-hour attempt to capture the excitement of the big-band era, but it was long and sloppy. Its most successful moments were film clips of such performers as Duke Ellington, Louis Armstrong, Glenn Miller, Benny Goodman and his band, and Frank Sinatra with the Lucky Strike Hit Parade Orchestra conducted by Mark Warnow.

Giggles and guffaws were plentifully provided by NBC on March 22 when the Rutles appeared on the home screen in a giddy parody of the Beatles called "All You Need Is Cash." Written by Monty Python star Eric Idle, the program satirized every stage of the Beatles' rise and demise, its most brilliant moments the songs by Neil Innes that uncannily captured the sound of the Beatles and, as *New York Times* reviewer John J. O'Connor commented, "turned it to mush."

For those who preferred musical elegance to parody, on the same evening PBS offered Herbert

von Karajan conducting La Scala of Milan chorus and orchestra, soloists Leontyne Price, Fiorenza Cossotto, Luciano Pavarotti, and Nicolai Ghiaurov in a luminous performance of Verdi's *Requiem.*

On March 26, André Previn hosted a fascinating mix of music and interviews on the first of a series featuring himself and the Pittsburgh Symphony Orchestra. The multitalented Mr. Previn discussed and conducted music by Prokofiev, Korngold, Walton, and Copland and interviewed composer John Williams who then led the Pittsburgh in a portion of the *Star Wars* theme.

Dolly Parton, Rod Stewart, and the Tubes joined Chér in "Chér . . . Special" on April 3 on ABC. Chér's heralded television comeback featured the glamorous songstress doing what she does best—having a marvelous time living out her fantasies onstage.

Later that same evening the Academy of Motion Picture Arts and Sciences put on its annual awards show, Oscar sharing the spotlight this year with the *Star Wars* robots C3PO and R2D2, as well as Mickey Mouse.

"The World's Largest Indoor Country Music Show" on April 5 was an NBC Big Event featuring Kenny Rogers and Dottie West as emcees, such country stars as Roy Acuff, Red Sovine, Porter Wagoner, Don Williams, Minnie Pearl, and an enthusiastic audience of some 65,000 at Pontiac Michigan's Silverdome.

"Pat Boone and Family," a pleasant musical evening, on ABC April 8, featured Debby neatly stealing the show from the rest of the Boones, including dad.

"Ringo," starring Ringo Starr on April 26, was an interesting approach to a television music special. Ringo loosely adapted *The Prince and the Pauper* theme, making the prince a rock star (Ringo) and his double, Ognir Rrats, a poor street-corner map vendor. The show featured the singing debut of a surprisingly strong-voiced Carrie Fisher.

On May 4, NBC telecast "The First Annual Rock 'n' Roll Sports Classic," in which an assortment of stars, including Rod Stewart, Kenny Loggins, Billy Davis, Marilyn McCoo, and many others, competed in various sports events. The biggest winner was Jackie Jackson, who ran off with four trophies, closely followed by Ronald LaPread of the Commodores and the Runaways' Sandy West who won three trophies each in contests as fiercely fought as any race for the top of the charts.

Above: Fiery performer Bruce Springsteen was welcomed back in 1978 with well-earned adulation, particularly in New York, where three concerts sold out in an hour. Left: The Commodores' Lionel Ritchie always gives an ecstatic performance. The band's success in 1978 included the hit "Three Times a Lady." Opposite: One of rock's great talents, Eric Clapton continued his success in 1978 with the platinum album Slowhand and the gold single "Lay Down Sally."

Clockwise from upper right:
*James Taylor won applause in 1978
at appearances with wife Carly Simon.
Crystal Gayle's Grammy-winning "Don't it
Make My Brown Eyes Blue" was one of the year's
most frequently programmed songs, as was her 1978
release "Talking in Your Sleep." With his album*
Foot Loose and Fancy Free *a top-charted winner
for months, several TV appearances, and
some touring, Rod Stewart remained very
much in the public eye. Opposite, top:
Charlaine Woodard and Andre De Shields dance
up a storm in the Tony-winning* Ain't Misbehavin',
*one of Broadway's 1978 smashes. Below: The
success of their collaboration on "Too
Much, Too Little, Too Late" led to
the teaming of Johnny Mathis and
Deniece Williams on* That's
What Friends Are For,
a top-twenty album.

Above: *Liza Minnelli—whose bravura performance in* The Act
*won her a Tony Award for Best Actress in a Musical—performing in
a benefit performance for New York City at Studio 54.* Opposite: *For
Jefferson Starship's inimitable lead singer Grace Slick, 1978 was a
year of illness and bouts with alcoholism, causing concern to
the rest of the band and her millions of fans.*

On May 8, ABC aired "The Stars Salute Israel at 30," featuring Pat and Debby Boone, Barry Manilow, Sammy Davis, and Barbra Streisand.

Patti Smith shared her views of the rock scene with Tom Snyder on his May 11 "Tomorrow" show on NBC. On May 23, ABC aired the "Academy of Country Music Awards Celebration," cohosted by Kenny Rogers, Donna Fargo, and Barbara Mandrell. A two-part "Country Night of Stars," an NBC presentation shown on May 23 and May 30, featured cohosts Charley Pride and Tennessee Ernie Ford on Part One and Crystal Gayle and Eddy Arnold on Part Two. Slick entertainments, they featured such top country names as Jeannie C. Reilly singing "Harper Valley PTA," Johnny Paycheck in his big black hat singing his hit "Take This Job and Shove It," a lovely Barbara Mandrell singing "Woman to Woman," and Conway Twitty singing "Wolverton Mountain."

Narrator William Holden led viewers through "Bing Crosby: His Life and Legend," a two-hour memorial to the late crooner aired by ABC on May 25. Interviews with many of Bing's friends, including Fred Astaire, Dean Martin, Bob Hope, Dinah Shore, Mary Martin, Grace Kelly, Frank Capra, Jimmy van Heusen, Ethel Merman, and Rosemary Clooney gave insights into what Holden described as Crosby's "remarkable naturalness and easy charm."

That program was followed four days later by a three-hour salute to Bob Hope called "Happy Birthday, Bob," featuring another stellar lineup that included Lynn Anderson, Pearl Bailey, Lucille Ball, George Burns, Charo, Kathryn Crosby, Mac Davis, Redd Foxx, Elliott Gould, Alan King, Dorothy Lamour, Carol Lawrence, Fred MacMurray, Tony Orlando, Donny and Marie Osmond, Telly Savalas, George C. Scott, David Soul, Elizabeth Taylor, Danny Thomas, and an interview with John Wayne, recovering from his heart surgery. The most moving moment occurred when Dolores Hope sang "On a Clear Day" with graceful assurance, obviously pleasing her husband enormously.

On May 31, NBC telecast the premiere of David Frost's "Headliners." Frost interviewed the Bee Gees, who revealed that they wrote the music for *Saturday Night Fever* in two weeks, and, when handed guitars, performed an impromptu version of "Massachusetts." Frost also interviewed a personable John Travolta in the star's DC3 airplane.

Beginning June 19, Dick Cavett on PBS presented an illuminating week-long songwriters'

Lynn Goldsmith

panel, featuring Paul Simon, Sammy Cahn, Joe Raposo, and Arthur Schwartz talking openly about the challenges and rewards of their craft.

On July 15, American television once again attempted to capture the success of Thames TV's 1976 hit "Rock Follies" but failed miserably with "The Rock Rainbow." That program simply lifted the British plot scene by scene, transplanted it to America, and turned what had been a mature, crisp comedy/drama into a soggy, whiny mess.

Portions of Cal Jam II appeared on television as a series of four one-hour specials on Metromedia beginning July 26. The programs included excellent footage of the acts.

On August 9, producer/director Kip Walton's speedy "Hot City" disco came to Metromedia. The first show featured Linda Clifford and The Sylvers, the second starred Aretha Franklin.

On August 22, NBC presented ninety minutes devoted to the music of Irving Berlin. "A Salute to Irving Berlin" starred Steve Lawrence and Eydie Gormé and featured Carol Burnett, Sammy Davis, and jazz pianist Oscar Peterson performing a collection of such shining all-American classics as "Puttin' on the Ritz," "Anything You Can Do," "Alexander's Ragtime Band," and "Cheek to Cheek." PBS gave America a chance to participate in the celebration of Leonard Bernstein's sixtieth birthday on August 25. The program was hosted by William Schuman, Lauren Bacall, and Lillian Hellman and featured Bernstein conducting the National Symphony Orchestra with cellist Mstislav Rostropovich, violinist Yehudi Menuhin, and pianist André Previn in a performance of Beethoven's Triple Concerto.

Left: *Barry Manilow displays exuberance during his 1978 television show, "The Second Barry Manilow Special."* Above: *John Belushi of "Saturday Night Live" deadpans with singer Art Garfunkel in one of the wacky scenes that keep viewers tuning in to the show week after week.*

Tony Korody

153

Theater

Martha Swope

Big, splashy musicals continued to breathe life into the Broadway scene in 1978. Successful holdovers from previous seasons, including 1977's *Annie, Beatlemania, I Love My Wife, The King and I,* and older confections like *A Chorus Line, For Colored Girls, The Magic Show, Grease,* and *The Wiz,* continued to sparkle. They were met and matched by new song and dance shows that were long on music if sometimes short on plot: out of ten Broadway musicals, six were revues or had only flimsy excuses for plot lines.

Could the number of skimpy plots have inspired what the Dramatists Guild interpreted as a snub in the presentation of this year's Tony awards? During the television presentation, award-winning writers, librettists, lyricists, and composers were denied the opportunity to enjoy a solo spotlight. Their awards were either presented offstage or in conjunction with award winners in other categories. Stephen Sondheim, president of the Dramatists Guild, threatened that the Guild would withhold permission to perform songs from nominated shows if the practice hasn't been changed by 1979.

Broadway musicals were so appealing that even January and February's frigid snowstorms could not daunt New Yorkers eager to see plays. Realizing that such inclement weather was likely to mean cancellations by those foolish or unfortunate enough to live out of town, intrepid New Yorkers snowshoed, skied, or plowed their way to the Great White Way to see whether they could grab abandoned tickets to *Annie, A Chorus Line,* or *The Act.*

The money-making potential of long-running Broadway musicals such as *The Wiz* and *Grease*— which, in its seventh year on Broadway, received an unexpected box-office boost from the movie and edged out *My Fair Lady* as the third-longest-running show in Broadway history—was understood by at least one major entertainment corporation in 1978. Warner Communications joined with Regency Communications to form Warner-Regency, a new company that intends to find and produce theatrical properties. Stephen Friedman and Irwin Meyer, who coproduced 1977's Tony-winning *Annie,* head the new firm.

The season started off on October 29, when high-octane Liza Minnelli stormed into New York with *The Act.* Given its rocky background, it was a wonder the musical arrived on Broadway at all. Many observers detected terminal anguish out of town, where critics hated it, where director Martin Scorsese was replaced by Gower Champion only a few short weeks before the scheduled opening, and where some $200,000 worth of costumes and scenery were discarded along with two songs and two original titles. Critics in New York were less than kind, but, as Bob Fosse pointed out in the *New York Times,* "Whatever the faults and failures, people are seeing a superstar, and they don't get a chance to do that very often." It was Liza's show, and she accounted for advance ticket sales of $2 million and theater-goers' continuing willingness—nay, eagerness—to plunk down $25 each for orchestra seats. As Michelle Craig, a performer obsessed with fame, Liza was onstage almost all evening, belting out one powerhouse show-stopper after another, giving audiences everything she had. Although the show was brickbatted, she was adored, winning a Tony for her performance. But she couldn't keep it up for long. There were several evenings during the winter when Liza was too sick to perform. The tour de force ran until early summer.

On February 19, *On the Twentieth Century* steamed grandly into New York's St. James Theatre. Although critics were somewhat mean-spirited about it, sizable audiences took to it immediately and the glittery production won a cloud of Tonys. Betty Comden and Adolph Green's adaptation of Ben Hecht and Charles MacArthur's 1932 comedy won them Tonys for the Best Musical Book. Cy Coleman's bigger-than-life, semioperatic score won for the Best Musical Score. John Cullum won for Best Performance in a Musical by an Actor for his role as Oscar Jaffee, the down-on-his-luck but never downhearted theatrical producer, and Kevin Kline's Tony was awarded for Best Featured Actor in a Musical. Robin Wagner's lavish scenery won him a Tony for Best Scenic Design. This big, sometimes hilariously funny musical opened with Madeline Kahn as tempestuous Hollywood Star Lily Garland in an oddly uneven performance. She dropped out after a couple of months and was replaced by Judy Kaye, who became

Preceding pages: *Onstage for almost the entire performance, it was Liza Minnelli's presence that dominated* The Act *and her Tony-award-winning performance that audiences came to see.* Opposite: *Madeline Kahn and Tony-award-winner Kevin Kline in* On the Twentieth Century.

Martha Swope

Above: *Eartha Kitt appreciates the biceps of Mr. Universe, Tony Carroll,
as the princesses look on in* Timbuktu!*, Geoffrey Holder's restaging of* Kismet.
Opposite: *Perennially radiant Carol Channing appeared once more as Dolly
in* Hello, Dolly *in a national tour and a limited Broadway run.*

Martha Swope

an overnight sensation. Imogene Coca won raves for her performance as a daffy religious fanatic.

Sinuous Eartha Kitt, feline as ever, starred in *Timbuktu!,* Geoffrey Holder's all-black revival of *Kismet.* Holder's direction, choreography, and costumes were flashy and full of zing, but critics insisted that a true spark was missing. Once again, audiences who were eager to see Eartha Kitt and Melba Moore onstage ignored the caveats of the critics, and by March 10 the show had earned a million dollars in advance ticket orders. The familiar songs such as "Stranger in Paradise," "Baubles, Bangles and Beads," and "And This Is My Beloved" kept their old magic.

March saw the triumphant return of Carol Channing in the role of the eternal matchmaker, Dolly Gallagher Levi, the character she created in *Hello, Dolly!* back in 1964. She played the original Dolly for a

United Press International Photo

record-breaking 1,273 performances before leaving the show in 1967. This current version, produced by the Houston Grand Opera, opened last June and received standing ovations wherever it played on its twenty-five-city road tour. It drew adoring audiences to its Broadway home through the beginning of July. Based on the play *The Matchmaker* by Thornton Wilder, the show's music and lyrics are by Jerry Herman.

With music by such an assortment of composers as Johann Sebastian Bach, George M. Cohan, Neil Diamond, Jerry Leiber and Mike Stoller, Johnny Mercer and Harry Warren, Louis Prima, Carol Bayer Sager and Melissa Manchester, Barry Mann and Cynthia Weil, John Philip Sousa, Cat Stevens, Edgar Varese, and Jerry Jeff Walker, Bob Fosse brought an

159

evening of pure Terpsichore to Broadway on March 27. Featuring a troupe of dancers headed by the gorgeous Ann Reinking, *Dancin'* was completely plotless, a brilliantly inventive collection of every kind of dance: modern, classical ballet, rock, jazz, tap, acrobatic, soft-shoe. Imaginative and surprising, the show attracted a large audience for such innovative numbers as "Fourteen Feet," in which Mr. Fosse had seven dancers nail fourteen shoes to a board, step into them, and dance—displaying how many graceful and amusing moves a human body can perform even when feet are still.

A show that did not fare as well as other musical entries was *A History of the American Film.* A parody of American films from their earliest day, this revue by Christopher Durang, with music by Mel Marvin, was successful neither as parody nor as music, and, despite winning performances from Gary Bayer, Brent Spiner, April Shawhan, Swoosie Kurtz, and Joan Pape, it did not last long.

On May 9, Broadway was treated to *Ain't Misbehavin',* a collection of Fats Waller's robust songs performed with exuberance by the exceptionally talented Ken Page, Andre De Shields, Nell Carter (who won a Tony for Best Supporting Actress in a Musical for her part in this show), Armelia McQueen, and Charlaine Woodard. Based on an idea by Murray Horowitz and Richard Maltby, Jr., the show originally opened at the tiny Manhattan Theatre Club. Its dazzling success there sent it to Broadway, where the show drew unqualified raves from both critics and SRO audiences. It came as no surprise to anyone that the show won a Tony as Best Musical of the Year. Such numbers as Armelia McQueen's baby-doll parody, "Squeeze Me," Andre De Shields gloriously stoned performance of "The Viper's Drag," Nell Carter's sensational trumpeting voice in "I've Got a Feeling I'm Falling," and, of course, the title song, all added up to an evening of sensational musical enjoyment.

Very different in style and substance was

Martha Swope

Opposite: *Ann Reinking got the opportunity for some exuberant high kicking in Bob Fosse's revue* Dancin'. *Above: Armelia McQueen, Ken Page, Charlaine Woodard, Andre De Shields, and Nell Carter display the infectious energy that made* Ain't Misbehavin' *such a smash Broadway success.*

Roger Greenawalt

Elizabeth Swados's *Runaways,* the cabaret-style show she wrote, composed, and directed. Often abrasive and harsh, sometimes painful, *Runaways* is an unromanticized look at the life-style and needs of stray children. Ranging in age from eleven to early twenties, the cast includes some professional actors, some ghetto children, and a couple of genuine runaways. Ms. Swados's music for the show, a vivid combination of rock, reggae, and salsa, conveyed the street experience with bite and bravado. Ms. Swados, at age twenty-seven, has worked with Ellen Stewart at La Mama, Etc., with Peter Brook in Paris, Africa, and America, and collaborated with Andrei Serban on *The Greek Trilogy, Good Woman of Setzuan, The Cherry Orchard,* and *Agamemnon.* She has received two Obies (the off-Broadway equivalent of a Tony) and an Outer Critics Circle Award.

Working, a short-lived musical version of Studs Terkel's powerful, best-selling book of the same name, was a spotty endeavor, its low points outnumbering its high ones. Stephen Schwartz, who wrote the music and lyrics for such Broadway hits as *Godspell, Pippin,* and *The Magic Show,* was responsible for the adaptation and direction of this one. James Taylor, Mary Rodgers, Micki Grant, and Craig Carnelia helped with the music and lyrics. Despite strong moments by Bobo Lewis as a teacher, Patti Lupone as a call girl, Matt Landers as a fireman, and Susan Bigelow as "Just a Housewife," in the eyes of most viewers, *Working* simply didn't work, and it closed after a short run.

A livelier play, and a more-than-moderate

success, was *The Best Little Whorehouse in Texas,* which was snapped up by Universal Pictures even before it got to Broadway. The rollicking musical that first opened in April at the 499-seat Entermedia Theatre moved to Broadway on June 19. The play was based on an article by Larry King, published in *Playboy,* about the closing of a Texas bordello, the famed Chicken Ranch of La Grange, Texas. The book was by Larry King and Peter Masterson, with music and lyrics by Carol Hall, who wrote the 1972 Marlo Thomas television special, "Free to Be . . . You and Me." The whoop-it-up spirit was provided by the inventive direction of Masterson and Tommy Tune. The show's unusual subject matter and its country-music score—played onstage by a bluegrass band—were largely responsible for its great success.

Musical theater was healthy all around the country in 1978. In Los Angeles on April 21 Lena Horne, Josephine Premice, and Clifton Davis heated up the Ahmanson Theatre with an all-black version of the Rodgers and Hart classic *Pal Joey.* Although the story was updated (in this version Joey borrows money from Vera, played by Lena Horne, so he can open a disco), songs like "Bewitched, Bothered and Bewildered," "I Could Write a Book," and "This Can't Be Love," were just as powerful as ever. And Lena Horne was superb.

In addition to *Pal Joey,* Los Angeles enjoyed *Pippin* in 1978, while San Fransisco got *Side by Side by Sondheim, Annie,* and *Chicago* with Gwen Verdon, Chita Rivera, and Jerry Orbach. The D'Oyly Carte Opera company swung Gilbert and Sullivan treats through some dozen cities, while Washington, D.C.,

Above: *A noble experiment that didn't quite succeed,* Working *was Stephen Schwartz's attempt to set Studs Terkel's study of American attitudes about work to music.* Opposite: *Elizabeth Swados (with guitar) sits surrounded by the cast of* Runaways, *the show she wrote, composed, and directed.*

savored road companies of *Annie* and *The Wiz*.

Summer theater offered a wide range of vital musicals. Sammy Davis displayed his inimitable high energy in *Stop the World I Want to Get Off* and brought it into New York for a limited run. *Out on a Limb,* a revue based on James Thurber's works and starring Douglas Fairbanks, Jr., made the rounds of northeastern summer theaters. *Seven Brides for Seven Brothers,* a stage version of the MGM film, with Jane Powell and Howard Keel recreating their original film roles, toured the South and Southwest during the summer and made a major sweep through the country in the fall.

The Berkshire Theater's fiftieth anniversary season began with *Let 'Em Eat Cake,* the 1933 George S. Kaufman/Morrie Ryskind/George and Ira Gershwin musical sequel to *Of Thee I Sing.* It starred Tony Roberts and Arnold Stang. The Massachusetts Playhouse finished its summer season with *Vagabond Stars,* a musical play by Nahma Sandrow and Allan Albert. At the Goodspeed Opera House in East Haddam, Connecticut, the summer season included *Whoopee,* a rave-gathering revival of the 1928 Ziegfeld show that starred Eddie Cantor.

Westport, Connecticut, audiences appreciated *Side by Side by Sondheim* with Arlene Francis and *Guys and Dolls* with Julius La Rosa and Jo Sullivan. Milford, New Hampshire, saw the premiere of *Bandstand,* a slam-bang musical revue. And out on Wantagh, Long Island, a fresh and bright Lucie Arnaz threw off sparks in *Annie Get Your Gun* at the Jones Beach Theatre.

The year 1978 saw Broadway shows traveling in ever-increasing numbers to the smaller towns across the country. The successes of national road companies and bus-and-truck tours have convinced producers that heartland audiences—once thought too unsophisticated to appreciate Broadway fare— are more than ready to welcome and support gypsies from Tin Pan Alley. If the present trend continues, Broadway soon will have changed from a street into a superhighway that stretches from coast to coast.

Courtesy Jeffrey Richards Associates

Opposite: *Lena Horne starred in Rodgers and Hart's* Pal Joey '78, *directed by Michael Kidd.* Above: *Carlin Glynn was seen as the tough madam of* The Best Little Whorehouse in Texas, *a play based on a true story.*

Richard Creamer

Trends

The most noticeable trends in the music world during 1978 were extramusical, reflections of changing social patterns, life-styles, and goals.

The dramatic growth in the number and strength of women musicians has been perhaps the most significant musical direction of the past few years. *Billboard* magazine reports that by the beginning of 1978 the number of female vocalists with singles on the charts had increased 90 percent since early 1976. The explosion of women soloists who have won major awards and gold and platinum records includes such performers as Linda Ronstadt, Barbra Streisand, Olivia Newton-John, Crystal Gayle, Donna Summer, Debby Boone, Natalie Cole, Dolly Parton, Deniece Williams, Emmylou Harris, Loretta Lynn, Roberta Flack, Rita Coolidge, Bette Midler, Liza Minnelli, Carly Simon, Donna Fargo, Helen Reddy, Diana Ross, Carol King, Millie Jackson, Yvonne Elliman, and Joni Mitchell. There are also successful members of duos, such as Toni Tennille, Karen Carpenter, Marie Osmond; focal points of groups include Rufus's Chaka Khan, Stevie Nicks and Christine McVie of Fleetwood Mac, Heart's Ann and Nancy Wilson, Debby Harry of Blondie. Successful all-women groups include the Emotions and Hot. And in 1978 newcomers such as Dianne Steinberg, Dyan Diamond, Stargard, the Runaways, and Carlene Carter began to rise. While some women battle for the Equal Rights Amendment, these women performers have long understood that it's talent and determination, not legislation, that lead to success.

In 1978, there were also more women disk jockeys, music-industry executives, first and second engineers, and producers. There even appeared several all-women labels, the largest being Olivia Records and Urana Records.

Songs by male/female duos were some of the year's greatest successes. Roberta Flack and Donny Hathaway had a top soul and pop hit with "The Closer I Get to You," Kenny Rogers and Dottie West topped the country charts with "Every Time Two Fools Collide," Johnny Mathis won his first number-one song with "Too Much, Too Little, Too Late," his duet with Deniece Williams, and John Travolta and Olivia Newton-John had two top smashes from the movie

Grease, "Summer Nights" and the platinum-awarded "You're the One That I Want."

With America's highways and byways clogged with joggers, runners, and bicyclists, and with gyms, sports arenas, health spas, and tennis courts springing up everywhere, it's no surprise that in 1978 body consciousness permeated the music world as well. Performers, whose life-styles demand abundant energy and stamina, have responded enthusiastically to the national sports craze. On March 1 through 3, such stellar names as Rod Stewart, Kenny Loggins, Marilyn McCoo and Billy Davis, Jr., Freddy Fender, Leif Garrett, Anne Murray, Tanya Tucker, the Alessi Brothers, and members of such groups as Boston, the Jacksons, Earth, Wind and Fire, the Commodores, and the Runaways took part in "The First Annual Rock 'n Roll Sports Classic." Tapes of the events, which included swimming, running, the long jump, bicycling, and a massive tug of war, were telecast on May 4. The event, created by the production team of Bill Aucoin, Alvin Ross, and Bob Finkel-Teram, was a treat for viewers and participants.

Rock stars have embraced the game of soccer, long the favorite sport of Elton John, (although he appears in a cricket uniform on the jacket of *Elton John's Greatest Hits, Volume II),* Rod Stewart, and Leif Garrett. Peter Frampton, Rick Wakeman, and Paul Simon are part-owners of the Philadelphia Furies soccer team, and Atlantic Records President Ahmet Ertegun is also president of the New York Cosmos.

Traditional all-American sports have not been neglected by the music world. Softball games between recording groups and radio station staffers are popular pastimes, and the most highly publicized softball battle of 1978 was the May 7 struggle between the Eagles and *Rolling Stone* magazine that the Eagles won 15 to 8.

Atlanta radio station WQXI sponsored a March of Dimes Walkathon on April 1, and with the help of Leif Garrett raised close to $200,000. Ian Anderson of Jethro Tull sponsored a car in Long Beach, California's April 2 Grand Prix. Driven by Ian Ashley, the car was painted to look like the cover of the *Heavy Horses* album, Jethro Tull's latest.

Los Angeles disk jockey Roger Carroll regularly

Preceding pages: *Women were big news in the music world in 1978: Ann and Nancy Wilson sing at Cal Jam II.* Opposite, top: *Janice Johnson and Hazel Payne of Taste of Honey.* Bottom: *Carlene Carter, June Carter Cash, and Emmylou Harris celebrate Carlene's sold-out shows at New York's Bottom Line.*

Ebet Roberts

Merry Alpern/Goldsmith Studios

broadcasts his KMPC-AM weekend programs live from the Los Angeles Coliseum or the Anaheim Stadium before the Los Angeles Rams or the California Angels games. And on Meat Loaf's hit single, "Paradise by the Dashboard Light," the voice in the background is that of Yankee sportscaster Phil Rizzuto giving a spirited baseball play-by-play. (Radio station WRKO in Boston, home of the Yankee's archrivals, plays a version featuring a Red Sox announcer.)

Formerly used only as promotional devices, records pressed on colored vinyl—and even more technically sophisticated picture disks, on which a picture (usually the album cover) is pressed into the vinyl—became available to the public for the first time in 1978. The first company to do this was Fotoplay Corp., a tiny Arizona label that issued *To Elvis: Love Still Burning,* a collection of eleven musical tributes to Presley written since his death. The initial May pressing of 6,000 copies was gone in three weeks, and the disk with artist Marge Nichols's rendering of Presley's face was quickly picked up for national distribution by Pickwick. Mushroom records followed with a special limited edition of Heart's *Magazine* in June. CBS Canada made picture albums of Meat Loaf's *Bat Out of Hell,* and in August Capitol Records released a limited-edition picture disk of the Beatles' *Sgt. Pepper's Lonely Hearts Club Band* as well as red, white, and blue disks of *The Beatles 1962–67, The White Album,* and *The Beatles 1967–70.* ELO's single "Sweet Talkin' Woman" appeared in bright purple. (It was supposed to glow in the dark, but, alas, the process had not yet been perfected. In August, however, Mushroom released a glow-in-the-dark album, *Lights from the Valley*, by Chilliwack.) Horslips' single "Sure the Boy Was Green," was pressed in green vinyl. Despite high prices for the novelty disks, the limited editions sold well as collectors' items.

Nostalgia continued to be popular in 1978. Hits of the sixties are so frequently played on many radio stations, both in original and updated versions, that they sometimes seem like contemporary tunes. There was a spate of successful movies about the 1950s—*American Hot Wax, The Buddy Holly Story,* and *Grease.* In Philadelphia, Joe Niagra of radio station WPEN staged a 1950s charity promotion and raffle. He played 1950s songs, and winners of the raffle won poodle skirts. One of Miami Beach's most successful clubs, the Swinger Lounge in the Marco Polo Hotel, began featuring 1950s groups exclusively in early 1978 and has been fabulously successful with

them. Radio station WDJZ in Bridgeport, Connecticut, plays top hits of the thirties, and radio station WWIW in New Orleans plays music of the big band era ranging from the 1930s to the early 1950s.

In the year 1978, Jamaican reggae gained in popularity. It became a favorite of American college students, and the Rolling Stones signed reggae artist Peter Tosh to their record label. And although Bob Marley's 1978 album *Kaya* was not a best-seller, his United States tour was a great success. His April 22 Jamaican peace concert, at which he brought together Jamaican Prime Minister Michael Manley and bitter opponent Edward Seaga and persuaded them to shake hands, made news in the United States. *Kaya,* a Jamaican word for marijuana, has been criticized by some of Marley's early supporters who maintain that he has given up on politics. In an interview with *New York Times* reporter Robert Palmer, Marley smiled at those accusations, saying that his music is about freedom, not politics.

In the year 1978, music on the streets continued to grow in visibility and audibility. In major cities across the country, there were itinerant musicians playing not only violin, flute, guitar, and harmonica, but also other more elaborate and unique instruments.

On New York City's upper west side, one musician interpreted Bach on a portable keyboard plugged into a small speaker; another New York busker, calling his music Celestial Vibrations, endlessly strummed an electrified autoharp plugged into a portable tape recorder. New York's classical radio station WNCN established a $15,000 kitty from which it donated a daily stipend to alfresco musicians the station considered worthy of support and encouragement.

Not only did solo efforts flourish, but outdoor duets, trios, and even quartets blossomed. In major cities, everything from symphony orchestras to salsa bands were heard full volume on the streets, blasting from the latest, biggest, most technologically advanced transistor radios available. Music was in the air, making even the grimiest urban sections brighter and more beautiful.

Clockwise from top left: *Jackson Browne rounds the bases in the Eagles-*Rolling Stone *softball game. Bob Marley brings Jamaican political rivals Prime Minister Michael Manley and Edward Seaga together. Peter Frampton signs a soccer ball for a delighted fan while Rick Wakeman looks on in the background.*

Richard Creamer

Chuck Pulin

Chuck Pulin

Concerts, Events, and Tours

Concerts and Events

November 1977

The month of November began with a flute treat for Floridians as Jethro Tull transported almost 23,000 fans at the Jai Alai Fronton in Miami on November 4 and 5. On November 11, as part of his farewell tour with the Four Seasons, Frankie Valli appeared with them and with Roberta Flack in a stunning concert at Las Vegas's Aladdin Hotel.

November's biggest concert, the first Miami Music Festival of the Arts, was three days of free music beginning November 11 and lasting to November 13. Neil Young celebrated his thirty-second birthday with his new twenty-four-piece Gone With the Wind band and 125,000 fans who came to hear him, the Ozark Mountain Daredevils, Lake, Dr. Hook, Tight Squeeze, Point Blank, Mark Farner and his band, and the Outlaws, who paid tribute to Lynyrd Skynyrd.

Also on November 11, in Honolulu, John Denver treated islanders to his first live concert in more than a year at the Blaisdell Arena. Backed by a superlative seven-piece band, John's shining performance had the audience spellbound.

Kansas and Nazareth packed more than 17,000 fans into Pittsburgh's Civic Arena on November 10; Queen jammed 15,000 into the Garden in Boston on the twelfth; and, also on the twelfth, Aerosmith and Nazareth drew 17,500 rocking fans to the Civic Center in St. Paul, Minnesota.

On November 20, in the first of many such concerts, the Los Angeles Philharmonic Orchestra conducted by Zubin Mehta offered music lovers a dazzling spectacle called Music from Outer Space at the Hollywood Bowl. Ninety-six onstage microphones fed a 100-channel mixing board the sounds of *Star Wars, Close Encounters, 2001,* and other space epics, while lasers slashed the air.

On November 23, the elegant Lou Rawls clip-

David Weiss

Lynn Goldsmith

Top: *On November 20, 1977, patrons of the Hollywood Bowl were transported by a laser-lit production called Music From Outer Space. Above: Shaun Cassidy was number one in the hearts of his fans, who loved him even with a new short haircut. Opposite: Individual albums by each member of Kiss shipped a million copies each.*

172

clopped into Broadway's Hellinger Theatre in the Anheuser-Busch float behind a team of six sturdy Clydesdale horses. For two weeks he entertained audiences with his polished show.

On the nights of November 24 and 25, New York City's Madison Square Garden was filled with 36,000 fans who jumped and boogied to the intricate rhythms of Earth, Wind and Fire in a concert that also featured perky Deniece Williams and Pockets.

If you were lucky, acted fast, or had connections, you could have gotten yourself an authentic 1977 Bette Midler T-shirt commemorating her six-night stint at Bimbo's, a North Beach San Francisco night spot. From November 29 to December 4, for twelve slam-bang performances, audiences were treated to the devilish wit and major talent of the Divine Miss M.

December 1977

On December 1 and 2, Queen dominated Madison Square Garden for two and a half hours each night, giving their revved-up audiences a sparkling show.

On December 6, at San Francisco's Boarding House, you could have closed your eyes and thought you were back in the sixties as Roger McGuinn took the stage with Gene Clark, David Crosby, and Chris Hillman—four-fifths of the original Byrds—and sweetly sang such Byrds' classics as "Turn, Turn, Turn," "Feel a Whole Lot Better," "You Ain't Goin' Nowhere," and "So You Wanna Be a Rock and Roll Star."

Other sold-out concerts in December included Aerosmith and Styx at the Coliseum in New Haven, Connecticut, on the seventh and eighth; Kiss solo at the Memphis, Tennessee, Mid-South Coliseum on the ninth, and with Detective at the Henry Levitt Arena in Williamsburg, Virginia, on the tenth; Rod Stewart with Air Supply at the Sports Arena in San Diego, also on the tenth, and Earth, Wind and Fire at the Oakland Coliseum on the ninth through the eleventh.

On Christmas Eve, the irrepressible Shaun Cassidy emceed a WRKO Boston benefit for the Kennedy Memorial Hospital. He was joined at the Boston Garden by the Bay City Rollers, Andy Gibb, and England Dan and John Ford Coley.

On Christmas night, the Apollo Theatre reopened, featuring Millie Jackson, the Manhattans, and Harold Melvin and the Blue Notes in an unleashed, let-your-hair-down show.

On New Year's Eve, audiences cheered in 1978 with Jackson Browne and Bonnie Raitt at the Forum

Ebet Roberts

Merry Alpern/Goldsmith Studios

174

in Inglewood, California, with Willie Nelson, and Jerry Jeff Walker at the Summit in Houston, with Santana, Journey, Eddie Money, and Starwood at the Cow Palace in San Francisco, with Heart, Sammy Hagar, Greg Kuhn, and Earthquake at the Coliseum in Oakland, with the Grateful Dead at Winterland in San Francisco, and with Patti Smith at the CBGB Theatre in New York.

January

The big concert events in January were Bob Seger's thunderous sets, both with and without opening band Rockets. Seger jammed St. Louis's Kiel Auditorium on the first and second, Freedom Hall in Louisville, Kentucky, on the third, the Municipal Auditorium in Kansas City, Missouri, on the fourth, Roberts Stadium in Evansville, Indiana, on the fifth. Kansas and Cheap Trick drew frenzied fans to do their sold-out dates at the Coliseum in Rutland, Oregon, on the second, Seattle's Coliseum on the third, and the Henry Levitt Arena in Wichita, Kansas on the seventh.

On January 5, the Sex Pistols made their American debut at the Great South East Music Hall in Atlanta, Georgia, with a thunderously repetitive show that left their audience dazed, damp, but happy.

On the seventh, Joan Jett, Lita Ford, Vickie Blue, and Sandy West—the Runaways—treated audiences at New York's Palladium to some diamond-hard rock and roll.

On January 13, Ronnie Milsap pleased his audience at Harrah's in Lake Tahoe with a sparkling blend of pop, R & B, and country.

On the twenty-fourth, Ted Nugent and Golden Earring drew 17,000 Gonzo freaks to the Checkerdome in St. Louis to hear Ted chomp their heads off with his multi-decibel assault. They loved it. Kiss and Rockets enticed 17,500 fans to the Memorial Auditorium in Buffalo, New York, in another of their towering stage shows.

Earth, Wind and Fire, Deniece Williams, and Pockets appeared at the Hollywood Sportatorium on January 20, sending their cosmic message out to nearly 20,000.

Opposite, top: *Bob Seger and the Silver Bullet Band maintained a white-hot touring schedule throughout 1978.* Bottom: *Singer/songwriter/pianist Warren Zevon pounded out fierce rock and roll in 1978.* Left: *Joe Frazier sings at Madison Square Garden's tenth birthday.*

February

The biggest concert in a month of top-name events was Earth, Wind and Fire's February 3 blast at the Superdome in New Orleans, where they drew more than 18,000 fans to hear dynamic music and watch a dramatic stage show. On the fourth, Emerson, Lake and Palmer appeared at the Boston Garden before a sold-out house, and the Grateful Dead sold out three concerts at Chicago's Uptown Theatre on February 2, 3, and 4.

On the seventh, Lou Rawls and Donna Summer began an eight-day run at the Las Vegas Hilton. Summer was onstage dynamite and Rawls was mellow.

Eric Clapton and Player drew 14,500 fans to Oakland's Coliseum on the tenth, did a sizzling show at the Santa Monica Civic Center on the eleventh. Waylon Jennings, the Waylors, Jessi Colter, and Don Williams crooned to a crowd of more than 12,000 at Denver's McNichols Sports Arena on the eleventh, and Parliament/Funkadelic, Kool and the Gang, and Grand Jury played for 11,600 fans at Baltimore's Civic Center.

On February 14 and 15, Muddy Waters treated patrons of New York's Bottom Line to two evenings of his smooth show, performing such classics as "I'm Your Hootchie Coochie Man," "Baby, Please Don't Go," "Mannish Boy," and "Got My Mojo Working." Johnny Winter joined in for one scorching set.

Maryland audiences at the Capitol Centre in Largo enjoyed the onstage antics of Parliament/Funkadelic, Mother's Finest, and Cameo on February 18. Shaun Cassidy, who had begun his first tour of the United States on February 4 in Salt Lake City, left 'em screaming for more at the Baltimore Civic Center on the twenty-fifth.

On the twenty-third, a post-Grammy-awards celebration drew 3,000 notables to Los Angeles's Hotel Baltimore, where Count Basie performed.

March

In March, the big one was, of course, Cal Jam II. On March 18, at a cost of almost two million dollars, the Ontario Speedway in Ontario, California was turned into the seventh-largest city in the state. That city's populace grooved for fifteen hours to a thunderous rock-and-roll show, during which they heard such rock favorites as Bob Welch's "Ebony Eyes," Dave Mason's "We Just Disagree," Santana's "Black Magic Woman,"

Heart's "Barracuda," Ted Nugent's "Cat Scratch Fever," Foreigner's "Feels Like the First Time," and Aerosmith's "Toys in the Attic." Executive Coordinator Don E. Branker described the event as "the ultimate concert. This is as far as you can take it," undoubtedly laying down a challenge to producers everywhere.

Enjoyment of a concert, of course, isn't necessarily measured by the number of people attending or the decibel level reached. Glen Campbell's return to the Versailles Room at the Riviera Hotel in Las Vegas was a luminous entertainment, sending the sophisticated Vegas crowd into a state of delight.

On the third, March's second-largest event packed 19,000 frenzied fans into Madison Square Garden for an evening of the zany musical antics of Sha Na Na.

The elegant Boettcher Concert Hall, Denver's glamorous new home for its symphony orchestra, opened March 4 with Van Cliburn as featured soloist.

Sprightly lady of music Sarah Vaughan delighted audiences at the Los Angeles Music Center on that same evening, treating them to a show spiced by her relaxed wit and inimitable style.

On the eleventh, Johnny Cash held a sold-out crowd in the palm of his hand at the Convention Center in Anaheim, California, as he sailed through such oldies but goodies as "Ring of Fire" and "Folsom Prison Blues," assuring his audience, "As long as you keep enjoying them, I'll keep on singing them as if it were the first time."

On March 16 and 17, John Denver thrilled New Yorkers at Madison Square Garden with his polished show, mixing his own songs with such works as Eric Andersen's "Thirsty Boots" and Tom Paxton's "Bet on the Blues."

On the twenty-third, Santana, Bob Welch, and Eddie Money packed 12,000 rock and rollers into the Municipal Auditorium in Mobile, Alabama, giving them a high-energy show. On the twenty-fourth, the Coliseum in Riverfront, Ohio, jumped to the crystal-clear rock of poet Jackson Browne as almost 14,000 people came to hear him perform.

Art Garfunkel, with Dan Hill as an opener, put on a fine show at a sold-out Carnegie Hall on the twenty-fourth, and Willie Nelson turned the Forum in Inglewood, California, into an annex of Texas with a whooping good show on the twenty-ninth.

Natalie Cole treated New Yorkers to four days of her polished vitality March 30 through April 2 when she appeared at Long Island's Westbury Music Fair.

On March 31, the irrepressible Liberace brought his two Rolls Royces (he drove onstage in one, drove off in the other), rings, mirrored piano, spangled suit, and dancing waters to the Las Vegas Hilton where he performed his inimitable blend of comedy and music before a transfixed audience.

April

On April 4, Gladys Knight and the Pips slipped into the Aladdin Hotel in Las Vegas, where delighted audiences made them and their spirited stage show more than welcome for two weeks.

Songstress Teresa Brewer, Dizzy Gillespie, and Stephane Grappelly—along with a top band featuring such musicians as Steve Marcus, Grady Tate, and Al Gray—turned Carnegie Hall into a jazz lovers paradise on April 4.

Warren Zevon pounded on his piano and howled for all he was worth at the Roxy on April 6, setting out a tasty rock dish for the cheering Los Angeles crowd. Across the country on that same date, Bootsy's Rubber Band, Raydio, and T Connection performed their outrageous hijinks for a crowd of 20,000 at the Capitol Centre in Largo, Maryland.

On April 8, Parliament, the Bar-Kays, and Cold Fire set Kansas City, Missouri, jumping with a dazzling show for 16,000 at the Kemper Arena. On the ninth, Foghat and Eddie Money let 'er rip before a sold-out crowd of more than 18,000 at the Forum in Inglewood, California. In Houston on that same date, Steve Martin with Steve Goodman had two sold-out shows at the Hofheinz Arena.

The extraordinary genius of Stevie Wonder was the attraction at Osko's in Los Angeles on April 11, when the king of soul climaxed a reception given by his publishing and management companies with a sensational concert.

On April 11 and 12, New Yorkers basked in the sunny glow of Crystal Gayle's talent, taking advantage of the rare opportunity to see her live and up close at the Bottom Line. On the thirteenth, a singing lady of vastly different style, Natalie Cole, brought musical cheer to the good folk of Buffalo, New York, belting out a high-energy show at the Kleinhans Music Hall.

Foghat, Eddie Money, and No Dice blasted out a sizzling concert at San Francisco's Cow Palace on April 14, repeatedly bringing the audience of 14,500 to its feet.

On April 14 and 15, singer/songwriter Peter Allen

treated capacity crowds at Rancho Nicasio in Nicasio, California, to a warm, enthusiastic performance of some of his finest songs, including "Love Crazy," "I Honestly Love You," and "Everything Old Is New Again."

On the eighteenth, Helen Reddy and Jose Feliciano played the Las Vegas Hilton, Feliciano offering a supercharged set and Reddy projecting with a new power. The big one on that date was the Jackson Browne/Karla Bonoff celebration at the St.Paul, Minnesota, Civic Center Arena, where more than 17,500 fans cheered and stamped. Another big one in April was Foghat and No Dice at the Coliseum in Seattle, Washington, on the nineteenth, drawing 15,000 people for an evening of blues-flavored rock.

On April 20, Engelbert Humperdinck brought a set of show stoppers, including some effective impressions, to the MGM Grand in Las Vegas, the first time he's ever performed there. On the twenty-first, a massive sold-out crowd of 18,250 rocked and rolled with REO Speedwagon, the Babys, and the Hounds at the Market Square Arena in Indianapolis, Indiana. On the twenty-first, in New York, Hubert Laws and Noel Pointer brought a crisp jazz show to Carnegie Hall.

New Yorkers danced in the aisles on April 22 as Chic and headliner Rufus dazzled with a fast and furious show. Across the country in Las Vegas on that same night, Olivia Newton-John and Kenny Rogers were cheered on by audiences at Las Vegas's Riviera Hotel in a dynamic evening of glorious singing.

The month ended with Bob Seger and the Silver Bullet Band raising sold-out audiences to a fever pitch at the Market Square Arena in Indianapolis on April 28 and at the Rupp Arena in Lexington, Kentucky on April 29.

May

Events musical, extramusical, and supermusical categorized the sunny month of May.

On the first, Garland Jeffreys brought some dynamic New York street energy to Los Angeles to the delight of both transplanted East Coasters and native Californians who jammed the Roxy for his nonstop show.

On May 15, the Bee Gees, Robert Stigwood, and David Frost met with Henry R. Labouisse, executive director of UNICEF, to announce that the Bee Gees would give a televised concert in January 1979, called Music for UNICEF, from the General Assembly. All profits from that concert will go to UNICEF.

On May 4, Carly Simon threw strawberries, chocolate kisses, and more than a handful of fine songs to crowds at New York's Bottom Line. She and husband James Taylor sang several songs together, as they did later in the month when they joined Bonnie Raitt and Jon Hall for a Karen Silkwood benefit at New York's Palladium

The stars came out May 7 to Los Angeles's Dorothy Chandler Pavilion to celebrate Israel's thirtieth birthday. Zubin Mehta and John Williams each led the Los Angeles Philharmonic; Debby and Pat Boone, Barry Manilow, Sammy Davis, and Barbra Streisand all performed at the gala, which was televised the next night.

Sun Day was celebrated in May all over the country. Katy Moffatt, John McEuen of the Dirt Band, and Breakaway celebrated with President Jimmy Carter as special guest in Denver, Colorado. In Boulder, the Beach Boys, Firefall, Bob Welch, and Journey entertained 35,000 Coloradans on May 13.

On the thirteenth, in the Forum at Inglewood, California, Parliament, the Bar-Kays, and Faze-o stupefied 17,400 fans with a knock-out show, and on the same date in the Jefferson Civic Coliseum in Birmingham, Alabama, Aerosmith and Mahogany Rush laid down some sizzling, hard-as-nails rock. On the fourteenth, the Grateful Dead wove smooth tunes for a capacity crowd of 13,370 at the Civic Center in Providence, Rhode Island.

Courtesy A & M Records

On May 20, Bootsy's Rubber Band brought its inspired musical lunacy to the Summit in Houston. Preceded by Stargard and Raydio, the band had the sellout crowd of more than 16,000 dancing in the aisles. On the twenty-first, the O'Jays, Con Funk Shun, and Faze-o brought a firecracker evening of rhythm and blues to Memphis's Mid-South Coliseum.

On May 28, Margaret Whiting, Rose Marie, Rosemary Clooney, and Helen O' Connell, billing themselves as 4 Girls 4, performed at a Johnny Mercer Tribute at Savannah, Georgia's, Civic Auditorium.

Also on the twenty-eighth, in Wolf Trap Park in Vienna, Virginia, President Carter and wife Rosalynn proudly watched ten-year-old Amy make her violin debut with a solemn rendering of "Twinkle, Twinkle Little Star."

On May 29, Bob Seger and the Silver Bullet Band, heading a dynamite bill including Foreigner, Nazareth, and Toby Beau, set the Iowa Fairgrounds ablaze with a ferocious rock-and-roll show, leaving 33,500 fans screaming for more.

June

The beginning of the summer concert season, June was a bonanza for music fans, featuring superstars of the highest magnitude.

On June 1, no less a legend than Bob Dylan mesmerized audiences at the Universal Amphitheatre in Universal City, California, in the first of seven sold-out shows, performing his classics in brilliant new versions. It was a magical series of concerts, with the Dylan genius filtered through a new performing warmth.

The entire Osmond family romped and played for three weeks at the Las Vegas Hilton, letting SRO crowds join in their fun.

On June 3, in one of the month's big ones, Bootsy's Rubber Band, Enchantment, and Raydio blared their sounds to 18,000 people at the Inglewood Forum.

Also on June 3, Bruce Springsteen returned to screaming fans at Long Island's Nassau Coliseum in his first appearance in New York for two years. He performed a faultless, high-energy set, as always giving his fans more than their money's worth.

On June 4, the world premiere of *Grease* drew celebrities and celebrity-seekers. The star-studded evening was capped by a glittering party—the Rydell High School Prom—at Paramount Studios.

178

Left: *With a sparkling stage presence and an armload of memorable songs (including "I Honestly Love You," the song that won Olivia Newton-John a performing Grammy in 1974), singer/songwriter Peter Allen's career is ready to take off.* Right: *Barbra Streisand celebrates Israel's thirtieth birthday.*

Robert Scott

On June 8, George Clinton and his group, Parliament/Funkadelic, gave funk lessons to New York City at Madison Square Garden. On the ninth and tenth, the Jefferson Starship lit up the Nassau Coliseum with electric excitement.

And then June really got raucous. The Rolling Stones arrived with their entourage and their no-nonsense rock and roll. Beginning their tour on the tenth at the Lakeland, Florida, Civic Center, the baddest band in the land went on to mix small and large concerts, from a few thousand at the Capitol Theatre in Passaic, New Jersey, on the fourteenth to ninety thousand at Philadelphia's JFK Stadium on the seventeenth. Every concert was an event.

On June 17, President Carter celebrated the twenty-fifth anniversary of the Newport Jazz Festival with *A Tribute to Jazz,* a White House event featuring such top names as Dizzy Gillespie, Lionel Hampton, Herbie Hancock, George Benson, Stan Getz, Dexter Gordon, and a host of others.

On the seventeenth, Donna Summer began a three-night engagement at the Universal Amphitheatre, during which she sang, danced, showed off a variety of costumes, and proved herself a dynamic talent.

On the weekend of the seventeenth, New York's Westchester County rang with the sounds of an authentic sixties-style folk festival, featuring such stars as Arlo Guthrie, Pete Seeger, Kate and Anna McGarrigle, Leon Redbone, and a host of other international acts. Called the *Great Hudson River Revival,* the purpose of the festival was to raise money to clean up New York's Hudson River.

On June 17, Bob Marley and the wailers drew a racially diverse crowd of 19,000 people to New York's Madison Square Garden to enjoy his sizzling reggae sound.

On June 19, Lynda Carter made her stage debut as a singer at Denver's Turn of the Century. Lynda provided a dramatic stage show and a shrewd choice of music that showed off her fine voice to good advantage.

Alice Cooper, with all his props intact (the guillotine, a mammoth television screen, dancing chickens, and huge black widow spiders), provided a bizarre show for some 10,000 fans at the Buffalo, New York, Memorial Auditorium on June 20.

On June 21, queen of soul Aretha Franklin began her first Las Vegas engagement in eight years. That night and the following four she delivered a varied, well-paced, powerhouse of a show.

On the twenty-fifth, 61,000 fans of rock and roll turned up for the first concert at Giants Stadium in the Meadowlands, New Jersey. The Beach Boys, Steve Miller, and Pablo Cruise raised up the audience with straight-ahead rock and roll shows.

Closing the month at New Orleans' Tropicana night club was a breakneck performance by sizzling Tina Turner on June 30.

July

There were two huge concert events in July, the Rolling Stones' record-breaking indoor draw of 80,173 fans on July 13 to the New Orleans Superdome and Bob Dylan's concert for 250,000 in Hampshire, England on the fifteenth.

On July 1, a scintillating collection of stars joined the Doobie Brothers at Santa Cruz's Catalyst in a benefit for the late Will Geer. The two shows included David Soul—with Norton Buffalo in his back-up band—the Captain and Tennille, who rocked and rolled in uncharacteristic but quite successful fashion, and a surprise performance by Martha & the Vandellas, together onstage for the first time in ten years.

July began with the celebrated Newport Jazz Festival, a glorious collection of concerts in New York City and Newport, Rhode Island, featuring jazz greats from Dizzy Gillespie to George Benson.

On July 5, at the Greek Theatre, Shaun Cassidy began a four-night engagement with a capacity crowd of shrieking young girls to whom he tossed various pieces of his clothing. They loved it. He loved it.

Barry Manilow performed at the Garden State Arts Center in Asbury Park, New Jersey, between July 3 and July 8. Kris Kristofferson and Rita Coolidge sold out four nights at Los Angeles's Universal Amphitheatre beginning July 12. On July 12, the O'Jays celebrated their twentieth anniversary as a band at the Greek Theatre in a joyful show overflowing with good feelings and good humor. Fleetwood Mac began their summer tour in Troy, Wisconsin, at the Alpine Valley Music Theatre on July 17. Their three sold-out concerts pulled more than 54,000 Fleetwood fans for a radiant set.

On July 23, Aerosmith, Foreigner, Pat Travers, Van Halen and, AC DC pulled 57,500 music fans for a glorious Bill Graham-produced Day on the Green at the Oakland California Stadium.

Top: Robert Stigwood, Maurice, Barry, and Robin Gibb, and David Frost, at the U.N. announce their forthcoming concert to benefit UNICEF. Bottom: Every concert given by the O'Jays was a celebration in 1978, their joy increased by the double platinum sales of the album So Full of Love.

Waring Abbott

Sandy Spieser

Hot summer weather and good-time music were made for each other, and the crowd of 60,000 that jammed into the stadium at Oakland, California, on July 26 for the fourth edition of Bill Graham's Day on the Green series was ready both for the heat of the day and the heat of the music churned out by the Stones, Santana, Eddie Money, and Peter Tosh. Other massive crowd-gatherers in July were the Eagles, Linda Ronstadt, and Dan Fogelberg, who drew more than 54,000 people to Kansas City, Missouri's, Arrowhead Stadium on July 30, making that concert the largest grosser in the city's history. The Eagles, Steve Miller, and Jesse Winchester captured the cheers of more than 38,000 at Boulder, Colorado's, Folsom Field on July 29.

Smaller but just as eager crowds of music lovers cheered Frankie Valli at Las Vegas's Aladdin Hotel on July 13. A perennially smooth, cool, and charming Perry Como entranced audiences at Los Angeles's Greek Theatre from July 19 through 22 in a show featuring such nostalgic classics as "You'll Never Walk Alone," "Without a Song," and "Temptation." New Yorkers got the opportunity to become re-acquainted with ex-New York Doll David Johansen, who gave a firecracker rock performance at the Bottom Line on July 20, singing some Dolls songs, some new songs, and presenting a vivid rock personality to adoring crowds. The Crusaders sizzled in a trio of sellout concerts from July 28 to 30 at Los Angeles's Roxy.

August

The Eagles were the big honchos in August, sharing honors with Steve Miller and Pablo Cruise at a bash for 65,000 at Bloomington, Minnesota's, Metropolitan Stadium on the first. On August 6, Aerosmith, Ted Nugent, Journey, and Mahogany Rush brought 51,000 of their fans to Giants Stadium in New Jersey, and ELO, Heart, and Trickster performed for 57,000 on August 12 and 13 at Pontiac, Michigan's, Silverdome.

From August 4 to 14, the city of Chicago hosted the August Lakefront Festival, known this year as Chicagofest. Half a million people came to see and hear the Atlanta Rhythm Section, Waylon Jennings, Andy Gibb, Frankie Valli, Helen Reddy, Eddie Money, the Spinners, Journey, Muddy Waters, John Lee Hooker, Asleep at the Wheel, Stanley Turrentine, Sonny Rollins, Herbie Mann, and many others.

On August 3, Genya Ravan rocked at the Bottom Line, her considerable thunder almost stolen by opener Benny Mardones, who set the stage with a flamboyant assault. Finishing her show at the Forest Hills West Side Tennis Stadium on August 7 with a sensational "You're No Good," Linda Ronstadt displayed her full voice and a range of music from albums past and present.

New York deejay George Michael's special, "Elvis Memories," was presented over ABC radio on August 13. The three-hour tribute was a moving documentary of the man's life and his music.

Other August high spots included Bruce Springsteen's conquest of New York City on August 21 through 23. The whole town was abuzz with astonished descriptions of his flat-out, no-holds-barred shows at Madison Square Garden. Black Sabbath, a group that hasn't appeared in New York for years, drew 20,000 of their strong-eared, devoted fans to Madison Square Garden on August 27. Van Halen, opening the show, succeeded

Wide World Photos

Above: *Olivia Newton-John and John Travolta were the main attractions at the star-studded premiere of* Grease *one of the hottest musical movies of 1978.* Right: *Dizzy Gillespie, Stan Getz, and Mel Tormé perform together during New York City's famed Newport Jazz Festival.*

in winning the crowd with a flamboyant set. On August 29, California's Universal Amphitheatre rang with the sounds of Peter Yarrow, Paul Stookey, and Mary Travers, reunited after nearly eight years apart. The sellout crowd welcomed the trio, who combined solo numbers, group efforts, and both old and new songs in a nostalgic set. Boston closed the month at Madison Square Garden. Originally scheduled for only one performance, the band easily added a second sold-out show.

September

To commemorate the anniversary of Elvis Presley's death, the Las Vegas Hilton presented an Always Elvis Festival. Held from September 1 to September 10, the event featured music (but no Presley imitators), booths selling all manner of Elvis memorabilia, and a life-sized bronze statue of the singer sculpted by Carl Romanelli.

The Grateful Dead and Willie Nelson performed a crackling show at New Jersey's Giants Stadium on September 2. That same evening, Teddy Pendergrass held a midnight concert for women only at New York's Avery Fisher Hall. Other September concerts included two sold-out evenings of Yes at Madison Square Garden

on the seventh and eighth. Bob Seger brought his band and power-packed show to the Nassau Coliseum on September 8. B. B. King and his guitar were the attractions at New York's Felt Forum on September 23. On September 27 and 28, Barry Manilow performed at Philadelphia's Spectrum, and on those same dates Neil Young and Crazy Horse were at Madison Square Garden. Bob Dylan's three months of extra touring included instant sellouts of two New York shows at Madison Square Garden and one at the Boston Garden.

October

On October 1 and 2, the O'Jays and the Commodores appeared at Madison Square Garden. Billy Joel performed his usual high-energy show at Philadelphia's Spectrum on the third. On the eighth and ninth, Madison Square Garden belonged to Jethro Tull. From October 5 to 11, New Yorkers were treated to the slick soul of Diana Ross at Radio City Music Hall. On October 20, Van Morrison tore it up at Philadelphia's Spectrum.

TOURS

Unless otherwise indicated, all dates are 1978.

Aerosmith: Ended lengthy fall tour December 22, 1977, at Capitol Center in Largo, Maryland; began 1978 tour March 24 in Columbus, Ohio.

Atlanta Rhythm Section: Began October 1977 at Pennsylvania State College in Mansfield; ended December 31, 1977, at Fox Theatre in Atlanta, Georgia. Began March 11 at Civic Center in Ozark, Alabama; ended July 29 in Atlanta, Georgia.

Average White Band: Began October 27, 1977, at Convention Center in Tucson, Arizona; ended November 21, 1977, at Power Theatre in Philadelphia, Pennsylvania. Began April 7 in San Antonio, Texas; ended July 1 in San Carlos, California.

Beach Boys: Began November 11, 1977, in Johnson City, Tennessee; ended December 17, 1977, in Eugene, Oregon. Toured major stadiums throughout the summer.

George Benson: Toured Far East March 10 through 26.

Blackbyrds: Began October 15, 1977, in Buffalo, New York; ended January 13 at Carnegie Hall in New York City. Began April 22 in Kansas City, Missouri; ended June 11 in Detroit, Michigan.

Blue Öyster Cult: Ended lengthy fall tour January 14 in New Haven, Connecticut. Went back on the road in March and July.

Debby Boone: Began May 5 in Louisville, Kentucky; ended August 28 in Syracuse, New York.

Boston: Began August 10 at Pittsburgh, Pennsylvania, Civic Arena; ended third week in November for break; resumed in December.

Jackson Browne: Began March 18 in Dallas, Texas; ended May 3 in Washington, D.C.

Jimmy Buffett: Began March 4 at Calley College in Rockford, Illinois; ended April 11 at University of Montana in Missoula, Montana. Began June 9 in San Jose, California; ended June 29 in Phoenix, Arizona.

Captain & Tennille: Toured Europe November 26 to December 15, 1977.

Shaun Cassidy: Began "weekends only" tour February 25 in Baltimore, Maryland.

Eric Clapton: Began February 1 in Vancouver, Canada; ended April 9 at Maple Leaf Gardens in Toronto.

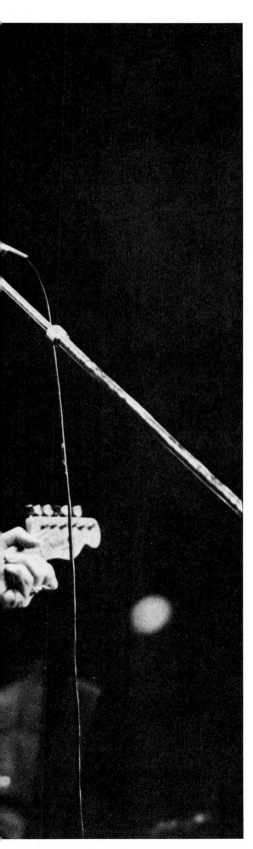

Chuck Pulin

Left: *Bob Dylan toured more extensively in 1978
than ever in his career. Here seen at Westfalia Hall
in Dortmund, Germany, on June 26, one stop on his
European tour.* Above: *In concert at a benefit for Karen
Silkwood, from left: John Hall, John Payne, Carly
Simon, James Taylor, Dennis Whitted, Bonnie Raitt, Freebo.*

Bootsy Collins: Began October 5, 1977, in Cheney, Pennsylvania; ended November 25, 1977, in Kalamazoo, Michigan. Began March 17 in Greensboro, North Carolina; ended June 8 in Oakland, California.

Commodores: Began August 26,1977, in Savannah, Georgia; ended November 19, 1977, in Dallas, Texas. Began July 14 in Louisville, Kentucky; ended November 23 in Montgomery, Alabama.

Con Funk Shun: Began December 9, 1977, in Jacksonville, Florida; ended December 31, 1977, in Houston, Texas. Began June 8 in Baton Rouge, Louisiana; ended September 3 in Norfolk, Virginia.

Rita Coolidge: Began August 8, 1977, in Detroit, Michigan; ended November 22, 1977, in Cookville, Tennessee. Toured Europe April 13 to May 12. Began August 2 at Memorial Auditorium in Buffalo, New York.

Elvis Costello: Began April 29 at Massey Hall in Toronto; ended June 7 at Winterland in San Francisco, California.

Pablo Cruise: Began October 9, 1977, in Seattle, Washington; ended December 4, 1977, at Freedom Hall in Louisville, Kentucky. Began April 23 in Fresno, California; ended July 28 at Rich Stadium in Buffalo, New York.

John Denver: Began March 13 in Portland, Maine; ended May 15 at the Forum in Los Angeles, California.

Neil Diamond: Began July 27 in Providence, Rhode Island; ended August 10 in Detroit, Michigan.

George Duke: Toured Europe November 6 to 18, 1977. Began June 9 in Houston, Texas; ended July 29 in Phoenix, Arizona.

Bob Dylan: Played June 1 through 7 at Universal Amphitheatre in Los Angeles, California. Toured Europe June 15 through July 15. Began September 15 in Augusta, Maine; ended December 15 in Miami, Florida.

Eagles: Began July 23 in Edmonton, Canada; ended August 6 in Toronto.

Earth, Wind and Fire: Began October 20, 1977, in Pittsburgh, Pennsylvania; ended February 23 in Cleveland, Ohio.

Electric Light Orchestra: Began June 30 at Civic Auditorium in Omaha, Nebraska; ended September 30 at the Forum in Montreal.

Yvonne Elliman: Began October 20, 1977, in Niles, Illinois; ended August 27 at Valley Forge Music Fair in Devon, Pennsylvania.

England Dan and John Ford Coley: Began February 17 at Joffa Mosque in Altoona, Pennsylvania; ended April 29 at Carowinds in Charlotte, North Carolina. Began July 14 in Jackson, New Jersey; ended September 3 in Kansas City, Kansas.

Roberta Flack: Began March 24 in Cleveland, Ohio; ended May 7 at Valley Forge Music Fair in Devon, Pennsylvania.

Fleetwood Mac: Toured Far East November 7 to December 10, 1977. Began July 17 at Alpine Valley Music Theatre in Milwaukee, Wisconsin.

Foghat: Began February 14 in Duluth, Minnesota; ended July 19 in Fort Pierce, Florida.

Foreigner: Toured world March 30 to April 28. Began June 2 in Greensboro, North Carolina; ended August 27 at Reading Festival in England.

Art Garfunkel: Began February 10 at Memorial Auditorium in Portland, Maine; ended May 1 at Carnegie Hall in New York City.

Andy Gibb: Began June 9 in San Francisco; ended July 9 in Miami Beach, Florida. Began July 29 in Honolulu; ended September 4.

Heart: Began June 9 in Bismarck, North Dakota; ended July 1 in Dallas, Texas.

Dan Hill: Began March 4 in Lakeland, Florida; ended March 31 in Milwaukee, Wisconsin.

Isley Brothers: Began May 26 in Biloxi, Mississippi; ended September 17 at the Von Braun Center in Huntsville, Alabama.

Millie Jackson: Began October 22, 1977, in Orlando, Florida; ended January 2 in Brooklyn, New York. Began February 24 in Compton, California; ended May 3 in Boston, Massachusetts.

Bob James: Began April 8 in Washington, D.C.; ended April 30 in Marshall, Missouri. Toured Japan July 18 to 27.

Jefferson Starship: Began May 13 in Minneapolis, Minnesota; ended June 10 at Nassau Coliseum in Uniondale, New York.

Billy Joel: Began September 28, 1977, in Boulder, Colorado; ended December 11 at Nassau Coliseum in Uniondale, New York. Toured Europe March 3 to 19. Toured Far East April 1 to 24.

Journey: Began March 1 in Racine, Wisconsin; ended July 8 in Chicago, Illinois.

Kansas: Began October 21, 1977, at Memorial Coliseum in Tuscaloosa, Alabama; ended January 20 at Winterland in San Francisco. Toured Europe February 28 to March 25. Began June 23 in Atlanta, Georgia; ended August 16 in Phoenix, Arizona.

Kiss: Began November 15, 1977, at Myriad Convention Center in Oklahoma City, Oklahoma;

According to Rolling Stone *magazine, Andy Gibb's mother once told him he should move around more onstage. Although it's hard to believe that Andy ever needed such advice, his performances make it obvious that he now knows what moves to make to win an audience of female fans.*

ended January 30 at Nassau Coliseum in Uniondale, New York.

Kris Kristofferson: Began August 23, 1977, in Atlanta, Georgia; ended November 22, 1977, in Cookeville, Tennessee. Toured Europe April 13 to May 12. Began July 12 at Universal Amphitheatre in Los Angeles, California; ended September 3 in Du Quoin, Illinois.

Little River Band: Began June 9 in Edmonton, Canada; ended August 27 in Vancouver, Canada.

L.T.D.: Began November 25, 1977, at Municipal Auditorium in Mobile, Alabama; ended December 29, 1977, at the Forum in Los Angeles. Began May 12 at Myriad Convention Center in Oklahoma City, Oklahoma; ended September 4 at the Omni in Atlanta, Georgia.

Barry Manilow: Began June 24 at the Civic Center in Providence, Rhode Island; ended September 3 at the Greek Theatre in Los Angeles, California.

Marshall Tucker Band: Began November 30, 1977, in Lakeland, Florida; ended January 15 in Niagara Falls, New York. Began April 28 in Scranton, Pennsylvania; ended August 26 in Denver, Colorado.

Steve Martin: Began October 4, 1977, in Philadelphia, Pennsylvania; ended December 10, 1977, in San Diego, California.

Johnny Mathis: Began October 19, 1977, in Honolulu; ended February 24 in Dallas, Texas. Toured Europe March 20 to April 9. Began May 1 in Cleveland, Ohio; ended September 17 in Lake Tahoe, Nevada.

Maze: Began March 17 in Jackson, Mississippi; ended July 28 in Oakland, California.

Meat Loaf: Began March 11 in Poughkeepsie, New York; ended April 22 in Montreal. Began July 19 in Toronto; ended September 1 at Nassau Coliseum in Uniondale, New York.

Bette Midler: Began November 29, 1977, in San Francisco, California; ended January 29 in Cleveland, Ohio. Toured Europe September 19 to October 18.

Steve Miller: Began July 23 in Dallas, Texas; ended August 26 in Anaheim, California.

Eddie Money: Began November 18, 1977, in San Antonio, Texas; ended December 31, 1977, in San Francisco, California. Began July 1 in Dallas, Texas; ended August 26 in St. Louis, Missouri.

Ted Nugent: Ended lengthy fall and winter tour February 18 in Johnson City, Tennessee. Toured Far East May 17 to 23. Began June 8 in Marquette, Michigan.

O'Jays: Began July 21 in Lafayette, Texas; ended September 1 at the Superdome in New Orleans, Louisiana.

Teddy Pendergrass: Began July 27 at the Centroplex in Baton Rouge, Louisiana; ended September 3 at Jones Beach Theatre in Jones Beach, New York.

Tom Petty and the Heartbreakers: Began November 26, 1977, at Tower Theatre in Philadelphia, Pennsylvania; ended December 3, 1977, in Chicago, Illinois.

Player: Began February 24 in Louisville, Kentucky; ended April 9 in Toronto. Began June 30 in Eureka, Missouri; ended August 6 in Lakeland, Florida.

Queen: Began November 11, 1977, in Portland, Maine; ended December 22 at the Forum in Los Angeles, California.

Raydio: Began April 1 at the Felt Forum in New York City; ended June 4 in San Diego, California.

Lou Reed: Began March 7 in Boston, Massachusetts; ended May 21 at the Bottom Line in New York City.

R.E.O. Speedwagon: Began March 10 in San Diego, California; ended June 30 in Pine Bluff, Arkansas.

Rolling Stones: Began June 11 at the Fox Theatre in Atlanta, Georgia; ended July 26 in Oakland, California.

Rufus: Began March 17 in Houston, Texas; ended June 10 in Lake Tahoe, California.

Samantha Sang: Began July 19 in Spartansburg, South Carolina; ended September 30 in Detroit, Michigan.

Boz Scaggs: Toured Far East February 3 to March 4. Began June 8 in Saskatoon, Canada; ended July 9 in Des Moines, Iowa.

Bob Seger: Began March 29 at the Onendoga War Memorial at Syracuse, New York; ended October 15 in Oklahoma City, Oklahoma.

Sex Pistols: Began January 5 at the Fox Theatre in Atlanta, Georgia; ended January 14 at Winterland in San Francisco, California.

Patti Smith: Began April 21 at the Paramount Theatre in Wilkes Barre, Pennsylvania; ended August 5 at Convention Hall in Asbury Park, New Jersey.

Bruce Springsteen: Began May 23 at Shea's Theatre in Buffalo, New York; ended September 13 at the Civic Center in Springfield, Virginia.

Rod Stewart: Ended lengthy fall tour December 19, 1977, at the Cow Palace in San Francisco.

Styx: Ended lengthy fall and winter tour April 7 in Lake Charles, Louisiana.

James Taylor: Began November 21, 1977, at Marin Civic Center in California; ended December 3, 1977, at Neal Blaisdell Center in Honolulu.

Robin Trower: Began October 15, 1977, at the Spectrum in Philadelphia, Pennsylvania; ended December 10, 1977, at the Coliseum in Houston, Texas.

Bonnie Tyler: Began July 6 at the Roxy in Los Angeles, California; ended July 17 at the Bottom Line in New York City.

Van Halen: Began March 17 in Louisville, Kentucky; ended April 26 at the Calderone Theatre in Hempstead, New York. Toured United Kingdom May 16 to June 4.

War: Began October 7, 1977, in San Diego, California; ended November 11, 1977, in Roanoke, Virginia.

Grover Washington, Jr.: Began January 13 in Vancouver, Canada; ended June 23 in San Diego, California.

Bob Welch: Began May 20 in Louisville, Kentucky; ended July 6 at Convention Hall in Asbury Park, New Jersey.

Deniece Williams: Began October 15, 1977 in Oklahoma City, Oklahoma; ended February 12 at Nassau Coliseum in Uniondale, New York.

Warren Zevon: Began May 12 in Cleveland, Ohio; ended May 21 in Minneapolis, Minnesota.

Dagmar

The graffiti on this Bruce Springsteen poster in Los Angeles was provided by the singer and assorted henchmen from his E Street band. Following page: Linda Ronstadt with her new short hairdo and powerful voice sent audiences into raptures at New York's Forest Hills stadium.

189

UPDATE

ROCK

On September 7, the rock world was shocked and saddened by the death of Keith Moon, whose thunderous drums powered the success of the Who. Ironically, his death came just as their new album, *Who Are You,* and its title single were storming their way up the charts.

In the fall of 1978, rock continued to be drawn by its past. The Beatles once again appeared center stage. Songs from the soundtrack album of *Sgt. Pepper's Lonely Hearts Club Band,* including Earth, Wind and Fire's percussive "Got to Get You Into My Life," Robin Gibb's sublimely sweet "Oh, Darling," and Aerosmith's powerful "Come Together," were hits. There was also a sharp sales increase of the Beatles original *Sgt. Pepper,* which shinnied up the charts with the momentum of a newcomer, even before Capitol released its special picture disk. Capitol also released a single from the album, the title song backed by "With a Little Help From My Friends." Natalie Cole sang "Lucy in the Sky with Diamonds," and on the road, the Broadway Show *Beatlemania* drew large audiences wherever it played.

Memories of Elvis remained strong, with a Las Vegas Always Elvis exposition commemorating the first anniversary of his death. Throughout the month of August, the city of Memphis was jammed with fans, and the city announced plans to build an Elvis Presley Museum.

In New York's Central Park, an August 16 concert by Dickie Betts and Great Southern at the Dr. Pepper Music Festival climaxed with an onstage reunion of four members of the original Allman Brothers Band. Ten thousand flabbergasted fans whooped with appreciation as Greg Allman, Jai Johnny Johnson, Butch Trucks, and Betts, joined by members of Betts's band, recreated Allman goodies.

The Rock 'n' Roll Flea Market, Record Meet and Film Festival, featuring rare rock records, collectors' items, a rock film festival, and special guest stars, was a lively and well-planned event. Held at New York's Statler-Hilton Hotel on the weekend of September 16 and 17, the festival was crammed with exuberant rock fans.

The hottest rock album of the fall was Boston's *Don't Look Back* with its smash title single. Other hit songs included Exile's "Kiss You All Over," Bob Seger's "Hollywood Nights," and Eddie Money's "Two Tickets to Paradise."

RHYTHM AND BLUES

R & B chart toppers in the fall of 1978 included such songs as "Get Off" by Foxy, "Holding On" by L.T.D., "Shake and Dance" by Con Funk Shun, "Got to Get You Into My Life" by Earth, Wind and Fire, "You and I" by Rick James, "What You Waitin' For" by Stargard, "Take Me I'm Yours" by Michael Henderson, "It's a Better than Good Time" by Gladys Knight and the Pips, "Brandy" by the O'Jays, "Dance" by Sylvester, "One Nation Under a Groove" by Funkadelic, and "It Seems to Hang On" by Ashford and Simpson.

Hit albums included *Come Get It* by Rick James and the Stone City Band, *Blam* by the Brothers Johnson, *Get Off* by Foxy, *The Concept* by Slave, *In the Night Time* by Michael Henderson, *Sunbeam* by the Emotions, *Jass-ay-lay-dee* by the Ohio Players.

COUNTRY AND WESTERN

Top country singles in the fall of 1978 included "Rake and Rambling Man" by Don Williams, "Rose Colored Glasses" by John Conlee, "Blue Skies" by Willie Nelson, "I've Always Been Crazy" by Waylon Jennings, "Boogie Grass Band" by Conway Twitty, "Hello Mexico (and Adios Baby to You)" by Johnny Duncan, "Womanhood" by Tammy Wynette, "If You Got Ten Minutes (Let's Fall in Love)" by Joe Stampley, "Who Am I to Say" by the Statler Brothers, "It's Been a Great Afternoon" by Merle Haggard, "Heartbreaker" by Dolly Parton, "Let's Take the Long Way Around the World" by Ronnie Milsap, "Cryin' Again" by the Oak Ridge Boys, "Another Goodbye" by Donna Fargo, and "Ain't No California" by Mel Tillis.

Top album chart-burners included *Let's Keep it That Way* by Anne Murray, *Heartbreaker* by Dolly Parton, and *Elvis Sings for Children and Grownups Too* by Elvis Presley.

DISCO

Disco action kept heating up through the end of 1978. More than eight thousand boogiers descended on the Miami Beach Convention Center on July 29 to compete in a disco dance marathon. Called Discorama, the contest featured live entertainment by Vickie Sue Robinson, Peter Brown, Bionic Boogie, and the Crown Heights Affair. On Labor Day, the Palace Country Club in Oldridge, New Jersey, drew close to ten thousand people to the Woodstock of Disco for a day of dancing, swimming, tennis, and basketball on the grounds of the twenty-two-acre club. Cab Calloway recorded a disco version of his 1931 hit "Minnie the Moocher," with hi-de-hos intact.

Disco hits that moved dancers to their feet included "Keep on Jumpin'" by Musique, "Think it Over/Warning Danger/ Somebody Should Have Told Me" by Cissy Houston, and "Victim" by Candi Staton.

EASY LISTENING

Tunes that soothed the psyches of easy listeners in late 1978 included Chris Rea's "Fool (If You Think It's Over)," Crystal Gayle's "Talking in Your Sleep," Olivia Newton-John's "Hopelessly Devoted to You," John Paul Young's "Love Is in the Air," Carly Simon and James Taylor's "Devoted to You," Billy Joel's "She's Always a Woman," Gerry Rafferty's "Right Down the Line," Kenny Loggins' "Whenever I Call You 'Friend'."

JAZZ

Jazz festivals that closed the summer and continued into early fall included a British arm of the Newport Jazz Festival, performed in a Middlesbrough football field by such notables as Ella Fitzgerald, Dizzy Gillespie, and Lionel Hampton. On September 9, the ubiquitous Diz, Max Roach, Zoot Sims, Bobby Brookmeyer, and a host of others performed in Philadelphia's Penn's Landing Jazz Festival in the city's new Riverside Park. Beginning September 12, the Los Angeles Playboy Club inaugurated a series of jazz jam sessions from five to seven P.M. on the first and third Tuesdays of each month. The Russian River Jazz Festival, held in the redwood country north of San Francisco on September 23 and 24, featured Ornette Coleman and the Fred Mathis Quintet.

Successful jazz albums included *Blam!* by the Brothers Johnson, *You Send Me* by Roy Ayers, and *Freestyle* by Bobbi Humphrey.

CLASSICAL

On August 25, Leonard Bernstein celebrated his sixtieth birthday with an intimate party of some six thousand friends; the festivities were telecast by PBS to an audience around the country. At Wolf Trap Farm Park, America's greatest and best-loved composer/conductor was honored by classical and musical-theater greats. Featured were performances of several of his works. It was a warmly gratifying tribute to Bernstein, much-needed balm after the loss of his wife, Felicia Montealegre, earlier in 1978.

Other classical events included the release of several early recordings by the late Maria Callas, live radio broadcasts by the San Francisco Opera of its complete 1978 season, and a slew of television classical offerings.

MOVIES

Although 1978 began with an explosion of musical movies, the year finished with only a few. In late August, *Who'll Stop the Rain,* the United Artists release starring Nick Nolte, featured Creedence Clearwater's song of the same name. In October, Paramount released *The Secret Life of Plants,* with a soundtrack by Stevie Wonder. A musical soundtrack was also prominent in November's *Slow Dancing in the Big City* from United Artists. Columbia's *Remember My Name,* featuring blues singer Alberta Hunter, was planned for autumn release.

THEATER

Stimulated by the notable successes of several recent Broadway musicals, theatrical producers planned a cornucopia of musical treats for fall and winter 1978. In September, Vinnette Carroll's adaptation of the works of Lewis Carroll, a musical with a long and stormy history, appeared as *But Never Jam Today* at New York's Off Broadway Urban Arts Theatre. Music was by Robert Larrimer, and Marilynn Windbush was featured as Alice. *Eubie!,* a revue directed by Julianne Boyd and featuring music by Eubie Blake, opened September 20.

On November 12, Alexis Smith showed up in *Platinum,* playing a faded movie queen who begins a new career as a rock singer. Book was written by Will Holt and Bruce Vilanch, and music and lyrics were written by Holt and Gary William Friedman. Paramount Pictures, seeing cinematic potential in the play, provided 25 percent of its capitalization.

Opening in December, *Ballroom,* based on Jerome Kass's 1975 television drama "Queen of the Stardust Ballroom" featured Dorothy Loudon and Vincent Gardenia, a book by Kass, music by Billy Goldenberg, lyrics by Alan and Marilyn Bergman. *Ballroom* was originally scheduled to be produced by Joseph Papp, who decided it wasn't appropriate for the New York Shakespeare Festival. Remaining with the Festival was *Alice in Wonderland;* this version of the Carroll classic featured music and staging by Elizabeth Swados and starred Meryl Streep. Another December offering was *A Broadway Musical,* with book by William F. Brown and music and lyrics by Charles Strouse and Lee Adams.

Other musical-theater events scheduled for winter were *They're Playing Our Song,* a Neil Simon effort with music by Marvin Hamlisch and lyrics by Carol Bayer Sager. The two-person musical starred Lucie Arnaz and John Rubenstein and opened in December in Los Angeles's Ahmanson Theatre. *Evita,* the fanciful biography of Eva Peron, was slated for Broadway by Robert Stigwood. With book and lyrics by Tim Rice and music by Andrew Lloyd Webber, the play was originally a London smash.

Cy Coleman, perhaps looking for a little crossover action, recorded disco versions of several songs from Tony-winner *On the 20th Century.*

TELEVISION

September's most exciting musical offerings were classical music programs. On September 24, NBC offered "Horowitz—Live!" starring Vladimir Horowitz and hosted by Edward Villela. On September 17, PBS kicked off its "Evening at Pops" series with Arthur Fiedler and the Boston Pops and dancer Noel Parenti. The same night, the network presented the first of a series of live recitals from the White House, starring cellist and music director of the National Symphony Orchestra, Mstislav Rostropovich, who was accompanied on piano by his daughter, Elena. September 20 saw the beginning of the PBS "Great Performances/Live from Lincoln Center" series, featuring Zubin Mehta conducting the New York Philharmonic Orchestra, with Rudolf Serkin as guest pianist. Steven De Groote, the winner of the 1977 Van Cliburn International Quadrennial Piano Competition, was featured on "Evening at Pops" on September 24.

PBS began a quartet of operatic broadcasts called "Live from the Met" with Verdi's *Otello* starring Renata Scotto, Jon Vickers, and Cornell MacNeil on September 25. Conductor Herbert von Karajan returned to "Great Performances" on September 27, conducting the Berlin Philharmonic in a program featuring cellist Mstislav Rostropovich.

The perennially youthful Dick Clark offered a preview of his NBC "Live Wednesday" series on September 6, featuring live performances by Les Paul, José Feliciano, Lou Rawls,

Above: *Eddie Money won gold with his first album and had a hit with his song "Two Tickets to Paradise."* Opposite, top: *Teddy Pendergrass, who has a heart line on his hands that indicates love for the world, proved it in his For Women Only concerts in New York and Philadelphia.* Bottom: *At Las Vegas's Always Elvis exposition fans could buy all manner of memorabilia of the King, from T-shirts to records.*

Paul Anka, and Little Richard.

A stellar group of performers, including Leslie Uggams, Cheryl Ladd, Charley Pride, Donny and Marie Osmond, and Sha Na Na helped make ABC's "General Electric's 100th Anniversary Celebration" a festive evening. Young viewers were delighted to see the Bay City Rollers become new hosts of NBC's "Krofft Superstar Hour." On September 17, CBS presented "The 30th Annual Emmy Awards." The following night, CBS introduced a new series, "WKRP in Cincinnati," revolving around a struggling easy-listening station that changes to a top-forty format.

PBS dominated music lovers' screens for most of October. On the fourth, the New York City Opera's new production of Rossini's *The Turk in Italy* was seen on "Live from Lincoln Center." Leontyne Price starred in the second "Recital Performance at the White House" on October 8. October ninth saw the beginning of a new season of "Evening at Symphony." The acclaimed contemporary music series "Soundstage" offered four top performers in October: Leo Sayer on the tenth, Emmylou Harris on the seventeenth, Journey on the twenty-fourth, and Jackson Browne on the thirty-first. On October 19, PBS presented "Ormandy and His Orchestra: Japanese Odyssey," a film of the Philadelphia Orchestra's spring tour of Japan. The rocking fifties were authentically recreated by the "Grease Band," taped in Asbury Park, New Jersey, and aired October 26.

Kiss, the masked sensations, starring in their first film, displayed acting as well as musical talents in an NBC "Movie of the Week" called *Kiss Meets the Phantom,* on October 28.

On October 29, the new musical director of the Los Angeles Philharmonic, Carlo Maria Guilini, conducted a performance of Beethoven's Ninth Symphony live over PBS. In October, the Country Music Association presented the "12th Annual Country Music Awards" live from Nashville on CBS.

Smetana's *The Bartered Bride* was aired "Live from the Met" on November 21 over PBS, starring Teresa Stratas, Nicolai Gedda, Jon Vickers, and Martti Talvela. On ABC, balladeer Pat Boone and his family starred in a special broadcast in November.

December 14 offered a taste of holiday viewing on NBC with Ann-Margret hosting "Rockette: A Holiday Tribute to the Radio City Music Hall," celebrating the New York landmark. PBS's "Live from the Met" featured Shirley Verrett, Luciano Pavarotti, Cornell MacNeil, and Fernando Corena in *Tosca* on December 19.

Each of the three commercial networks outdid itself in making the 1978 holiday season a memorable one for viewers. ABC featured Perry Como and John Davidson in their own specials; "The Carpenters' Christmas Portrait" starred the brother/sister duo; "Christmas at the Grand Ol' Opry" was hosted by John Ritter and starred Minnie Pearl, Ronnie Milsap, Crystal Gayle, Chet Atkins, Barbara Mandrell, and the Statler Brothers; and, to end the year in grand style, "New Year's Rockin' Eve" starred Dick Clark.

CBS took the season to outer space with the ninety-minute musical "Star Wars Holiday Special." The network also offered two animated programs, "Frosty the Snowman" and "Twas the Night Before Christmas." Bing Crosby's holiday annuals were fondly remembered with "Bing, the Christmas Years," and country music was heard on the "Johnny Cash Christmas Show" and "A Country Christmas," starring Roy Clark, Jim Stafford, Loretta Lynn, the Oak Ridge Boys, and many others.

A remarkable musical version of the Scrooge story was shown by NBC as "The Stingiest Man in Town." The program

featured the singing debuts of Walter Matthau, his son
Charles, and Tom Bosley, as well as stars Theodore Bikel,
Robert Morse, and Dennis Day. Also from NBC were new
musical adaptations of "Gift of the Magi" and "Amahl and the
Night Visitors."

The Captain and Tennille, Roy Clark, Cheryl Ladd, Barry
Manilow, and the Osmonds hosted specials on ABC. The
network saluted black music in a two-hour special from the
Apollo Theatre called "Uptown." Busy Dick Clark presented
his "American Music Awards" and "The Heroes of Rock 'n'
Roll" on ABC.

Annie star Andrea McArdle portrayed the young Judy
Garland on "Rainbow," an NBC special. Mac Davis, Dean
Martin, Bette Midler, Tony Orlando, and Helen Reddy were a
few of the music luminaries to host musical specials on NBC.
That network also presented "The Tenth Anniversary of Hee
Haw," featuring Loretta Lynn and Tennessee Ernie Ford; "The
First 100 Years of Recorded Music," starring Andy Williams,
Glen Campbell, Ethel Merman, and Henry Mancini; and "Dick
Clark's Good Ol' Days, Part II."

Dagmar

Dagmar

Top Sellers

(From October 1977 through September 1978)

Platinum Record Awards

Albums
(Indicates sales of more than 1 million copies)

Endless Flight, Leo Sayer
Shaun Cassidy, Shaun Cassidy
Cat Scratch Fever, Ted Nugent
Free for All, Ted Nugent
In Flight, George Benson
The Floaters, the Floaters
Ol' Waylon, Waylon Jennings
Chicago XI, Chicago
Simple Dreams, Linda Ronstadt
In Concert, Elvis Presley
Anytime...Anywhere, Rita Coolidge
Elton John's Greatest Hits, Vol. II, Elton John
Out of the Blue, Electric Light Orchestra
Barry White Sings for Someone You Love, Barry White
James Taylor's Greatest Hits, James Taylor
Here at Last...Bee Gees...Live, Bee Gees
Kiss Alive II, Kiss
Point of Know Return, Kansas
Elvis Sings "The Wonderful World of Christmas,"
  Elvis Presley
In Full Bloom, Rose Royce
Down Two, Then Left, Boz Scaggs
All 'n All, Earth, Wind and Fire
Street Survivors, Lynyrd Skynyrd
I'm Glad You're Here with Me Tonight, Neil Diamond
Draw the Line, Aerosmith
You Light Up My Life, Debby Boone
Born Late, Shaun Cassidy
Changes in Latitudes—Changes in Attitudes,
  Jimmy Buffett
Greatest Hits, Olivia Newton-John
"Live" Bullet, Bob Seger and the Silver Bullet Band
Foghat Live, Foghat
Foot Loose and Fancy Free, Rod Stewart
Too Hot to Handle, Heatwave
The Grand Illusion, Styx
Aja, Steely Dan
News of the World, Queen
Saturday Night Fever, Bee Gees
The Stranger, Billy Joel
Greatest Hits, Etc., Paul Simon

We Must Believe in Magic, Crystal Gayle
Even Now, Barry Manilow
Running on Empty, Jackson Browne
Slowhand, Eric Clapton
London Town, Paul McCartney and Wings
Waylon and Willie, Waylon Jennings and Willie Nelson
Here You Come Again, Dolly Parton
French Kiss, Bob Welch
Showdown, Isley Brothers
The Best of Jethro Tull, Jethro Tull
Weekend in L.A., George Benson
Funkentelechy vs. the Placebo Syndrome, Parliament
Earth, Jefferson Starship
Grease, original soundtrack
Let's Get Small, Steve Martin
FM, original soundtrack
Son of a Son of a Sailor, Jimmy Buffett
I Want to Live, John Denver
Double Platinum, Kiss
Feels So Good, Chuck Mangione
Carolina Dreams, Marshall Tucker Band
Stranger in Town, Bob Seger and the
  Silver Bullet Band
So Full of Love, O'Jays
Magazine, Heart
Star Wars and other Galactic Funk, Meco
Thank God It's Friday, original soundtrack
Shadow Dancing, Andy Gibb
City to City, Gerry Rafferty
Central Heating, Heatwave
Teddy Pendergrass, Teddy Pendergrass
Thankful, Natalie Cole
Double Vision, Foreigner
Some Girls, Rolling Stones
Darkness on the Edge of Town, Bruce Springsteen
You Light Up My Life, Johnny Mathis
Agents of Fortune, Blue Öyster Cult
Sgt. Pepper's Lonely Hearts Club Band,
  original soundtrack
Ten Years of Gold, Kenny Rogers
Greatest Hits, ABBA
Double Live Gonzo, Ted Nugent
Takin' It to the Streets, Doobie Brothers
Flowing Rivers, Andy Gibb
Boys in the Trees, Carly Simon
But Seriously, Folks, Joe Walsh
The Album, ABBA

Natural High, Commodores
Songbird, Barbra Streisand
Life Is a Song Worth Singing, Teddy Pendergrass
Bat Out of Hell, Meat Loaf
Don't Look Back, Boston

Singles
(Indicates sales of more than 2 million copies)

"You Light Up My Life," Debby Boone
"Boogie Nights," Heatwave
"Stayin' Alive," Bee Gees
"Emotion," Samantha Sang
"We Are the Champions," Queen
"Night Fever," Bee Gees
"Star Wars Theme/Cantina Band," Meco
"Shadow Dancing," Andy Gibb
"You're the One that I Want," John Travolta and
    Olivia Newton-John

Gold Record Awards

Albums
(Indicates sales of more than 500,000 copies)

Simple Things, Carole King
Welcome to My World, Elvis Presley
Luna Sea, Firefall
Love You Live, Rolling Stones
Southern Nights, Glen Campbell
From Elvis Presley Boulevard, Memphis, Tennessee,
    Elvis Presley
American Stars 'n Bars, Neil Young
Jailbreak, Thin Lizzy
Love Songs, the Beatles
Elvis—A Legendary Performer, Vol. II, Elvis Presley
The Johnny Cash Portrait/His Greatest Hits, Vol. II,
    Johnny Cash
Rock and Roll Love Letter, Bay City Rollers
Eric Carmen, Eric Carmen
Street Survivors, Lynyrd Skynyrd
You Light Up My Life, original soundtrack
Captured Angel, Dan Fogelberg
Let it Flow, Dave Mason
Anthology, Steve Miller Band
Something to Love, L.T.D.
2112, Rush
A Farewell to Kings, Rush
All the World's a Stage, Rush
In City Dreams, Robin Trower
Dedication, Bay City Rollers

Galaxy, War
The Turning Point, John Mayall
Moonflower, Santana
His Hand in Mine, Elvis Presley
Elvis Country, Elvis Presley
The Story of Star Wars, original cast with
    narration by Roscoe Lee Browne
Bay City Rollers/Greatest Hits, Bay City Rollers
Once Upon a Time, Donna Summer
Friends and Strangers, Ronnie Laws
Greatest Hits, Captain and Tennille
Tupelo Honey, Van Morrison
Daytime Friends, Kenny Rogers
Viva Terlingua, Jerry Jeff Walker
Masque, Kansas
A Chorus Line, original cast
Feelin' Bitchy, Millie Jackson
Action, Blackbyrds
Works, Vol. II, Emerson, Lake and Palmer
Best of Z.Z. Top, Z.Z. Top
Bee Gees Gold, Bee Gees
Brass Construction III, Brass Construction
Close Encounters of the Third Kind,
    original soundtrack
Diamantina Cocktail, Little River Band
New Season, Donny and Marie Osmond
Waylon Live, Waylon Jennings
Reach for It, George Duke
Spectres, Blue Öyster Cult
Little Criminals, Randy Newman
Leif Garrett, Leif Garrett
It Was Almost Like a Song, Ronnie Milsap
Don Juan's Reckless Daughter, Joni Mitchell
When You Hear Lou, You've Heard it All, Lou Rawls
Street Player, Rufus
Blue Lights in the Basement, Roberta Flack
Watermark, Art Garfunkel
Countdown to Ecstasy, Steely Dan
Bootsy? Player of the Year, Bootsy's Rubber Band
Golden Time of Day, Maze
It Feels So Good, Manhattans
Emotion, Samantha Sang
Chic, Chic
Carole King...Her Greatest Hits, Carole King
Champagne Jam, Atlanta Rhythm Section
Heavy Horses, Jethro Tull
Excitable Boy, Warren Zevon
Player, Player
Endless Wire, Gordon Lightfoot
Rock 'n' Roll Animal, Lou Reed
Together Forever, Marshall Tucker Band
Infinity, Journey
The Sound in Your Mind, Willie Nelson
Secrets, Con Funk Shun

Flying High on Your Love, Bar-Kays
Warmer Communications, Average White Band
Menagerie, Bill Withers
Van Halen, Van Halen
The Best of Rod Stewart, Rod Stewart
And Then There were Three, Genesis
Disco Inferno, Trammps
Greatest Stories Live, Harry Chapin
Don't Let Me Be Misunderstood, Santa Esmeralda
The Best of Dolly Parton, Dolly Parton
Octave, Moody Blues
Stone Blue, Foghat
Send It, Ashford & Simpson
Togetherness, L.T.D.
Sounds...and Stuff Like That, Quincy Jones
Love Me Again, Rita Coolidge
Worlds Away, Pablo Cruise
You Can Tune a Piano, But You Can't Tuna Fish,
    REO Speedwagon
Street Legal, Bob Dylan
It's a Heartache, Bonnie Tyler
Eddie Money, Eddie Money
You're Gonna Get It, Tom Petty and the Heartbreakers
Natalie Live, Natalie Cole
That's What Friends Are For, Johnny Mathis and
    Deniece Williams
Stardust, Willie Nelson
Pyramid, Alan Parsons Project
Elite Hotel, Emmylou Harris
Blam!, Brothers Johnson
Under Wraps, Shaun Cassidy
A Taste of Honey, Taste of Honey
Macho Man, Village People
Heartbreaker, Dolly Parton
Reaching for the Sky, Peabo Bryson
Come Get It, Rick James
Who Are You, the Who
Don't Look Back, Boston
Love Shine, Con Funk Shun
Get it Out'cha System, Millie Jackson
Sleeper Catcher, Little River Band

Singles
(Indicates sales of more than 1 million copies)

"It's Ecstasy When You Lay Down Next to Me,"
    Barry White
"Strawberry Letter 23," Brothers Johnson
"Telephone Man," Meri Wilson
"Nobody Does it Better," Carly Simon
"I Feel Love," Donna Summer
"Don't it Make My Brown Eyes Blue," Crystal Gayle
"Swayin' to the Music," Johnny Rivers

"Heaven on the 7th Floor," Paul Nicholas
"How Deep Is Your Love," Bee Gees
"(Everytime I Turn Around) Back in Love Again," L.T.D.
"Baby Come Back," Player
"My Way," Elvis Presley
"Hey Deanie," Shaun Cassidy
"Short People," Randy Newman
"Blue Bayou," Linda Ronstadt
"Here You Come Again," Dolly Parton
"We're All Alone," Rita Coolidge
"You're In My Heart," Rod Stewart
"Love Is Thicker than Water," Andy Gibb
"Dance, Dance, Dance," Chic
"Sometimes When We Touch," Dan Hill
"Just the Way You Are," Billy Joel
"Always and Forever," Heatwave
"Our Love," Natalie Cole
"Can't Smile Without You," Barry Manilow
"Lay Down Sally," Eric Clapton
"Flash Light," Parliament
"Jack and Jill," Raydio
"The Closer I Get to You," Roberta Flack and
    Donny Hathaway
"If I Can't Have You," Yvonne Elliman
"Too Much, Too Little, Too Late," Johnny Mathis and
    Deniece Williams
"Use Ta Be My Girl," O'Jays
"It's a Heartache," Bonnie Tyler
"Dust in the Wind," Kansas
"The Groove Line," Heatwave
"Baker Street," Gerry Rafferty
"Last Dance," Donna Summer
"Two Out of Three Ain't Bad," Meat Loaf
"Miss You," Rolling Stones
"Grease," Frankie Valli
"Take a Chance on Me," ABBA
"Boogie, Oogie Oogie," Taste of Honey
"Shame," Evelyn "Champagne" King
"An Everlasting Love," Andy Gibb
"King Tut," Steve Martin
"Hopelessly Devoted to You," Olivia Newton-John
"Summer Nights," John Travolta, Olivia Newton-John,
    and cast of *Grease*

Major Awards

Billboard's #1 Music Award Winners

(Presented December 11, 1977, by *Billboard* Magazine)

Soundtrack of the Year: *A Star Is Born*

Top Easy Listening Artist: Barbra Streisand

Top Jazz Artist: George Benson

Top Disco Artist: Donna Summer

Top Soul Artist: Stevie Wonder

Top Country Artist: Waylon Jennings

Top New Artist: Foreigner

Top Pop Group: Fleetwood Mac

Top Pop Female Artist: Linda Ronstadt

Top Pop Male Artist: Stevie Wonder

Top Pop Single: "Tonight's the Night," Rod Stewart

Top Pop LP: *Rumours*, Fleetwood Mac

Dick Clark's American Music Award Winners

(Presented January 16, 1978, by Dick Clark)

Favorite Pop/Rock Male Vocalist: Barry Manilow

Favorite Pop/Rock Female Vocalist: Linda Ronstadt

Favorite Pop/Rock Duo or Group: Fleetwood Mac

Favorite Pop/Rock Album: *Rumours*, Fleetwood Mac

Favorite Pop/Rock Single: "You Light Up My Life," Debby Boone

Favorite Country Male Vocalist: Conway Twitty

Favorite Country Female Vocalist: Loretta Lynn

Favorite Country Duo or Group: Loretta Lynn and Conway Twitty

Favorite Country Album: *New Harvest, First Gathering*, Dolly Parton

Favorite Country Single: "Lucille," Kenny Rogers

Favorite Soul Male Vocalist: Stevie Wonder

Favorite Soul Female Vocalist: Natalie Cole

Favorite Soul Group: the Commodores

Favorite Soul Single: "Best of My Love," the Emotions

Favorite Soul Album: *Songs in the Key of Life*, Stevie Wonder

Golden Globe Award Winners

(Presented January 28, 1978, by the Hollywood Foreign Press Association)

Best Original Score for a Motion Picture: John Williams for *Star Wars*

Best Original Motion Picture Song: "You Light Up My Life"

Grammy Award Winners

(Presented February 23, 1978, by The National Academy of Recording Arts and Sciences)

Record of the Year: "Hotel California," Eagles; Bill Szymczyk, producer; Asylum

Album of the Year: *Rumours*, Fleetwood Mac; Fleetwood Mac, Richard Dashut, Ken Caillat, producers; Warner Brothers

Song of the Year: "Love Theme from A Star Is Born (Evergreen)," Barbra Streisand and Paul Williams, songwriters; "You Light Up My Life," Joe Brooks, songwriter

New Artist of the Year: Debby Boone, Warner Brothers/Curb

Pop Vocal Performance, Female: "Love Theme from A Star Is Born (Evergreen)," Barbra Streisand, Columbia

Pop Vocal Performance, Male: "Handy Man," James Taylor, Columbia

Pop Vocal Performance by a Duo, Group or Chorus: "How Deep Is Your Love," Bee Gees, RSO

Pop Instrumental Recording: *Star Wars*, John Williams conducting London Symphony Orchestra, 20th Century

R & B Vocal Performance, Female: "Don't Leave Me This Way," Thelma Houston, Motown

R & B Vocal Performance, Male: *Unmistakably Lou*, Lou Rawls, Philadelphia Intl/Epic

R & B Vocal Performance by a Duo, Group or Chorus: "Best of My Love," Emotions, Columbia

R & B Instrumental Performance: "Q," Brothers Johnson, A&M

R & B Song: "You Make Me Feel Like Dancing," Leo Sayer, Vini Poncia

Jazz Vocal Performance: *Look to the Rainbow*, Al Jarreau, Warner Brothers

Jazz Performance by a Soloist: *The Giants*, Oscar Peterson, Pablo

Jazz Performance by a Group: *The Phil Woods Six—Live From the Showboat*, Phil Woods, RCA

Jazz Performance by a Big Band: *Prime Time*, Count Basie and his Orchestra, Pablo

Country Vocal Performance, Female: "Don't It Make My Brown Eyes Blue," Crystal Gayle, UA

Country Vocal Performance, Male: "Lucille," Kenny Rogers, UA

Country Vocal Performance by a Duo or Group: "Heaven's Just a Sin Away," the Kendalls, Ovation

Country Instrumentalist of the Year: Hargus "Pig" Robbins, Elektra

Country Song: "Don't It Make My Brown Eyes Blue," Richard Leigh

Instrumental Composition: "Main Title from Star Wars," John Williams

Original Score Written for a Motion Picture or a Television Special: "Star Wars," John Williams, 20th Century

Instrumental Arrangement: "Nadia's Theme (The Young and the Restless)," Barry DeVorzon; Harry Betts, Perry Botkin, Jr., and Barry DeVorzon, arrangers; Arista

Arrangement Accompanying Vocalist(s): "Love Theme from A Star Is Born (Evergreen)," Barbra Streisand; Ian Freebairn-Smith, arranger; Columbia

Arrangement for Voices: "New Kid In Town," Eagles; Eagles, arrangers; Asylum

Engineered Recording (non-classical): *Aja*, Steely Dan; Roger Nichols, Elliot Scheiner, Bill Schnee, Al Schmitt, engineers; ABC

Album Package: *Simple Dreams*, Linda Ronstadt; Kosh, art director; Asylum

Album Notes: *Bing Crosby: A Legendary Performer*, George T. Simon, annotator, RCA

Producer of the Year: Peter Asher

Gospel Performance, Contemporary or Inspirational: *Sail On*, Imperials, Dayspring/Word

Gospel Performance, Traditional: "Just a Little Talk With Jesus," Oak Ridge Boys, Rockland Road

Soul Gospel Performance Contemporary: "Wonderful!" Edwin Hawkins & the Edwin Hawkins Singers, Birthright

Soul Gospel Performance, Traditional: *James Cleveland Live at Carnegie Hall*, James Cleveland, Savoy

Inspirational Performance: *Home Where I Belong*, B. J. Thomas, Myrrh/Word

Ethnic or Traditional Recording: *Hard Again*, Muddy Waters, Blue Sky/CBS

Latin Recording: *Dawn*, Mongo Santamaria, Vaya

Recording for Children: *Aren't You Glad You're You*, Christopher Cerf and Jim Timmens, Sesame Street

Comedy Recording: *Let's Get Small*, Steve Martin, Warner Brothers

Spoken Word Recording: *The Belle of Amherst*, Julie Harris, Credo

Cast Show Album: *Annie*, Charles Strouse, Martin Charnin, composers; Larry Morton, Charles Strouse, producers; Columbia

Album of the Year, Classical: *Concert of the Century*, Leonard Bernstein, Vladimir Horowitz, Isaac Stern, Mstislav Rostropovich, Dietrich Fischer-Dieskau, Yehudi Menuhin, and Lyndon Woodside; Thomas Frost, producer; Columbia

Classical Orchestral Performance: *Mahler: Symphony No. 9*, Carlo Maria Giulini conducting the Chicago

Symphony Orchestra; Gunther Breest, producer; DG

Opera Recording: *Gershwin: Porgy and Bess*, John DeMain conducting Sherwin M. Goldman/Houston Grand Opera; Thomas Z. Shepard, producer; RCA

Choral Performance, Classical (Other Than Opera): *Verdi: Requiem*, Sir Georg Solti conducting the Chicago Symphony Orchestra; Margaret Hillis, Choral Director of Chicago Symphony Chorus; RCA

Chamber Music Performance: *Schoenberg: Quartets For Strings*, Juilliard Quartet, Columbia

Classical Performance Instrumental Soloist or Soloists (With Orchestra): *Vivaldi: The Four Seasons*, Itzhak Perlman, violin; Itzhak Perlman conducting the London Philharmonic Orchestra; Angel

Classical Performance Instrumental Soloist or Soloists (Without Orchestra): *Beethoven: Sonata For Piano No. 18; Schumann: Fantasiestücke*, Artur Rubinstein, piano, RCA

Classical Vocal Soloist Performance: *Bach: Arias*, Janet Baker; Neville Marriner conducting Academy of St. Martin-in-the-Fields; Angel

Engineered Recording, Classical: *Ravel: Boléro*, Solti conducting the Chicago Symphony; Kenneth Wilkinson, engineer; London

Hall of Fame:

Bach-Stokowski: Toccata & Fugue in D Minor, Leopold Stokowski conducting the Philadelphia Orchestra. Released in 1927 (Victor No. 6751).

The Genius of Art Tatum, Vols. 1-13, Art Tatum. Released 1954 through 1955 (Verve, 13 LPs)

I Can Hear It Now, Edward R. Murrow. Released 1948 through 1950 (Columbia, album series)

My Blue Heaven, Gene Austin. Released 1928 (Victor No. 20964)

Strange Fruit, Billie Holiday. Released in 1939 (Commodore No. CMS-526)

Award Winners for Best-Selling Records
(Presented March 20, 1978, by the National Association of Recording Merchandisers)

Album: *Rumours*, Fleetwood Mac

Movie Soundtrack Album: *A Star Is Born*, Barbra Streisand and Kris Kristofferson

Broadway Cast Album: *A Chorus Line*

Album by a Group: *Rumours*, Fleetwood Mac

Album by a Male Artist: *Silk Degrees*, Boz Scaggs

Album by a Female Artist: *Simple Dreams*, Linda Ronstadt

Album by a Male Country Artist: *Moody Blue*, Elvis Presley

Album by a Female Country Artist: *Simple Dreams*, Linda Ronstadt

Album by a Black Group: *Commodores*, the Commodores

Album by a Black Male Artist: *Songs in the Key of Life*, Stevie Wonder

Album by a Black Female Artist: *I Remember Yesterday*, Donna Summer

Jazz Album: *In Flight*, George Benson

Comedy Album: *Let's Get Small*, Steve Martin

Classical Album: *Suite for Flute and Jazz Piano*, Jean-Pierre Rampal and Claude Bolling

Children's Album: *The Rescuers*

Economy Album: *Christmas Album*, Elvis Presley

Album by a New Artist: *Foreigner*, Foreigner
Shaun Cassidy, Shaun Cassidy
You Light Up My Life, Debby Boone
Too Hot to Handle, Heatwave

Single Record: "You Light Up My Life," Debby Boone

Pop Instrumental Album: *Star Wars*

Academy Award Winners
(Presented April 3, 1978, by the Academy of Motion Picture Arts and Sciences)

Best Original Music Score: *Star Wars*, John Williams

Best Original Score Adaptation: *A Little Night Music*, adapted by Jonathan Tunick

Best Original Song: "You Light Up My Life," music and lyrics by Joseph Brooks

Academy of Country Music Award Winners

(Presented April 27, 1978, by the Academy of Country Music)

Bass: Larry Booth and Curtis Stone

Fiddle: Billy Armstrong

Drums: Archie Francis and George Manz

Guitar: Roy Clark

Keyboard: Hargus "Pig" Robbins

Steel Guitar: Buddy Emmons

Specialty Instrument: Charlie McCoy

Radio Station of Year: KGBS, Los Angeles

Disk Jockey of Year: Billy Parker, KVOO, Tulsa

Country Night Club: Palomino Club, North Hollywood

Band of the Year (Touring): Asleep at the Wheel and Sons of the Pioneers

Band of the Year (Non-Touring): Palomino Riders

Top New Female Vocalist: Debby Boone

Top New Male Vocalist: Eddie Rabbitt

Top Vocal Group: Statler Brothers

Album of the Year: *Kenny Rogers*, Kenny Rogers

Top Male Vocalist of Year: Kenny Rogers

Top Female Vocalist of Year: Crystal Gayle

Single Record of Year: "Lucille," Kenny Rogers

Entertainer of the Year: Dolly Parton

Song of the Year: "Lucille," Kenny Rogers

Career Achievement: Johnny Paycheck

Jim Reeves Memorial Award: Jim Halsey

Pioneer Award: Sons of the Pioneers

Tony Award Winners

(Antoinette Perry Awards presented June 4, 1978, by the American Theatre Wing and the League of N.Y. Theatres and Producers)

Best Musical: *Ain't Misbehavin'*, music by Fats Waller, produced by the Schubert Organization

Best Musical Book: *On the Twentieth Century*, book by Betty Comden and Adolph Green

Best Musical Score: *On the Twentieth Century*, music by Cy Coleman, lyrics by Betty Comden and Adolph Green

Best Actor in a Musical: John Cullum, *On the Twentieth Century*

Best Actress in a Musical: Liza Minnelli, *The Act*

Best Featured Actor in a Musical: Kevin Kline, *On the Twentieth Century*

Best Featured Actress in a Musical: Nell Carter, *Ain't Misbehavin'*

Best Director of a Musical: Richard Maltby Jr., *Ain't Misbehavin'*

Best Choreographer: Bob Fosse, *Dancin'*

Best Scenic Designer: Robin Wagner, *On the Twentieth Century*

Lawrence Langner Award: Irving Berlin

NAACP Image Award Winners

(Presented June 9, 1978, by the NAACP)

Best Group: the Commodores

Best Male Vocalist: Stevie Wonder

Best Female Vocalist: Natalie Cole

Entertainer of the Year: Ben Vereen

Best Jazz Artist: Ella Fitzgerald

Best Gospel Artist: James Cleveland

Best Blues Artist: B. B. King

Best Musical Score: Curtis Mayfield, *Piece of the Action*

Emmy Award Winners

(Presented September 17 by the Academy of Television Arts and Sciences)

Comedy-Variety or Music Series: "The Muppet Show"

Comedy-Variety or Music Special: "Ol' Red Hair Is Back," Bette Midler

Classical Program in the Performing Arts: "American Ballet Theatre: *Giselle* Live From Lincoln Center"

Continuing or Single Performance by a Supporting Actor in Variety or Music for a Continuing Role in a Regular or Limited Series: Tim Conway in "The Carol Burnett Show"

Continuing or Single Performance by a Supporting Actress in Variety or Music for a Continuing Role in a Regular or Limited Series: Gilda Radner in "Saturday Night Live"

Directing in a Comedy-Variety or Music Series; a Single Episode of a Regular or Limited Series: Dave Powers for "The Carol Burnett Show" (with Steve Martin and Betty White)

Directing in a Comedy-Variety or Music Special: Dwight Hemion for "The Sentry Collection Presents Ben Vereen: His Roots"

Writing in a Comedy-Variety or Music Series; a Single Episode of a Regular or Limited Series: Ed Simmons, Roger Beatty, Rick Hawkins, Liz Sage, Robert Illes, James Stein, Franelle Silver, Larry Siegel, Tim Conway, Bill Richmond, Gene Perret, Dick Clair, Jenna McMahon for "The Carol Burnett Show" (with Steve Martin and Betty White)

Writing in a Comedy-Variety or Music Special: Lorne Michaels, Paul Simon, Chevy Chase, Tom Davis, Al Franken, Charles Grodin, Lily Tomlin, Alan Zweibel for "The Paul Simon Special"

Outstanding Achievement in Music Direction for a Single Episode of a Series, or a Special Program, Variety or Music: Ian Fraser for "The Sentry Collection Presents Ben Vereen: His Roots"

Art Direction or Scenic Design for a Comedy-Variety or Music Series; for a Single Episode of a Regular or Limited Series: Roy Christopher for "The Richard Pryor Show"

Art Direction or Scenic Design for a Comedy-Variety or Music Special: Romain Johnston (Art Direction) and Kerry Joyce (Scenic Design) for "The Sentry Collection Presents Ben Vereen: His Roots"

Outstanding Achievement in Music Composition for a Series (Dramatic Underscore) for a Single Episode of a Regular or Limited Series: Bill Goldenberg for "King"

Outstanding Achievement in Musical Composition for a Special (Dramatic Underscore): Jimmy Haskell for "See How She Runs, G.E. Theater"

Outstanding Achievement in Costume Design for a Music-Variety Special: Bob Mackie for "Mitzi Zings into Spring"

Outstanding Achievement in Choreography for a Music-Variety Special: Ron Field for "The Sentry Collection Presents Ben Vereen: His Roots"

Special Musical Material: Stan Freeman and Arthur Malvin for "The Carol Burnett Show, mini-musical called High Hat" and Ken Welch and Mitzi Welch for "The Sentry Collection Presents Ben Vereen: His Roots"

Country Music Association Awards

(Presented October 9, 1978 by the Country Music Association)

Entertainer of the Year: Dolly Parton
Single of the Year: "Heaven's Just a Sin Away," the Kendalls
Album of the Year: *It Was Almost Like a Song*, Ronnie Milsap
Song of the Year: "Don't It Make My Brown Eyes Blue," by Richard Leigh
Female Vocalist of the Year: Crystal Gayle
Male Vocalist of the Year: Don Williams
Vocal Group of the Year: The Oak Ridge Boys
Vocal Duo of the Year: Kenny Rogers and Dottie West
Instrumental Group of the Year: The Oak Ridge Boys Band
Instrumentalist of the Year: Roy Clark

STARS OF
YEAR IN M

THE
USIC

2

A

ABBA

Anni-Frid (Frida) Lyngstad–Vocals

Benny Andersson–Piano , vocals

Björn Ulvaeus–Guitar

Agnetha (Anna) Faltskog/Ulvaeus–Vocals

Since 1974, when their song "Waterloo" won top prize in the nineteenth Eurovision song contest, ABBA has sold more than 50 million records. In 1978, the phenomenal worldwide success of this Swedish supergroup is more characteristic of a powerful international cartel than a rock and roll band. Financial wizard Stig Anderson, their manager, writer, and producer, arranged for countries in Eastern Europe and Russia to pay the band in oil rather than cash. ABBA uses the precious commodity to run some of their facilities—their art gallery, film theater and studio, hotels and restaurants. According to a Swedish business publication, ABBA is the most profitable corporation in Sweden.

When you talk about ABBA you're talking huge numbers. When they toured Europe in 1977, they received 3.5 million mail-order requests for seats at a London concert where only 12,000 seats were available. Every single they release soars to the top of the European charts within days. At one point in their career they had five records in the top ten in Australia. Their smooth, danceable harmonies sent millions of fans spinning to disks like "Mama Mia," "I Do, I Do, I Do, I Do, I Do," "Fernando," "Dancing Queen," and 1978's smash singles, "The Name of the Game" and "Take a Chance on Me," from their latest collection, *ABBA—The Album*.

In 1978, they appeared on Olivia Newton-John's television special. In return, the band played host to Olivia when she toured Europe and Scandinavia. Late in the year they released *ABBA—The Movie*, a semidocumentary musical extravaganza that was filmed partly in Australia during their sold-out tour of February 1977. With twenty songs, a believable and interesting plot, high-quality photography and editing, the film did fabulously in Europe. They also won their first platinum album with their *Greatest Hits*.
1978 Discography: *ABBA—The Album*

AEROSMITH

Steven Tyler–Vocals

Joe Perry–Guitar

Brad Whitford–Guitar

Tom Hamilton–Bass

Joey Kramer–Drums

The stern New England bastion of Sunapee, New Hampshire, may seem an unlikely cradle for a fledgling rock band, but the summer of 1970 found Steven Tyler, Tom Hamilton, and Joe Perry in a local hangout called, appropriately enough for Sunapee, The Barn, with a local group called the Jam Band. The three musicians were drawn together by their similar musical taste, and with the addition of Joey Kramer and Brad Whitford, the rocky hills of Sunapee were soon ringing with the embryonic sounds of Aerosmith.

From the beginning, the five of them were dedicated to their music and were determined to make it on that alone. At the end of the first summer, realizing that serious musical advances, both artistically and financially, could come only in a large city, they moved to Boston—the nearest major city. For the duration of 1971 the five of them and their equipment lived squashed together in a small apart-

ment. They discovered the only positive thing about starving: The five of them couldn't have existed in that apartment at all if any one of them had been fatter.

They played wherever they could, with Steven Tyler's rave-up onstage antics attracting attention almost immediately. Many of the concerts they played were free, but they began to win a local following. In July of 1972, they signed with managers Leber-Krebs, and in August Clive Davis signed them to Columbia Records. So great was the group's in-person impact that both signings took place after the principals had seen them perform only once.

From then on, it was a steady climb to the top. *Aerosmith*, released at the beginning of 1973, sold moderately; 1974's *Get Your Wings* hustled a few more copies; and by the time their third LP, *Toys in the Attic*, was released in 1975, *Get Your Wings* had gone gold. *Toys in the Attic* soon went gold, followed quickly by the first album. By the summer of 1975, Aerosmith had become a top touring band, selling out halls across the country. By December, *Toys in the Attic*, which stayed on the charts for two years, had earned platinum.

In May 1976, their fourth album, *Rocks*, a heavy metal venture, was released, and at the beginning of 1978, *Draw the Line*, their fifth album, became their second platinum-winner. The year 1978 saw Aerosmith touring, including a powerpacked performance at Cal Jam II, Ontario, California's, belated answer to Woodstock.

ATLANTA RHYTHM SECTION

Barry Bailey–Lead guitar

J. R. Cobb–Rhythm and slide guitar, vocals

Dean Daughtry–Keyboards, vocals

Paul Goddard–Bass

Ronnie Hammond–Lead vocals, organ

Robert Nix–Drums, vocals

When the Atlanta Rhythm Section was formed in 1970 in the small town of Doraville, Georgia, each band member was sure the group's unquestionable musical excellence would zip them to success in no time. That sought-after success took seven hard years to materialize, but long before that the six musicians absorbed the hard knowledge any businessman must learn. As J. R. Cobb puts it, in words that echo from Dale Carnegie, "…you have to go out and tell people about your music, show them—you can't just wait for them to find you."

So, the group set out to tour the country. For any new band, this is the acid test; the seemingly endless trudge from one unknown small town, one identical motel room to another. For the Atlanta Rhythm Section, with years of individual experience as session men, with the respect and admiration of other musicians, and with two albums out in the stores (*Atlanta Rhythm Section* and *Back Up Against the Wall*), it was particularly difficult, as Dean Daughtry recalls, "…to hit a new city and find out we were billed as 'The Atlantic Rhythm Boys' or something similar and that few people knew our music. We would think, 'What the hell are we doing this for?'"

They probably didn't get any answer, except for a shared grin and a shrug as they strapped on their guitars for the next show. They kept slugging away in those small halls through *Third Annual Pipe Dream*, their critically acclaimed third album, through the cult favorite *Dog Days*, and through *Red Tape*, their fifth album. And then, with all the force of something that's been pent up for too long, their slow, moody, beautiful love song "So in to You" flashed its way up the charts, and the album it came from, *A Rock and Roll Alternative*, became their first million-seller and one of 1977's ten most programmed albums in America. Climaxing that year was their triumphant return to Atlanta in September, where fifty thousand fans hollered and stomped and cheered them on at the Dog Day Rock Fest. It was one of those magic performances they always aim for. "Our goal, whenever possible," says lead singer Ronnie Hammond, "is to make the audience feel a part of us."

ABBA

Atlanta Rhythm Section

Aerosmith

Ron Pownall

205

Average White Band

Their triumphs in 1978 include *Champagne Jam* (half a million sold and still going strong), their top pop single "Imaginary Lover," and a world tour.
1978 Discography: *Champagne Jam*

THE AVERAGE WHITE BAND

Roger Ball–Keyboards, synthesizer, saxophones

Malcolm "Molly" Duncan–Tenor saxophone

Steve Ferrone–Drums

Alan Gorrie–Bass, guitar, vocals

Onnie McIntyre–Rhythm guitar, vocals

Hamish Stuart–Guitar, bass, lead vocals

They tour hard, logging hundreds of thousands of miles as they crisscross the United States, the Far East, Japan, Australia, Great Britain, Germany, Holland, Sweden, and Switzerland, leaving behind them a trail of blissed-out fans. Grinning widely, the band charges right into the next engagement, always giving their all. Onstage, the Average White Band is a canny collection of Scotsmen who somehow, even in Glasgow, Dundee, and Brighton, cut their musical teeth on American R & B, jazz, and the Motown hits of the sixties.

From this music they drew the inspiration that led them to such extraordinary achievements as their 1975 debut album, *Average White Band,* and its red-hot single, "Pick Up the Pieces." Both were million-sellers, and "Pick Up the Pieces" was nominated for a Grammy Award and named Top Instrumental Single by *Record World.* Their second LP, *Cut the Cake,* was another gold-winner, and *Soul Searching,* their third LP, became their first platinum disk.

At the beginning of 1977, perhaps as a reward for those fans who crave them in concert, AWB released a live double LP, *Person to Person.* The album was quickly certified gold, just before the release of *Benny and Us,* their historic performance with the legendary Ben E. King. In 1978, the half-million sales of *Warmer Communications* displayed that the album was yet another step on their sizzling road.
1978 Discography: *Warmer Communications*

B

THE BEACH BOYS

Brian Wilson–Vocals

Carl Wilson–Vocals, guitar

Dennis Wilson–Vocals, drums

Mike Love–Vocals

Al Jardine–Vocals, guitar

It's sometimes hard to believe that before 1961 there were no Beach Boys. Their good-time songs, such as "Fun, Fun, Fun," "Surfin' Safari," "Little Deuce Coupe," "I Get Around," "Help Me, Rhonda," "California Girls," "Wouldn't It Be Nice," "Barbara Ann," "Don't Worry Baby," and "I Can Hear Music," feel as if they've been around forever. But it was in 1961 that surfer Dennis Wilson suggested to brother Brian that Brian write a song about surfing. Brian, who had studied music, sat down and batted out a little number called "Surfin'." The brothers, with cousin Mike Love and schoolmate Al Jardine, recorded a demo, took it to the small Candix label, and dubbed themselves the Beach Boys (to go with the song, of course).

For the next few years, they churned out one hit after another and kept up a brutal touring pace. By the end of 1965, Brian, the group's

Bee Gees   Waring Abbott

George Benson   Courtesy Warner Brothers Records

The Beach Boys

Courtesy Caribou Records

The Blackbyrds

Courtesy Fantasy Records

Leonard Bernstein

207

admitted musical center, began to suffer from the strain of constant touring. He had a nervous breakdown early in the year and announced he would tour no longer. Bruce Johnston became his replacement, and Brian, left to himself, brooded about becoming a serious, respected musician, began to take a lot of acid, and collaborated with intellectual Van Dyke Parks. He created *Pet Sounds,* an advanced studio album that failed in the United States. Despite the fantastic reaction to "Good Vibrations" in 1966, Brian was crushed by the response to his attempts at serious composition.

For the next ten years the Beach Boys traveled the world, singing their old songs with unfailing verve and gathering millions of ever-younger fans. Brian turned out a handful of powerful songs, including "Surf's Up," "Sail on Sailor," and "Heroes and Villains."

Although he returned to touring in the late seventies, Brian was usually passive onstage. But in 1978 there were some changes. The Beach Boys left Warner Brothers, their record label of seven years, switching to Caribou, a Columbia label. They toured even more vigorously than usual to standing-room crowds, jaunting from California to Australia and New Zealand, hitting the Southwest during April and thirty large stadiums during the summer. In some of those concerts, notably their June appearance at the new Giants Stadium in New Jersey's Meadowlands Sports Complex, an animated, energetic Brian showed 63,000 fans his best side.

As usual, the Beach Boys too were in top form. Uncannily, despite perennial rumors of imminent break-up, despite Mike Love's moonlighting gig with a band called Celebration, despite the thousands of times they've performed the songs , their show was fresh and jumping. They've got that magical ability to take a crowd of fifty thousand people and make each of them glad to be alive.
1978 Discography: *M. I. U.*

THE BEE GEES

Barry Gibb–Vocals, guitar

Maurice Gibb–Vocals, bass

Robin Gibb–Vocals

Alan Kendall–Guitar

Dennis Byron–Drums

Blue Weaver–Keyboards

In the year 1978 there was Gibb music everywhere. For the first six months of the year, charts, record stores, and airwaves were completely dominated by the infectious boogies and fiercely sweet harmonies of *Saturday Night Fever,* the Robert Stigwood-produced epic that has grossed more than a hundred million dollars. "How Deep Is Your Love," the first single from the soundtrack album released in November 1977, "Stayin' Alive," (well on its way to three million in sales, a staggering figure in this day of weak singles sales), and "Night Fever" were record-breaking singles. As if that wasn't enough, two other songs from the musical extravaganza, "If I Can't Have You" and "More Than a Woman," performed by the Tavares and Yvonne Elliman, became hits for those artists. In addition, the Gibb song "Emotion" helped Samantha Sang rise to fame, and Andy Gibb's "Love Is Thicker than Water" was cowritten by brother Barry, who also had a hand in Andy's other 1978 hits, "Shadow Dancing" and "An Everlasting Love."

You might imagine that with all this frenzied buying of singles the album sales would suffer, but in 1978 *Saturday Night Fever* became the best-selling LP of all time, staying number one on the charts for twenty-three weeks. At least one radio station, New York's WXLO, at one point threw up their hands in despair and declared one weekend in May a Bee-Gee-free weekend. Such total domination of the music scene has not been seen since the Beatles.

The Bee Gees, who began singing and playing in Australian speedway ovals in 1958, had a local following in Queensland and their own television show. But their first attempt at the Australian big time failed. A dozen singles released by Festival Records in Sydney went unnoticed. In 1967, the entire family packed up for England, just as their last single, "Spicks and Specks," recorded for an Australian fan who happened to own a recording studio, was on its way to becoming a number-one hit in Australia.

Their first week in England they met Robert Stigwood, who has masterminded their career. He released "New York Mining Disaster, 1941," in April 1967, and it became their first hit in Britain and the United States. During that summer their songs "To Love Somebody" and "Holiday" also became hits. Their first three albums, *Bee Gees First, Horizontal,* and *Idea,* with top-ten singles like "Massachusetts," "I've Gotta Get a Message to You," and "I Started a Joke," were all successful.

But, as the brothers admitted to David Frost on his program "Headliners," they were not ready for stardom then. They were too young, and they broke up early in 1969. Robin tried for a solo career; Barry and Maurice recorded together for a while and then broke up.

In late 1971, they came together again and began a second try for fame and fortune with the smash "Lonely Days." They followed this with such memorable songs as "How Can You Mend a Broken Heart," "Don't Want to Live Inside Myself," "My World," and "Run to Me." Their albums *Two Years On* and *Trafalgar* were successful, but it wasn't until producers Albhy Galuten and Karl Richardson added the spice of R & B to their music that they really began to soar to the top. From the hit albums *Main Course* and *Children of the World* came the number-one songs "Jive Talkin'," "Nights on Broadway," and "You Should Be Dancing." *Here At Last...Bee Gees...Live,* a million-selling two-record set with twenty-two of their greatest hits, captured the excitement of their live tour of the United States in 1976.

To add an extra fillip to their year, the Bee Gees appeared in *Sgt. Pepper's Lonely Hearts Club Band.* In another unprecedented step, the Bee Gees announced they would donate their earnings from a new composition to UNICEF. In January 1979, the group will participate in the inauguration of the International Year of the Child, a gala event that will be telecast on NBC from the General Assembly of the United Nations. The program will be sent by satellite around the world, and profits from the soundtrack will be donated to UNICEF.

The Bee Gees admitted to *Crawdaddy* interviewer Greg Mitchell that they are still as scared as they've always been about writing songs and that they worked twice as hard and as long on *Spirits,* their follow-up to *Fever,* as they have on anything else. They like it at the top and want to prove to the world that they can stay there.
1978 Discography: *Spirits*
Sgt. Pepper's Lonely Hearts Club Band

GEORGE BENSON

It's quite a distance from strumming a ukulele in a Pittsburgh candy store to cutting albums that sell in the millions, win Grammies, and collect honors from such publications as *Rolling Stone, Downbeat, Billboard, Record World, Cash Box,* and *Playboy.* George Benson took the giant step in 1976, when his album *Breezin'* sold more than 2 million copies, a stratospheric leap for the experienced guitarist and a sales figure that set the jazz world on its ear. The jazz revival that has sparked the success of so many performers in 1977 and 1978 was begun in 1976 by George Benson, whose crystal-clear, bubbling guitar lines lit up the single "This Masquerade."

Benson was no stranger to recording, having begun his professional career at the ripe old age of ten, when he was signed by RCA. He was already a seasoned musician at that advanced age, having begun his candy store workouts to appreciative audiences when he was only eight. He sang as well as played guitar, but guitar was the focus of his attentions for many years. "While I was at CTI Records they didn't want me to sing, they just wanted me to play the guitar. A lot of people never knew I could sing, because I just wasn't given the opportunity to express myself vocally," he reports.

When Benson was twenty he joined with Jack McDuff's small group, where he broadened his mastery of R & B. In 1965, he went on to form his own band, with Lonnie Smith on organ, Ronnie Cuber on baritone sax, and Phil Turner on drums. It took eleven long, hard years of mastering his craft before his 1976 breakthrough, but that has been followed by an unbroken string of successes. In 1977, *In Flight*

Blue Öyster Cult

Debby Boone

Boston

Peter Brown

became his second platinum album, and in June of 1977 he spent a long weekend in New York that will be talked about for years. Billed as Benson X Four, the series of performances included a guitar duel with Bucky Pizzarelli, Les Paul, and Gabor Szabo at the Metropolitan Museum of Art. At the Palladium Theatre he appeared with Minnie Riperton, at Avery Fisher Hall with the Dance Theatre of Harlem, and again at Avery Fisher Hall he performed with Alphonso Johnson, Harvey Mason, Ralph McDonald, Joe Sample, and Grover Washington, Jr.

The year 1978 has been another nonstop one, featuring his third platinum album, the double-record live set *Weekend in L.A.,* another pop, soul, and jazz winner; his top-ten single "On Broadway"; a tour of Europe, Japan, and Australia as well as some fine American concert appearances.

1978 Discography: *Weekend in L.A.*

Jackson Browne   Jimmy Wachtel

LEONARD BERNSTEIN

The 1970s have been a frustrating time for Leonard Bernstein. Although in 1977 he completed *Songfest,* a musical celebration of America's artistic past, between 1970 and 1978 he devoted his time and labors to four stillborn pieces for musical theater. In this decade there have been more creative failures than successes for the composer who in a breathtaking career has written three symphonies, three ballets, a one-act opera, the score for the film *On the Waterfront,* many orchestral, chamber, and choral works, and, for Broadway, the scores to *On the Town, Wonderful Town, Candide,* and, of course, *West Side Story.*

You would think that Bernstein might be disappointed or bitter about these recent failures, but as he told John Ardoin in the *New York Times,* "…it makes me only want to do more." After becoming the first American-born musician to attain the pinnacle of music director of the New York Philharmonic, a position he held from 1958 to 1969, Mr. Bernstein looks to the years ahead as the opportunity to catch up with the composing he feels he's missed in the past.

Born in Lawrence, Massachusetts, in 1918, Mr. Bernstein was brought up in Boston, where he studied piano. He graduated from Harvard in 1939 and continued his studies at the famed Curtis Institute. He spent his summers at Tanglewood, a student of and assistant to Serge Koussevitzky.

He was made assistant conductor of the New York Philharmonic in 1943, and during the years that followed he served as music director of the New York City Symphony, headed the conducting faculty at the Berkshire Music Center, and was Professor of Music at Brandeis University. Between 1945 and 1958 Bernstein conducted most of the world's major orchestras.

The vigor Bernstein still demonstrates has been evident throughout his extraordinarily prolific career. He has written three best-selling books, *The Joy of Music, Leonard Bernstein's Young People's Concerts,* and *The Infinite Variety of Music;* he has introduced children to the world of music through his televised "Young People's Concerts" with the New York Philharmonic; and he has recorded more than 240 albums with fifteen different performing groups on seven record company labels. Throughout the years audiences have heard Mr. Bernstein's interpretations of the most exalted works of music mature and grow.

In 1978, he conducted the Vienna State Opera performing *Fidelio.* It was the first live telecast from the Opera and was seen via Eurovision in many countries around the world. During the year Mr. Bernstein conducted for the Vienna State Opera and Philharmonic Orchestra; Holland's Concertgebouw; at the Spoleto Festival; and with the New York Philharmonic in Washington, D.C., New York, Japan, and Korea.

Jimmy Buffett   Courtesy ABC Records

210

THE BLACKBYRDS

Kevin Kraig Toney–Keyboards

Keith Killgo–Drums, percussion

Joseph S. Hall III–Bass

Orville Saunders–Guitars

Stephen Johnson–Saxophone, flute

The Schwann catalog lists the Blackbyrds as a jazz group. It's understandable that Schwann would classify them that way. After all, they were founded by educator and jazz great Professor Donald Byrd. But Kevin Toney, who plays keyboards for the dynamic group, told Conrad Silvert in *Down Beat* magazine, "Our records usually end up on most of the charts—easy listening, R & B, jazz. I think we're just basically pop."

Four years ago Donald Byrd took a handful of Howard University students who, although young, had amassed among them years of experience playing with such jazz titans as Stan Getz, Sonny Stitt, Sonny Rollins, McCoy Tyner, Woody Shaw, Marcus Belgrave, Miles Davis, Joe Henderson, Herbie Hancock, and George Benson. Byrd encouraged them to listen to all kinds of music and to stretch themselves by playing new, unexpected riffs. Byrd's shrewd philosophy has always been that music is a business, and he groomed the Blackbyrds to understand the mechanics of the business as well as of the music. Perhaps it was that combination of musical and mercantile knowledge that led guitarist Orville Saunders to once tell a *Billboard* reporter, "We believe that certain chords make money and certain chords do not."

What Orville says may not be too far from the truth. Of the six albums the Blackbyrds have made with little promotional fanfare, the last three—*City Life, Unfinished Business,* and *Action*—have won gold awards.

BLUE ÖYSTER CULT

Eric Bloom–Vocals, guitar

Albert Bouchard–Drums, vocals

Joe Bouchard–Bass, vocals

Allen Lanier–Keyboards, guitar

Donald (Buck Dharma) Roeser–Lead and rhythm guitars, vocals

For years, squadrons of New York taxicabs sported mysterious stickers that read "Blue Öyster Cult." Bemused riders wondered whether the signs announced a new religious group, a highly specialized ecological concern, or a fanatic gourmet society. Today there are few riders who don't recognize the name as that of one of America's most determined and decibel-happy heavy-metal bands, a group whose core of Long Island, New York, fans has grown to an international army of Blue Öyster Cult admirers, snapping up their last three albums—*On Your Feet Or on Your Knees, Agents of Fortune,* and *Spectres*—to the golden tune of half a million each and in 1978 pushing *Agent of Fortune* into the platinum stratosphere.

Of course, Blue Öyster Cult didn't begin at the top. Indeed, they didn't even begin as Blue Öyster Cult. In the late 1960s, with original members Allen Lanier and lead guitarist Donald Roeser, they were known as the Soft White Underbelly. After a few years of personnel changes and small-time scuffling, the band had put together its current lineup and, as the Stalk Forrest Group, was signed by Columbia Records.

Writer Sandy Pearlman, an early supporter who later became their manager, dubbed them Blue Öyster Cult, and their first album, *Blue Öyster Cult,* was released in 1972. That disk, with its combina-

tion of violence and slightly demented humor, paved the way for their spot on Alice Cooper's Killer Tour. Inspired by the well-stitched Cooper stage show, the boys developed their own costumes: leather thongs and cape for Eric Bloom and pure white for Donald Roeser. The band's reputation as heavy-metal monsters was increased by their next two albums, *Tyranny and Mutation* and *Secret Treaties.* In 1975, their double-live set, *On Your Feet Or on Your Knees,* a wicked collection of rave-up material (including some live classics that they had never before committed to vinyl) was their first to win gold.

After that, they felt they could afford some breathing time, and their next album, *Agents of Fortune,* proved to be their most successful to date, as the group members allowed each other space to create their own compositions.

In May of 1976, the Cult took their $100,000 laser light show out to shock audiences. It achieved that goal, but their 1978 show, accompanying their album *Spectres,* was far more elaborate and startling, even jolting a government agency into warning the group that it must tone down the lasers to protect their audience.

1978 Discography: *Live*

DEBBY BOONE

Judging from the size of the grin on his face these days, Pat Boone must be one proud father. Debby, the third of four Boone daughters, after years of singing with her sisters, broke out on her own last year with the monumental winner "You Light Up My Life," only the fourth single in twenty years to stay number one on the pop charts for nine weeks. Joe Brooks's gorgeous song from the movie of the same name won honors by the armload. It tied with "Evergreen" as Song of the Year in the Grammy voting; it won the American Music Award as Favorite Pop–Rock Single. Debby, flashing her smile that looks like bubbling laughter, walked off with a Grammy as New Artist of the Year and won the Academy of Country Music Award as Top New Female Vocalist.

Of course, as the daughter of Pat Boone and granddaughter of country-and-western star Red Foley, Debby didn't have to suffer the dues-paying trials of most fledgling musicians. Musical genes and early training provided a solid base, but no parental influence could have pushed her song to its glorious heights. And the poised, shining loveliness she conveys on stage is Debby's own, her natural beauty surviving a period when poor eating habits nearly did her in.

Her career began in 1969, when she and her sisters traveled to Japan, accompanying their father on a tour he was headlining. They sang "What the World Needs Now Is Love." Debby quickly became the lead singer in that quartet. When she decided that she was serious about a music career, she discussed it with her parents. "My father told me it was a hard life for a girl but he never did say, 'Please don't do it.'" As she and her sisters grew up, two married, one entered college, and touring as a group became difficult. The year 1977 seemed like the right one for Debby to step out on her own.

The decision to team her with producer Mike Curb was a natural one. He had been after her for a record for him for years. In 1978, Debby was the leading light of "Pat Boone and Family," an ABC-TV special shown on April 5; she sang on the premiere of *Grease,* won the $5,000 gold prize for "God Knows" at the Seventh Tokyo Music Festival in June, and toured with her dad during the summer.

BOSTON

Tom Scholz–Guitar, keyboards

Bradley Delp–Vocals

Barry Goudreau–Guitar

Fran Sheehan–Bass

Sib Hashian–Drums

Boston is one of those rare bands that did everything backward and achieved extraordinary success in the bargain. Before making the big time, most groups must endure years of disappointment, rejections from record companies, and playing either to half-empty houses or as opener for name acts. Not so Boston. They had never played together once when their first album, *Boston,* was released.

When that disk came out in 1976 it seemed to have a life of its own. It quickly sold more than 4 million copies, an unheard of response to a debut album. The fans who sent its sales figures soaring didn't seem at all concerned to hear·that the group had never performed together. Not only did these Boston fans buy the album, they also set cash registers jingling as they scooped up armloads of the two singles from the album, "More Than a Feeling" and "Peace of Mind."

Of course, although the band may seem to be an overnight sensation, if you look closely at their history you'll find that mechanical engineer Tom Scholz paid his musical dues, beginning back in 1968, when he and singer Bradley Delp suffered rejection of their demonstration records. MIT graduate Scholz, who worked by day as a research assistant for Polaroid and played guitar in Boston clubs at night, decided to set up his own twelve-track home studio. Using his new equipment, Scholz mixed tracks that had been independently recorded by the musicians who would eventually comprise the group. New tapes met with a deluge of new rejections, so Scholz turned for help to independent record producers Paul Ahearn and Charlie McKenzie. Ahearn and McKenzie hustled Scholz's tracks successfully, first getting airplay in the Boston area and finally signing the group to Epic Records.

Once *Boston* was released, fans began figuratively to beat down the doors for the live Boston experience. So the five musicians got together, rehearsed for a couple of weeks, and took off on a fiery four-month tour, during which they knocked out audiences and critics with a powerhouse show. Bradley Delp emerged as a high octane lead singer, and Tom Scholz's electronic wizardry kept everything cooking. In 1978, their long-awaited second album, *Don't Look Back,* and its title single were instant hits.

1978 Discography: *Don't Look Back*

PETER BROWN

Named Best New Male Vocalist of 1977 by *Record World* magazine, Peter Brown has come a long way from the Chicago teen-ager who taught himself to play the drums by listening to hit records again and again. Today, with his first single, 1977's "Do You Want to Get Funky With Me," the first twelve-inch disk ever to win gold certification, and the top-ten successes of "Dance With Me" and *Fantasy Love Affair,* it looks like Peter's rock-hard determination has carried him to his goal: to become a top music star.

Once Peter had taught himself drums and played in a few local bands, he set his sights on the Jorgensen Rangerettes, a high school baton twirling corps that played rock and roll instead of marching songs. Peter loved that idea, but the corps already had a drummer. Undaunted, Peter, at age sixteen, taught himself piano. Successfully reaching his goal once again, Peter played with the Rangerettes for five years and eventually became their musical director.

After high school, Peter attended the Art Institute of Chicago but found himself devoting more time to music than to commercial art. He began to compose songs, learned more instruments, and recorded at home on a four-track tape recorder, working to reproduce the songs he heard in his head.

At the suggestion of a friend, he sent his first tape to TK Records' producer Cory Wade. Wade was impressed by what he heard and encouraged Peter to learn more about recording. Peter left the Art Institute, bought himself a synthesizer, a piano, a drum kit, some dozen percussion instruments, moved his home recording studio to a larger room, and spiffed up his first tape.

After hearing the new version of "Do You Want to Get Funky With Me," Wade signed Peter to TK. The astonishing success of that homemade single was the first step in what is sure to become an equally astonishing career.

JACKSON BROWNE

Although he was born in Heidelberg, Germany, and brought up in Los Angeles, Jackson Browne's musical roots are firmly in the late 1960s musical stew of New York City. He arrived there in the winter of 1967, and friend Tim Buckley helped him get a job as accompanist to Nico, who had just left the Velvet Underground. While in New York he began writing songs, and when he returned to Los Angeles such artists as the Nitty Gritty Dirt Band, Tom Rush, Steve Noonan, Linda Ronstadt, Johnny Rivers, the Byrds, and Brewer & Shipley were eager to record them.

In 1970, he went on his first concert tour, opening the show for Laura Nyro, and in 1971, thanks in part to the friendly support of Tom Rush, a great fan of Browne's, his first album for Asylum Records was released. During 1972 Browne was on a heavy touring schedule, first in the United States and Europe with Joni Mitchell, then on his own. Closing the year were three concerts with the Eagles and J. D. Souther. *For Everyman,* featuring good friend David Lindley, was released in October 1973. *Late for the Sky* was his 1974 album and his first to reach gold sales. *The Pretender,* his late 1976 album, shipped gold and soon reached platinum, as his earlier albums achieved gold status as well.

Running on Empty, released late in 1977, is a tight and thrilling collection of passionate rock-and-roll songs about life on the road. One of 1978's hot records, it zoomed into the top ten on the charts and soon sold more than a million copies.

In addition to composing a string of memorable songs, such as "Doctor My Eyes," "Rock Me on the Water," "These Days," "Song for Adam," "Here Come Those Tears," and "The Pretender," Browne has added record producing to his list of achievements. He produced buddy Warren Zevon's first album and coproduced Zevon's second, *Excitable Boy,* drawing an impressive response for his impeccable work.

JIMMY BUFFETT

One of the most freewheeling of today's musicians, Jimmy Buffett somehow manages to combine a devil-may-care life-style with a totally professional commitment to his music. The result is a refreshingly bouncy music, buoyant as Buffett's newly purchased *Euphoria II,* the oceangoing sailboat that he recently took on a two-month ocean cruise, his first real vacation in five years.

Jimmy's had little time for vacations since the platinum success of his fifth ABC album, 1977's *Changes in Latitudes—Changes in Attitudes,* and the gold award won by "Margaritaville," the hit single from that album. As a result of those awards, Jimmy's 1978 album, *Son of a Son of a Sailor,* shipped gold and immediately zoomed to platinum. His joyful performance of "Livingston Saturday Night" was a high point of the movie *FM* and contributed to the success of the film's soundtrack album.

Success has not changed Jimmy's quirky, offbeat humor. Despite his unquestionable arrival in the ranks of pop stardom, he still lists his occupation as Professional Misfit, perhaps thinking of the years when he had to battle people who tried to fit him into a mold. Born Christmas Day, 1946, he grew up in Mobile, Alabama, earned a degree in journalism from the University of Southern Mississippi, and then traveled to Nashville in the late 1960s. He found his style a bit pinched by Nashville's definition of country-and-western music, however. He cut a couple of albums for Andy Williams' Barnaby Records but was disillusioned when the first, *Down to Earth,* didn't sell well —and the master tapes for the second mysteriously disappeared.

Buffett made off to Florida, settled in Key West, and found his music coming to life. He signed with ABC-Dunhill and cut several records for them that enjoyed increasingly good sales. *A White Sports Coat and a Pink Crustacean, Living and Dying in 3/4 Time, A1A,* and *Havana Daydreamin',* with song titles like "A Pirate Looks at 40" and "Life Is Just a Tire Swing," paved the way for his mass acceptance today.

1978 Discography: *Son of a Son of a Sailor*

Captain and Tennille Courtesy A & M Records

Carpenters Courtesy A & M Records

Johnny Cash Courtesy Columbia Records

CAPTAIN & TENNILLE

Some songs become instantly recognizable classics—you only have to hear the first few notes to be immediately swept up by their familiarity. Such a song is "Love Will Keep Us Together," Neil Sedaka's syncopated ballad that was popularized by the Captain and Tennille to the tune of 2.5 million copies and a Grammy.

Such astonishing success seems to be the pattern for the sparkling duo, whose four albums each have a little extra going for them besides being gold. Their first—*Love Will Keep us Together*—was on the charts for two years and has sold more than a million copies. The second, *Song of Joy,* provided them with three gold singles—"Lonely Night," "Shop Around," and "Muskrat Love." Their third, 1977's treat, was a golden *Come in from the Rain,* and their fourth, *Greatest Hits,* achieved the gold standard early in 1978.

Toni Tennille was born in Montgomery, Alabama. In 1962, she moved with her family to Los Angeles, where she worked as a file clerk and put her musical background (singing with her sisters and nine years of classical piano training) to use in the South Coast Repertory Theatre, where she cowrote a musical called *Mother Earth.*

Shaun Cassidy Courtesy Warner Brothers Records

The show ran in San Francisco to good reviews; during its run there, she met Daryl Dragon—son of conductor Carmen Dragon—who entered the show as a keyboard player. (His credentials include *ten* years of classical piano training.) He and his brothers had recorded a single for Capitol, but they were an instrumental group, the Beatles had just become popular, and, as Daryl observes, "You had to sing to get any jobs in those days."

Daryl and Toni then toured together with the Beach Boys (Toni became the first Beach Girl). On one of those tours, Mike Love began calling Daryl Captain Keyboard because of the naval captain's cap he always wore onstage. The name stuck.

Their television series was inspired by the enthusiasm of Fred Silverman, who, impressed by their concert charisma, asked them to host an ABC-TV summer special. The show's high rating led to a contract with ABC for the successful "Captain & Tennille Show." Their television performances in 1978 included *"Captain and Tennille in New Orleans,"* aired in April. "I'm on My Way," their 1978 single, became a top-ten easy-listening hit.
1978 Discography: *Dream*

THE CARPENTERS

With their latest album, *Passage,* the traditionally hearts-and-flowers Carpenters have injected a little more spice and variety into their music without doing violence to the kind of songs their millions of fans expect and want. Those songs include such classic beauties as "Rainy Days and Mondays," "Superstar," "For All We Know," Close to You," "Yesterday Once More," and "We've Only Just Begun." Characterized by the full, haunting loveliness of Karen's voice and the lush arrangements brother Richard provides, the music of the Carpenters has won them three Grammy awards, seventeen gold records, and sales of more than 30 million singles and albums, as well as years' worth of sold-out concerts throughout the world.

The Carpenters, a hard-working duo, are eager to shed their saccharine image. But it will take more than one album to do that. Although *Passage* contained the witty, jazzy, Latin-flavored "Bwana She No Home," the dazzling "Don't Cry for Me, Argentina," a sly, calypso treatment of "Man Smart, Woman Smarter," and the surprising electronic inventions of "Calling Occupants of Interplanetary Craft," it was "Sweet, Sweet Smile," one of the more traditional cuts on the album, that became a top-ten easy-listening and country hit in 1978.
1978 Discography: *Passage*

JOHNNY CASH

One look at his face can tell you the story of his life. The lines etched around his mouth, the intense look in the deep-set eyes are not the marks of soft and easy years. Cash has worked hard all his life, both at physical labor and in emotional battle with inner demons that seemed determined to snatch success away from him. One look at his face and you know that the voice and the songs he sings come from his heart and his experience. One look at his face and you know that he has gone as deep into himself as any person can go and has pulled out truths that he is not ashamed to show.

His universal appeal has raised him from dirt-poor beginnings on a cotton farm in Kingsland, Arkansas, to concert appearances ranging from Europe's elegant concert stages to the prison yards of San Quentin. Musically and professionally he won acceptance from others without much difficulty. When he was with the air force in Germany during the early 1950s, he wrote the first of his songs, including "Folsom Prison Blues," one of his most famous. When he returned to the States, he married and then enrolled in radio school, hoping to become a country-music disk jockey.

He found, however, that he enjoyed performing and felt that his future lay in that direction. After many attempts, he finally persuaded Sam Phillips of Sun Records to agree to record him, and with his first two songs, "Cry, Cry, Cry" and "Hey Porter," in June 1955, his career was on its way.

Success came easy, but he didn't cope with it well. Afraid that he wouldn't measure up, he began to take amphetamines to bolster his confidence and keep him going at top speed. Soon he was hooked into the amphetamine-barbiturate circle; his first marriage broke up; he would develop psychosomatic laryngitis and simply not show up at scheduled concerts. By the mid-sixties he seemed headed for oblivion, hitting bottom when he almost died of a drug overdose soon after being arrested for transporting pills across the Mexican border.

It was then that June Carter, one of the singing Carter family and part of the Johnny Cash Show, stepped in. In 1968, she called on the help of Dr. Nat Winston, former head of the Tennessee Department for Mental Health, who agreed to see Cash through the long drug withdrawal process. During that painful time, Cash rediscovered the Christianity that had been part of his childhood, and in 1971 he and June took a film crew to Israel, where he wrote and produced a feature-length film called *Gospel Road*, distributed successfully by Billy Graham's World Wide Pictures.

His prolific recording career includes such classic hits as "I Walk the Line," "Orange Blossom Special," "Jackson," "A Boy Named Sue," "The Lady Came from Baltimore," and many others. He continues to perform ten to twelve prison shows per year. He has written a book about his experiences and philosophy called *Man in Black*. He appears on television frequently and records one or two albums a year. In 1978, "There Ain't No Good Chain Gang," performed with Waylon Jennings, became a top-ten country single.
1978 Discography: *I Would Like to See You Again.*

SHAUN CASSIDY

At only nineteen his first two albums have already sold more than 5 million copies. His first, *Shaun Cassidy,* was the first debut album ever to be certified triple platinum by the Recording Industry Association of America. His 1978 concert tour grossed millions, his contract with ABC-TV as costar of "The Hardy Boys" was renewed; Shaun Cassidy posters, magazines, books, lunch boxes, pajamas, and a host of other instant products are snapped up by eager preteen fans as quickly as they can be shoved out; he has become master of the quick getaway after his concerts and the clever disguise for his other travels. But Shaun Cassidy is no raw youngster about to be turned around by his astounding fame. He accepts it with a certain wryness ("It's a rotten job but somebody has to do it," he remarked with a straight face to *People* magazine) and a mature grasp of what he has to do if he wants to stay on top.

Cassidy, son of Shirley Jones and the late Jack Cassidy, half brother of the once-famous David, comes to the business with excellent credentials and outstanding talent. In 1975, he toured with his mother in the musical "On a Clear Day," and he sang the theme song "Comin' Home Again" for ABC's 1976 television movie *Dawn, Portrait of a Teenage Runaway.*

His first record hits, "Morning Girl" and "That's Rock 'n' Roll," were released in Europe and became top-twenty smashes there. It wasn't until May of 1977 that "Da Doo Ron Ron" blasted its good-time rockin' 'n' rollin' message across American airwaves, becoming his first gold single, followed by "That's Rock 'n' Roll" and "Hey Deanie," also gold monsters.

In addition to his talent, his maturity and clear-sightedness sometimes seem too good to be true. Coworkers praise his decency and intelligence. He himself takes a long-term view of his success, realizing that it can't go on forever and looking for things he can do that will be worthy follow-ups to his hit songs and albums.

Although fans eagerly and sometimes heartbrokenly wonder about Shaun's love life, according to him there is no special lady—there just isn't the time.
1978 Discography: *Under Wraps*

CHIC

Bernard Edwards–Bass

Nile Rodgers–Guitar

Tony Thompson—Drums

Norma Jean Wright—Vocals

Crack critic Vince Aletti, writing for *Record World,* called Chic's debut single "relaxed and invigorating . . . the ideal combination for a dance record you'll never get tired of." And enthusiastic disco crowds all over the country agreed, as they sent "Dance, Dance, Dance" spinning into a golden orbit. Chic's debut album, called *Chic,* was also swept up in the golden fever. In response, the group that calls itself Chic hollers "Yowsah, yowsah, yowsah," quoting the good-time message of their winning disco tune.

Leader Bernard Edwards says of their music, "We're not trying to deliver any heavy message, just entertainment—when you're off from work, come and see us and have a good time. No moral issues, no heavy problems—you just come to see us, have a good time, and split—that's it." Bernard met fellow Chic member Nile Rodgers in 1972 when they were part of the Big Apple Band, back-up band for a group called New York City. They had much in common. Both had been raised in New York, both had extensive instrumental backgrounds and a love for the same kind of funky R & B.

When New York City disbanded (the band—despite threats, the city still stands) they continued to play with the Big Apple Band, recording and backing up other artists. In early 1977, they laid down rhythm and vocal tracks for "Everybody Dance," which was played at New York's Night Owl disco and soon gained an underground reputation. "Dance, Dance, Dance " had come to the attention of several record companies, and in the fall of 1977 the group was signed to Atlantic.

While these tunes were cooking away, drummer Tony Thompson and vocalist Norma Jean Wright added to the chemistry of the group, bringing it to its current lineup.

ERIC CLAPTON

The swift, scintillating tones of Eric Clapton's guitar weave their legendary way through the music of the past fifteen years. His awesome guitar style rings out in the music of the Yardbirds, John Mayall's Bluesbreakers, Cream, Blind Faith, and Derek and the Dominos. Perhaps more in demand that any other guitar player of his generation, he has played in person and on record with such an assortment of musicians as the Beatles, the Rolling Stones, Delaney and Bonnie, Stephen Stills, George Harrison, John Lennon, Leon Russell, Dr. John, and the Mothers of Invention. His influence on the sound of rock has been unequalled, and more than one generation of aspiring superstars has attempted to coax sounds resembling Clapton's from their own guitars.

During the mid-seventies, the most prominent guitarist in rock fell into a deep depression and became addicted to heroin. Through his own determination, the help of friends, and treatment by a London acupuncturist, he was finally able to defeat the need for the drug.

When he felt steady once more, he walked into Robert Stigwood's office and told Stigwood he wanted to record again. Stigwood sent him to Florida, where Clapton cut *461 Ocean Boulevard,* from which came the hit "I Shot the Sheriff," written by Bob Marley. Two more albums followed, but Eric's next big breakthrough came in 1978, when his single "Lay Down Sally" sold a million copies and his album *Slowhand* flamed its way to double-platinum sales. His 1978 tour, gracefully scaled down to small, continually sold-out houses, was wonderful, revealing the guitarist to be in his best shape in years.
1978 Discography: *Slowhand*

NATALIE COLE

Natalie Cole was surrounded by music and musical talent from the beginning of her life. Daughter of the late Nat King Cole, her father's house was filled with the highest names of the jazz world. Musical greats like Pearl Bailey, Nancy Wilson, Ella Fitzgerald, Sarah

Vaughan, Count Basie, and Harry Belafonte were frequent visitors. When she was a teen-ager, she played in a small combo and listened avidly to the music of the sixties—the Jefferson Airplane, Janis Joplin, Sly Stone, the Beatles, and Stevie Wonder. At the University of Massachusetts, she would spend her summers waiting on tables at a local club and singing with a band on weekends.

"It was just for fun," she says. "I never planned on being a singer back then." But the calling was there, and after college she began singing in bigger and better clubs, appearing on local television, and growing as a performer. Singing didn't become a serious profession for her until she attended a church service at the invitation of producers Chuck Jackson and Marvin Yancy. At that service Natalie says, "It was almost like the Lord turned me around and said, 'There's something for you to do.' I was almost in tears."

She was quickly signed to Capitol Records, and her success began with her first album, *Inseparable,* which went gold, topped the R & B charts, and was on the pop charts for more than a year. It also won her two Grammy Awards, one for New Artist of the Year and one for Best R & B Female Vocal Performance, for "This Will Be," a single from that album. *Natalie,* released in May 1976, also went gold. One of its big singles, "Sophisticated Lady," won her a third Grammy for Best Female R & B Vocal Performance.

The year 1977 was a particularly fine one for Natalie. Professionally, her career continued to grow. Her third album, *Unpredictable,* was a platinum smash, a number-one R & B hit, and a top-ten pop hit. The album's first single, "I've Got Love on My Mind," was a goldwinner.

In addition, her personal life began to take on more shine. On Valentine's Day in 1977, she announced her seven-and-a-halfmonth-old secret marriage to Marvin Yancy; and on October 15, 1977, her first son, Robert Adam Yancy was born.

The year 1978 promises to be a continuation of joy and fulfillment. It began when she won the American Music Award as America's Favorite Female Vocalist. *Thankful,* released in late 1977, became her second platinum album, and the best-selling single "Our Love" also clinched a gold disk. "Annie Mae," a second single from that album, became a top-ten soul single, while *Natalie Live* soared to gold.

About all this, Natalie says, "I'm thankful for all the blessings I've been lucky enough to receive, not only professionally but personally. I have a wonderful husband and a beautiful new baby. The joy I feel right now makes me feel like singing about love and thankfulness."
1978 Discography: *Natalie Cole Live*

BOOTSY COLLINS

"If you fake the funk, your nose got to grow," proclaims the Pinocchio Theory of Funk Professor Bootsy Collins, who in the guise of a not-so-mild-mannered bass player has single-handedly transformed the face of funk with his 1978 monster single, "Bootzilla," from the top soul LP (number one after only four weeks on the chart) *Player of the Year.*

Born and raised in Cincinnati, the formerly shy, blue-jeaned bass player served an eight-year apprenticeship with master funkifiers James Brown and George Clinton. He took the flash of those inspired loonies, filtered it through his own cheerful, reckless madness, and emerged with a unique sizzle—funk-honed, refined, and raised to a spacey art form.

In 1976, Bootsy and some equally raunchy henchmen put out an album called *Stretchin' Out in Bootsy's Rubber Band,* which quickly went into a golden orbit. His second album, *Aah...the Name is Bootsy, Baby,* also achieved gold status and won him the devoted fervor of the world's Geepies. As Bootsy explains them, "Geepies" are "younger kids who are turned on without drugs. They're so deep, they're past D all the way to G. That's what makes them geep."
1978 Discography: *Player of the Year*

Eric Clapton

Natalie Cole

Commodores

Chic

Bootsy Collins

217

COMMODORES

Walter "Clyde" Orange–Vocals, drums

Thomas McClary–Guitar

Ronald LaPread–Bass, trumpet

Lionel Richie–Saxophone

William King–Trumpet

Milan Williams–Keyboards, trombone, drums, guitar

At the end of 1977 the Commodores' *Live* album zipped to the top five of the soul and pop charts; early in 1978 their single "Too Hot ta Trot" became a number-one soul single; in June 1978, *Natural High,* their seventh album, shipped double platinum and in July their soft ballad "Three Times a Lady" became a number one soul and pop single. But these awards come as no surprise. For ten years this crackling good band has been turning out the kind of crisp R & B that invariably means gold, platinum, and the top of the charts.

They began making music together in 1968, when, as freshmen at Tuskegee Institute in Alabama, they allowed themselves to be coerced into performing by a group of upperclassmen, who rewarded them with water-filled balloons, whoops of laughter, and other audience responses dear to musician's hearts. Born hams, the sextet would have taken *any* response as a good sign, so they agreed to stick together as a band, calling themselves the Jays.

Before long the hard-playing group had developed a local reputation. As the result of a foray to New York, where they played Small's Paradise in Harlem, their reputation began to spread along the East Coast. Motown heard them, signed them, changed their name to the Commodores, and recorded their first album, *Machine Gun.* The title single was their first million-seller.

The Commodores followed it up with monsters like "The Bump," "Slippery When Wet," "This is Your Life," and "Sweet Love." On worldwide tours they knocked out audiences in Africa, the Philippines, Japan, Manila, and Nigeria. Their funky soul sound creates near riots wherever they appear.
1978 Discography: *Natural High*

CON FUNK SHUN

Michael Cooper–Guitar, sitar, timbales, percussion, vocals

Karl Fuller–Trumpet, flugelhorn, vocals

Paul Harrell–Saxophones, flute, vocals

Cedric Martin–Bass, vocals

Louis McCall–Drums, vocals

Felton Pilate–Trombone, bass trumpet, piano, synthesizer, acoustic guitar, vocals

Danny Thomas–Clavinet, piano, synthesizer, organ, vocals

They can trace their musical roots back to the glory days of the late 1960s Memphis Stax sound: a blast of horns and a get-up-and-move rhythm. Although their sound was born in Memphis, Con Funk Shun hails from California. In San Francisco, pianist Mike Cooper and drummer Louis McCall formed a high school band called Project Soul, which began with just the two of them but eventually expanded to its current lineup.

As usual with new young bands, it was not easy for them to find work and support themselves, so when they were approached to back the Stax group the Soul Children, they jumped at the chance. In 1972, they moved to Memphis and officially adopted the name Con Funk Shun. Through the next few years they developed their sound as an opening act for Stevie Wonder, Lynyrd Skynyrd, Tower of Power,

and others. In 1976, they cut their first album, *Con Funk Shun,* which sold encouragingly.

Secrets, their second album, with its bouncy single called "Ffun," quickly leaped to gold. Con Funk Shun sashayed out on tours that wowed the nation. In 1978, their single "Shake and Dance" was a top-ten soul single and their album *Loveshine* leaped up the soul and pop charts with vigor.
1978 Discography: *Loveshine*

RITA COOLIDGE

In 1976, Rita Coolidge cut the album that was destined to place her squarely in the top rank of female singers. *Anytime...Anywhere*—now a double-platinum monster—showcased Rita's stirring voice in a collection of songs that seemed made for her to sing. The first single from the album, Jackie Wilson's "Higher and Higher," became an international hit in 1977 as Rita's sensuous rendition, completely different from Wilson's original up-tempo fling, recreated the song for a new generation of listeners. In 1978, singles from the album were still going strong, as "We're All Alone" became her second gold single and "The Way You Do the Things You Do" rose high on the pop charts and became a top-ten easy-listening winner. Her 1978 album, *Love Me Again,* was instant gold, and "You" quickly became a top-five easy-listening hit.

Nashville-born Rita began singing at an early age. She first performed in her minister-father's church choir, then with sisters Priscilla and Linda as the Coolidge Sisters. They won at state fairs and talent contests but eventually went their separate ways. Rita went to Florida State University to study art, and it was only to pay for art supplies that she took up singing again.

One of her jobs was for a jingle company in Memphis, for which she recorded a solo single, "Turn Around and Love You." She so impressed rockers Delaney and Bonnie when they visited Memphis that they took her back to Los Angeles with them, where she appeared on their *Accept No Substitutes* album. In Los Angeles she was surprised to find that her single had been a top-ten hit there and that she was already somewhat of a celebrity.

In 1969, she toured with Joe Cocker's Mad Dogs and Englishmen, a rowdy assortment of musicians, roadies, friends, and hangers-on who trucked across country in a celebrated tour that marked the close of a decade of rock growth. Back in L.A., at tour's end, she found herself in great demand, singing on albums by Stephen Stills, Eric Clapton, and Dave Mason. These same musicians contributed some stellar back-up work on her first single album for A & M, *Rita Coolidge.*

As she concentrated on finding her own voice and style, she discovered what her strengths were. "I realized I didn't need rock and roll to move an audience," she explains. "I found my strength lay in ballads, songs. I came out of that searching period learning you could touch people's hearts and it could have as much impact as making them dance in the streets."

At the end of 1970, on a flight to Memphis, Rita met Kris Kristofferson. He was headed to Nashville for a cover story interview in *Look* magazine. He never made it to Nashville, however, as Rita got off at Memphis and Kris deplaned with her. They married soon after, have a daughter, Casey, have cut two albums together, and tour together frequently in a supercharged stage show.
1978 Discography: *Love Me Again*

ELVIS COSTELLO

Elvis Costello, he of the thin intense face, oversized stare, and wicked insights, is a unique proposition, make no mistake. He first came to the attention of CBS Records when he picketed their convention in London in 1976 because they wouldn't listen to his songs. He is honest, and his songs, from the tender "Alison" to the crisp "Less than Zero," tell the truth as he sees it. He doesn't romanticize romance or street life.

Con Funk Shun

Rita Coolidge

Billy "Crash" Craddock

Elvis Costello

Although he's reticent about his past influences and the way his music developed, he's anything but shy about his own talent and his belief in himself. He recalls the months and months of hustling his demo tapes and the reaction—or nonreaction—he got, until Britain's Stiff Records saw the light and signed him on. "I never lost faith. I'm convinced in my own talent," Costello says, without a trace of braggadocio. He is not without supporters of his opinion, his hard, spare songs winning critical praise and vigorous audience reaction.

He has great faith in the power of the song itself, ignoring the virtuoso solo, the extended riff, and anything else that might distract his listeners from the pure experience of the song.

He signed with Columbia late in 1977, toured to promote *My Aim Is True,* his first album, at the end of 1977 and the beginning of 1978, and, judging from the determination in his words and the look in his eyes, Elvis Costello is going to be a name to reckon with.

1978 Discography: *This Year's Model*

BILLY "CRASH" CRADDOCK

When you see Billy "Crash" Craddock leap onstage like a human dynamo and whip his audience into a frenzy, when you count up his eighteen top-ten country singles, it's hard to believe that in 1971 he came home after a show and told his wife, "That's it—I quit." But it's true that the road to success for this native of Greensboro, North Carolina, was not an easy and smooth one.

Born of poor, hard-working parents, Billy played and sang to an audience of barnyard chickens when he was a child. One of his brothers caught an early show and urged Billy to keep singing. Heartened by his brother's encouragement, Billy bought a second-hand guitar and taught himself to play. In high school, he and two of his brothers began playing together. They won a local talent contest thirteen weeks straight, until the promoter politely asked them not to come back.

So Billy, a brother, and two high school friends formed a band called the Four Rebels. A representative from Columbia Records heard them and offered Craddock a recording deal. Delighted, Craddock headed for Nashville in 1959. But things didn't work out well with that first contract. "They tried to make another Fabian out of me," recalls Craddock. At that time, country and pop were widely separated. There was too much country in Craddock for him to make it as a pop singer. Added to that difficulty was Craddock's dislike of Nashville and its atmosphere. So he went back home, worked in a cigarette factory, raced stock cars (hence the nickname "Crash"), and later took a job hanging Sheetrock at local construction sites. He kept his musical hand in by playing local gigs. But after a local concert where the presence of successful, established stars made him feel that he was not achieving what he wanted, he made his decision to quit.

Two weeks later, Craddock got a call from Dale Morris, who had seen him perform two years before. Morris, who had just started his own record label, Cartwheel Records, was looking for a young, exciting male recording artist. He tapped Craddock, who leaped out of retirement, eager for the chance to record again. On a shoestring, Cartwheel put out "Knock Three Times," and nine weeks after it was released, it had raced to number one on the country charts. That was followed by "Ain't Nothin' Shakin'" and "Dream Lover," two more country smashes, and a string of others. Television, touring, and awards followed.

In the fall of 1977, Craddock signed with Capitol Records, called in a sizzling good collection of Nashville pickers to back him, and recorded his first album, *Billy "Crash" Craddock,* a vigorous collection of rock, country, and ballads. The first single from that album, "I Cheated on a Good Woman's Love," quickly swept its way to the top ten of the country charts, and Craddock today is riding high. His greatest worry is getting safely back to his tour bus after a performance without being mauled by female fans.

1978 Discography: *Billy "Crash" Craddock*

JOHN DENVER

One of music's most consistent winners, John Denver is popular with a wide range of fans. He is one of the few artists whose records continually charge to the top of the pop, country, and easy-listening charts, whose concerts are packed by an audience of all ages and musical tastes. In an era of fragmentation and specialization, Denver does not sing rock or country or R & B. He simply makes fine, upbeat, refreshing music.

Perhaps his breathtaking success was in the stars. He was born on New Year's Eve, 1943, in Roswell, New Mexico, and one can speculate that a particularly strong configuration of planets blessed him on that pivotal night. Denver's childhood, as Henry John Deutchendorf, Jr., was spent traveling with his air force pilot father from one military base to another, giving John an early experience of the varieties of life in America. When he was eight years old, his grandmother presented him with a guitar, and from that time to this, music has been his passion.

He studied architecture at Texas Tech, but in his junior year he packed up his 1955 Chevrolet and followed the lure of music to Los Angeles, where he changed his name to that of his favorite city and began playing and singing in clubs. New York was the next stop. There, he replaced Chad Mitchell of the Chad Mitchell Trio, touring with them until 1969, when his song "Leaving on a Jet Plane" became a hit for Peter, Paul, and Mary. John was ready to go out on his own.

On the college circuit he was a solid hit, but his first real success came when "Take Me Home, Country Roads," from the album *Poems, Prayers, and Promises,* struck a responsive chord in the heartland of America, zipped quickly to the top of the charts to become his first gold-winning single, leading the album on to gold. It was the first of thirteen gold albums that have sold a total of more than 30 million copies. But gold and platinum records tell only part of the John Denver success story.

In addition to his support of the vinyl industry, John is a popular television personality. His 1975 special, "Rocky Mountain Christmas," was watched by 30 million viewers, and every other one of his television programs has been an event. His concerts are always sold out; announcement of his 1976 engagement with Frank Sinatra at Harrah's in Lake Tahoe, Nevada, generated 600,000 phone calls for reservations. His songs are performed by a wide variety of other music titans, ranging from Frank Sinatra to the Osmonds.

In 1978, Denver kept right on piling up successes. Late in 1977, the album *I Want to Live* became his thirteenth gold-winner. Three singles from that album—"How Can I Leave You Again," "It Amazes Me," and the title song—became top-ten easy-listening hits; tickets for a whirlwind tour of forty-seven cities in sixty days were grabbed by avid fans. His first concert appearance at New York's Madison Square Garden in a year saw twenty thousand paying fans jam into that arena to experience the Denver magic. This year he received Madison Square Garden's Golden Ticket Award for sales of over 100,000. Two successful television specials, February's "John Denver in Australia" and September's "Alaska, American Child" drew huge audiences.

NEIL DIAMOND

Personal joy and professional success. Who could ask for anything more? Certainly not Neil Diamond, who continued his growth in 1978 with a little of both. In early 1978, his album *I'm Glad You're Here with Me Tonight,* from the television special aired late in 1977, became his third platinum LP. "Desirée," a single from that album, became a number-one easy-listening hit. To ice the cake, in February wife Marsha gave birth to a son, Michael Joseph.

Diamond is a rare musical animal—one who thinks in addition to

George Duke

John Denver

Bob Dylan

making music. When he decided to retire from performing at the end of 1972, most observers thought that Diamond would not be able to resist the lure of the stage for very long. But they didn't know that Diamond had a firm plan in mind. He knew he needed the time to return to personal and creative vigor, needed it for his family and for himself, for reflection and increased self-knowledge. He had endured thirteen years of intense pressure: six years of almost constant touring and recording, preceded by seven years of rejection—a time when, although he wrote constantly and continually, he could not make the slightest impression on the music business he so longed to conquer.

It was in New York City that he sweated through those years, sometimes working at short-lived gigs with music publishing companies, most of the time slaving away in a $35-a-month attic office on Broadway, writing morning, noon, and night. Finally, at the end of those lean years, he turned to performing locally as a way of getting his music heard. One fateful night in a Greenwich Village coffeehouse he was heard by record producers Jeff Barry and Ellie Greenwich, who signed him to their small, independent label, Bang Records. At his first studio session Diamond recorded "Solitary Man," "Cherry, Cherry," and "I Got a Feeling," destined to be his first three hits.

His next contract was with Uni Records. During the five years he recorded for them, he turned out eight albums, each of which won gold certification. In 1973, Columbia Records made him a multimillion-dollar, five-year, five-album offer; the first album he produced for them under that agreement, *Jonathan Livingston Seagull,* became a huge best-seller here and overseas.

When Diamond returned to performing in 1976, there was a vast public waiting eagerly to see and hear him. His first comeback concert, held in Auckland, New Zealand, set an all-time attendance record of 37,500. When he returned to New York's Forest Hills Tennis Stadium in June of 1976, *Variety* raved, "Neil gave a brilliant performance, holding a crowd of around 15,000 in the palm of his hand throughout." In 1976, he also released *Hot August Night,* recorded live during his eight-night engagement in 1976 at Los Angeles's Greek Theater. This album sold 8 million copies, ranking it among a small handful of titanic album sellers.

GEORGE DUKE

George Duke's love of music began early in his life. He pinpoints it at age four, when his mother took him to a Duke Ellington concert. "That's what did it," he says. "I don't remember it too well, but my mother told me I went crazy. I ran around saying, 'Get me a piano.'" Eventually she did, and by the time George was seven and a half years old he was taking piano lessons.

Throughout his teen years he was fascinated by the piano. By the time he reached high school, he was working professionally, first with a rock band, later a Latin group, then with a band called the Jazz Co-op. At sixteen he was leading his own trio.

The piano isn't his only musical passion, however. At the San Francisco Conservatory, the multi-talented Duke majored in trombone and composition and minored in piano. He sharpened his musical skills working with his trio at two local clubs, the Halfnote and the nearby Both/And. After he disbanded the trio, he worked for six months in 1968 with Don Ellis's big band.

George then used the same persistence with which he had won a piano from his mother to gain a place on the disks and tours of Jean-Luc Ponty, a violinist he greatly admired. While touring, the Jean-Luc Ponty Experience and the George Duke Trio were booked into some small rock clubs. It was at one such venue that George was forced into playing the electric piano for the first time, as that was the only keyboard the club had. In a matter of minutes, George had begun to enjoy the electric piano; he made plans to record there a week later.

That live session turned into a major event. Among the audience luminaries was Frank Zappa, who asked George to play with the Mothers of Invention. He stuck with Zappa for a year, but found the experience hard to take. "It was the first time," he says, "I was ever involved with a band that was *too* far out for me. I couldn't figure out why we'd be playing '50s rock and roll when the night before we had been playing contemporary classical with the L.A. Philharmonic."

In 1970, after a year with the Zappa zanies, Duke replaced Joe Zawinul in Cannonball Adderley's band, with which he played for two years. In 1972, he rejoined a more mature Zappa as a more mature Duke and found the experience far more rewarding than the first trip had been. It was Zappa who persuaded George to sing and to play synthesizers, two very important aspects of George's performances today. For a short time after the Mothers broke up, Duke and dynamo drummer Billy Cobham joined forces in a quartet.

Today George fronts his own band, creating music that is a meld of soul, jazz, hard rock, and funk. That this blend is a winner is clear from his sales figures. *Reach For It,* his 1977 album, was his first gold LP and a top soul album; "Dukey Stick" was a top-ten soul single in 1978; and *Don't Let Go,* his 1978 album, soared to the top ten on the soul charts.
1978 Discography: *Don't Let Go*

BOB DYLAN

Since 1961, when his first album, *Bob Dylan,* was released, the singer/songwriter has always been at the center of controversy and stunned acclaim. His musical importance in the early 1960s cannot be overestimated. Just a list of those early song titles has mythic importance. Such works as "Mr. Tambourine Man," "Blowin' in the Wind," "The Times They Are A-Changing," "Ballad of a Thin Man," and "Positively Fourth Street" were more than anthems. Their themes and images provided a direction for the decade.

In 1978, Bob Dylan is once again in the center, as he came out of semiretirement at the beginning of June to give his first solo performance in four years at the Universal Amphitheatre, Universal City, California. The seven sold-out shows were amazing. Dylan performed his old songs—in completely new, vivid, up-tempo versions—as well as material from his new album, *Street Legal,* which has quickly become his sixteenth gold album.

Everything he did in 1978 left no doubt that the Dylan magic was still there. His trip to Japan was a bombshell of exploding rock energy. When he gave a concert at Earl's Court in England in the middle of June, twenty thousand tickets were bought the day they went on sale. Even though the four-hour version of his enigmatic movie, *Renaldo and Clara,* released early in 1978, was not well received, the new Bob Dylan was willing to cut it down to two hours and release it again.

Perhaps this illustrates the biggest change in Dylan—his attitude toward his public. Dylan seems more aware today of the value of a performance. He doesn't snarl and ignore his audiences as he used to; instead, he seems eager to win them to his side. Sporting a white sequined thunderbolt on one costume, he regaled his audiences at the Universal Amphitheatre with what Cameron Crowe in *Rolling Stone* called "earnest between-song patter," saying hello to celebrities in the audience, giving brief introductions to his songs, and like the fine street hustler he's always been, being sure to mention the title of his new album.
1978 Discography: *Street Legal*

E

THE EAGLES

Glenn Frey–Guitars, vocals

Don Felder–Guitars

Don Henley–Drums, vocals

Tim Schmit–Bass, vocals

Joe Walsh–Guitars, vocals

At the end of February, Elektra/Asylum records took an inside back cover ad in *Billboard.* It featured a caricature of Irving Azoff, the Eagles' manager; dressed in a pair of yellow and white plaid overalls and a T-shirt reading "Big Shorty," he was holding a stack of records on a plate, like hotcakes, high above his head. According to the ad, the Eagles had sold a million records a month for the eighteen months preceding that ad.

That's a breathtaking ride, but the supermen of laid-back, Los Angeles rock took it in stride. It was all part of their growing luster that included a Grammy for *Hotel California* as Record of the Year and a second Grammy for the vocal arrangements on "New Kid in Town." On May 7, in a highly publicized softball game, they even whupped *Rolling Stone* magazine by an embarrassing (for *Rolling Stone* staffers) 15 to 8.

Founded in 1972 when Glenn Frey, Don Henley, Randy Meisner, and Bernie Leadon came together at the urging of Linda Ronstadt's manager, John Boylan, the group hit immediately with the gentle "Take It Easy," a softly melodic rocker. *Desperado* followed in 1973, and in 1974 they swept up an armful of honors as "Best of My Love," a top pop, country, and MOR song, won them a gold record, a Grammy nomination, an American Music Award, and a Nashville Songwriter's Award. That top song was from *On the Border,* the album that introduced Don Felder on slide guitar.

In 1975, they scored with another smash hit, "Lyin' Eyes," preceded by *One of These Nights,* a swift gold-winner. By the end of 1975, Bernie Leadon had decided to leave the group, and former James Gang rocker Joe Walsh was brought in. In 1976, they scored with "Take It to the Limit," and *Their Greatest Hits, 1971-1975,* shipped platinum; and *Hotel California* dominated the charts in 1977 with its title single and "Life in the Fast Lane."

EARTH, WIND AND FIRE

Maurice White–Vocals, kalimba, drums

Verdine White–Vocals, bass, percussion

Philip Bailey–Vocals, congas, percussion

Larry Dunn–Piano, organ, Moog synthesizer

Al McKay–Guitars, percussion

Ralph Johnson–Drums, percussion

Johnny Graham–Guitars

Andrew Woolfolk–Flute, tenor and soprano saxophones

Fred White–Drums, percussion

They are elemental spirits. Their name announces it; their music throbs with it. In 1977, with a little help from magician Doug Henning, their sold-out stage show vibrated with elemental illusions, including the levitation of bass player Verdine White. Perhaps more than any-

thing else, the magic of levitation symbolizes the message of Earth, Wind and Fire. Just as Verdine White floated mysteriously above the stage, their positive outlook and spiritual vitality lift up their listeners with a rush. It is this message, combined with their unique blend of rock, jazz, sophisticated African rhythms, and Southside Chicago soul, that has led to their great success. Since signing with Columbia Records in 1973, the band has earned six gold albums, four of which have gone on to earn platinum, three double platinum. They have also been awarded three gold singles, a Grammy award, two Rock Music awards, and an American Music award.

In 1978, following in the footsteps of *Last Days and Time, Head to the Sky,* and *Gratitude,* their album *All 'n All* was awarded double-platinum certification. "Serpentine Fire," the single from the album, was a number-one soul single. In addition, Earth, Wind and Fire won the American Music award as 1977's Favorite Soul Group. 1978 Discography: *All 'n All*

ELECTRIC LIGHT ORCHESTRA

Jeff Lynne–Guitar, vocals

Bev Bevan–Drums

Richard Tandy–Keyboards

Mik Kaminski–Violin

Hugh McDowell–Cello

Kelly Groucutt–Bass

When the Electric Light Orchestra, known as ELO to its millions of fans all over the world, appeared at London's Wembley Empire Pool during the first two weeks of June 1978, they received rave reviews from Britain's *Evening Standard, Daily Express,* and the respected music paper *Melody Maker.* The breathless adulation was not only for their music and their playing, but for their stage show as well. During their 1978 tour, which included forty-four dates in the United States, ELO began each set with a giant spaceship shrouding the stage. The huge saucer slowly lifted off to reveal the band accompanied by a flashing laser light show. An occasional flying saucer would swoop over the heads of the audience. And onstage, immersed in this extraordinary visual experience, ELO blasted out their complex, artful rock to totally involved crowds.

The ambition of ELO has always been to produce music that would blend classical influences with rock and roll. From the beginning of 1972, when guitarists Roy Wood and Jeff Lynne of Britain's hard-rocking the Move joined with drummer Bev Bevan and cellist Hugh McDowell to create the Electric Light Orchestra, the aim of the group has been to cement a relationship between the lushness of strings and the hard edge of a rock combo to create a full, vibrant sound, unlike anything anyone had heard before.

Their first album, the experimental *The Electric Light Orchestra,* was a success in Britain, and it looked as though the band was off to a flying start. But, in 1972, Wood and McDowell left. Lynne and Bevan recreated the band, gathering a total of nine musicians with an assortment of musical backgrounds. This band really clicked. *ELO II,* their 1973 effort, contained their smash rework of Chuck Berry's classic "Roll Over Beethoven."

Although their recorded sound had reached a fine peak, onstage the band had trouble with their strings. It took time and experimentation before they found the direct amplifiers that gave the strings the power to hold their own against the rock instruments.

The group's reputation continued to grow throughout their third album, *On the Third Day,* and their fourth, *Eldorado.* Their fifth album, *Face the Music,* was their first gold-seller, as was the single from it, "Evil Woman." Their next three albums, a greatest-hits collection called *Olé ELO, A New World Record,* and 1977's *Out of the Blue,* were all platinum-winners.

Eagles

Earth, Wind and Fire

Bruce W. Talamon

225

Yvonne Elliman

Electric Light Orchestra

England Dan and John Ford Coley

YVONNE ELLIMAN

Yvonne Elliman's career began with a flash of excitement when, during her very first job, singing at a London club, she was spotted by Tim Rice and Andrew Lloyd Webber, authors of *Jesus Christ Superstar,* who at that very moment were looking for a female singer to play Mary Magdalene. Yvonne was hired. As a member of the original cast, she recorded the album, performed the role in the world's major theaters, and appeared in the motion picture. For her performance in the film, Yvonne was nominated for the Golden Globe Award by the Hollywood Foreign Press Association.

After recording one album for Decca in New York, Yvonne decided she was feeling stifled by the role of Mary and returned to London, where she cut a second solo album with the help of Peter Townshend. Her return to America came at a fortuitous time. Eric Clapton was recording in Miami; Yvonne dropped into the studio to

hear him work. He needed a strong female voice for "I Shot the Sheriff," and he called on Yvonne. The song was a success, and Yvonne worked with Eric on his next five albums, including *Slowhand,* his 1978 double-platinum smash.

During her years with Eric, Yvonne was still determined to have a solo career. Signing with RSO Records, she recorded an album for them called *Rising Sun.* From her second album, *Love Me,* came two singles, the title cut and "Hello Stranger," both top-twenty hits.

In 1978, her strong, rich voice, sparked by the songwriting talents of the Brothers Gibb, won Yvonne her first gold record with the number-one smash from *Saturday Night Fever* "If I Can't Have You." Her first tour as a headliner in early February was a triumph.
1978 Discography: *Night Flight*

ENGLAND DAN AND JOHN FORD COLEY

This talented team from Texas has expanded its musical repertoire in 1978. The gentle harmonies and ballads that swept them to fame are now accompanied by hammer-hard rock, R & B, and jazz, much to the delight of their fans. In 1978, their fans were also pleased by the blazing success of their single "We'll Never Have to Say Goodbye Again," which raced up the charts with blinding speed. By the end of its first week of release, more than 75 percent of America's radio stations were playing the song, which was a cut from their 1978 album *Some Things Don't Come Easy.*

In addition to their records and fabulously successful concerts, England Dan and John Ford Coley wrote the theme for "James at 16," the engaging television series. Their appearance on that program was just one in a series that has included "David Soul and Friends," "The Lynn Anderson Special," "Dinah!," "The Tonight Show," "Midnight Special," and the Merv Griffin and Mike Douglas shows. In addition, their title song for the movie *The Time Has Come,* their first movie song, was nominated for an Academy Award.

The successful team met as teen-agers. Music was prominent in both their backgrounds: England Dan (real name: Danny Wayland Seals—his brother is Jimmy Seals of Seals and Crofts) played upright bass in a trio with his father on guitar and brother on fiddle; John Ford Coley played classical piano and added guitar later. While still in high school, the boys had their first taste of success with a local group called the Southwest F.O.B. and a song called "The Smell of Incense," which appeared on the national charts. When the group broke up, Dan and John set out for California, signed with A & M Records, and were soon given the golden opportunity to tour with Elton John. They were well received and toured nationally with other top acts, from Carole King to Three Dog Night. After their second A & M album, Dan and John took some time off and, in 1976, cut *Nights Are Forever,* their first gold.
1978 Discography: *Some Things Don't Come Easy*

DONNA FARGO

She was a high school English teacher in Southern California, writing a little music on the side, when producer Stan Silver met her. He had a feeling that there was something special about Donna Fargo, taught her to play guitar, became her first songwriting critic and, eventually, her producer. Donna began performing country songs in local clubs, and before long her success with audiences made her decide to go into music full time.

In 1972, her song "The Happiest Girl in the Whole U.S.A." soared straight to the top of the country and pop charts, winning her a gold record and slews of music awards (from the National Association of

Donna Fargo

Roberta Flack

Fleetwood Mac

227

Foghat

Foreigner

Peter Frampton

228

Record Merchandisers, the Music Operators of America, the Country Music Association, the Academy of Country Music, and *Billboard*). Fame had come upon her when she was barely looking.

But the bright-eyed ex-tomboy from Mt. Airy, North Carolina, didn't let fame knock her off course. She kept at her writing and performing, and "Happiest Girl" was followed by a string of number-one country hits, including "Funny Face," "Superman," "You Were Always There," and "Little Girl Gone." Her sparkling good humor is evident in the loving treatment she gives songs by such a variety of songwriters as Shel Silverstein, Neil Sedaka, Harry Chapin, Paul Simon, Elvis Presley, and many others.

In 1978, she scored a top-ten country hit with "Do I Love You (Yes in Every Way)," toured fairs, and made a rip-roaring appearance at Wembley Stadium for the tenth anniversary of Wembley's Country Festival. Her blossoming career was interrupted in the summer of 1978, when she was stricken with a difficult-to-diagnose neurological ailment. As of this writing, Donna's doctors are confident that she will be able to resume her professional activities in a short time.

ROBERTA FLACK

"Whatever you write about me," Roberta Flack has said, "should be reflective of what I feel rather than statistical." The statistics, however, are too staggering to ignore. They include nine gold records—eight of them swooped up in a mere two and a half years, the ninth earned by 1978's smash "The Closer I Get to You," her smooth duo with Donny Hathaway. "If Ever I See You Again," the second single from the album *Blue Lights in the Basement,* was a top-ten easy-listening hit.

Those statistics also include earlier success with Hathaway. In 1973, their performance of "Where Is the Love" won them each a Grammy for Best Pop Vocal by a Duo. In addition, her recording of "First Time Ever I Saw Your Face" was voted Record of the Year and Song of the Year in 1973. In 1974, her recording of "Killing Me Softly" walked off with Grammies as Record of the Year, Song of the Year, and Best Pop Vocal by a Female.

But, of course, those statistics have their basis in feelings that began in Arlington, Virginia, when nine-year-old Roberta took piano lessons and sneaked away to the Baptist Church down the street to drink in the music of Sam Cooke and the Soul Stirrers, the Five Blind Boys, and Mahalia Jackson. Throughout her teens she listened to every type of music, from R & B to classical, and at age thirteen her playing of a Scarlatti sonata won her second place in a statewide piano contest for black students.

Education and music have always been integral to her life. At fifteen she entered Howard University on a full music scholarship to study piano. Before she graduated, she changed her major to music education, and after graduation she taught music. While teaching, she got her first professional performing experience playing piano at Washington, D.C.'s Tivoli Club, accompanying opera stars. She was soon snatched away by club owner Henry Jaffe, who made her happy by paying her forty dollars an afternoon to perform. She loved it. "All of my interest was in learning new songs, making them better, knockin' 'em dead," she says of those times. "It was very pure, very simple, very honest."

But that pure simplicity was not to last. In the summer of 1968, Les McCann heard her sing and nearly fell out of his seat with excitement. Within days he had arranged for her to audition for Joel Dorn, a producer for Atlantic Records. With typical energetic determination, Flack recorded thirty-nine tracks in nine hours, and her debut album, *First Takes*, was completely recorded by November. It was released in June, 1969. The Flack power steadily built through two solo albums and then finally smashed through to an eager public in 1972.

Flack's extraordinary energy inspires all her projects. In addition to her performing and recording schedule, Flack is a producer, having coproduced several albums for others, as well as two of her own albums—1975's *Feel like Makin' Love* and 1978's *Blue Lights in the Basement.* She is also working toward a Ph.D. from the University of Massachusetts. Her goal beyond that degree is to reshape the way children in the inner cities are taught.

1978 Discography: *Blue Lights in the Basement* (with Donny Hathaway)

FLEETWOOD MAC

Christine McVie–Keyboards, vocals

Lindsey Buckingham–Guitar, vocals

Stevie Nicks–Vocals

John McVie–Bass

Mick Fleetwood–Drums

For twenty-nine weeks in 1977, *Rumours,* Fleetwood Mac's seventeenth album, sat proudly at the top of the charts, gathering honors, awards, fabulous sales figures, and setting a record for the longest time any contemporary rock record has been number one. It has sold 11 million copies worldwide to date, won a Grammy, the American Music Award, and *Billboard*'s award as Album of the Year. Fleetwood Mac was voted Group of the Year by *Billboard* and won the American Music Award as the year's favorite group. On Thanksgiving Day, the first annual North American Rock Radio Awards were broadcast to 258 FM radio stations. It was no surprise that the recipient of their top album award was *Rumours*.

Closing 1977 with a screaming SRO tour of Australia, Fleetwood Mac could look back on the year as a succession of pinnacles. The showmanship, perseverance, and sheer musical excellence of this ten-year-old hard-trucking band had finally paid off in the kind of success every musician dreams about.

Success began for them in 1975, when their album *Fleetwood Mac,* sparked by the chemistry of new members Stevie Nicks and Lindsey Buckingham, rocketed to sales of more than 4 million copies. Three songs from the album—"Over My Head," "Rhiannon," and "Say You Love Me"—were top singles. If there had been the slightest question of whether the new group could work together, it was answered in performance. As Christine McVie remembers, "We could tell by the first concert we ever did that it was going to be good. That first show went down a complete storm; there was something about the combination of people on the stage that was very special."

The band had always had a devoted cadre of hard-core fans from the beginning in 1967, when guitarist Peter Green, bass player John McVie, and drummer Mick Fleetwood left John Mayall's Bluesbreakers to form Peter Green's Fleetwood Mac. Guitarists Jeremy Spencer and Danny Kirwan rounded out the band's electric blues sound.

They had some hits during their first three years: the Britons loved their instrumental "Albatross," and the Americans took to "Oh Well" and "Green Manalishi." But instead of being able to build on that early success, the close-knit band had to cope with some stormy and painful changes. Peter Green left, his departure cushioned by the addition of Christine McVie. Jeremy Spencer disappeared during a 1971 tour to become a member of the Children of God; Peter Green stepped into the breach briefly, and Bob Welch filled in admirably. Their music was becoming more melodic and more sophisticated when Danny Kirwan left.

In 1973, their former manager, Clifford Davis, put together a band to tour in America and called them Fleetwood Mac, socking the original Mac another low blow until an injunction stopped the impostors. Just when everything seemed to be smoothed out, Bob Welch left to form his own band.

None of this kept them from turning out one well-respected, modestly successful album after another: *Kiln House, Future Games, Bare Trees, Penguin, Mystery to Me,* and *Heroes Are Hard to Find.* It wasn't until 1975, however, when Nicks and Buckingham added their magic that the mix finally jelled into something superlative.

The year 1978 began as a leisurely one, spent in preparing a new album and celebrating bass player John McVie's marriage to Julie Rubens in April. A summer tour, joined for several performances by Bob Welch, was greeted with great enthusiasm.

FOGHAT

Lonesome Dave Peverett–Guitar, vocals

Rod Price–Slide guitar

Roger Earl–Drums

Craig MacGregor–Bass, keyboards

The enthusiastic R & B offered by Foghat has its immediate roots in Savoy Brown, a British blues band of the late sixties. But guitarist Dave Peverett, drummer Roger Earl, and bass player Tony Stevens, who broke away from their fourth Savoy Brown partner in order to create Foghat, have never forgotten their deepest source—American rhythm and blues. To honor their inspirations, in the fall of 1977 in New York City they staged the Foghat Blues Tribute, which included appearances by such blues masters as John Lee Hooker and Muddy Waters.

Their early days as a band featured a long, painful search for a guitarist. They auditioned for months until they heard fellow blues freak Rod Price, whose tasty playing meshed beautifully with their sound. Once they found him, the four quickly blended into a hard-playing unit, driven to perform with crisp enthusiasm. "We always figured," says drummer Roger Earl, "that if we had a twenty-minute set to do, we'd go out and do the best twenty minutes possible." Their ability to heat up audiences soon made them a highly sought-after opening act.

In 1974, they made their breakthrough, when *Energized* qualified as a gold album, the first of seven in a row. Numbers four, five, and six—*Night Shift, Fool for the City,* and *Foghat Live*—have gone on to score platinum plaudits. The year 1977 saw Craig MacGregor join the group on bass. In 1978, *Stone Blue* became their seventh gold album, and their concert tours throughout the States were sold-out events.
1978 Discography: *Stone Blue*

FOREIGNER

Mick Jones–Lead guitar, vocals

Ian McDonald–Guitars, keyboards, horns, vocals

Lou Gramm–Lead vocals

Al Greenwood–Keyboards, synthesizer

Ed Gagliardi–Bass, vocals

Dennis Elliott–Drums

If you were anywhere in the civilized world in 1977 you heard the music of Foreigner. This potent combination of British and American musicians blasted out a supercharged music that was snapped up with dazzling speed. Their debut album, *Foreigner,* sold 3 million copies in less than a year, and each single from the album—"Feels like the First Time," "Cold as Ice," and "Long, Long Way from Home"—sailed effortlessly to the top of the charts. They scooped up an armload of awards as the best new group of the year from such publications as *Rolling Stone, People, Circus, Creem, Billboard, Cashbox, Record World* and walked off with honors for their songs and album as well. They continued their success in 1978, as their second album, *Double Vision,* was instant platinum and "Hot Blooded," the album's first single, a top-five single.

Because they wanted to be a successful live band, they played together for months before they recorded. That practice paid off with sold-out performances and ecstatic reviews for 1977's American tour and 1978's forty-two-day world tour, which included concerts in Australia, Japan, Germany, Greece, and England.

It's rare that a new group is so instantly successful. But when you look at the credentials of the individual musicians who make up the band, it's clear that the potential was there. Mick Jones had played with Spooky Tooth and Leslie West; Ian McDonald, in addition to being a successful producer, had also been part of King Crimson. When the two met, Mick knew that they could be the core of a successful endeavor. At his urging, McDonald agreed to join with him. Together they set out to find other talented musicians who were experienced but still fresh. Al Greenwood was recruited, and then Lou Gramm. Dennis Elliott and Ed Gagliardi joined forces with them to create their tight, melodic, audience-pleasing hard rock.
1978 Discography: *Double Vision*

PETER FRAMPTON

The year 1978 was another full one for singer/songwriter/guitarist/producer/movie star Peter Frampton. The twenty-eight-year-old whose 1976 album, *Frampton Live,* was a multimillion seller, starred as Billy Shears in Robert Stigwood's film adaptation of *Sgt. Pepper's Lonely Hearts Club Band.* Just a few weeks before the film's glamorous, star-studded premiere, Peter was in an automobile accident and sustained a broken arm, several broken ribs, and multiple cuts and bruises.

To the disappointment of the thousands of fans who hoped to catch a glimpse of him at the premiere, Peter was still too bruised to appear. However, fans were relieved to see him up and about a few weeks later.

It would take more than a car accident to keep Peter Frampton down. From the beginning, his career has been marked by the kind of energy and determination that has been the envy of the record world. His career began in the late sixties, when he played mean guitar with an English band called the Herd. His guitar often took a back seat, however, as Peter was promoted as the Face of 1968, an accolade that proved more of a hindrance than an aid, as Peter had to battle to prove he was a gifted musician and not just another pretty face.

With the breakup of the Herd, Frampton was freed to form Humble Pie with Steve Marriot. He played with them until 1971, when he left to go solo. In 1972, after contributing guitar work to albums by George Harrison, Harry Nilsson, and John Entwistle, Peter released his first solo album, the brilliant *Wind of Change.* That album was followed by three others: *Frampton's Camel, Somethin's Happening,* and *Frampton.* None made much progress on the charts, but they slowly built an adoring audience for the ace guitarist.

In 1976, that audience and millions of others were jolted out of their seats by *Frampton Comes Alive,* the live album that rocketed to the top of the charts, stuck in the number one spot for more than eighteen weeks, and broke through several platinum milestones before slowing down at about 8 million copies. During 1977, Peter released the self-produced album *I'm In You,* a mixture of soul, jazz, ballads, and rock; toured the United States, Europe, and Japan; and filmed *Sgt. Pepper's Lonely Hearts Club Band.* The year 1978 began with a much-needed vacation and ended with a major tour.

G

ART GARFUNKEL

"I love singing," states Arthur Garfunkel. After twelve years of sharing the limelight with partner Paul Simon as the harmony voice in one of the most famous and best-selling duos of the 1960s, Art Garfunkel still loves singing and continues to do what he loves.

Art began singing at age four, when his father brought home one of the first wire recorders. Like any young child, Art was excited over the possibilities of being able to record his voice and hear it played

Crystal Gayle

Courtesy United Artists Records

Larry Gatlin

Art Garfunkel

Courtesy Columbia Records

Leif Garrett

231

back. But unlike most young children, Art didn't tire of his new toy and put it away after a week. By the time he was eleven he was singing Everly Brothers songs at school talent shows with friend and schoolmate Paul Simon.

Pop music shifted to rhythm and blues, and the first 1950s rock-and-roll stars came along when Simon and Garfunkel were in high school. Paul and Art thought they had the stuff to make the big time. "We made demos in Manhattan and knocked on all the doors of the record companies with our hearts in our throats...just a couple of kids," Art recalls. As Tom and Jerry they got a contract, and their first single, "Hey! School Girl," was a top forty hit.

The two got their feet wet in the music business and learned a lot, but then separated and went on to college. Each continued to make music, but each focused on a career that was somehow more serious and certain. In 1962, the two old friends met again and found the performing magic of their sweet harmonies as strong as ever. This time the two of them sang and Paul was acknowledged the songwriter. For the next eight years Simon and Garfunkel spun some of the most beautiful music of the 1960s. Their classic best-selling albums include *Wednesday Morning 3 A.M.; Sounds of Silence; Parsley, Sage, Rosemary and Thyme; The Soundtrack from The Graduate; Bookends;* and *Bridge Over Troubled Water.* In 1977, the duo went to England, where they were given the prestigious Britannia award for the finest single piece of recorded music over the last twenty-five years as voted by the music industry of Great Britain. That prize was for *Bridge Over Troubled Water,* the album and the single.

Because each of them was interested in exploring other areas, the partnership broke up amicably in 1970. Art acted in *Catch-22* and *Carnal Knowledge,* receiving high praise for those performances. In 1973, his first album, *Angel Clare,* was released. His next, *Breakaway,* contained the singles "Breakaway," "I Only Have Eyes For You," and, with Paul, "My Little Town."

In 1978, Art released his third album, *Watermark,* much of which was written by Jimmy Webb. "(What a) Wonderful World," written some twenty years ago by Herb Alpert and recorded with the help of Paul and James Taylor, became a number-one easy-listening single. Art also gleefully embarked on his first tour since Simon and Garfunkel's 1970 farewell concerts. Delighted to be back on the road, he thrilled his audience with impeccably polished, totally professional, yet warm and engaging sets. He was obviously doing what he loved best and radiated that enjoyment to his audiences.
1978 Discography: *Watermark*

LEIF GARRETT

In late 1977 an album by Leif Garrett, yet another young, blond, Southern California singer came out. Ho hum. But surprise! The boy could sing. Garrett had been acting since the age of five, when he made his film debut in *Bob and Carol and Ted and Alice* and in succeeding years had appeared in *Macon County Line,* the *Walking Tall* series, and many television programs. Most recently, he starred in the Universal Picture *Skateboard* and the NBC-TV pilot "Peter Lundy and the Medicine Hat Stallion."

But for the last couple of years, Leif has had his eyes on the music scene, listening to and admiring the Rolling Stones and Led Zeppelin and getting advice and encouragement from fellow soccer fan Rod Stewart. From *Leif Garrett,* his first album, no less than two gold singles emerged—brilliant remakes of "Surfin' USA" and "Runaround Sue." In February 1978, the album itself achieved gold status.

Leif, as his role in *Skateboard* demonstrates, is a great athlete. He's a favorite of young fans, regularly appearing in a host of teenage publications. A recent high school graduate, he completed four years in two while maintaining a straight A average.

LARRY GATLIN

The praise that means the most to country singer/songwriter Larry Gatlin is not that of critics or fans, but the praise he receives from his peers. Johnny Cash, Kris Kristofferson, and other artists who have recorded his songs will tell you Gatlin is one of the outstanding songwriters of our time. Johnny Mathis describes Larry as the best singer he's heard in twenty years, and Marty Robbins calls him the best singer/songwriter since Merle Haggard.

Only twenty-six, Larry Gatlin has been in love with music since he was a baby. When he was six, he and younger brothers Steve and Rudy sang in a gospel group at church gatherings. Music and religion provided the stability Larry needed in his childhood, as his oil-driller father moved frequently from state to state. When Larry was attending the University of Houston, he seized an opportunity to work with the Imperials, a gospel group. Through them he met country singer Dottie West who half-jokingly suggested that Larry try to write some songs. "I sent her eight songs and a month later she sent me an airplane ticket to Nashville," he recalls.

That was in May of 1971. For the next three years Larry wrote songs for Dottie and other country singers. She played one of Larry's tapes for Kris Kristofferson, who was so excited that he called Fred Foster, president of Monument Records, who signed Larry and his younger brothers. In 1974, *The Pilgrim* was released, followed by *Rain Rainbow.* His third album, *Larry Gatlin with Family and Friends,* features his first number-one country single, the Grammy-winning "Broken Lady." From his next, *High Time,* comes his number one smash "Statues Without Hearts."

Throughout 1977 and into 1978 Larry's career has continued to heat up, with one country hit after another rocketing to the top of the country charts. In 1977, his album *Love Is Just a Game* produced two number-one hits, "I Don't Wanna Cry" and the title single. Early in 1978, he hit the top again with "I Just Wish You Were Someone I Love," and in the spring "Night Time Magic" repeated the performance. His latest album, *Oh! Brother,* is another sensitive winner.
1978 Discography: *Oh! Brother*

CRYSTAL GAYLE

On the cover of the June 5 issue, *People* magazine touted the relationship of Loretta Lynn and Crystal Gayle as a rivalry, but the story inside seemed to say that Crystal Gayle and Loretta Lynn share a warm sisterhood. After all, it was Loretta and husband Moony who gave baby sister Crystal her first breaks in the business. And Crystal's crossover successes don't threaten Loretta's image as the queen of country. Crystal's pop achievements led her to her first platinum album early in 1978, *We Must Believe in Magic.* "Don't It Make My Brown Eyes Blue," her 1977 country monster, was a number-one pop hit as well. The song also earned her a Grammy and her second Top Female Vocalist award from the Academy of Country Music.

In 1978, everything just kept rolling Crystal's way. Her "Ready for the Times to Get Better" was a top-ten easy-listening and a number-one country single. Her 1978 album, *When I Dream,* leaped onto the country charts at number twenty-one and quickly shot to the top, as did her summer single "Talking in Your Sleep." Her television appearances included the usual country roster, as well as such plums as her spot on "Dick Clark's New Year's Rockin' Eve." She was also included as part of a *Ladies Home Journal* tribute to the American Woman.

Crystal's career is one that started out with success and just kept smoothly rolling. After cutting her teeth in performances for churches, local charities, and lodges with three of her four brothers, her very first single, "I've Cried (the Blue Right Out of My Eyes)," (a song sister Loretta had originally written for Brenda Lee, who, unfortunately, has brown eyes) climbed right into the country top twenty in 1970. She and Loretta toured county fairs and festivals for the next few years, and in 1973 Crystal signed with United Artists. Her first album, *Crystal Gayle,* provided the hit single "Restless," and from her second album, *Somebody Loves You,* came her first chart-topper, "I'll Get Over You."

In 1975, the Academy of Country Music, knowing embryonic success when they saw it, voted her the Most Promising Female Vocalist of the Year. Crystal continues to fulfill that promise.
1978 Discography: *When I Dream*

ANDY GIBB

What do you do with your life if you're Andy Gibb and your older brothers are the increasingly fabulous, legendary, mythical titans the Bee Gees? Well, if you're Andy Gibb you up and carve yourself a musical career—and *you* become a fabulous, legendary, mythical titan yourself, even faster and more stunningly than your elder siblings. With a brilliant songwriting gift and a sexy onstage presence, Andy has amply shown the cynical music business that he can make it on his own.

Nineteen-year old Andy, who snakes his way into a song with polished dynamism, has been playing guitar since the age of nine and traveling the world and performing in clubs with his own band since fourteen.

In 1976, Andy signed with pop mastermind Robert Stigwood. Early in 1977, with the help of brother Barry, he cut his first single, the number-one "I Just Want to Be Your Everything," and his first album, *Flowing Rivers*. Both quickly became gold-sellers, followed hot on their heels by "Love Is Thicker than Water," another swift gold. His second LP, *Shadow Dancing*, and the title single both broke the gold pattern—zipping quickly to platinum. His summer single "An Everlasting Love" was another rocket to the top of the charts.

Throughout 1978 Andy graced many television programs and kept himself in good fighting trim with constant touring. His performances were lessons in the art of teen heartthrob, arousing piercing squeals from his mainly female audiences.
1978 Discography: *Shadow Dancing*

EMMYLOU HARRIS

For Emmylou Harris, 1978 has meant one hit after another. From her country album, *Quarter Moon in a Ten Cent Town*, a rapid top ten on the country charts, came the singles "To Daddy" and "Two More Bottles of Wine," both top country hits. A springtime tour with Willie Nelson was a refreshment for the country lady, one of those stars whose meteoric overnight success was preceded by eight singing but unsung years of hard work.

In 1967, she took guitar in hand and wandered through what was left of the East Coast folk scene. "It wasn't really the most opportune time to try to make it as a singer-songwriter," she says laughingly, but she was a familiar figure on college campuses and in the coffeehouses. In 1969, she was signed by Jubilee Records, but her first album arrived at the same time as her daughter, and daughter Hallie took precedence over a career. For a year Emmylou was out of the music scene, but in 1971, with a folk-country band backing her, she began to appear in clubs in Washington, D.C.

At Washington's Cellar Door she was heard by the Flying Burrito Brothers, who asked her to join them. Unfortunately, the Burritos were on the verge of breaking up. Good ultimately came of the meeting, however, as Gram Parsons got to hear Emmylou and tapped her to help him with his first solo album. After months of waiting she finally received a ticket to Los Angeles in the mail and joined with Parsons for his album *G.P.*, a tour in the spring of 1973, and his last album, *Grievous Angel*.

Parsons' death in late 1973 was a blow to Emmylou, but she pulled herself together, began to play on her own, and organized Angelband. Warner Brothers, with impeccable timing, stepped in and offered her a contract. With Brian Ahern (Anne Murray's producer) as producer, and members of Elvis Presley's band as back-up musicians, *Pieces of the Sky* emerged early in 1975 as a gorgeous success, a number-one country record, from which came the hit single "If I Could Only Win Your Love."

Her second album, *Elite Hotel*, was her first gold-winner, featuring three top country singles—"Together Again," "Sweet Dreams," and "One of These Days." Her appearance on Bob Dylan's album *Desire* won her added respect and admiration, and in 1977 she won a Grammy for Best Vocal Performance, Female, for *Elite Hotel*.

Luxury Liner was her 1977 chart-topper, a rocker with a strong country flavor.
1978 Discography: *Quarter Moon In a Ten Cent Town*

HEART

| Ann Wilson—Lead vocals |
| Nancy Wilson—Lead guitar, vocals |
| Michael Derosier—Drums |
| Howard Leese—Keyboards |
| Roger Fisher—Lead guitar |
| Steven Fossen—Bass |

After a year of bickering over who owned the rights to the album *Magazine*, recorded by Heart when they were still under contract to the Mushroom label, Heart and Mushroom came to an amicable agreement in 1978. *Magazine* was released, and, to no one's surprise, least of all to fans of the Wilson sisters and their musical henchman, the album quickly sold platinum. Their 1978 single, "Heartless," did not do as well, but the album and their blasting performance at Cal Jam 2 more than made up for it.

The trip to the top was one of hard, steady work for this powerhouse of a rock band. They hail from Seattle where they spent several years breaking in their act before being signed by Mushroom Records in 1975. The small label could afford little in the way of promotion, and their distribution was certainly not powerful, but with Heart doggedly slamming out sizzling rock and roll in clubs, halls, auditoriums, and theaters for the better part of a year, that first album, *Dreamboat Annie*, racked up sales of more than 3 million copies.

In 1976, a disagreement with their label nudged Heart in the direction of a CBS Records subdivision, Portrait, for whom they cut their second album, 1977's platinum-winner, *Little Queen*.
1978 Discography: *Magazine*
Dog and Butterfly

HEATWAVE

| Johnnie Wilder, Jr.—Vocals |
| Keith Wilder—Vocals |
| Mario Mantese—Bass |
| Rod Temperton—Keyboards |
| Bilbo Berger—Drums |
| Roy Carter—Guitar |
| Billy Jones—Guitar |

Platinum singles don't come easy. It's especially startling for a group to have its first single sell the required 2 million copies. But, in 1977, a carefree disco tune called "Boogie Nights," the first American single by a rollicking band called Heatwave, dominated airwaves and record bins for months. Proving that they were no mere flash in the pan, Heatwave's first album, *Too Hot to Handle*, also sold 2 million copies in the United States. And, proving that the band really had staying power, "Always and Forever," the second single from the album, ran away with gold certification. *Central Heating*, Heatwave's second album, became its second platinum-winner, and "The Groove Line," its third gold single. With a history that goes back nearly a decade

Emmylou Harris

Dan Hill

Heatwave

Heart

and roots reaching into two continents, there's little chance that Heatwave will fade to obscurity.

Leader and founder Johnnie Wilder, Jr., hails from Dayton, Ohio, and has sung all his life. In the army in Heidelberg, West Germany, at the beginning of 1969, Johnnie formed a five-man vocal group that sang a cappella at service clubs on weekends. In a short time he had joined with a group of German musicians who called themselves the Soul Sessions.

After his discharge in 1972, Johnnie returned to the States; but two months later he was back in West Germany, singing with Soul Sessions for another half year. In Germany he met up with fellow American Tommy Harris, a drummer who was leading a group called the Upsetters. In Zweibrücken they began playing together in a small room where a nonstop radiator poured out heat twelve months a year. It was that radiator that inspired the name Heatwave.

During the next few years the band went through several changes of name and changes of personnel. Their first break came in 1976, when GTO founder Dick Leahy discovered them in Great Britain. Leahy offered to finance the cutting of some master tapes; two of their songs, "Super Soul Sister" and "Ain't No Half Steppin'," were released in Britain. In January 1977, "Boogie Nights" was released as a single and soared to the number-one spot on the British pop, soul, and disco trade charts. Epic Records then brought "Boogie Nights" to the United States, where it was equally successful.

1978 Discography: *Central Heating*

DAN HILL

"I love to sing...I feel like I'm flying sometimes when I'm singing," says twenty-four-year-old, Canadian-born singer/songwriter Dan Hill. "I love performing. I love going out there and telling stories to the audience and making people laugh. I love that as much as making them cry...and relaxing them and drawing them closer to me and setting up a real warmth that sets up the songs."

It is the intense quality of his onstage communication that has made Dan Hill a major concert attraction in Canada, where his first two albums, *Dan Hill* and *Hold On,* achieved gold status; his third, *Longer Fuse,* achieved double platinum. In 1976, he won Canada's respected Juno Award as Best New Singer, and in 1978 he swept up three Junos: one as Top Male Vocalist, one as Composer of the Year, and one for his best-selling album *Longer Fuse.*

The son of a black father and a white mother, Dan was born and raised in a white suburb of Toronto, where his mixed racial background was the source of much confusion and anxiety during his childhood. Dan was not destroyed by those feelings, however. "I look at it as a blessing, insofar as I think I was forced to be very aware of...things that were going on around me so I could understand exactly how I fit in...and through that awareness, I think, I became a much stronger human being and a better writer for it." One of his most personal songs, "McCarthy's Day," is a tribute to his parents' courage in choosing each other and a life together.

His moving, intelligent songs, often explorations of the pain and beauty of love, are written with great sensitivity and perception. They have won unqualified praise from both Canadian and American critics. Audiences, too, have discovered Dan's music. His compelling single "Sometimes When We Touch," cowritten with hit-maker Barry Mann, quickly became his first American gold-winner. Dan received the news of that success during a superior tour of America with Art Garfunkel, a tour that found audiences held spellbound by the magical intensity of Dan's voice, guitar work, and songs.

VLADIMIR HOROWITZ

On February 26, 1978, Vladimir Horowitz, whose professional career has spanned fifty-seven years and has been full of remarkable pinnacles, appeared as a special guest artist at a recital at the White House. President Carter declared Horowitz "a national treasure," and

Engelbert Humperdinck

Vladimir Horowitz

the recital was aired on radio and given a delayed telecast over more than one hundred Public Broadcast stations.

That, perhaps, was the peak of Horowitz's 1978 triumphs. They included the fiftieth anniversary of his American debut on January 8, when he performed the Rachmaninoff Third Concerto with the New York Philharmonic conducted by Eugene Ormandy. It was his first concert with any orchestra in twenty-five years, and the resulting album was a number-one classical chart-topper. On March 12 and 19, Horowitz gave afternoon Carnegie Hall recitals. The demand for tickets was so great that Horowitz fans began lining up the night before they went on sale, repeating their eager response of April 1965, when Horowitz announced his return to the concert stage after a self-imposed retirement of twelve years. On September 24, Horowitz performed the Rachmaninoff for a national television audience, appearing live from Lincoln Center with The New York Philharmonic conducted by Zubin Mehta.

The pianist, who has won fourteen Grammies in his career, was delighted by the response to his appearances and to the recordings he has released this year.

1978 Discography: *Rachmaninoff Third Concerto*
Golden Jubilee Recital

ENGELBERT HUMPERDINCK

His records have sold more than one hundred million copies, he has more than one hundred fan clubs in the United States, and fans travel hundreds of miles to catch his shows. Given the fabulous statistics of his career today, it's hard to believe that Engelbert Humperdinck struggled for years before he got a break.

Engelbert, born Arnold George Dorsey in India on May 2, 1936, spent the early 1960s performing in small clubs, sending tapes of his songs to record companies, and battling unsuccessfully to get his soaring love songs heard above the din of British rock. His style and the ballads he sang were the antithesis of the most popular music of the day, and Engelbert met with one disappointment after another.

One man, however, friend and manager Gordon Mills, believed in Engelbert's talent and appeal. In 1967, Gordon placed Engelbert on the top British television show "Saturday Night at the London Palladium." Engelbert sang his new single, "Release Me," and within minutes after the handsome singer had left the stage, phone lines to the station were jammed by eager callers. The response was so powerful that Engelbert was called back the following week and given star billing, something that had never happened before in the twelve-year history of the show.

For Engelbert that was just the beginning. Throughout the years he has collected fifteen gold singles as well as twenty-one gold and two platinum albums for his treatments of an assortment of beautiful love songs, including "There Goes My Everything," "The Last Waltz," and "Les Bicyclettes de Belsize." Working with new manager Harold Davison, in 1977 Engelbert was on the road for nine months, and in 1978 his active itinerary kept him moving to places as exotic as Kuala Lumpur, Singapore, Manila, and Hong Kong.

1978 Discography: *Last of the Romantics*

I

THE ISLEY BROTHERS

Ronald Isley–Lead vocals

Rudolph Isley–Vocals

Kelly Isley–Vocals

Ernie Isley–Guitar, drums

Marvin Isley–Bass

Chris Jasper–Keyboards, ARP

The names of their albums tell it all: *Live It Up, The Heat Is On, Go for Your Guns,* and their latest platinum powerhouse, *Showdown*. Since 1959, when group founders Ronald, Rudolph, and Kelly recorded "Shout," the dynamic Isleys have been spinning out tight, aggressive R & B. Such hit singles as "(Who's) That Lady," "Twist and Shout" (made famous by the Beatles), and "It's Your Thing," have won them the applause and adulation of millions of fans.

They trained hard for their success, soaking up knowledge and experience from everywhere. In the early sixties they played with Jimi Hendrix; in 1966 they signed with Motown, where they learned about production, songwriting, and the financial aspects of the music world.

The brothers came out of this informal schooling as consummate musicians and shrewd businessmen, becoming one of the first groups to form their own record label at the end of the 1960s. The creation of T-Neck Records coincided with the addition of brothers Ernie and Marvin and brother-in-law Chris Jasper, enabling the Isleys to abandon the horns and background instruments that appeared on their earlier records. Their newer sound was pared-down and clean, a direct and classic R & B statement.

The title of their 1978 number-one soul single, "Take Me to the Next Phase," reflects their desires for the future. As Ernie Isley explains it, "We do hope that the scope of our music will not always be limited by such restrictive classifications as top forty, MOR, pop, or R & B, but will fall into a broader category known simply as rock 'n' roll."

1978 Discography: *Showdown*

The Isley Brothers   Courtesy Epic Records

J

MILLIE JACKSON

The earthy Millie Jackson is another one of those singers who comes from a highly unlikely background. She was raised by her grandparents in a small town in Georgia. Her grandfather was a strict and stern preacher. "Man," Millie recalls, "I was in church six days a week. On Saturday we didn't go to church—we had a prayer meeting at home." Millie wasn't allowed to watch soap operas or westerns; for a time she was allowed to watch Tennessee Ernie Ford because Tennessee Ernie closed his show with a hymn. "But my grandfather finally came to the conclusion that the only reason he sang the hymn at the end was to make up for the lies he told for the other twenty-five minutes," she says. "That was the end of Tennessee Ernie Ford." So Millie did what any normal adolescent would do—when she was fourteen she ran away from home and lived with a friend for a few months.

Although her father sent for her a few months later, Millie didn't stay with him long, but moved to New York to finish high school. A model before black models became chic, Millie became a singer quite by chance in 1964. Attending a night club with friends, she was dared to go onstage and sing. She took the dare, and, she admits with a laugh, "I've been singing ever since."

She appeared in several clubs, and in 1969 she recorded her first single, "A Little Bit of Something," for MGM Records. That didn't do too much for her, and she soon signed with Spring Records.

In the next few years Millie turned out several albums. Her first, *Millie Jackson,* won her the National Association of Television and Radio Artists' award as the Most Promising Female Vocalist of 1972. In 1973, her single "It Hurts So Good" was featured in the movie *Cleopatra Jones.* The album of the same name won her *Cash Box*'s Best Female R & B Vocalist Award.

Her next album, *Millie,* contained some philosophical songs and also prepared the way for her first completely conceptual album, the gold-winning *Caught Up,* in which Millie explores the emotions of a love triangle: On one side she sings the role of the wife whose husband has a lover; on the other side she explores the role of the mistress. She developed this theme further on *Still Caught Up,* and the extended monologue, or as Millie calls it, "A Musical Soap Opera," has become her trademark.

On her next two albums, *Free and In Love* and *Lovingly Yours,* Millie displayed a positive sense of joyful abundance. With *Feelin' Bitchy,* her 1977 album, she won gold, and from that album came the gold single "If We're Not Back in Love by Monday," also a country winner for her.

Millie and her two daughters live in a ten-room house in New Jersey, from which she runs her own music-publishing company, Double Ak-Shun Music, and manages and produces the Facts of Life, a four-piece R & B group.
1978 Discography: *Get It Out'Cha System*

BOB JAMES

At the age of four Bob James sat down at his first piano, and he hasn't stopped playing since. As composer and arranger for many jazz greats, he has made major contributions to jazz's return to popularity. Born in Marshall, Missouri, he put together his first jazz trio while attending the University of Michigan. Their first public appearance, at the Notre Dame Jazz Festival in 1962, brought him to the attention of Quincy Jones, one of the festival's judges. Quincy was enthusiastic about James's group, and James was signed to Mercury Records.

He began working with electronic compositions and live improvisation, documented on the album *Explosions.* For the next four and a half years he was Sarah Vaughan's musical director and then worked as an arranger to some of the greatest soul vocalists, including Dionne Warwick, Morgana King, Roberta Flack, and Aretha Franklin. He worked with producer Creed Taylor at CTI Records, arranging and composing albums for such jazz notables as Hubert Laws, Eric Gale, Stanley Turrentine, Hank Crawford, Ron Carter, and Johnny Hammond. He arranged, conducted, and contributed several songs to Grover Washington, Jr.'s, two gold crossover albums, *Mister Magic* and *Feels So Good.*

In 1976, James accepted a position at CBS Records, where he began expanding out of the confines of jazz. He worked with million-selling pop artists, including Paul Simon, for whom he orchestrated the Grammy-winning "Still Crazy After All These Years."

At the beginning of 1977 he began a new label, Tappan Zee Records, giving him the opportunity to create new music. His own album for that label, *Heads,* became a top jazz LP at the beginning of 1978. About his future Bob says, "To me, music is a responsibility we musicians have to the public. I like that responsibility of communicating. Basically, I just want to keep on making records, and play the kind of music that people will enjoy."

JEFFERSON STARSHIP

Grace Slick–Vocals, keyboard

Paul Kantner–Vocals, guitar

Marty Balin–Vocals

Craig Chaquico–Lead guitar

David Freiberg–Vocals, keyboards, bass

John Barbata–Drums

Pete Sears–Bass, keyboards

The archetypal San Francisco band of the sixties, the Jefferson Airplane was known for exploratory journeys into acid-influenced hard rock that were anthems for a generation. In the early seventies, however, the band began to fragment. Key vocalist Marty Balin left the group in 1970; the energies of Jack Casady and Jorma Kaukonen were channeled into their new blues-oriented band, Hot Tuna; Grace Slick and Paul Kantner turned their attentions to several solo albums. It looked as though the Airplane was about to become a casualty of the new decade.

But, strangely, some subtle cord continued to tie Grace Slick, Paul Kantner, and Marty Balin together, and in 1974 there emerged a shimmering album called *Dragonfly* by the Jefferson Starship, with Grace, Paul, a new rhythm section, and with one song by Balin. His complete return to the group in 1975 marked a new growth for the band. With him, they cut the album *Red Octopus,* a smashing 2.5-million-seller and their first number-one album, sliding in and out of first place for the entire year.

The Starship, its lineup of fine musicians finally firmly established, continues to reach greater and greater heights. In 1978, RCA released their album *Earth* with an unprecedented broadcast of the entire disk to a listening audience of more than 10 million over select radio stations. *Earth* more than repaid RCA's faith in it, becoming the Starship's second platinum album, zipping to a top-ten pop chart position, and producing a top-ten single, the soaring "Count On Me."
1978 Discography: *Earth*

WAYLON JENNINGS

Kris Kristofferson calls Waylon Jennings "the best country singer in the world." Even if you had never heard his darkly mellow voice wrap itself warmly around his songs, a look at his musical credentials makes it clear that millions of music fans share Kristofferson's assessment of Waylon's talent. Highlights of his fabulous career include his mammoth 1960 country hit "Only Daddy That'll Walk the Line," his superior pop crossovers "This Time" and "I'm a Ramblin' Man," and his historic 1976 album *The Outlaws,* on which he, his wife Jessi Colter, Willie Nelson, and Tompall Glaser officially established a new, renegade voice in country music. It was the first country album ever to sell a million copies. Since the early 1960s when he first began singing with his own group, the Waylors, Waylon has been a record maker and record breaker.

Waylon has spent his professional life in the music world. From the age of twelve until he was twenty-one he was a disk jockey in his home town of Littlefield, Texas. In addition to spinning records, Waylon hosted local talent shows and even sang on occasion. When he was twenty-one, he moved to Lubbock, Texas, where he continued to spin platters until rock-and-roll star Buddy Holly asked him to join his group.

Waylon agreed gladly and traveled with Holly as a singing member of the Crickets through 1958. Fortunately, he passed up the plane flight that so tragically took young Holly's life in 1959.

Waylon's next step was to move to Phoenix, Arizona, where he formed the Waylors, a country, folk, and rock act. They were a top local attraction, and Waylon's reputation grew until he was ready to step out on his own. By the end of the sixties, Waylon had become a

Millie Jackson

Jefferson Starship

Bob James

Waylon Jennings

fixture in the country charts' top ten, a position he maintained in the seventies.

In 1978, his rapidly burgeoning career took more fabulous leaps. *Waylon Live,* 1977's big hit, became his fifth gold LP. At the end of 1977 he won *Billboard's* Country Artist of the Year Award. In 1978, he and Willie Nelson released an album called *Waylon and Willie,* which quickly won them their first platinum award as a duo. From the album came the top country single "Mamas, Don't Let Your Babies Grow Up to Be Cowboys." Another successful collaboration in a year of heavy touring was his top country single with Johnny Cash, "There Ain't No Good Chain Gang." Waylon also scored with his winning country album and single of the same name, *I've Always Been Crazy.*
1978 Discography: *Waylon and Willie* (with Willie Nelson)
  I've Always Been Crazy

JETHRO TULL

Ian Anderson—Flute, guitar, vocals

Barriemore Barlow—Drums

John Glascock—Bass

David Palmer—Saxophone, keyboards

The manic flute dances of Ian Anderson, an errant sprite, continue to pack the houses and slay 'em in the aisles. For eleven years now, Ian Anderson has been prancing between his audience and his band, brandishing his flute like an ancient woodland instrument and creating rare and original musical moments, living up to his early vow to make a different kind of rock and roll.

Not only do concert audiences respond to the raffish musician's onstage antics (in 1978 he was awarded a gold ticket by Madison Square Garden, signifying ticket sales of more than 100,000), but record buyers by the millions grab his disks off the shelves with unbridled enthusiasm. Take, for example, his latest gold album, *Heavy Horses,* which thundered onto the pop charts at number fifty; or his latest platinum, a collection called *The Best of Jethro Tull;* or the five platinum, five gold albums he's earned in the past.

Anderson and his band gained acclaim easily. Their first few albums—*This Was, Stand Up,* and *Benefit*—were like nothing anybody had ever heard. His was a new voice, blending jazz, rock, and a classical spirit with a growingly outrageous persona. This persona began to overstep its bounds for the critics with the album *Aqualung,* which stunned with its lead single about decadence and perversion (albeit a highly successful track, musically and commercially) and with one side devoted entirely to Anderson's views of organized religion.

Thick as a Brick and *Passion Play* were soundly trounced by the critics. Anderson decided to retire from performing for a while and took his band to Switzerland, where they remained two years while making the album *War Child,* which sold more than a million copies. Late in 1974, Jethro Tull emerged from seclusion and took to the welcoming road once again. Since then, they have played to sold-out houses wherever they go, continuing to win new fans as they go on pleasing their old ones.
1978 Discography: *Heavy Horses*

BILLY JOEL

Trained for twelve years as a classical pianist, Billy Joel is today one of the great names of rock and roll. His fourth album for Columbia Records, *The Stranger,* glided early to platinum sales, sparked by such superb hits as the rock-hard "Movin' Out" and the soft ballad "Just the Way You Are."

Billy's recording career began in 1968, after several years of pounding the ivories in Long Island, New York, bar bands. His first solo album, *Cold Spring Harbor,* was recorded in 1971 and made only small ripples in the musical pond. Soon after, Billy moved to Los Angeles, where he played piano in a bar called The Executive

Lounge. Under the name Billy Martin he made music, absorbed the California scene, and wrote the songs that were eventually to appear on his first Columbia album, *Piano Man.* The album, with its real-life pictures of a musician's trials, soon went gold. *Cash Box* named him the Best Male Vocalist of 1974, and Billy began to tour as a headliner, playing in such respected arenas as Carnegie Hall in New York and the Kiel Opera House in St. Louis.

During the summer of 1974 he wrote and recorded *Streetlife Serenade* in Hollywood, but in 1975 he said goodbye to the Golden West and headed back for home base. In June of 1976 his third album, *Turnstiles,* was released. *Turnstiles* didn't quite ship gold, but by the end of its first week it had sold half a million copies to catch that coveted gold ring.

From the summer of 1976 through June of 1977, Billy played to sold-out halls all across the country. The hard-working singer/pianist/songwriter finished 1977 with a fifty-four-date blitz of the United States and Canada and began 1978 playing to packed houses in Europe and Japan.

ELTON JOHN

After years of phenomenal best-selling albums and scores of rollicking singles, including such instant wake-ups as "Crocodile Rock," "Saturday Night's Alright for Fighting," "Bennie and the Jets," "Island Girl," "Honky Cat," and "Don't Go Breaking My Heart," the years 1976 through 1978 have been relatively quiet ones for Elton John. His rest from performing was broken in 1977 by four appearances at London's Rainbow Theatre, a free concert for five hundred students at Shoreditch Teacher Training College near London, and a surprise appearance in New York's Central Park with protégée Kiki Dee.

During 1978, the British musician who began teaching himself to play piano when he was only four and who was playing with a band called Bluesology at age fourteen, has continued to keep a low profile. He's changed record labels, was interviewed by David Frost, and made some appearances kicking a soccer ball around. Other than that, Elton has continued his well-earned rest. After seven years of nonstop, sold-out performing and an extraordinarily prolific writing and recording career, it is certainly time.

It's hard to believe that with all his musical talent and the force of his personality Elton John should have had a difficult time getting started in the business, but after he left his first band, Bluesology, which eventually played as back-up band for John Baldry, it took him a long time to find work. He met Bernie Taupin in the late sixties, and the lyricist and composer worked well together. They worked on salary for years in the offices of music publisher Dick James, trying to turn out top-forty middle-of-the-road material.

Elton and Bernie finally decided the only way to succeed was to do what they liked best, which happened to be hard, fast, no-nonsense rock and roll. Their first album, *Empty Sky,* was released in 1969, and the second, *Elton John,* in 1970. This was the first album to be issued in the United States; with it, Elton felt he was ready to show America how a real star of the seventies acted. His first appearance, in August 1970, at Los Angeles's famed Troubadour Club, did just that. By the end of the evening, cynical critics were jumping all over each other in their search for adjectives to describe the juggernaut that was Elton John. From that night on there was no stopping him. It was hit single after hit single, from albums like *Tumbleweed Connection; 17 – 11 = 70;* the soundtrack to the movie *Friends; Madman Across the Water; Honky Chateau; Don't Shoot Me, I'm Only the Piano Player; Goodbye Yellow Brick Road; Blue Moves.* Then, in 1975, Elton debuted as the Pinball Wizard in Ken Russell's outrageous film spectacular *Tommy,* based on the Who's rock opera. His record company, Rocket, has also flourished.

QUINCY JONES

His 1978 album, *Sounds and Stuff Like That,* featuring the talents of

Ian Anderson

Billy Joel

Elton John

Journey

Quincy Jones

241

such contemporary giants as Hubert Laws, Herbie Hancock, Ashford & Simpson, and Chaka Khan, leaped onto the pop charts as number forty-six and climbed rapidly from there, quickly becoming his third gold LP. "Stuff Like That" became a number-one soul single. The zip with which those disks achieved success is a reflection of the fierce energy with which Quincy Jones has always poured his soul into music. Born in Chicago, raised in Seattle, Quincy was playing trumpet for Billie Holiday and writing and arranging with buddy Ray Charles by the time he was fourteen. At the age of fifteen he was ready to hit the road with Lionel Hampton, but Mrs. Gladys Hampton pushed him off the bus with a heartfelt "Get that child out of here. Let him finish school!!"

Quincy won a scholarship to the Berklee College of Music in Boston, where he somehow managed to cram in ten courses a day in addition to playing in strip joints at night to pay his rent. He soon began adding weekends in New York, where he played with the titans of jazz: Art Tatum, Thelonious Monk, Charlie Parker, Miles Davis. He toured Europe with Lionel Hampton's Premier Band and fell in love with Paris, where he worked as musical director at Barclay Disques and studied classical composition with the famed Nadia Boulanger. While in Paris he swept up European awards as Best New Arranger and Composer.

Back in New York in 1961, Quincy began working for Mercury Records, where he starred as vice-president, recording artist, arranger, and producer. During those years he produced, arranged, and wrote for a galaxy of stars, including Ray Charles, Frank Sinatra, Sammy Davis, Sarah Vaughan, Andy Williams, Johnny Mathis, Tony Bennett, Glen Campbell, B. B. King, and Count Basie.

He expanded his musical repertoire even further when he wrote the score for Sidney Lumet's film *The Pawnbroker*. Since then he has scored more than thirty major motion pictures and numerous television shows, gathering Academy and Emmy awards. His most recent was the 1977 Emmy for "Roots." His most recent film score was for *The Wiz*. During his twenty-five-year career he has won thirty-seven Grammy nominations and seven Grammies.

In 1976, he once again broadened his musical world when he collaborated with the Brothers Johnson, helping them win a platinum album.
1978 Discography: *Sounds and Stuff Like That*

JOURNEY

Steve Perry—Vocals

Aynsley Dunbar—Drums

Ross Valory—Bass

Gregg Rolie—Keyboards, vocals

Neal Schon—Guitars

Journey's musical adventures began at the end of 1973 when Gregg Rolie, Neal Schon, Aynsley Dunbar, and Ross Valory made their crackling debut on New Year's Eve in San Francisco's Winterland. Following that appearance, they seared 100,000 music fans on New Year's Day, 1974, at Hawaii's annual Sunshine Festival. Their combination of hard-rock punch and wicked Latin rhythms captivated audiences from the very beginning.

All of the group's original members have stellar credentials. Gregg Rolie was a cofounder of Santana and played on four of that band's platinum albums. Neal Schon, who at the advanced age of sixteen declined Eric Clapton's offer to play with Derek and the Dominos, cut two albums with Santana and played with Graham Central Station. Aynsley Dunbar, a Liverpudlian, played with John Mayall's Bluesbreakers, formed two bands of his own—Retaliation and Blue Whale—and then joined with the Mothers of Invention. He accompanied Flo and Eddie when they left Frank Zappa's lunatic bunch and worked on sessions with Jeff Beck, Lou Reed, and David Bowie. Ross Valory, a veteran of San Francisco's 1960s Haight Ashbury scene, worked with the Steve Miller Band. Steve Perry, Journey's newest addition, was a member of Tim Bogart's band. His

dramatic vocals add a soulful dimension to Journey's instrumental sound.

The band's reputation has built slowly and steadily through three masterful albums—*Journey, Looking Into the Future*, and *Next*. Their latest, *Infinity*, was their first gold disk, and at this writing is steaming along toward platinum.
1978 Discography: *Infinity*

K

KANSAS

Kerry Livgren—Guitar, keyboards

Robby Steinhardt—Violins, vocals

Steve Walsh—Keyboards, vocals

Phil Ehart—Drums, percussion

Dave Hope—Bass

Rich Williams—Guitars

For those of us whose knowledge of Kansas comes from *The Wizard of Oz*, it might be hard to believe that a group of flatlanders could create such intense blasts of white-hot rock, combining classically influenced melodies with laser-precise rhythms. As Kansas's composer and cofounder Kerry Livgren explained to *Seventeen* magazine, "Our band sounds the way it does because we grew up in a place—Topeka, Kansas—that had absolutely no musical tradition." So the six high school chums (four of them knew each other from junior high) drew on all the music they had ever heard and began their own tradition, blending rock with classical overtones and creating a blistering meld that is entirely unique.

After becoming a group in 1971, Kansas paid their dues in nonstop tours of wild and woolly midwestern and southern clubs. They got their first break when Don Kirshner heard them and signed them to his label at the end of 1972. Their first three albums—*Kansas, Song for America*, and *Masque*—were modest sellers, but in 1977 their fourth album, *Leftoverture*, smashed through to a fabulous 2 million plus in sales. "Carry on Wayward Son," the single from the album, became a top-ten pop hit. In 1978, their juggernaut continued, as *Point of Know Return* sailed to double-platinum certification and their haunting single, "Dust in the Wind," became a top-ten hit as well.

In late 1977 and early 1978, they swept through fifty-four American cities in a large-scale tour. Tickets for their March tour of Europe were snapped up in hours, and SRO audiences throughout the continent cheered them on. A June 29 concert at Madison Square Garden was greeted by the joyful howls of hard-to-please New Yorkers, who agree that the Midwest has something quite special in Kansas.
1978 Discography: *Point of Know Return*

THE KENDALLS

Royce Kendall—Vocals, guitar

Jeannie Kendall—Vocals

Born and raised in the crushing poverty of northern Arkansas at the tail end of the depression, Royce Kendall began playing guitar when he was five. By the time he was eight, he was playing on the radio with his brother. But music wasn't Royce's choice of a career. After the army and several civilian jobs, Royce got married, and he and wife Melba finally settled down in St. Louis, where they ran a barbershop/beauty salon.

Although Royce had decided not to pursue music as a profes-

Kansas

The Kendalls

Kris Kristofferson

Kiss

sion, he did a lot of singing around the house. When daughter Jeannie became a teen-ager, the two of them began singing harmony at home. Royce and his wife realized that he and Jeannie had voices that naturally blended, and, based on his early radio experiences, he felt they could succeed in Nashville if they gave it a try.

So, in 1969, backed by the encouragement of friends and neighbors, the Kendalls took a trip to Nashville and cut a custom record. They were promptly signed by Pete Drake to his STOP Records, a small Nashville label. At the urging of folk-fan Jeannie, the duo cut a country version of "Leavin' On a Jet Plane," which became a top-twenty success on the country charts. With this positive indication, the Kendalls packed away their tonsorial gear and moved to Nashville for good.

It was the right move. Their sweet country harmonies were immediately in demand, and their singles hit the country charts again and again. They signed to one of Nashville's hottest labels, ABC/Dot, where they stayed for three years and enjoyed success with several country hits. But disagreements caused them to move to United Artists, where they found the situation not much better. "Jeannie always said, 'If we don't like our own records, how can anyone else like them?'" Royce recalls, "So, we just decided if we couldn't record the way we thought was right, we wouldn't record at all."

For several months they were without a recording contract. Then, in 1976, they met Brian Fisher, a producer for Ovation who was looking for a strong act to kick off that company's move into country. Their first single for Ovation, "Making Believe," did well on the charts until it met resistance from Emmylou Harris's version of the same song. Then, in the middle of 1977, they released a second single, "Live and Let Live," which did respectably but was not a smash. However, they began to get reports that when the B side, "Heaven's Just a Sin Away," was played, radio stations were besieged by phone calls.

Before long the song was a firm country number one and remained so for four weeks. The album of the same name became a top-five country hit. And that was just the beginning of the big country fame that had eluded the Kendalls on two top country labels. That big song won them a Grammy for Best Country Vocal Performance by a Duo. It was followed by "It Don't Feel Like Sinning to Me," another top-ten country single, and "Pittsburgh Stealers," their summer smash. Their 1978 LP, *Old Fashioned Love*, was another top-ten country winner.

1978 Discography: *Old Fashioned Love*

KISS

Paul Stanley—Guitar
Ace Frehley—Guitar
Gene Simmons—Bass
Peter Criss—Drums

After five years of increasingly sensational stage shows, five platinum albums, and a barrage of articles proclaiming them the most outrageous rock band in the world, Kiss took the opportunity of a small, free concert at Magic Mountain Amusement Park in Los Angeles to announce a year's wait between albums. Although there are plans for individual albums by each member of the band—and for television and film projects—there will be no group album until June, 1979.

The fans took it well. To sustain them, they have *Alive II* and the ironically titled *Double Platinum*, the latest platinum efforts, NBC-TV's Halloween special, "Kiss Meets the Phantom," to say nothing of Kiss warm-up suits, a second Kiss superhero comic book, bubble gum cards, and, best of all, Kiss dolls. There was also the titillating gossip about Gene Simmons and Cher to keep fans from losing interest. But there will be a definite gap in the touring rosters and the record bins with no new Kiss product to set the blood boiling in young heads.

Since 1973, when their flaming madness first erupted on stages across the country, Kiss has been worshipped by a riotous group of young teen-agers, whose roaring response to their onstage antics

sometimes competed with the music of the band. Those fans took Kiss to their hearts with the ferocious love of the very young. They emulated their heroes by donning imitations of their bizarre makeup, even going so far as to endanger life and limb by aping Gene Simmons's fire-breathing tricks.

From the beginning, the band wanted to create and project a strong image. At their first concerts in a club called Coventry, in Queens, New York, Kiss began to experiment with their makeup. They were soon spotted by TV producer Bill Aucoin, who saw their potential, became their manager, and signed them to Neil Bogart's Casablanca Records. They were Casablanca's first act, and although their first three albums—*Kiss, Hotter than Hell,* and *Dressed to Kill*—did well, it was *Alive,* their first live recording, that was the commercial breakthrough, selling well over 2 million copies in the United States alone.

After that, the Kiss express just kept on screaming along: *Rock and Roll Over, Love Gun,* and *Alive II* sold millions; Kiss products, from T-shirts to love guns, were eagerly snapped up; a 1977 Gallup poll named them the number-one band; the *New York Times* called them an outrage. Kiss is unique, and their fans look forward to their 1979 incarnation.

1978 Discography: *Double Platinum*

KRIS KRISTOFFERSON

Kris Kristofferson's training is light-years away from the background of most country stars. Born the son of a major general in Brownsville, Texas, he attended Pomona College in California, majoring in creative writing and winning the top four out of twenty prizes offered in *The Atlantic Monthly* short-story contest. He then went on to Oxford University as a Rhodes Scholar for two years. At Oxford he began to write songs, but after a stint in the army he planned to teach English literature at West Point. A temporary detour to Nashville turned into a five-year stay in Music City paying his dues—working as a janitor in Columbia's Recording Studios and bartending at the landmark Tally Ho Tavern.

In 1969, his dues-paying period ended resoundingly when the posthumous release of Janis Joplin's recording of his song "Me and Bobby McGee" became a best-seller. By 1970, the *New York Times* was calling Kristofferson "the hottest thing in Nashville." In that year Kristofferson won the Country Music Song of the Year Award, and the Nashville Songwriter's Association gave him the Songwriter of the Year Award as well. His hit songs since that period have included such moving ballads as "Sunday Mornin' Comin' Down," "Help Me Make It Through the Night," "Loving Her Was Easier (Than Anything I'll Ever Do Again)," "Josie," and "The Pilgrim, Chapter 33." At the end of 1977 he and Combine Music Publishing Company received awards from BMI for 3 million performances of "Me and Bobby McGee," "Help Me Make It Through the Night," and "For the Good Times."

In addition to his singing career, Kristofferson now has a blossoming acting career as well. Since his well-reviewed debut in the film *Cisco Pike,* he has been featured or starred in such films as *Alice Doesn't Live Here Any More, Pat Garrett and Billy the Kid, Bring Me the Head of Alfredo Garcia, Blume in Love, Vigilante Force, The Sailor that Fell from Grace with the Sea, A Star Is Born, Semi-Tough,* and 1978's *Convoy.*

In 1973, he married Rita Coolidge, and when he's not touring (often with his lovely wife), working on a film, or recording, he retires to his Malibu Beach home where he and Rita live with daughter Casey.

1978 Discography: *Easter Island*

RONNIE LAWS

At the beginning of 1978, Ronnie Laws' brilliant 1977 album, *Friends* and Strangers, became his first gold-winner. Of course, anyone who had observed the Laws family throughout the years would have needed no precognitive talents to know that musical success would touch Ronnie. Music is in his genes. The thriller-killer saxophone player was born to Miolla Laws, a gospel pianist who lived and breathed music. She brought up older brother Hubert to become a world-famous jazz and classical flutist and older sister Eloise to be a successful actress/singer. Although these three had awesome credentials for Ronnie to live up to, they also provided a milieu of music in which his talents could flourish.

For Ronnie there was never any doubt that he would pick up a musical instrument. When he was twelve he chose the alto sax, switching from alto to tenor sax in high school and mastering the flute in college. Music was his companion throughout his teen-age years. When other kids in Houston were playing hide and seek, Ronnie was watching a group of local teen-agers rehearse their jazz band. The group later became the Crusaders, and through them Ronnie became a part of the varied and busy Houston music scene.

Although Ronnie won a total of $18,000 in scholarships from Berklee College of Music and Juilliard, he chose to stay in Texas and attend Stephen F. Austin University. After two years there, feeling he would learn more from actual playing experience, he and his new wife Karmen moved to Los Angeles.

There his jazz background was enriched by rock and rhythm and blues as he played with hard-rocking Von Ryan's Express, as well as with Quincy Jones, Walter Bishop, and the dynamic Earth, Wind and Fire. After a stint with Hugh Masekela, Laws freelanced, playing with several bands. He soon signed with Blue Note, where his first album, Pressure Sensitive, became the largest-selling debut album in that label's history.

In 1976, he won awards from Record World and Billboard and applause from fellow performers such as Elton John, Jeff Beck, Lamont Dozier, and Eric Clapton.

Pressure Sensitive was followed by the hard-edged Fever, and his third, Friends and Strangers, even more pop oriented than his earlier disks, became his first gold album.

GORDON LIGHTFOOT

Gordon Lightfoot's music shimmers with the light of lakes and mountains. In gently beautiful songs like "Early Morning Rain," "If You Could Read My Mind," "Sundown," and "The Last Time I Saw Her," he creates a mood of lush nostalgia. Following in the tradition of those finely crafted songs is his 1978 hit, "The Circle Is Small."

Gordon's musical career began stumblingly in 1960, when he began to write in a country mode. The early Dylan, as he did for so many others, enlightened Gordon to the wider possibilities of songs. His music became more personal and expressive of himself. And the words began to flow. Today he has written more than four hundred songs. Often, in the early days, you could find an intensely concentrating Gordon, locked in a hotel room for five days at a stretch, creating at a furious rate.

Today, he says, that pace has slowed down somewhat. "Now," he relates, "I usually settle into an abode somewhere, and live there for about a year or so before moving on. What I have written by the end of that period is usually what appears on my current album." Gordon writes from his own experience, blending past and present in vivid word pictures.

Until a few years ago, when he chose to slack off his touring pace, Gordon would do more than seventy concerts a year. He creates his performances with great care, saying, "I try to set up a coffeehouse atmosphere at center stage, a small, intimate space where everyone's thoughts are focused on the same thing at the same time. I always keep in mind that everyone has to go through the hassle of buying the ticket and getting to the hall and all that, so it's up to me to give out a good feeling in return—musically, emotionally,

sound-wise, etcetera. I try never to give my audience less than they expect, nor do I ever take them for granted." As the gold award given to Endless Wire, his latest LP, testifies, Gordon's fans never take him for granted, either.
1978 Discography: Endless Wire

LITTLE RIVER BAND

Glenn Shorrock—Lead vocals

Beeb Birtles—Vocals, guitars

David Briggs—Lead guitar

Graham Goble—Guitars

George McArdle—Bass

Derek Pellicci—Drums and percussion

Like a growing number of international music stars, Little River Band hails from down under. The group formed in Australia in 1975, although the four original members of the band had first met in England in 1974, where three of them had been playing with a group called Mississippi. Their first album, Little River Band, was recorded in Melbourne, and in mid-1976 the band toured the United States, Germany, and Great Britain, quickly establishing themselves as serious contenders in the battle for the pop musical crown. With their main influences being the Buffalo Springfield, Crosby, Stills, Nash & Young, and Poco, it's no wonder that their sound is heavily laced with sweet vocal harmonies. Their three lead guitars are used with tasteful imagination; the sound is always crisp and clean.

In 1977, they released Diamantina Cocktail, which sold more than 1 million copies around the world and was a gold-winner in the United States. The group toured for a back-breaking five-month stretch in 1977, hitting North America, Europe, and Japan. In 1978, Sleeper Catcher, their current album, was also a million-copy international seller before it was released. Their 1978 tour, a little less bonecrushing than 1977's, was a three-month summer circuit, followed by a European tour later in the fall.
1978 Discography: Sleeper Catcher

L. T. D.

Arthur Lorenzo Carnegie—Saxophones

Henry Davis—Bass, piano, flute, saxophone

Jake Riley, Jr.—Trombone

Abraham Joseph "Onion" Miller, Jr.—Saxophones

Carle Vickers—Trumpet, flugelhorn, saxophones, flute

Johnny McGhee—Guitar

Jeff Osborne—Lead vocals, drums

Billy Osborne—Lead vocals, percussion, keyboards

Jimmy "J. D." Davis—Piano

Melvin Webb—Percussion

It takes the qualities of Love, Tenderness, and Devotion—abbreviated to L. T. D.—for a nine-man group to stay together for almost a decade, through all kinds of adversity, trauma, and trials. Luckily, when they first began making music together in North Carolina in 1968, they couldn't foresee the hard scuffling they would have to do before they achieved success.

The band worked in Florida for a while, then traveled up and down the East Coast, settling in New York in 1969. There they played top-forty music in bars and clubs, trying all the time to develop their own sound. In 1970, after meeting with rejection from all the major

Gordon Lightfoot

Loretta Lynn

Ronnie Laws

L.T.D.

246

Little River Band

record companies in the East, they drove to California. But the coast was not golden for them, and it was back to fifty-dollar gigs to pay the rent.

At the end of 1971, with a lot of gruelling L.A. night club experience behind them and an armload of rejections from West Coast record companies, the band took some time off to work in Japan for ten weeks, where they were adored—a welcome relief from the frustrations they were facing in the United States.

Finally, in 1973, they signed with A & M. Although their first two albums, *Love, Togetherness and Devotion* and *Gittin' Down,* were not chart-burners, the group gained experience and a growing audience as they began to tour with name bands, opening for the O'Jays, Average White Band, Bob Seger, Aerosmith, and Harold Melvin and the Blue Notes.

Their third album, *Love to the World,* contained their first number-one R & B hit, "Love Ballad." With their first success came business problems, dislocation, and an internal crisis that almost broke them up. But luck was with them, as they were introduced to arranger/producer Bobby Martin, who inspired their first gold album, *Something to Love,* with its chart-topping gold single "Back in Love Again." Their success story continues in 1978 as *Togetherness,* their latest album, was a gold-winner and fast climber on the pop charts.

1978 Discography: *Togetherness*

LORETTA LYNN

If double-platinum awards were given for books, Loretta Lynn's autobiography, *Coal Miner's Daughter,* would have one. The fascinating story of her life has now sold more than 2 million copies in the United States alone. Filming of the book began this year, and its release in 1979 should see the first lady of country music win millions of new fans.

Loretta's career has never stopped building. Married when she was thirteen, she and husband Mooney Lynn immediately began to raise a family. Singing had always come naturally to her, and after she, her husband, and her growing brood moved to Custer, Washington, Mooney encouraged her to continue writing and to develop her singing.

Before long she was singing in a local club, and her first record, "Honky Tonk Girl," was the one she and Mooney decided to push. They would pack up their old car with kids and bologna sandwiches and drive around the countryside. With Loretta's bubbly determination tearing down the resistance of hardened DJs, they finally agreed to listen to her song. The DJs liked what they heard and played it on the air; before long the song had climbed into the country top ten. Soon, all Loretta's songs were making it not only to the top ten but to number one on the charts.

Determination was the ingredient that got her songs heard, but it was musical talent that created such top country masterpieces as "One's on the Way," "You Ain't Woman Enough to Take My Man," "Don't Come Home A-Drinkin' (With Lovin' on Your Mind)," "Coal Miner's Daughter," "She's Got You," and her 1978 hit "Out of My Head and Back in My Bed" from the album of the same name.

In 1978, Loretta also scored with appearances with Conway Twitty, first at performances at the Montgomery Civic Center in Alabama, where they became the first country act ever to sell out that hall. In April, she and Conway appeared at the White House in a country-music performance for President and Mrs. Carter and some two hundred guests. "From Seven till Ten/You're the Reason Our Kids Are Ugly" was a top-ten country single for the team. In 1978, she won the American Music Award as the Favorite Female Country Vocalist, and she and Conway Twitty won as Favorite Country Duo. Her concert successes included her debut as a headliner at the Aladdin Theatre in Las Vegas, where she did so well during her first engagement that she was invited back to perform for seven more weeks during the year, plus additional weeks at Harrah's in Reno and Lake Tahoe.

1978 Discography: *Out of My Head and Back in My Bed*

M

CHUCK MANGIONE

Why is this man smiling so ecstatically in all his 1978 photographs? First of all, *Feels So Good,* his 1978 jazz–pop winner, has sold half a million copies and has achieved gold status, a rarity among jazz recordings. Add to that the Grammy Award he picked up in 1977 for Best Instrumental Composition for *Bellavia,* the success of his second 1978 album, *Children of Sanchez,* his numerous television appearances, the many scores he's composed for television shows, and his warm, fulfilled family life and it's easy to see why all photos of Chuck Mangione reflect an entirely joyful expression.

Mangione's exciting success in 1978 was the culmination of a life of hard work and dedication to music, a life that began in 1940 in Rochester, New York. After closing his grocery store at night, Chuck's father, an avid jazz fan, would take Chuck and his brothers to hear jazz greats at nearby clubs. After the show, he would introduce himself to the musicians and invite them home for dinner. Mrs. Mangione would serve up a spaghetti sauce so good that Chuck still has supplies of it delivered to him on the road.

After seeing the film *Young Man with a Horn,* Chuck chose the trumpet as his instrument and began lessons at the age of ten. In high school he and his brother Gap formed a quintet called the Jazz Brothers and cut several albums for Riverside. College was the prestigious Eastman School of Music, where Chuck was dissatisfied at the lack of a jazz program. Today he wishes he had taken more advantage of the many opportunities the school offered for learning other types of music. Despite his dissatisfaction, he did accomplish many things at Eastman, not the least of which were his mastering of the flugelhorn and his composition of "Feel of a Vision" for classmate Lew Soloff, who went on to play trumpet with the original Blood, Sweat and Tears.

In 1965, after a year of teaching music in Rochester, he traveled to New York to free-lance; late in that year he landed the trumpet spot with Art Blakey and the Jazz Messengers. He stayed with them for two and a half years in a quintet featuring Keith Jarrett, and (later) Chick Corea. He then returned to Rochester, where he wrote for a rock group; when the group broke up, he taught at the Hochstein School of Music in Rochester.

His career really began to take off when, while teaching at Eastman in 1969, Chuck hired fifty musicians and staged a concert of his music. The concert, called *Kaleidoscope,* attracted the attention of Rochester Philharmonic Orchestra manager Tom Iannaccone, who invited Chuck to conduct the Philharmonic in a concert of Chuck's music. *Friends and Love,* as the May 9, 1970, concert was called, was a terrific success. A live album of the concert was also successful and led to a recording contract, a Grammy nomination, and the beginning of hard touring, recording, television appearances, and, eventually, his contract with A & M Records.

1978 Discography: *Children of Sanchez*

BARRY MANILOW

It's been another one of those years for Barry Manilow—so jammed with one astounding success after another that one wonders when he finds the time to compose. He ended 1977 with a top-ten easy-listening song, "Daybreak." In November, he won the American Music Award as Favorite Pop–Rock Vocalist. His lilting single "I Can't Smile Without You" was a top-ten pop, a number-one easy-listening hit, and his fourth gold single. His album *Even Now,* a top-ten LP its fourth week on the charts, became gold, and the title single from the album was a number-one easy-listening hit and a top-ten smash. The bouncy, 40s-flavored disco tour de force "Copacabana" was a top-ten hit, and "Ready to Take a Chance," from the film *Foul Play,* was another success. As a matter of fact, at the beginning of 1978 Barry Manilow's albums sold 3 million copies in ten weeks. And, oh, yes,

Chuck Mangione Courtesy A & M Records

Barry Manilow Gene Trindel

The Marshall Tucker Band

"The Second Barry Manilow Special," aired on ABC-TV at the end of February, featuring the legendary Ray Charles, was universally applauded.

All of this is simply the way Barry's career has evolved, with its roots in a Brooklyn childhood in a house where there was always music, including early accordion lessons for him. But although he loved music, it wasn't until he had worked in the advertising field that he decided music was his life.

Once he had made that decision, he switched from City College of New York to New York College of Music and finally to Juilliard. To support himself while going to school at night, he worked during the day in the mailroom at CBS. There a director asked him to do some arranging for a television production, and from that moment on there was no stopping the nervy kid from Brooklyn.

His career seemingly has had no dull or rough spots. Instead it's been one highlight after another, ranging from his association with Bette Midler as musical director, arranger, and pianist (he coproduced and arranged her first, Grammy-winning LP, *The Divine Miss M*) to his gold and platinum LPs (*Barry Manilow Live, Tryin' to Get the Feeling,* and *This One's for You* have now reached the double platinum mark), to the music he's written for such songs as "It's a Miracle," "This One's for You," and "Daybreak" and his thrilling performances of such smashes as "Mandy," "Tryin' to Get the Feeling Again," "This One's for You," "Weekend in New England," "Looks Like We Made It," and "I Write the Songs."

On March 2, 1977, ABC-TV presented Manilow's first network television show, "The Barry Manilow Special," which drew an estimated audience of 37 million viewers. He has also appeared on Broadway and for his brief sold-out engagement won a special Tony, Broadway's equivalent to the Oscar.

1978 Discography: *Even Now*
Barry Manilow's Greatest Hits

THE MARSHALL TUCKER BAND

Tommy Caldwell–Bass, vocals

Toy Caldwell–Guitars, vocals

George McCorkel–Guitar

Doug Gray–Vocals, percussion

Paul Riddle–Drums, percussion

Jerry Eubanks–Saxophone, flute, vocals

In May, the Marshall Tucker Band's 1978 album, *Together Forever,* became their sixth gold-winner, and *Carolina Dreams,* 1977's big one, became their second platinum. Since 1970, when the band came together in Spartanburg, North Carolina, as the Toy Factory, they've been turning out a blistering fusion of rock, country, R & B, and western swing that has always set audiences jumping.

In 1972, after growing from a trio to the current sextet, they changed their name, adopting that of a blind piano-tuner friend from their hometown. In 1973, they signed with Capricorn, label of the then all-mighty Allman Brothers. The Marshall Tucker Band, touring for the first time as openers for the Allmans, gave them some powerful competition. Reviewers and audiences, expecting to be able to chatter mindlessly during the opening act, found themselves swept up and carried away by the dead-ahead, fierce energy of Marshall Tucker. No ordinary opening band, this.

Realizing that the place for them to win fans was on the road, the band toured three hundred days a year for the first few years, doggedly tuning up and blasting out in nightclubs, colleges, auditoriums, small theaters, outdoor venues, and wherever else they could gather an audience.

Their heavy touring paid off. Their first album was an immediate success, and they had achieved fame almost entirely through albums and tours. In 1977, "Heard It in a Love Song" became their first hit single.

1978 Discography: *Together Forever*

STEVE MARTIN

Steve Martin and his happy feet have been tickling risibilities with a combination of wacky wit and physical comedy for more than sixteen years. At age sixteen, billed as Mouth and Magic, Steve Martin wowed 'em while performing at Disneyland's Golden Horseshoe Revue. Today, with his first album, *Let's Get Small,* a Grammy-winner and a platinum monster and his top-charted single "King Tut" a delightful surprise, Steve's at the top of his form.

His fans attend his concerts with phony arrows stuck through their heads and sport glasses with funny noses attached, just as he does in his routines. They respond gleefully to his loony escapism and his complete lack of hostility. Unlike the sharp comedians of the early sixties or the socially conscious ones of the late sixties and early seventies, Martin is part of a new breed of comics whose humor comes from poking gentle fun at the overinflated—including themselves. Hearing his off-the-wall routines, it's hard to believe that Martin majored in metaphysics, logical positivism, and semantics at Long Beach State College before switching to UCLA, where he began to major in theater.

He worked as a comic in local clubs and then was tapped by the Smothers Brothers to write for their television series. Martin was immediately successful as a comedy writer. After the Smothers Brothers program folded he wrote for "The Glen Campbell Good-Time Hour." (He quit that one after two weeks because he thought it was dumb.) Then he wrote for Ray Stevens, Sonny and Cher, Pat Paulsen, John Denver, and Dick Van Dyke.

Writing, however, wasn't enough for him. "I did a couple of summer shows and then I realized . . . I gotta get back to performing."

Although all his friends advised him against it, Martin persisted, choosing the most difficult route possible for his first performances: working as an opener for rock acts. The last thing rock fans wanted to see was a comedy act, and Martin suffered the inglorious fate of inattention.

In 1973, Martin left Los Angeles, lived with a girl friend in Santa Fe for a year, and then settled in Aspen. He changed his image to his current white-suited one and swore he would never do another opening act.

His stage show grew in daffiness and popularity, and by the end of 1975 he was a sellout in San Francisco's well-known Boarding House. In the fall of 1976, he made his national breakthrough with a Home Box Office special and his first guest-host appearance on "Saturday Night Live."

1978 Discography: *A Wild and Crazy Guy*

JOHNNY MATHIS

Since 1957, the magical warmth of Johnny Mathis's voice has been casting its romantic spell on lovers the world over. In 1978, an inspired pairing with Deniece Williams on the song "Too Much, Too Little, Too Late" has given his career a new boost. The single zipped to number one on soul, easy-listening, and pop charts, becoming, surprisingly enough, Johnny's first top-charted hit in twenty-one years and winning the two singers their first gold record as a duo. For Mathis, 1978's honors included his own television special on PBS and a tour of the United Kingdom with Deniece Williams, capped by a sold-out command performance for Prince Charles at the London Palladium. His latest album, *You Light Up My Life,* became his tenth gold-winner and scored top-ten success on the soul and pop charts.

This, of course, is not the first time such exciting success has touched Mathis. Beginning in 1957, when Mitch Miller, then an executive for Columbia Records, spotted him singing in a local club, Mathis's made-for-lovers voice and music have won him millions of fans. His career has included such unforgettable songs as "Wonderful! Wonderful!" "Chances Are," "It's Not for Me to Say," "The Twelfth of Never," and other loving ballads that have become indelibly wed to his style and his voice. His best-selling album, 1958's *Johnny's Greatest Hits,* remains to this day the only pop album ever to be on the charts for 490 consecutive weeks—more than nine years! About this,

Steve Martin

Johnny Mathis

Zubin Mehta

Maze

251

Bette Midler

Liza Minnelli

Ronnie Milsap

Steve Miller

David Alexander

Joni Mitchell

Norman Seeff

252

Johnny comments wryly, "I think I can say my style has done pretty well for me through the years."

His 1978 success represents a new direction for Mathis. Always an R & B fan, Mathis and producer Jack Gold decided it was time for him to reach that market. They reasoned it would be easier if they teamed Mathis with someone already well known to the R & B audience. Deniece Williams was a natural choice, and the excitement sparked by the two singers was mutually beneficial, winning the R & B crowd for Johnny and scoring pop success for Deniece.

1978 Discography: *You Light Up My Life*
That's What Friends Are for (with Deniece Williams)

MAZE FEATURING FRANKIE BEVERLY

Frankie Beverly–Vocals, rhythm guitar

Ronald "Roame" Lowry–Vocals, congas

McKinley "Bug" Williams–Vocals, percussion

Wayne Thomas–Lead guitar

Robin Duhe–Bass

Sam Porter–Keyboards

Ahaguna G. Sun–Drums

Throughout 1977, *Maze Featuring Frankie Beverly*, by the band of the same name, quietly sold three-quarters of a million copies. Its steadily swelling sales were not the result of a frenetic advertising campaign or inflated media hype; this was a low-budget first album. But the disk was backed by a summer of hard touring: In city after city the soulful, driving songs of Frankie Beverly and Maze sent hundreds of thousands of new fans skidding into record stores to buy the album.

Two strong hit singles, "While I'm Alone" and "Lady of Magic," made forays into the soul and pop charts, and in addition to those hits, Maze enjoyed a disco success with "Time Is on My Side," winning them the title the Most Promising Disco Group at the 1977 Popular Music Disco Awards show in New York City.

It may seem that Maze sprang out of nowhere to achieve swift success, but Frankie Beverly, the band's founder, songwriter, and leader, has been singing and creating music since he began to talk. The Philadelphia-born soulman went on to form numerous groups in his late teens. These evolved into Frankie Beverly and Raw Soul, a band that recorded two singles for RCA in the early 1970s and toured extensively with Kool and the Gang, Mandrill, and Isaac Hayes.

In San Francisco in 1972, where they had been living for several years, paying their dues in small rock clubs, honing down the group to its present core, they finally attracted the attention of Marvin Gaye, who loved their sound and offered them creative guidance and support. Maze got the opportunity to open for Gaye and backed him in several concerts.

Maze was signed to Capitol Records in 1976 and, after the success of their first album, released *Golden Time of the Day* at the beginning of 1978. The album has already earned gold certification, and its first single, the driving "Working Together," leaped into the top ten of the soul charts.

1978 Discography: *Golden Time of the Day*

ZUBIN MEHTA

In the fall of 1978, renowned conductor Zubin Mehta continued his illustrious career as music director of the New York Philharmonic.

For the past fifteen years he was music director of the Los Angeles Philharmonic Orchestra (at twenty-six, he was that orchestra's youngest permanent conductor). His career has included such highlights as winning the First International Conductors' competition in Liverpool, England, in 1958; performing or recording in such diverse places as the Salzburg Festival, the front line during the 1973 Middle East War, before audiences at a Southern California men's prison; conducting the London Royal Opera House production of *Die Fledermaus,* the first opera transmitted by satellite from Europe to the United States; conducting for the Metropolitan Opera; in 1977 and 1978, leading the Los Angeles Philharmonic in a series of laser-lit concerts called Music from Outer Space; and on September 24 conducting the New York Philharmonic and Vladimir Horowitz in a performance of the Rachmaninoff Third Piano Concerto, telecast live from Lincoln Center by ABC.

Born in Bombay in 1936, the son of the founder of the Bombay Symphony, Mehta was, as he puts it, "brainwashed with classical music from the cradle." At age seven he began studying violin and piano, and, by the time he was eleven, he was helping his father with orchestral chores.

Mehta's father, however, seeing little future for Western music in India, pushed his son into premedical courses. But Zubin could never ignore music. It was in his blood and on his mind. "Every time I sat down to write an exam or cut up a dog-fish," he remembers, "there I was with a Brahms symphony running through my head." So, when he was sixteen, Zubin left Bombay for Vienna, where he studied piano, composition, string bass, and finally conducting, at the Academy of Music.

In 1978, his performance of Stravinsky's *The Rite of Spring,* his first recording with the New York Philharmonic, was released by Columbia Masterworks as its February 1978 Record of the Month selection and became a classical best-seller.

1978 Discography: *The Rite of Spring*
Music from Star Wars and Close Encounters

BETTE MIDLER

When the Divine Miss M shakes her improbable red curls, bumps and grinds her impossibly voluptuous body, belts out songs with inexhaustibly lusty pipes, and banters with her inimitable raunchiness, audiences are simply swept away by the infectious charge of frantic energy. Bette (pronounced Bet, not Betty) struts and prances and dances, displaying every side of herself; she is adored because her audiences see in her endless possibilities for having a good time.

From her fabled discovery at New York's Continental Baths to her $1.8-million Broadway success in her *Clams on the Half-Shell Revue,* it's been a Cinderella story for this Hawaiian-raised trouper. She had always loved the theater, and she financed her early career attempts with the usual series of odd jobs—typing, filing, department store clerking, even a stint of go-go dancing. But she was always on the lookout for acting work, and she achieved her first success in the Broadway production of *Fiddler on the Roof,* where she began as a member of the chorus and left three years later in the important role of Tzeitel, Tevye's oldest daughter.

It was that role that focused her on singing rather than acting. She went on to the Baths, where her campy style was perfect for its homosexual clientele, who adored her. It wasn't long before Saturday nights at the Baths became the hottest ticket in New York, and Bette's local fame was fanned by appearances on national television and open-mouthed critical acclaim. No one had ever seen anyone quite like her, and her first album, *The Divine Miss M,* won her a Grammy as Newcomer of the Year.

After that million-seller came *Bette Midler, Songs for the Depression, Live at Last,* and *Broken Blossom,* her latest. Because her later albums did not make so big a splash as her first, in 1977 there were rumors that her career was in decline. But millions of television viewers took Bette to their hearts in such memorable spectaculars as "The Bette Midler Show," "Ol' Red Hair Is Back," and her refreshing song and patter on "Rolling Stone . . . The Tenth Anniversary Special." Late in 1977 she took off on a seven-city tour of small clubs to balance the television shows. In 1978, Bette also filmed her first motion picture musical, *The Rose.*

253

STEVE MILLER BAND

Steve Miller–Vocals, guitar, synthesizer
Gary Mallaber–Drums
Lonnie Turner–Bass
David Denny–Rhythm guitar
Greg Douglass–Slide guitar
Byron Allred–Keyboards

He doesn't look like a rock star, doesn't act like one, and prefers not to be treated like one. Fame is not important to Steve Miller. Music is.

"I expect to be working on music the rest of my life," Steve Miller told *Crawdaddy* reporter James Trombetta. Miller has been working on music since he was four years old, when he learned basic guitar from Les Paul, a friend of his father's. He continued to work on it when he was in school, at the age of twelve forming a band called the Marksmen Combo. At the University of Wisconsin he put together the Ardells, later known as the Fabulous Knight Train.

He studied literature in Copenhagen for a year, but it was music that pulled him when he got back to the States. In Chicago in the mid-sixties he jammed with such blues greats as Muddy Waters, Buddy Guy, Junior Wells, Otis Rush, Shakey Jake, and Magic Sam. With Paul Butterfield, Mike Bloomfield, and Barry Goldberg, he formed a band that received eleven recording offers the first night they performed.

The late sixties and early seventies found him in San Francisco, the quintessential sixties musical scene. There he formed the Steve Miller Blues Band, with whom he turned out a string of adventurous, fresh, but, alas, only marginally successful albums, including *Children of the Future, Sailor, Brave New World,* and *Your Saving Grace.* It wasn't until 1973 that his small following of devoted fans was able to shout, "I told you so," when Miller's *The Joker* exploded to the top of the charts and won gold honors for itself and the single of the same name.

Atypically, Miller did not follow up that success with a quickie album. "I didn't feel like I had anything really worthwhile to say at the time. I had to go on my own intuition. I had built up an audience over the years and I knew they wouldn't forget me overnight." His intuition was right, and when *Fly like an Eagle* was released two years and eight months after *The Joker,* it soared to the top of the charts, stayed there for more than a year, and sold more than 4.5 million copies around the world. *Book of Dreams,* released in May of 1977, sold more than 2 million copies. After its release, Miller spent most of the year touring the country, playing to audiences composed of new and old fans, who responded joyfully to Miller's hard-edged, highway rock.

At the end of the year, Miller was honored again. He received his fourth gold album for *Anthology,* and he celebrated ten years with Capitol Records. The label's present to him was an Arabian brood mare, a perfect addition to his 312-acre Oregon farm. On June 25, 1978, he and the Beach Boys shared the honor of playing the first rock concert ever in Giants Stadium at The Meadowlands, a mammoth new sports complex in New Jersey.

RONNIE MILSAP

In the fall of 1977, Ronnie Milsap walked off with the Country Music Association awards for Entertainer of the Year, Male Vocalist of the Year, and Album of the Year for his 1977 winner, *Ronnie Milsap Live.* This emphatic confirmation of Milsap's talents was not surprising. It was merely the next step in the natural growth of his phenomenal career, a perhaps predictable follow-up to his capture of the CMA's Male Vocalist of the Year award in 1974, given to him only two years after he began singing country music professionally.

Blind from birth, Ronnie Milsap grew up in Raleigh, North Carolina, where he attended the State School for the Blind. It was there that his innate musical gifts were discovered, and by the time he was twelve he had mastered the violin, piano, and guitar. Although the Raleigh School pushed Bach and Mozart, Ronnie was an avid country-rock fan, and he was suspended more than once for indulging in hot licks when the school felt he should have been engaging in more staid musical pursuits. Eventually, however, school officials realized that Ronnie's talents were too important to be subdued, and they gave his rock group, called the Apparitions, their blessing.

Later, Ronnie abandoned his prelaw studies—even giving up a scholarship to Emory University—so he could continue to perform. He formed his own band in 1966, recorded for Scepter Records, and delighted audiences with an energetic blend of country, rock, and jazz. He had some early record hits with "Denver" and "Loving You Is a Natural Thing," but he was dissatisfied with the music he was creating. He finally realized that he was longing for his roots: country music.

In the early 1970s, Milsap and his wife moved to Nashville. There he signed with Charley Pride's manager, Jack D. Johnson, and accepted a contract with RCA. His first release for them became the double-sided hit "(All Together Now) Let's Fall Apart" and "I Hate You." From then on, backing his country hits with a rolling piano, Milsap turned out one smash after another, including "The Girl Who Waits on Tables," "Pure Love," "Please Don't Tell Me How the Story Ends," "Legend in My Time," "Daydreams about Night Things," and "Let My Love Be Your Pillow."

He won a Grammy as the Best Country Vocalist (Male) for the album *(I'm a) Stand by My Woman Man,* and in 1978 the Milsap hits just kept coming. In February of 1978, *It Was Almost Like a Song* became his first gold album; "What a Difference You Made in My Life" was a number-one country single; his 1978 album, *Only One Love in My Life,* and its title single were top-ten country winners.
1978 Discography: *Only One Love in My Life*

LIZA MINNELLI

Daughter of Judy Garland and the Academy-Award-winning director Vincente Minnelli, Liza Minnelli is a brilliant performer whose career has been meteoric and sensational. An explosion of pure, unleashed energy, from the time of her Tony-awarded Broadway debut in *Flora, the Red Menace,* Liza has been making theatrical history. She was nineteen when she won that first Tony, the youngest actress ever to win for a musical role. In 1973, she captured a second Tony for breaking the box-office record at the Winter Garden in her one-woman show. Her third Tony was grabbed in 1978 for her bravura performance in *The Act.*

Liza also won an Academy Award nomination for her starring role in *The Sterile Cuckoo* and nabbed the best-actress Oscar for her breathtaking performance in the film *Cabaret.* She has also received the highest film awards from Great Britain and Italy.

In 1972, her television special, "Liza with a Z," received an Emmy for Most Outstanding Single Program—Variety and Popular Music. Also in 1972 she was named Female Star of the Year by the National Association of Theatre Owners; she's won the Las Vegas Entertainer of the Year Award for three consecutive years and the American Guild of Variety Artists Entertainer of the Year Award twice.
1978 Discography: *The Act.*

JONI MITCHELL

Her birthplace remains with her as a burr in her voice and a certain northern coolness in her outlook, but other than that there seems to be very little left of Roberta Joan Anderson, daughter of a schoolteacher mother and grocery-store-manager father. Born November 7, 1943, in Fort McLeod, Alberta, Canada, Joni was always regarded as an odd one in her adolescence. At the age of twenty-one she shed a first marriage but kept her new last name. As Joni Mitchell she sang in coffeehouses in Detroit, all the while gathering the strength and confidence to head for New York: a single woman, a fledgling, a future star.

New York was everything she dreamed it would be. She found a community of musicians that included David Crosby, Judy Collins, Buffy Sainte-Marie, and Tom Rush, all of whom loved her songs, recording such beautiful early Mitchell works as "Both Sides Now," "The Circle Game," and "Clouds." They also urged people to see her in person, and she began gathering a following of both the public and other performers.

In 1967, she signed with Reprise Records and in 1968 settled in California. Her four albums for that label, *Songs to a Seagull, Clouds, Ladies of the Canyon,* and *Blue,* featured such masterful pieces as "For Free," "Big Yellow Taxi," "Blue," and the haunting "Woodstock," a lasting love song to a generation and its unique state of mind.

Joni changed to Asylum Records in 1972 and made for them a series of increasingly complex and sophisticated albums, popular with the critics and public alike. In 1978, *Don Juan's Reckless Daughter,* released late in 1977, became her sixth gold album, proving that commercial success and artistic achievement are not necessarily contradictions.

Eddie Money Courtesy Columbia Records

EDDIE MONEY

Eddie Money is the first artist signed by starmaker Bill Graham to his new Wolfgang Productions. Graham sums up the hard-edged Eddie Money mystique with great perception. "Of all the people I've seen, he has all the elements necessary to make it today. Not only can he sing, write, and play, but he possesses two other factors not often seen on a rock 'n' roll stage—one is that he PERFORMS and it's natural and the other is that he's very, very hungry."

The hunger burns out of his eyes and sizzles in the raspy intensity of his performances. Born in Manhattan, Money grew up tough on the streets of New York, singing street-corner harmonies in Queens and Brooklyn from the time he was eleven. His father and his father's father were policemen, and Eddie too became one of New York's finest. But rock and roll possessed his soul, and there was no rest for the boy during the year that he was on the force.

Eddie moved to San Francisco and soon carved a place for himself in the rough, competitive Bay Area rock club circuit. He wanted to be able to perform more original material, so he formed his own band and called it Eddie Money. During its fiery performances he occasionally took over the keyboards, harmonica, or sax, playing them with the same electric energy that drives his singing.

In March 1977, the talented Money, for a change of pace, performed in a one-man play on San Francisco's Broadway. Called *Bakk Tracks,* it told the story of a ninety-year-old former rock star who is the last man on earth after the holocaust. Money's performance was riveting and fueled his determination to succeed. For the past two years he has been studying with vocal coach Judy Davis, who has helped in the development of such stars as Frank Sinatra, Grace Slick, Barbra Streisand, and Sammy Davis.

During early 1978, Eddie toured with Foghat to promote his first album, *Eddie Money,* a gold-winner in Canada and America.

Anne Murray Courtesy Capitol Records

MOODY BLUES

Justin Hayward–Guitar, vocals

Michael Pinder–Keyboards, vocals

Ray Thomas–Flute, vocals

John Lodge–Bass, vocals

Graeme Edge–Drums

In 1964, Mike Pinder, Ray Thomas, Graeme Edge, Denny Laine, and Clint Warwick got together to make some good old rhythm and blues.

An early single, "Go Now," was an international million-seller, and the five musicians were ready to sink back into a life of ease. But their next few singles did not fulfill the promise of their first smash. Denny Laine and Clint Warwick left the band, and Justin Hayward and John Lodge replaced them.

The band's popularity kept slipping, and they finally sat down and rethought their direction, coming up with the lushly orchestrated, complex *Days of Future Passed*, recorded with the London Symphony Orchestra. "Nights in White Satin," an extraordinarily successful single from the album, became a theme song for many a late-night disk jockey.

Throughout the years the Moodys continued to develop their strongly identifiable sound, inspiring many imitators and influencing the sounds of countless other bands. During 1973 they released the album *Seventh Sojourn* and took a successful world tour. But since that time they have each recorded separately or broken down into various smaller units. In 1978, satisfying their legions of fans, the Moody Blues produced *Octave*, another of their velvety treats, an instant gold-winner.

1978 Discography: *Octave*

ANNE MURRAY

Juggling motherhood and a career is never easy, but Anne Murray, after a year and a half of full motherhood, decided to combine the two. Judging by her radiant and relaxed stage presence and full, open voice, the combination is successful, the best of both possible worlds for this lovely singer.

Born and raised in Nova Scotia, Anne Murray has always sung. As a child she performed, played piano, and soaked up a wide variety of music, enjoying everything from classical to gospel. But when family and friends tried to persuade her to switch her teaching career for one in singing, she wasn't interested. "I thought they were crazy," she says. "Singing was something you did in the bathtub and around bonfires. I felt there was no security in singing." She allowed herself to be talked into cutting an album, *What about Me*, for a small Canadian label. It was not long before Capitol of Canada signed her up, and her 1970 single "Snowbird" became a huge worldwide hit. For the next six years Murray turned out a string of hits, including such singles as "He Thinks I Still Care," "Love Song," "Danny's Song," and albums like *Country, Highly Prized Possession*, and *Keeping in Touch*.

During that period she spent eight months of each year on the road, playing clubs and one-night stands. She loved the singing, the applause, and the honors—five year's worth of Canada's Juno Awards as Best Female Vocalist, a Grammy in 1974 for Best Female Performance by a Country Singer (for "Love Song"), and a list of international awards—but she didn't like the time on the road. In 1976, she decided, "Life is too short to stay on the road." Her first son was born in August 1976. Except for a few television spots and a couple of concerts, Murray spent all her time with son William until her return to Las Vegas's Aladdin Hotel in November, 1977.

Her comeback has been triumphant. She received rave reviews for her sold-out sets in Vegas; performances at New York's Bottom Line early in 1978 had fans hanging on every note she sang; "Walk Right Back" and "You Needed Me," singles from her 1978 album *Let's Keep It That Way*, were top-ten country singles. She toured the western United States in the early spring, appeared on more than a dozen television shows around the country, and toured her native Canada in April.

1978 Discography: *Let's Keep It That Way*

WILLIE NELSON

Willie Nelson, the king of country outlaws, idol of millions of fans,

continued to rule the country roost in 1978. The good ole singer/songwriter/guitarist, who was advised by Nashville pundits back in the fifties never to try to make it as a singer, racked up a king's ransom in gold and platinum in 1978. *Waylon and Willie* (performed with Waylon Jennings) and Willie's solo *Red Headed Stranger* both picked up platinum awards; *The Sound In Your Mind* became his second gold LP. As if that weren't enough, "Mamas Don't Let Your Babies Grow Up to Be Cowboys," from *Waylon and Willie*, was a number-one country hit early in the year. Nelson's gold-winner *Stardust* was a number-one country album for many weeks and "Georgia On My Mind," a number-one country single. "If You Can Touch Her at All" was a top-ten country hit.

Named to the Hall of Fame by the Nashville Songwriters Association in 1973, Willie had begun his professional career at the age of ten as a rhythm guitarist for a Bohemian polka band in a small Texas town. Music was his companion as he grew, but the realities of supporting himself, a wife, and daughter made him turn to a variety of odd jobs after his marriage in 1950. The musical talents he had inherited from the grandparents who raised him burned in his blood, however, and he sang and played whenever he got the chance.

He finally persuaded a radio station manager in San Antonio to take a chance on him as a disk jockey. He was a good one, and for the next few years he spun platters during the day and performed at night. With the constant exposure to music, songs began to pour out of him, and he scribbled them down on whatever scraps of paper he could grab.

Willie's next step was a move to Nashville, where he performed at a songwriters' hangout, Tootsie's Bar. He was quickly signed as a songwriter to Pamper Publishing, and his songs were immediately successful. Faron Young recorded his hit song "Hello Walls," and Patsy Cline did "Crazy," another smash. Ray Price, part-owner of Pamper Publishing and leader of Ray Price and His Cherokee Cowboys, turned "Night Life" and "Funny How Time Slips Away" into blockbusters. Throughout the years, Willie's songs have been recorded by such a variety of artists as Perry Como, Aretha Franklin, Little Anthony and the Imperials, Lawrence Welk, Stevie Wonder, Harry James, Eydie Gormé, Frank Sinatra, Al Green, and Elvis Presley.

But Willie, always a rebel, found Nashville's definition of country a great limitation, particularly the often expressed opinion that Willie shouldn't sing. In the early 1970s, he broke away from Nashville, began hosting mammoth Fourth of July picnics in the Texas hill country, and cutting country's rare platinum sellers, such as *The Outlaws*, his 1977 monster recorded with Waylon, Jessi Colter, and Tompall Glaser.

1978 Discography: *Waylon and Willie*
　　　　　　　　　　Stardust

RANDY NEWMAN

One radio station played it eighteen times in a row; others wouldn't play it at all. The Little People of America detested it; songwriters wrote rebuttals and parodies, but no one was indifferent. Somehow, much to the surprise of Randy Newman, who had no idea when he wrote it that it would create such a stir, "Short People," from the album *Little Criminals*, became his biggest hit to date, striding into the top ten and taking *Little Criminals* along with it.

Newman, a cult figure long worshipped by a few for his intelligent, funny, softly melodic songs, is a very private figure. Although his songs have been recorded by such diverse artists as Ringo Starr, Bonnie Raitt, and Harry Nilsson, and although he's provided some hits for others—"Mama Told Me Not to Come" for Three Dog Night, "I Think It's Going to Rain Today" for Judy Collins, and "Sail Away" for Ray Charles—Newman himself has kept a low profile.

Born in New Orleans into a musical family (three of his uncles are respected conductors and composers of film scores), he began studying music when he was twelve. His music is beautifully American, shining with influences of Stephen Foster, blues and country, Cole Porter, and George Gershwin. He has the uncanny knack of being able to condense a short story into the song format, revealing

Willie Nelson Courtesy Columbia Records

Randy Newman

Courtesy Warner Brothers Records

Ted Nugent Courtesy Epic Records

Olivia Newton-John

Courtesy MCA Records

an extraordinary amount in a line or a phrase.

His songs, however, do not fit into any categories, which perhaps explains why commercial success of his six albums has not been greater. His music is truly like no one else's except Randy Newman's, and it is cherished by a small group of serious pop music lovers.

OLIVIA NEWTON-JOHN

Her American career dates back only to 1973, but in five short years Olivia Newton-John has gathered an armload of awards, honors, gold and platinum singles and albums, and three Grammies. In 1978, the British-born, Australian-raised singer won another platinum album with her *Greatest Hits;* her top-charted duet with John Travolta from the movie *Grease,* "You're the One That I Want," went platinum, and was followed by two other sizzlers from that platinum soundtrack, "Hopelessly Devoted to You" and "Summer Nights," another duet with Travolta.

Olivia's career began when she was a teen-ager in Australia. She and three friends formed a group they called the Sol Four, but the group was disbanded when Olivia's academically oriented parents feared it was interfering with schoolwork. But even the pressure of being the granddaughter of a Nobel prize-winner and the daughter of a college headmaster could not dissuade Olivia from her desire for a musical career. She continued singing, and when she was sixteen won her first talent contest.

The prize was a trip to England, and for the next two years Olivia performed as part of a duo with another Australian, Pat Carroll. They appeared in cabarets and on many BBC television shows. When Pat's visa ran out she decided to return to Australia. Olivia opted to remain in England, where her first solo single—Bob Dylan's "If Not for You"—was an international smash. She followed this with "Banks of the Ohio," which won her the English Silver Disk and the Australian Gold Disk.

In 1973, her first records were released in America, and she won her first Grammy as Best Country Vocalist for the song "Let Me Be There." In 1974, she swept up two more Grammies for "I Honestly Love You," which was voted Record of the Year and won her the Country Music Association award as Top Female Vocalist of the Year.

The year 1977 was a hectic one for Olivia, beginning with an SRO tour of the eastern and midwestern states and her concert debut performance at New York's Metropolitan Opera House. A trip to Europe followed, during which Olivia taped her own BBC special in London and appeared as a special guest on the Silver Jubilee television show commemorating Queen Elizabeth's twenty-fifth year of reign. While in Europe she toured France and Germany. On her return to Los Angeles she plunged into the filming of *Grease.* Her winsome performance in that film won her critical praise and many new fans.

TED NUGENT

Ted Nugent—Guitar

Cliff Davies—Drums

Rob Grange—Bass

Derek St. Holmes—Vocals

"If they ain't foaming at the mouth after ten minutes then we've screwed up," snarls Ted Nugent, maintaining his legendary position as the king of eat-it-raw rock and roll. Nugent has always drawn out madness from his audiences—after one of his concerts your average rock arena looks more like a battleground than a concert hall. This powerhouse of nonstop rock and roll—who once prompted *New Musical Express* to run a front page headline proclaiming "Ted Nugent Is Jaws"—has always kicked out the jams. When he was fourteen he was cutting his teeth on killer rock as a member of a Detroit

group called the Lords. When he had attained manhood (at sixteen), Ted formed the original Amboy Dukes, who became legends in the sixties for their classics "Journey to the Center of Your Mind" and "Baby Please Don't Go." They toured more than two hundred days a year, suffered the pangs of four under-promoted albums, and absorbed a music business education the hard way.

Never one to wince and run away, Ted stuck with the music and, in the mid-seventies, formed the Ted Nugent Band. His name in lights seemed to be the winning ticket. Since signing with Epic Records as the Ted Nugent Band, each of his albums has been a gold-winner, including such raunch and roll masterpieces as *Ted Nugent, Free-For-All,* the howling *Cat Scratch Fever,* and 1978's ventures into vinyl mayhem, the platinum *Double Live Gonzo* and *Weekend Warriors.*

Ted wiped 'em out across the country in an end-of-1977 tour, and one of his most memorable bashes of 1978 was his appearance at Cal Jam II, drawing 250,000 paying customers to the Ontario Motor Speedway in Ontario, California.
1978 Discography: *Double Live Gonzo*
Weekend Warriors

OAK RIDGE BOYS

Bill Golden—Vocals

Duane Allen—Vocals

Richard Sterban—Vocals

Joe Bonsall—Vocals

During World War II, a country group called the Country Cut-Ups performed on weekends at the atomic energy plant in Oak Ridge, Tennessee. Their songs were for workers not permitted to leave the base for security reasons, and so the group was soon called the Oak Ridge Quartet. The songs they did then were gospel songs, but in their latest incarnation as the Oak Ridge Boys they perform country music, blending their fine voices in new and arresting harmonies.

As the Oak Ridge Quartet, they chalked up an impressive string of honors: three Grammies, fifteen Dove Awards, and a tour of the Soviet Union. Then, in the face of all this success, they dared to change from gospel to contemporary country sound—and were immediately successful. *Y'all Come Back Saloon,* their debut album, quickly became a top country disk and bobbed in and out of the top ten for months. Both the title single and "You're the One" became top-three country smashes. They were named Top New Vocal Group of the Year for Singles in *Record World's* 1977 Country Music Awards competition, and they were named Best Country Group at the Wembley Festival of Country Music in England. In the United States, their many television appearances include "The Dinah Shore Show," during which they sang a song they had composed for Mary Tyler Moore.

In 1978, they released their second album, the top-ten country *Room Service.* From it came the number-one country hit "I'll Be True to You."
1978 Discography: *Room Service*

O'JAYS

Eddie Levert—Vocals

Walter Williams—Vocals

Sammy Strain—Vocals

On July 12, 1978, the O'Jays celebrated their twentieth anniversary in a sold-out show at Los Angeles's Greek Theatre. The sensational response they received for a tight, professional, but warmly alive show represented the kind of audience reaction they've always worked hard to win.

The O'Jays began twenty years ago as a five-member group in Canton, Ohio. As the Mascots, Eddie Levert, Walter Williams, William Powell, Bobby Massey, and Bill Isles played the black "Chitterling Circuit" of Ohio for as much as twenty-five dollars a night. Cleveland deejay Eddie O'Jay caught their act, was impressed with them, and took them under his wing. He gave them polish and confidence, and, in thanks, they changed their name to the O'Jays.

But although they had a new name, a wealth of singing talent, and a drive that just wouldn't quit, they had only one big hit in the mid-1960s—a song called "Lonely Drifter," on the Imperial label. Disappointed by their lack of success, Bill Isles left the group. A lesser collection of men would have given up in disgust, but the remaining O'Jays hung in there. After a few years of filling in at some small R & B clubs, they signed with the newly formed Philadelphia International label, owned by hit-makers Kenny Gamble and Leon Huff.

By this time Massey had left the group, so it was as a trio that the O'Jays struck gold with the classic "Back Stabbers," written for them by Gamble and Huff. The smooth, slick, electric-tempo disk moved them right to the top; it was followed by two other huge hits from the album called *Back Stabbers*—"992 Arguments" and "Love Train."

From then on success came fast, with one gold album after another: *Ship Ahoy, Survival, Reunion.* In May of 1977, the O'Jays and their fans were deeply grieved by the death of William Powell. But, with replacement Sammy Strain, the band turned out 1978's double platinum-winner, *So Full of Love,* from which came the million-selling single "Use Ta Be My Girl."
1978 Discography: *So Full of Love*

The O'Jays   Courtesy Epic Records

The Oak Ridge Boys   Courtesy ABC Records

TONY ORLANDO

He pushed himself up from the ghetto to the pinnacle of show business success. In 1976, he had everything—a wife who loved him, his own television show, three smash singles with the female duo Dawn: "Knock Three Times," "Candida," and "Tie a Yellow Ribbon." He had ideas, energy, youth, health, and good friends like Freddie Prinze.

But within the space of a few short months everything fell apart for Tony Orlando. In November 1976, his television series was cancelled. Early in 1977, Freddie Prinze shot himself to death. Tony was shattered by his friend's suicide. He was overcome by fear, couldn't sleep, and had to take pep pills to get started in the mornings. He went through months of horrendous mood swings from extreme elation to the bottomless pits of depression, until on July 22, in a performance at Cohasset, Massachusetts, after beginning to talk about Freddie Prinze and being rebuffed by the shouts of the audience, Tony announced that he was retiring from show business.

It was shortly after this traumatic evening that Tony called on psychiatrist Ronald R. Fieve, author of the book *Moodswing,* to help him with his problem. He embarked on a course of intensive psychotherapy, including a stay in a mental hospital and convalescent home. Throughout his ordeal he was buoyed by friend Muhammad Ali, who supported and encouraged him. His wife Elaine, the most important person in his life, was by his side constantly. In November 1977, Tony made his comeback at the Circle Theater in San Carlos, California. Fans cheered his return, and Tony zipped into full gear, showing up at the beginning of December at the Riviera Hotel in Las Vegas. He gave a crackling performance, obviously charged with happy excitement over his return. Tony continued to tour throughout 1978 and completed an album, released in July.
1978 Discography: *Tony Orlando*

Tony Orlando

Courtesy Elektra Records

Donny and Marie Osmond

DONNY AND MARIE OSMOND

That remarkable family of musical stars, the Osmonds, whose rec-

Courtesy Polydor/Kolob Records

Pablo Cruise   Courtesy A & M Records

Johnny Paycheck

Courtesy Epic Records

Luciano Pavarotti

Dolly Parton   Chuck Pulin

Courtesy Columbia Records

Teddy Pendergrass

Parliament's George Clinton

Courtesy Casablanca Records

260

ords have sold a total of more than 70 million copies worldwide, has produced two even more rarefied animals, musical superstars, in brother and sister duo Donny and Marie. Donny is twenty-one and Marie is still in her teens, but the pair are seasoned performers and recording artists. Their well-known hits include such songs as "I'm Leaving it All Up to You," "Deep Purple," and "Aint Nothin' like the Real Thing."

Donny began singing professionally at age five, making his debut in 1963 on "The Andy Williams Show," a spot that most performers don't aspire to until they have years of experience. His performing brothers, Alan, Wayne, Merrill, and Jay, then known as the Osmond Brothers, were singing barbershop quartet music and Donny was a solo. Later that year, Donny joined his brothers in a television special called "The Seven Little Foys," and before long the group became a quintet.

At the end of the 1960s, during a European tour, Marie, then seven, stepped out onstage with her brothers and sang with them, transforming the Osmond Brothers into the Osmonds and adding a touch of country to the act. In 1970, the Osmonds switched to pop music, and they immediately became teeny-bopper rock sensations.

In 1971, Donny's first solo single, "Sweet and Innocent," was released. It was a huge hit for Donny, the first of ten gold records for his solo singles and albums. In addition, he and Marie together have won a number of gold albums, their most recent for 1977's *New Season*. Marie, who in 1978 is sporting a sophisticated new hairdo, has also won gold for her first solo album, *Paper Roses*, recorded in Nashville.

PABLO CRUISE

Cory Lerios–Keyboards, vocals

Dave Jenkins–Lead vocals, lead guitar

Steve Price–Drums

Bruce Day–Bass, vocals

It's no accident that the bright, sunny music of Pablo Cruise reflects a positive outlook and a search for life's natural highs. That good-time cheer is a consciousness they achieve in their lives as well as in their music. And, as the free-flowing album *Worlds Away*, 1978's gold-winner, illustrates, they reach beautiful musical highs again and again. The titles of their albums and songs reflect their search for natural beauty around them: *A Place in the Sun*, their first album; "Love Will Find a Way," "Sailing to Paradise," and "Worlds Away," from *Worlds Away*.

The exhilaration of sports and physical activity is a part of their lives. Cory and Steve met as members of the same high school band, rehearsing their music after football practice. Dave, who came to the West Coast during the sixties, is a sailor. The three of them came together in the band Stoneground. After their first album as Pablo Cruise, *A Place in the Sun*, their original bass player, Bud Cockrell, left. They recruited Bruce Day, whose credits include a stint with Carlos Santana. In 1977, they had a summer hit with the catchy "Whatcha Gonna Do" and, in 1978, "Love Will Find a Way" was a top-ten single.
1978 Discography: *Worlds Away*

PARLIAMENT-FUNKADELIC

Onstage, after a breathtaking arrival by flying saucer, dripping with ermine and feathers, swaggering on mighty golden platform boots, George Clinton as Doctor Funkenstein leads his outrageous gang of zanies in a superflash, superfunk extravaganza. As the Doctor has said about his second platinum album, *Funkentelechy Vs. the Placebo Syndrome*, "The message of Parliament on this album is YOU WILL DANCE." And, as the irresistible rhythms of advanced funk sail out over his audiences, the maggot brains (fans of p-funk) rise up and boogie.

Where does he come from, this insane perpetrator of funk-talk, funk-music, and—if all goes as planned—eventual supergroovalisticprosifunkstacation (that is, funk taken to its highest level) of the whole world? Clinton's madness began back in the fifties in a barbershop near Newark, New Jersey, where he and some teen-age jivers harmonized between haircuts. Out of these laid-back beginnings, the Parliaments were born. First signed by ABC, they then moved to Tamla/Motown and finally to the Revilot label, where they scored their first towering hit single in 1967—"(I Just Wanna) Testify."

Revilot was to pass out of existence in 1968, and with them went the Parliament's name. Clinton renamed his band the Funkadelics and developed them into a show band with a more aggressive beat, an overt black philosophy, and an irresistibly demented stage show that never stopped jumping. When the Parliament name again became available, Clinton signed his group of musicians to Casablanca as the Parliaments and to Warner Brothers as Funkadelic. This duality may cause some confusion, but there's no need to fear missing out on one or the other band—when Clinton leads, his pranksters are together.

In 1978, Clinton trucked his mammoth show to sold-out houses all around the country, raising his largely black fans to heights of delirium.

DOLLY PARTON

"My work is very important to me," says country/pop star Dolly Parton. The bountifully endowed blond singer, whose wigs, spiky eyelashes, and full-tilt sequins camouflage a mind as sharp as a steel blade, tossed her hat into the crossover arena in 1976. In 1978, the returns came in and Dolly was a winner. Her expanded pop repertoire on 1977's *Here You Come Again* helped propel the disk to platinum, her first. And even if the Country Music Association did ignore her in their 1977 awards (they had voted her Best Female Singer of the Year in 1975 and 1976), the Academy of Country Music bestowed on her their highest accolade, naming her Entertainer of the Year, only the second woman to win that honor.

Those weren't the only bright spots for Dolly. *New Harvest, First Gathering*, her mid-1977 album, won the American Music Award as the nation's Favorite Country Album. The title single from *Here You Come Again* won gold in 1978 and was both a top-ten easy-listening and pop hit. In May, her single "It's All Wrong, But It's Alright" zoomed to the number-one country spot. In April, she shared the stage with Cher on "*Cher…Special*." In June, *Best of Dolly Parton* became her second gold LP. It was a year when Dolly could be generous. Country singer Zella Lehr reached the country top ten with Dolly's song "Two Doors Down" because Dolly agreed to let Zella be the first to release her song as a single.

Dolly has been ecstatic. "Lately," she says, "I've found such happiness and new inspiration in being able to have the freedom to do what is so totally me." Of course, Dolly has always been a happy person, but even her sunniness must have been strained in 1976, after her break with the friends and relatives who made up her band and with Porter Wagoner, the country star who gave her her start and who was a supportive friend for many years. Her new success, however, has more than made up for any doubts and misgivings she might have felt.

Her ability to express herself in music dates back to her early childhood. She's been singing since she could talk and writing songs since before she began school. Her stardom is a result of the ambition that has always burned within her, an ambition that drove her from her poor Tennessee home to Nashville at the age of eighteen. It was there that she met Carl Dean, who soon became her husband, and there, in 1967, that Porter Wagoner gave her the chance to be part of his show.

In 1974, Dolly cut her first solo album, *Jolene,* which was a smash. She began more consciously to develop her songwriting, and some of her compositions were recorded by singers of such stature as Linda Ronstadt, Emmylou Harris, and Maria Muldaur. Through their interpretations of her songs she realized that she could appeal to a wider than country audience.

1978 Discography: *Heartbreaker*

LUCIANO PAVAROTTI

If it hadn't been for the wishes of Luciano Pavarotti's father, it's possible that one of the twentieth century's most compelling lyric tenors could have been lost to the world of music. Luciano's original desire was to teach, but because his natural talents could not be submerged, and because his father continually prodded his son to become an operatic tenor, Luciano Pavarotti took to the opera stage in 1961 and has not stopped singing since.

La Bohème was the opera in which he made his debut in 1961, and for the next two years he performed in Italy. In 1963, his fame began to spread across Europe. He appeared as Edgardo in *Lucia di Lammermoor* in Amsterdam and then traveled throughout Holland, to Vienna, and to Zurich, rousing opera fans to frenzies of applause with his voice. He sang *La Bohème* in England in the fall of that year, rocking the British with his thrilling performance.

Pavarotti made his North American debut in 1965. In that same year, he also toured Australia, where critics hailed him as one of the great tenors of all time. When he returned home, his birthplace of Modena, Italy, awarded him the Principessa Carlotta prize for his contribution to the arts.

In 1966, Pavarotti firmly established himself as the world's foremost lyric tenor. He made his debut at Milan's La Scala in *La Bohème,* conducted by Herbert von Karajan. Later in the year, he was chosen to sing in a performance of the Verdi *Requiem* conducted by von Karajan in honor of the centenary of the birth of Toscanini. He was also awarded the coveted Verdi d'Oro prize by the city of Parma.

Pavarotti's career has continued to grow throughout the years. In 1978, three of his albums were in the classical top ten: *Operatic Duets* with Joan Sutherland, *The Great Pavarotti,* and *The World's Favorite Tenor Arias.* His *La Bohème* with the Berlin Philharmonic under von Karajan was a new entry, rocketing onto the classical charts at number twenty-two.

1978 Discography: *La Bohème*
Bravo Pavarotti
Hits from Lincoln Center

JOHNNY PAYCHECK

Early in 1978, a construction crew in Rapid City, South Dakota, walked off the job when they heard Johnny Paycheck's "Take This Job and Shove It." Like Merle Haggard's sixties hit "Okie from Muskogee," Johnny's song struck a responsive chord in the hearts of workingmen across the country. It was exactly right for the feelings of 1978, and it jetted to the top of the country charts, taking the album by the same name up along with it. It also won Paycheck the Academy of Country Music Award for career achievement for "hanging in there."

Paycheck, as his seamed face testifies, has hung in there through some heavy going. He got his early training with George Jones and his first fame in 1967 with a hard-driving song called "A-11."

After that success he went off the track, losing himself in drink and drugs. In 1971, he shook off these habits and made a fabulous comeback. Since then there have been years of struggle, but in 1978 he is back at the top.

TEDDY PENDERGRASS

Teddy Bear to his fans, the incomparable Teddy Pendergrass, after a fabulously successful five years as lead singer of the Blue Notes, has been on his own since 1976. In 1978, with his first two solo albums certified platinum monsters, the growly-voiced bear has forged himself a new career so bright it dazzles.

Never a slacker, Teddy began singing at age two. He was an ordained minister at ten and a self-taught drummer by the time he was thirteen. In his home town of Philadelphia he sang in the city-wide McIntyre Elementary School Choir and the All-City Stetson Junior High School Choir. In his teens he was lead singer for a local group and eager for a singing career. A fast-talking sharpie, however, took a record Teddy had cut, promised him a fat recording contract, and disappeared without a trace. Disillusioned, Teddy began performing as a drummer with another Phillie group, the Cadillacs. A group called the Blue Notes hired the Cadillacs as back-ups, and Teddy came along on drums.

In 1970, during a tour of the French West Indies, the band split apart. A new singer was needed and Teddy was more than ready. The first release with Teddy's vocals was "I Miss You," which fell into the record world like a bombshell. It was followed by a string of gold singles featuring Teddy's unmistakable voice: "If You Don't Know Me by Now," "To Be True," "The Love I Lost," and "Bad Luck," as well as the albums *To Be True* and *Wake Up Everybody.*

At the end of 1976 Teddy left the Blue Notes and went out on his own. In 1977, his first solo album, *Teddy Pendergrass,* was a platinum smash. The memorable singles from the album, "I Don't Love You Any More," "You Can't Hide From Yourself," and "The More I Get the More I Want," were soul, pop, and disco hits. Teddy's second soulful album, the gold-awarded *Life Is a Song Worth Singing,* contains his number-one soul single "Close the Door."

1978 Discography: *Life Is a Song Worth Singing*

ITZHAK PERLMAN

One of the world's most sought-after musicians, Itzhak Perlman thrills audiences in performances with all of America's major orchestras as well as in concerts with such internationally renowned orchestras as the Berlin Philharmonic, the Vienna Philharmonic, the London Symphony, the Amsterdam Concertgebouw, and L'Orchestre de Paris. In addition to orchestral performances, Perlman regularly takes part in chamber music recitals with his colleagues at the major summer music festivals in the United States, Europe, and Israel, which he tours with his wife Toby and their three children.

Although he is only thirty-one years old, Perlman is often considered an elder statesman of the violin. He made his first major professional impact at age seventeen, when he captured the coveted Leventritt Memorial Award. Perlman has been winning lavish critical acclaim ever since.

Considered the foremost violinist of his generation, the Israeli-born virtuoso is master of a wide repertoire of music. Best known as a brilliant interpreter of nineteenth-century romanticism, he has recently expanded his repertoire to include the baroque and twentieth-century composers and even his own transcriptions of several Scott Joplin rags.

Many of his recordings, which encompass most of the literature for violin, are considered definitive performances. These exquisite showcases include the recently recorded Brahms Violin Concerto, performed with the Chicago Symphony Orchestra, conducted by Carlo Maria Giulini; the complete Paganini Caprices; concerti by Bach, Bruch, Dvořák, Mendelssohn, Paganini, Tchaikovsky, and Wieniawski; and sonatas by Franck and Prokofiev. With the renowned Vladimir Ashkenazy, Perlman performed the complete Beethoven Sonatas for Violin and Piano in concert during March 1978.

Itzhak Perlman

Tom Petty and the Heartbreakers

Charley Pride

Courtesy RCA Records and Tapes

Elvis Presley

TOM PETTY AND THE HEARTBREAKERS

Tom Petty–Rhythm guitar

Mike Campbell–Lead guitar

Ron Blair–Bass

Ben Tench–Keyboards

Stan Lynch–Drums

Tom Petty knows what rock and roll is all about. At twenty-six, the handsome, hollow-cheeked musician has been worshiping it since he was ten and turning it out with a variety of rocking bands since he was fourteen. Rock and roll is his heart and soul, and he's likely to snarl if anyone tries to affix the label punk or new wave on him. His music is simple, pure, hard as nails, rough, and tough. Its roots are in the fifties, but Tom knows that his impact is more like the eighties. With his melodic, energetic music, Petty is very much the wave of the future.

Born in Gainesville, Florida, Petty discovered Elvis Presley at the age of ten. An uncle took him to a Presley movie set, and when Presley stepped out of his white Cadillac and said hello to Petty, the boy was hooked. He spent the next few years of his life snatching up every Elvis record he could get. He also took inspiration from the Beatles, the Rolling Stones, and the Byrds (Roger McGuinn returned the compliment when he recorded Petty's song "American Girl").

When Tom was fourteen, he formed his first band, and for the next six years he and his group lived on the road, playing wherever they would get paid. Eventually Petty decided that it would be more pleasant to starve in Los Angeles than in New York, so he moved to the West Coast. There he met Leon Russell, moved into his house, and became an observer of the L.A. music scene. Although he felt there was good music coming out of Los Angeles, he knew it wasn't his style. The sound was too slick for him; he was looking for ways to capture the gritty energy of his live performances on record. So, coming together with band members who had been with him in the very earliest days, Petty cut his first album.

Released in 1976, *Tom Petty and the Heartbreakers* won critical acclaim but sold poorly. Undaunted, he and his band went on the road for some more touring. During all of 1977, they traveled throughout the United States, finally taking off for Europe. There they received an astonishing reception. The British loved them. "Breakdown" and "American Girl," two singles from the first album, became smash hits in England. ABC Records, his company, had just gone through a personnel shake-up; the new people in charge saw potential in Tom's music and began supporting him with some advertising. His second album, *You're Gonna Get It,* began attracting record buyers as well as critics and zoomed to gold sales.

1978 Discography: *You're Gonna Get It*

ELVIS PRESLEY

On August 16, 1977, the life of the recording industry's most phenomenal success came to an end. The shock wave created by that passing has continued to grow. Throughout 1977 and 1978, millions of Elvis fans helped keep his memory alive. Radio stations broadcast tributes to him; newspapers devoted special editions to his career and the way it changed the face of popular music; hundreds of thousands of tourists made the trek to Memphis to view his grave; in November of 1977 there were twelve Presley albums in the top thirty-two of the country top fifty, including *Elvis in Concert,* which became the number-one country LP during the month of August. *He Walks Beside Me* became a top-ten country album in April 1978. "Unchained Melody" became a top-ten country single in the same month. "My Way" became his tenth gold single and *His Hand in Mine* and *Elvis Country* became his thirty-second and thirty-third gold

albums; *Elvis Sings the Wonderful World of Christmas* became his third platinum LP in December 1977. In Russia, *Melodiya,* the state record company, included "Careless" and "True Love" on a compilation album.

The king may be dead, but his music lives on.

1978 Discography: *Elvis Sings for Children and Grownups Too*

CHARLEY PRIDE

It's a rare week when Charley Pride doesn't have a powerful song in the upper atmosphere of the country charts. The year 1978 was another nonstop success ride for this exceptional former big-league baseball player, as singles like "Someone Loves You Honey" and "When I Stop Leaving (I'll Be Gone)" reached the top country slot. His album *Someone Loves You Honey* was also a top-ten country LP.

Charley's early years had much in common with those of many other country singers. Born dirt poor in the small town of Sledge, Mississippi, Charley spent his early years picking cotton side by side with his parents and ten brothers and sisters. It didn't take long for Charley to make up his mind that picking cotton was not going to play an important part in his future.

He left Sledge at age seventeen to begin a baseball career in the Negro American League. After a short interruption for the army, he returned to baseball in 1961, playing outfield and pitching for the Los Angeles Angels. In the evenings, he played guitar and sang in Los Angeles night spots.

In 1963, Red Sovine, an important country star, encouraged Charley to take his singing seriously. Pride traveled to Nashville in early 1964 and cut some demo tapes for Chet Atkins. Atkins was excited by the tapes and signed Charley to RCA Records. His faith in the singing ballplayer was well-founded, and Charley's first single for the company, "Snakes Crawl at Night," launched him on his way.

From that time on, Charley has raked in honors and awards from such places as the Country Music Association, *Billboard, Cash Box,* and the Music Operators of America. He has won three Grammies for his performances both as a country and as a gospel performer. His dynamic onstage presence has made him a sought-after television performer; his credits include many appearances on "The Lawrence Welk Show," "The Kraft Music Hall," "Hee Haw," and "The Johnny Cash Show."

1978 Discography: *Someone Loves You Honey*
Burgers and Fries

QUEEN

Freddie Mercury–Vocals, keyboards

Brian May–Guitar, vocals

Roger Taylor–Drums, vocals

John Deacon–Bass

Queen ended 1977 with an SRO heavy-metal blitz at New York's Madison Square Garden. They began 1978 with their *News of the World* album achieving platinum, and, soon after, the hit single from that album—"We Are the Champions"—also went on to win a platinum disk. Not a bad way to start the year.

Queen began in 1970, when Freddie Mercury, Brian May, and Roger Taylor met in London. In 1971, they added bassist John Deacon. Most other groups at this point would have busied themselves trying to play the largest possible halls, but Queen had no intention of rushing anything. They quietly crafted their sound, work-

Queen   Christopher Hopper

Eddie Rabbitt   Anthony Friedkin

Gerry Rafferty

Jean-Pierre Rampal

Raydio

Lou Rawls

265

ing away in small halls, polishing their stage show and perfecting their material. It wasn't until they had a hard-as-nails, identifiable, unique sound that they approached Elektra Records, who jumped at the chance to record them. They released their first album, *Queen*, in 1973. With its two hit singles, "Keep Yourself Alive" and "Liar," the album quickly sold gold. The group toured England to ecstatic reviews, and in early 1974 they made *Queen II*.

In 1974, they toured America for the first time as opening act for Mott the Hoople. During the tour Brian was struck ill and the rest of the engagements were cancelled. Queen returned to England and created a fresh new album, *Sheer Heart Attack,* with the hit single "Killer Queen." In 1975, they hit platinum with *A Night at the Opera,* which contained a single called "Bohemian Rhapsody," a six-minute, complex work with operatic interludes and abrupt rhythmic changes. Although they were advised against releasing such a demanding song as a single, "Bohemian Rhapsody" became their biggest worldwide hit so far. *A Day at the Races* was released late in 1976, with the hit singles "Somebody to Love," and "Tie Your Mother Down."

R

EDDIE RABBITT

From the stage of Manhattan's Lone Star Cafe at the end of 1977, country singer Eddie Rabbitt let out a shout. "I left this town on a Greyhound bus, and I came back in a limousine!" The line scans with the rhythm of a country song, but Rabbitt's is not your usual country tale. Country singers are traditionally born in mountain shacks or towns so small you can blink them away. Eddie Rabbitt, a first-generation American born to Irish parents, was born in Brooklyn and raised in East Orange, New Jersey, where he learned two guitar chords from a New Jersey scoutmaster. Within a couple of years Rabbitt had parlayed those two chords into a bona fide piano-playing job in a New Jersey country bar.

For the next few years Eddie played the country bar circuit in New Jersey, but he began to see that he wasn't getting anywhere except older; he decided to make the move to Nashville. Once there, in a rundown hotel near the train station, Eddie, inspired by the meanness of his surroundings, wrote "Working My Way Up to the Bottom." The song became a hit for singer Roy Drusky and, in 1968, Rabbitt became a staff writer for Hill and Range, earning the princely sum of $37.50 a week. During those lean days he hung out with a group of other struggling young songwriter/singers, including such future stars as Kris Kristofferson, Billy Swan, and Larry Gatlin.

In 1970, Eddie faced a momentous decision. He had just won a recording contract with a major record company on the basis of "Kentucky Rain," a new song of his. But Elvis Presley was also eager to record "Kentucky Rain." Eddie now had to decide whether to keep the song for himself or give it to Elvis, with whom it would be a guaranteed best-seller. Eddie wisely decided to let Elvis record it. Although the song became Elvis's fiftieth million-seller, Eddie had to watch in dismay while the record company tore up his contract because he had given away his best tune.

Eddie shrugged and went back to his writing, figuring he had done the right thing and that his time would come. In 1973, Ronnie Milsap had a top country hit with Eddie's song "Pure Love," and soon afterwards Eddie signed to Elektra/Asylum's country division.

His first hit, "Forgive and Forget," led to the first album, *Eddie Rabbitt*. Three hit songs, "Drinking My Baby off My Mind," "Two Dollars in the Jukebox," and "Rocky Mountain Music," came from his second album, *Rocky Mountain Music*. In 1977, he had top country hits with "I Can't Help Myself" and "We Can't Go on Living Like This,"

both from his third album, *Rabbitt*—a top-five country record.

In December 1977, Rabbitt had a successful tour of England, Germany, and Holland, leading to a 1978 European tour with Dolly Parton. In March his "Heart's on Fire" became a top-ten country single, just as his most recent album, *Variations,* was released. He also was awarded the Academy of Country Music's award as Top New Vocalist of 1977.
1978 Discography: *Variations*

GERRY RAFFERTY

On July 8, 1978, the electric connection between the Bee Gees' *Saturday Night Fever* and the number-one spot on the pop album charts was broken by Gerry Rafferty. Rafferty's platinum album, *City to City,* hit the top spot just as his mysteriously sensual gold single "Baker Street" was nudging Andy Gibb's number-one "Shadow Dancing." After three years outside the musical limelight, Scottish singer/songwriter/guitarist Gerry Rafferty was emphatically in it again.

Rafferty's professional career began in 1968, when he and Billy Connolly formed the Humblebums. After they disbanded, Gerry cut a solo album, *Can I Have My Money Back?* In 1972, he and boyhood friend Joe Egan formed the core of what was to become Stealers Wheel. *Stealers Wheel,* their first album, contained the smash single "Stuck in the Middle With You," a major hit in Britain and in the United States.

The group released two more albums, *Ferguslie Park* and *Right or Wrong,* before managerial and personal problems split them apart. In 1978, Gerry Rafferty resurfaced with *City to City,* which looks like the beginning of a whole new career.
1978 Discography: *City to City*

JEAN-PIERRE RAMPAL

The sound of his flute leaves no doubt in any audience's mind that Jean-Pierre Rampal is the twentieth century's greatest flutist. In addition to his enormous classical repertoire, including every major work for the instrument, Rampal and Claude Bolling recorded *Suite for Flute and Jazz Piano* in 1976, a record that was on the classical best-seller list for more than two years. Several other recent recordings, including *In Concert, Three Concertos for Two Flutes, Greatest Hits,* and his most recent 1978 entry, *Sakura,* have also been top classical sellers.

Because of his youth and enormous vitality, Rampal is a hit with young concert-goers as well as more mature audiences. He made his American debut as a conductor in the early 1970s at the Mostly Mozart concerts held at New York's Avery Fisher Hall. Those concerts, which attract mainly a young audience, are always filled to overflowing when Mr. Rampal conducts.

Rampal received his early training from his father, a flutist who played with the Marseilles opera and symphony and taught at the local conservatory. At the beginning, however, Jean-Pierre had no intention of being a flutist. He planned to be a doctor, and it was only in his third year of medical school, when he was called up for military service during the German occupation of France, that the flute became his life. He went AWOL, hiding from the military authorities in Paris and attending flute classes at the Conservatoire, graduating in five months with the first prize in flute.

After the liberation of Paris, Rampal became first flute with the Paris Opera, gave solo recitals on the radio, and joined forces with harpsichordist Robert Veyron-Lacroix, with whom he toured the musical capitals of Europe.

Throughout the years he has produced a prodigious body of recordings: as a soloist, with chamber groups, with orchestras, and in duets with Robert Veyron-Lacroix at the keyboard. Several of his records have been awarded the Grand Prix du Disque, and all are best-sellers.
1978 Discography: *Sakura*

LOU RAWLS

Who else could sing the praises of a beer company on national television and in concert and come out of the experience not only unscathed but with added stature? Perhaps only Lou Rawls, who claims a genuine love for the beer he promotes; in fact, the title of a recent album, *When You Hear Lou, You've Heard It All,* is taken directly from the beer's ad.

He is successful as a spokesman because everything he does has the ring of authenticity. When Lou sends notes spinning out, audiences drink them up, because the words are real, the feelings are true. Lou never misrepresents. He conveys a sense of both professional polish and extraordinary warmth, intelligence, and humor in his supple voice. The career to which he's given so much of himself has repaid him amply in the coin all performers seek: the love of his audience, the sales of his records (*When You Hear Lou, You've Heard It All* was his fifth gold LP), and awards from his peers—the 1977 Grammy for "Unmistakably Lou" joins his two other Grammies for *Dead End Street* and *A Natural Man.*

Lou began singing at the age of seven in his Chicago church choir. With puckish humor he attributes his singing to extramusical concerns. "I discovered that the kids who sang in church got to go home early," he jokes, "so I said to myself, hey, that's for me." As a teen-ager he continued to develop his voice with the Pilgrim Travelers, a well-known Chicago gospel group. After a hitch in the army he sang at local service clubs and then toured the nightclub circuit in the Midwest.

A serious automobile accident that took place while touring with Sam Cooke in 1958 put Lou in a coma for five days. Perhaps it was the toughness he developed during his midwestern travels that pulled him through, because he surprised his doctors by recovering and going back out on the road far sooner than expected.

In 1959, Lou got his first taste of real success. Moving to Los Angeles, he appeared with Dick Clark at the Hollywood Bowl Show, after which he was acclaimed by critics as the most promising male vocalist of the year. During the sixties he lived up to that promise, producing such gold-winning albums as *Tobacco Road, Dead End Street,* and *Natural Man.* Lou ended 1977 with a tour of Europe, and in 1978 had two easy-listening hits, "Lady Love" and "One Life to Live."
1978 Discography: *Lou Rawls Live on Broadway*

RAYDIO

Ray Parker, Jr.–Guitars, vocals

Arnell Carmichael–Synthesizer, vocals

Jerry Knight–Bass, vocals

Vincent Bonham–Piano

R & B fans got a tasty new single to bite into at the end of 1977. Called "Jack and Jill," it was described by its creator, Ray Parker, with a sly grin as "an innocent but nasty song." Ray Parker, the supersonic ray of Raydio, dynamic new R & B winners, is no newcomer to the music world. Until now, however, he's always been in the background, his crisp guitar work featured on hits by such artists as Marvin Gaye, Stevie Wonder, Barry White, and Love Unlimited. "I don't know how many records I've played on," he reports. "Just a million hits. If you picked up a record magazine, every week in the top 100 there used to be at least 15 to 20 songs I played on."

Parker, who's been a professional musician for ten of his twenty-three years, taught himself to play guitar during a year when he was confined with a badly broken leg. At thirteen he formed his first group with Ollie Brown and Nathan Watts, two Detroit friends who have gone on to fame. When he was fourteen he toured with the Spinners and then, in tuxedo, lugged 150-pound amplifiers ("More than I weighed at the time," he recalls) through the wedding/bar mitzvah circuit with a group called Jeep Smith and the Troubadors. He graduated to appearances at the Twenty Grand in Detroit, where he and a small group backed such luminaries as Gladys Knight, Stevie Wonder, and the Temptations.

In 1972, Parker's career leaped ahead when he took part in the rollicking Stevie Wonder/Rolling Stones tour. Stevie recorded some of Parker's songs. As Parker puts it, "I decided to start writing because Stevie could go into the studio and play drums, play guitar, plus write these songs. He could do all that, and I was a bit jealous. So I went out and bought all these tape recorders and started to write songs."

Packing all his gear into his Lincoln Continental, Parker then trekked out to Hollywood, where he began selling his songs to such artists as Barry White and Nancy Wilson. His first big hit was the giant "You've Got the Love," written with Chaka Khan, recorded by Rufus.

From then on events moved into high gear for Parker, who started recording with and being recorded by such names as Boz Scaggs, LaBelle, Bobby Womack, Helen Reddy, and Seals and Crofts. Clive Davis, president of Arista Records, hearing Parker was looking for his own career, snapped him up. Parker brought together experienced musicians Arnell Carmichael, Jerry Knight, and Vincent Bonham, molded them into a group, and turned out a neat, driving top-ten soul LP, of which Parker says with a grin, "It just sounds like me. It's a hit sound."
1978 Discography: *Raydio.*

HELEN REDDY

Born in Melbourne, Australia, the daughter of show business parents, Helen Reddy began performing at the tender age of four. After winning a talent contest in Australia, Helen came to America in April of 1966. After settling in New York, she struggled for several months to get her career off the ground. Nothing happened.

At the end of 1966, discouraged and almost daunted, she met and married agent Jeff Wald. With his support she kept plugging away at singing while he kept trying to find her a big break.

In 1968, they moved to Chicago, where she worked in a comedy revue and cut a single for Mercury Records. Neither did anything to further her career. Then everything began to happen with a rush. She and Jeff had moved to California in 1969, and in 1970, thanks to the help of Flip Wilson, she made an appearance on the "Tonight Show" and was immediately signed by Artie Mogull of Capitol Records.

Her first single, "I Don't Know How to Love Him," a song from *Jesus Christ Superstar,* became a sizeable hit. Her second single, however, was her big breakthrough. "I Am Woman," Helen's own composition, was a powerful women's lib anthem that struck a responsive chord and sold 1 million copies.

In 1978, Helen can proudly point to three more gold singles: "Delta Dawn," "Leave Me Alone (Ruby Red Dress)," and "Angie Baby," as well as six gold and three platinum albums. In 1977, she appeared in the Walt Disney movie *Pete's Dragon,* and her version of the song "Candle on the Water" was nominated for an Academy Award. Helen also has the distinction of being one-half of one of the strangest star-producer teams extant. Her last album, *Ear Candy,* was coproduced by the legendary king of punk-rock, the wild and wicked Kim Fowley, Los Angeles's answer to Mick Jagger.

LOU REED

The legendary Velvet Underground, New York City's darkly powerful chronicler of the seamy underside of 1960s hippie life, was a short-lived flame. Lou Reed was there, perhaps its most important member, writing songs like "Heroin," "Waiting for My Man," "White Light/White Heat," "Sweet Jane," and "Rock and Roll," blistering, grimy portraits for Nico, John Cale, and the other Velvets.

Raised in the streets of New York, Reed was always a hard rocker. After a two-year hiatus following the Underground's split in 1970, Lou came back rocking stronger than ever. The album *Lou Reed* contained the knife-edged "Wild Child," "Ocean," "Walk It and

Talk It." The next album, the David-Bowie-produced *Transformer,* contained "Walk on the Wild Side," a rock-and-roll classic throbbing with insistent rhythms and Lou's insinuating vocals.

In the fall of 1973, Reed produced *Berlin,* a bold attempt to tell a tragic story as rock music. Its view of reality was harsh, and the album was a commercial failure. He seemed to bounce back with his next album, the recorded-live *Rock 'n' Roll Animal,* a raw blast of performing heat. Captured at New York's Academy of Music, this remains his best-selling album, reaching the half million mark and gold status in 1978.

After that, however, Lou fell into decline; his performances became increasingly bizarre; his work deteriorated. Ironically, as he sneeringly offered audiences parodies of himself, his popularity grew. The critically abused *Sally Can't Dance* was his first top-twenty album. He finally shook himself of fans by the thousands with *Metal Machine Music,* a grinding, aggressive disaster that RCA had to pull off the shelves. It led to the termination of their long contract with him.

In 1976, Reed signed with Arista Records and released *Rock and Roll Heart.* His 1978 album, *Street Hassle,* was hailed as a stunning achievement, but its rough language caused it to be banned from air play around the country. For Lou, whose powerful visions have influenced the entire new wave movement as well as such stars as Patti Smith and Bruce Springsteen, it is a sad irony that his latest album, reported to be his best by far, cannot be heard.
1978 Discography: *Street Hassle*

REO SPEEDWAGON

Kevin Cronin—Rhythm guitar, vocals

Gary Richards—Lead guitar

Neal Doughty—Keyboards

Bruce Hall—Bass

Alan Gratzer—Drums, percussion

REO Speedwagon is the name of a massive semitrailer truck, and anyone who has heard its namesake group pound out hard-driving music will understand the derivation of the name. Onstage, the band named REO Speedwagon delivers 450 horsepower of nonstop rock and roll. In 1977, the band captured that raw onstage vitality in a tough rocker called *You Get What You Play For.* That double album netted them their first gold disk and is still climbing.

It took REO eight hard-traveling years, blasting their howitzer drum beat and machine-gun guitar fire at audiences all over the country; it was eight years of life on the road, in small clubs and large halls, playing both as opening act and headliner, honing and polishing, writing and rewriting, rehearsing and working, working, working, before their tight core of midwestern fans grew to include the whole country.

The success of *You Get What You Play For* looks like the beginning of a new stage of REO's career. Their 1978 album, the self-produced *You Can Tune a Piano But You Can't Tuna Fish,* has won them their second gold disk. And 1978's powerhouse tour saw them rock the rafters of halls and auditoriums from coast to coast.
1978 Discography: *You Can Tune a Piano But You Can't Tuna Fish*

MARTY ROBBINS

When Marty Robbins appeared at the Palomino, Los Angeles's country night club, early in January 1978, his performance was just one huge hit song after another. They were all there, the whole impressive Robbins canon, from "Singing the Blues" to "Devil Woman," from "A White Sport Coat" to "My Woman, My Woman, My Wife," as well as

"El Paso" and some of his more current country monsters, such as 1977's "Don't Let Me Touch You."

Since 1957, when his first single, "A White Sport Coat," won him national acclaim, Robbins has turned out more than four hundred songs. While it's true that country songs seem to flow easiest from his pen, Robbins doesn't limit his output to the country style. He has sung and written straight ballads and blues, as well as Polynesian, Mexican, and gospel music in addition to good old-fashioned country and western.

During the three years he was stationed in the Pacific with the navy, the Arizona-born Robbins taught himself to play guitar and write songs. After his return to civilian life, he debuted as a singer with a friend's band back in Phoenix. He won over local audiences and his one-shot performance extended into a steady job as guitarist with the band.

Robbins's reputation grew, and he soon had his own radio show and a television program called "Western Caravan." In great demand as a guest on television shows today, he has appeared on most of the major ones and has starred in about a dozen movies. Marty is also a serious stock car racer and finds the time to compete in four or five major races each year. In 1976, he had the honor of driving the pace car in the Indianapolis 500.

In 1978, Marty's career continued on track with hits like "Return to Me" topping the country charts.

KENNY ROGERS

After years of making superior, top-charted music with the group the First Edition, Kenny Rogers burst out on his own and continued to make superior, top-charted music. *Daytime Friends,* his 1977 album entry, picked up gold certification at the end of 1977. His 1977 country and pop hit "Lucille" won him a Grammy for Best Country Vocal Performance, Male, the Single of the Year Award from the British Country Music Association, the American Music Award for Favorite Country Single, the American Country Music Association Awards for Single and Song of the Year, and the Academy of Country Music Awards for Record and Song of the Year. He was also named Top Male Vocalist by the Academy, and *Daytime Friends* was Album of the Year.

In 1978, Kenny added the duet form to his repertoire. With Dottie West, he cut a top-ten country album from which came a number-one country single of the same name, "Every Time Two Fools Collide."

But Kenny continued to win kudos on his own in 1978. His number-one country album, *Ten Years of Gold,* was also his first platinum album. The same week that *Ten Years of Gold* was number one on the country charts, *Every Time Two Fools Collide* was in the top ten, and *Daytime Friends* was number nineteen. His single "Love or Something Like It" from the pop and country album chart-topper of the same name, was also a number-one country winner.

Born in Houston, Texas, into a family that included seven brothers and sisters, Kenny began singing in the church choir while in high school. He also organized a high school group called the Scholars. Even in those days Kenny was marked for success, as the Scholars' first single, "Crazy Feeling," sold a million copies. Kenny wisely decided to stick to singing, gaining experience with the Bobby Doyle Trio and then the New Christy Minstrels. In 1967, he began a lengthy stay with the First Edition, who scored right off the bat with their first single, the wry "Just Dropped In to See What Condition My Condition Was In."
1978 Discography: *Ten Years of Gold*
　　　　　　　　　　Every Time Two Fools Collide (with Dottie West)
　　　　　　　　　　Love or Something Like It

Helen Reddy Courtesy Capitol Records

REO Speedwagon Courtesy Epic Records

Lou Reed Courtesy Arista Records

Marty Robbins Courtesy Columbia Records

Linda Ronstadt Courtesy Asylum Records

Kenny Rogers Courtesy United Artists Records

The Rolling Stones Courtesy Atlantic Records

THE ROLLING STONES

Mick Jagger—Vocals, guitar

Keith Richards—Guitar, vocals

Ron Wood—Guitar

Bill Wyman—Bass

Charlie Watts—Drums

From the very earliest days in 1962, when Mick Jagger and Keith Richards were scrabbling around London trying to put together a viable band, the Rolling Stones have been surrounded by an aura of perversity and evil. Their scruffy looks and aggressive music quickly won them the reputation of the world's foremost bad band, a reputation they gloried in for years. It was a reputation built on the songwriting genius of Jagger and Richards, the performing overdrive of Charlie Watts, Bill Wyman, and Brian Jones, and five years of screaming-down-the-line rock-and-roll songs, including such classics as "Satisfaction," "Get Off My Cloud," "Let's Spend the Night Together," "Paint It Black," "Jumpin' Jack Flash," "Sympathy for the Devil," "Street Fightin' Man," "Honky Tonk Woman," and "Midnight Rambler."

They were an unprecedented phenomenon in the 1960s. Elvis may have given the world a new sexuality in its music, but there had never been anything like the hard, bored meanness of the Rolling Stones. It was no surprise that two Rolling Stones events marked the end of the 1960s hippie dream. One was the mysterious drowning of guitarist Brian Jones on July 3, 1969, less than a month after he left the band. The other was the Altamont concert, designed as a climax to the decade, planned to be the biggest free-love, free-dope, free-music celebration of them all. Three hundred thousand people gathered at California's Altamont Speedway, but the glorious party was swiftly shattered. Sometime during the Stones's performance, a hapless black was killed in a scuffle. Three years later, audiences who had missed the real-life event could catch it on the big screen, as all its tawdry flash was captured in the Maysle brothers' film Gimme Shelter.

The Stones went on to produce two more powerful albums—Sticky Fingers, with the brilliant "Moonlight Mile" and the raunchy "Brown Sugar," and Exile on Main Street. But the following albums, Goat's Head Soup, It's Only Rock 'n' Roll, and Black and Blue, were critical and popular disappointments. The group's overhyped 1975 tour met with more questions than it could answer. The 1970s were shaping up as a lackluster decade for the band, and, although the word most often used to describe 1977's performances at Toronto's 350-seat El Mocambo Club was "dynamite," there was some speculation that the Stones were finished.

In 1978, however, there were some mighty bombshells from rock's original bad boys. There was a new, critically adored album, Some Girls, a swift million-seller, with a real old-fashioned hit single, "Miss You," and a grand concert tour of the United States, during which the Stones played large arenas like J.F.K. Stadium in Philadelphia as well as unannounced concerts in small halls like New York's Palladium and New Jersey's Capitol. Varying reports came back from the different concerts. Many found the Stones to be in excellent shape; others accused Jagger of conveying nothing but strained boredom, except when he performed songs from the new album. But there was an excitement that had not been apparent in years, from the usual near-riots when the Stones wouldn't do encores to riots by disgruntled fans who couldn't buy tickets to rumors of lawsuits for their unauthorized use of some famous faces on their album cover, and a record-setting indoor concert gross for their July 13 performance at the New Orleans Superdome. It was only rock 'n' roll, but fans loved it.
1978 Discography: Some Girls

LINDA RONSTADT

At the end of 1977, Linda Ronstadt had again outdone herself. From her platinum showcase, Simple Dreams, came "Blue Bayou" and "It's So Easy," both of which shot to the top ten, arriving there at the same time. It was the first time since the heyday of the Beatles that any artist had two singles in the top ten at once. A month later she won Billboard's Female Artist of the Year Award, and in January of 1978 she won the American Music Award as the nation's favorite pop/rock female vocalist. A 1977 concert she gave at the Summit in Houston was filmed for the movie FM, providing some of that picture's finest moments. In June 1978, "I Never Will Marry" was a top-ten country single.

Linda's gutsy, sensual voice has torn into such hits as "Long, Long Time," "You're No Good," "When Will I Be Loved," "I Can't Help It if I'm Still In Love with You," "Heat Wave," and "That'll Be The Day." To anyone who knows her well it came as no surprise that the shy young lady from Tucson, Arizona, made it to the top with such speed and style. Beneath her early insecurities there was always a strong sense of her own power and talents—and always the fierce drive to become a star.

Her career began in the 1960s, when she, Bob Kimmel, and Ken Edwards, as the Stone Poneys, had a huge hit with Monkee Mike Nesmith's "Different Drum." Linda's ambition drove her to leave the group and record her first solo album, the countrified Hand Sown, Home Grown, in 1969. Although the album did not sell spectacularly, it created for Linda a small but faithful group of fans and sent her out for the beginning of what were to be years of hard, intense touring.

Everywhere she went she captured new fans with her teasingly sensual stage presence. Silk Purse, her 1970 album, strengthened her position as a leading interpreter of country classics. In 1971, after winning over the Continent on a tour of England and France, she gathered together Glenn Frey, Don Henley, and Randy Meisner, soon-to-be Eagles, to add a rock-and-roll blast to Linda Ronstadt, her third album.

In 1973, Linda signed with Asylum Records. Her first album for them was Don't Cry Now, and Linda moved into a period of frenzied, nonstop touring that she has only recently allowed to slow down. It was in 1974, when producer Peter Asher began working with her albums, that she really made the breakthrough. Her first album with him, Heart Like a Wheel, sold more than a million copies, as did Prisoner in Disguise, Hasten Down the Wind, and Linda Ronstadt's Greatest Hits.

Today, with her career under control, her beach house at Malibu remodeled, her friends surrounding and supporting her, Linda can finally slow the frantic pace a bit and take the time to be with herself.
1978 Discography: Living in the U.S.A.

ROSE ROYCE

Kenji Chiba Brown—Lead guitar, vocals

Kenny "Captain Gold" Copeland—Trumpet, vocals

Gwen Dickey—Lead vocals

Freddie Dunn—Trumpet

Henry "Hammer" Garner—Drums, vocals

Lequeint "Duke" Jobe—Bass guitar, vocals

Michael Moore—Saxophone, vocals

Mike Nash—Keyboards

Terral "Powerpack" Santiel—Percussion, vocals

Phenomenal Phunk from L.A. characterizes Rose Royce, who tore into 1978 with a couple of number-one soul singles—"Do You Dance, Part One" and "Ooo Boy"—and a shining platinum award for In Full Bloom, their second album and their second platinum disk. Not bad

Diana Ross　　　　　　　　　　　　Bob Deutsch

plaudits for a group that first came together in 1976, but not their only honors by any means. They had already gathered such kudos as Cash Box's Number One New R & B Group of the Year and Number One Pop Group of the Year, the Golden Disco Award as the Number One New Group of the Year, a Grammy for the Best Original Sound Track, the Cannes Film Festival award for the Best Soundtrack of the Year, and *Record World*'s awards as Number One Top Vocal Group of the Year, Number One Sound Track of the Year, and Number One New Vocal Group. They made a big splash in 1976.

Of course, they had all had experience. Norman Whitfield, then one of Motown Records' brightest producers, responsible for the Temptations' hits, heard them backing up the Temps, Edwin Starr, and Yvonne Fair and immediately saw their potential. He took over the group, polished them up, taught them recording techniques, and sent them out to be winners. Duke Jobe points out, "Norman taught us

Rufus with Chaka Khan　　　　Courtesy ABC Records

Rose Royce

Courtesy Whitfield Records

271

not only how to produce records, but how to produce hit records." They had already begun to tour as Rose Royce when they realized that they needed a strong female voice to give a special spice to their sound. They found what they were looking for in Gwen Dickey, whose infectious spirit was just right for them. Together they make beautiful music.
1978 Discography: *Rose Royce Strikes Again*

DIANA ROSS

She began life as a skinny kid from Detroit with determination: "If I'm going to do something, then it's going to have to be the right thing because I'm going to work with everything I've got to make it right." That attitude was toughened in the poverty-stricken streets of her hometown, where she grew up a baseball-playing tomboy. Her other early love was singing, and she and classmates Mary Wilson and Florence Ballard would often harmonize after school.

The girls were no ordinary high school singing group, and Berry Gordy, who was then creating Motown Records, heard the promise in those voices when they rehearsed for him in 1960. He hired them and gave them the chance to learn about the possibilities and challenges of professional music as a back-up group for such other Motown acts as Marvin Gaye and Mary Wells.

Dubbed the Supremes, the trio went out on their first tour as soon as they had graduated from high school. Their first single—"Where Did Our Love Go?"—soared to the top of the charts. It was followed by a golden string of memorable hits, including such songs as "Baby Love," "Stop in the Name of Love," and "Come See about Me." With their sweet, driving harmonies, the Supremes were the cream at the top. Their future looked like an endless stream of smash songs.

But then, at the peak of their success, lead singer Diana announced that she was going to leave the group. The music world waited in stunned surprise, wondering what she could do as a solo that would equal the track record of the Supremes. Anyone who had doubts was underestimating Diana, who snapped right back to the top with her performance as Billie Holiday in *Lady Sings the Blues,* winning an Academy Award nomination. In 1976, the love song she sang in *Mahogany*—the bittersweet "Do You Know Where You're Going to?"—also won an Oscar nomination.

During 1977, Diana scored with her album *An Evening with Diana Ross* and the singles "Baby It's Me," a top-ten soul winner, and "Gettin' Ready for Love," a top-ten easy-listening single. In 1978, she toured busily, giving her fans the fiery performances they expect from her. Her single, "You Get It," was a top easy-listening hit, and her performance as Dorothy in the film *The Wiz* was a personal triumph.

RUFUS Featuring Chaka Khan

Chaka Khan–Vocals
Tony Maiden–Guitar
Bobby Watson–Bass
Kevin Murphy–Keyboards
David "Hawk" Wolinski–Keyboards
Richard "Moon" Calhoun–Drums

A nonstop powerhouse of a band, Rufus displays anew their dynamic mastery of slam-bang rhythm and blues in their latest album, the number-one soul, shipped-gold LP *Street Player*. With its top-ten soul single, "Stay," *Street Player* is another step forward for this relentlessly boogieing volcano.

Rufus got its first power boost from Stevie Wonder himself, who supplied them with a number of his songs for their second album. One of them, "Tell Me Something Good," sizzled its way up the charts in 1974, sold a million copies, and won a Grammy. From then on, it was as their second album proclaimed—*Rags to Rufus*. That album

skyrocketed to platinum, as did *Ask Rufus,* their 1977 monster. *Rufusized* and *Rufus Featuring Chaka Khan* were gold-winners as well.

Those are impressive credentials for a group that's been in existence for only six years. But the credentials of the six individuals who make up Rufus are impressive indeed. Lead singer Chaka Khan, with feline grace and a voice that packs a boilerhouse punch, left school when she was sixteen to sing, making her professional debut with a group called the Babysitters. Kevin Murphy, a professional musician for more than eighteen years, learned his craft with the Crystals, Del Shannon, and Brian Hyland and the American Breed. Fellow keyboard genius David "Hawk" Wolinski was a member of Minnie Riperton's band and cowrote the single "Take me Back to Chicago" with Danny Seraphine. Guitarist Tony Maiden, along with Bobby Watson, were part of Ray Charles's Rhythm Rebellion; drummer Richard "Moon" Calhoun has years of percussion experience in his native Tulsa. Together, they really cook.
1978 Discography: *Street Player*

SAMANTHA SANG

Samantha Sang is the newest Australian-born performer to zap the American charts. Early in 1978 her first release in the United States, the Barry and Robin Gibb song "Emotion," won her a gold record. Samantha, a star in Australia since her early teens, finally grabbed the opportunity to perform in the United States, a chance that had been denied her eight years before.

At the age of sixteen, Samantha, who began performing on Australian radio when she was eight, won the Australian Best Female Vocalist Award for her second record, "You Made Me What I Am." As a result of her success, she toured Europe, met Barry Gibb, and recorded his song "Love of a Woman." That one became an international million-seller, and Samantha became an international traveler. Because of her age, however, she was not permitted to enter the United States. Samantha continued to travel the world, performing in eleven European television specials and touring and winning awards in Europe, Tokyo, South Africa, Japan, and New Zealand.

Her first album, *Emotion,* was produced by Nick De Caro and Gary Klein, who produced such hit records as Dolly Parton's *Here You Come Again,* Glen Campbell's *Southern Nights,* and Barbra Streisand's *Superman.*
1978 Discography: *Emotion*

BOZ SCAGGS

It took him eighteen years to win his first platinum album and only a little more than one to get his second. The first of his sizzling successes, 1976's *Silk Degrees,* has gone on to sell 3 million copies. The second, *Down Two Then Left,* received its platinum award at the beginning of 1978.

From his early days performing and writing music with high school buddy Steve Miller, Scaggs has never abandoned music. Even during a two-year stretch in Europe in the mid-sixties, he continued to play and sing, cutting an album called *Boz,* still available only in Europe. Back in the United States in 1967, he became part of the Steve Miller Blues Band and stuck with them until the album *Sailor* was finished, at which point he felt he was ready to go out on his own.

Five albums followed—tight, professional, but of limited commercial success. *Boz Scaggs* was produced in Muscle Shoals, Alabama, with the help of *Rolling Stone* Editor Jann Wenner and includes the San Francisco favorite "Loan Me a Dime"; *Moments* contained the hit "We Were Always Sweethearts"; *Boz Scaggs and Band* was produced in England by Glyn Johns, producer of the

Rolling Stones and the Who; *My Time,* produced in Muscle Shoals again, contained the hit "Dinah Flo"; *Slow Dancer* was sweetly soulful; and then came *Silk Degrees,* with its Grammy-winning disco hit "Lowdown" and—finally—commercial recognition of Boz Scaggs as a major rock talent.

BOB SEGER

Bob Seger–Guitar, electric piano, vocals

Drew Abbot–Lead guitar

Robyn Robbins–Keyboard

Alto Reed–Saxophones, flute

Charlie Martin–Drums

He's been covered with intense praise in a very short time, but every flattering word in *Newsweek, Rolling Stone,* the *New York Times, New Musical Express,* and many other publications must give him particular satisfaction. It took years for this talented hard rocker to reach the pinnacle of his career because he stubbornly resisted the efforts of record companies to put him in a slick, neat package. Finally, after a decade of performing 300 days a year, his album, *Live Bullet,* shot him to national fame in 1976.

Seger had always been the darling of Detroit fans, who jammed into Detroit's Cobo Hall for his performances, and then stomped and hollered and shook themselves wild when he appeared. Those Motor City folk had eagerly snapped up 80,000 copies of *Beautiful Loser,* which gave Capitol Records a nudge in his direction. But it was *Live Bullet,* a spur-of-the-moment double album recorded at two sold-out shows at Cobo Hall, that captured the white heat of Seger's performance and the frenzy of his fans.

Live Bullet is now platinum, as is *Night Moves,* his 1976 album. *Stranger in Town* shipped platinum in 1978, and Seger toured to promote it in the winter of 1978. For Seger this is all a rare delight, but his new success has not gone to his head. He lives modestly, continues to call Detroit his home, and, realizing the vicissitudes of fame, says of his, "This is nice for a change."
1978 Discography: *Stranger in Town*

RUDOLF SERKIN

Born in Eger, Bohemia (now Czechoslovakia), in 1903, premiere pianist Rudolf Serkin celebrated his seventy-fifth birthday in 1978. It was a triumphant year, during which the pianist proved once again his mastery of the instrument and fortified the respect with which he is regarded in the United States. His first full-scale TV solo recital program, which opened the series "Tonight at Carnegie Hall," was a triumph, judged by the *New York Times* to be "Exemplary performances by one of the greatest artists ever to sit down before a piano." He was also seen on "Live from Lincoln Center," where he played Beethoven's *Emperor Concerto,* and became the first soloist to perform with Zubin Mehta in Mehta's new position as music director of the New York Philharmonic.

Serkin studied piano in Vienna with Professor Richard Robert and composition with Joseph Marx and Arnold Schoenberg. He made his debut with the Vienna Symphony at age twelve. His first appearance in the United States was in 1933, when he and his mentor, violinist Adolf Busch, played for a specially invited audience at the Coolidge Festival held at the Library of Congress. After his formal debut in New York, with Toscanini and the New York Philharmonic in 1936, he was hailed as one of the greatest living pianists.

The list of honors and awards he has won is long and impressive. He was the first artist to be invited by President and Mrs. Carter to perform at a White House State Dinner. He has been awarded honorary degrees from Curtis Institute in Philadelphia (where he taught between 1939 and 1975, and was director from 1968 to 1975)

and from Harvard University, Williams College, Temple University, University of Vermont, Oberlin College, Marlboro College, and the University of Rochester.

He tours the United States annually and makes regular tours of Europe, apearing in recital, with chamber ensembles, and with all the major orchestras. In addition, he has played in South America, Iceland, Israel, India, and throughout the Far East. He has recorded more than thirty-five albums for Columbia Records, concentrating on the great works of the Romantic composers.

SHA NA NA

Lennie Baker–Lead tenor vocals, saxophone

Jon (Bowzer) Bauman–Bass vocals

Johnny Contardo–Vocals

Denny Greene–Vocals

Jocko Marcellino–Drums, vocals

Danny ("Dirty Dan") McBride–Lead guitar

Scott (Santini) Powell–Guitar, vocals

David-Allan (Chico) Ryan–Bass

Scott (Screamin') Simon–Piano

Don York–Vocals, guitar, piano, drums

Watching their lunatic stage show or their zany television series, it's hard to believe that these ten madmen number among their combined educational experiences Juilliard, the Boston Conservatory, the Cavallaro School, Boston University, New York University, and Columbia University, where the band had its beginnings in 1969 as a twelve-man a cappella group called the Kingsmen. Four of that original twelve, drummer Jocko Marcellino and vocalists Denny Greene, Scott Powell, and Donny York are still with the band today.

At first, they did very few 1950s songs. But Columbia students went crazy over those oldies. So Sha Na Na called its first campus concert the *Grease Ball* and packed it full of doo-wops, yips, and booms. It was a phenomenal success.

Jammed into Steve Paul's club, the tiny but influential The Scene, they rocked music-industry executives and media with their tightly choreographed, brilliantly paced stage show. Their big break came when they performed at Woodstock, where they were cheered by hundreds of thousands; their version of "At the Hop" was included in the movie and Sha Na Na became a band in demand.

Ever since, they've traveled across the country, giving their audiences zany humor along with a serious treatment of rock-and-roll classics, with Lennie Baker bustling his massive girth around on stage, (belieing the title of their 1977 song, "Too Chubby to Boogie"), Jon Bauman flexing his lean muscles, and Scott Powell flashing his gold lamé jumpsuit.

Their successful television series, now beginning its third year, continues to add fuel to the flame of their already massive coast-to-coast popularity.

BEVERLY SILLS

Early in 1978, Beverly Sills announced that she will retire from her singing career in 1980 to become codirector of the New York City Opera. It's hard to imagine the vivacious soprano in the wings rather than center stage. Despite the demands of a best-selling autobiography (*Bubbles*) and a respected television series, Sills has always managed to perform and record frequently throughout each year.

Born Belle Silverman in Brooklyn, New York, she grew up sing-

Courtesy Norby Walters Associates

Samantha Sang

Boz Scaggs

Courtesy Columbia Records

Bob Seger and the Silver Bullet Band   Courtesy Capitol Records

ing. She performed on radio's "Major Bowes Capitol Family Hour" when she was only nine, soon graduating to the New York City Opera. After eleven years of singing various roles, she achieved the pinnacle of operatic superstardom with her brilliant performance of Cleopatra in Handel's *Julius Caesar.*

Other triumphs followed, including stunning performances in Donizetti's trilogy about British royalty, *Roberto Devereux, Maria Stuarda,* and *Anna Bolena.* She also flashed fire in the demanding *Lucia di Lammermoor* and revealed comedic gifts in her interpretations of Marie in *The Daughter of the Regiment* and Rosina in *The Barber of Seville.*

Miss Sills made her London debut at Covent Garden in 1970 and her Paris debut in 1971. Her long-awaited debut at the Met was a historic performance of Rossini's *The Siege of Corinth,* in April, 1975. Her professional credits include fifteen full-length opera recordings; several solo recital albums; a repertoire of more than seventy roles; and star appearances at the world's most respected opera houses. She won an Emmy in 1975 for a television program called "Profile in Music," produced by the BBC, and charmed American television viewers in the fall of 1976 when she appeared with Carol Burnett in a television special called "Sills and Burnett at the Met."

CARLY SIMON

Carly toured for only a month her first time out, and she didn't brave any hall with a capacity of more than 2500. And because her commitments to husband James Taylor and children Benjamin and Sarah are, she claims, more important to her than her career, her touring

Sha Na Na

Rudolf Serkin

Beverly Sills

Carly Simon

Paul Simon

was limited to the East Coast. But if her lone, brilliant 1977 performance at New York's Other End represented dipping her toe into the waters of performing, for Carly Simon the 1978 tour meant at least waist-high immersion. And, judging from the good time she had at New York's Bottom Line on May 4—when she threw strawberries and chocolate kisses to her devoted audience—Carly may be beginning to think the water's fine.

It is hard to believe that Carly, a daughter of Richard Simon, cofounder of Simon & Schuster, should have any fears. If you didn't know that she has always hated singing in public, a dislike that dates back to the performances she and sister Lucy gave as the Simon Sisters at Sarah Lawrence College, you might think that she was suppressing her natural ambitions so as not to be a threat to husband James Taylor. She did, after all, admit to Ed Ward in an interview in *Us* Magazine that she and James are fiercely competitive and that her marriage comes first. But as she revealed in Charles Young's provocative *Rolling Stone* interview, she now feels like a star.

Of course, she's always been one. From her first hit single, 1971's sensitive, perceptive "That's the Way I've Always Heard it Should Be," (it won her a Grammy as Best New Artist), through "Anticipation," through 1972's monster, "You're So Vain," to 1977's "Nobody Does It Better," Carly has always had a strong way with a song and an electrifying effect on those audiences fortunate enough to catch her live.

In 1978, her smooth love song, "You Belong to Me," became a top-ten single, and her album, *Boys in the Trees,* a top-ten gold-winner.

1978 Discography: *Boys in the Trees*

PAUL SIMON

There have been several times in the history of music (and, no doubt, in the history of every other human endeavor), when fortuitous accident has radically altered the shape of the future. One such fortuitous accident occurred when producer Tom Wilson, left to his own devices, sagely if whimsically decided to add electric guitar, bass, and drums to "The Sound of Silence," a cut from Simon and Garfunkel's first album, *Wednesday Morning 3 A.M.* The song became a major hit; Paul Simon quickly returned from London, where he had just completed recording *The Paul Simon Song Book,* an album of his songs accompanied by himself on acoustic guitar. The success of "The Sound of Silence" created great demand for the duo on the college circuit, and the incredible success saga of Simon and Garfunkel began.

Paul Simon was born in Newark, New Jersey, and raised in Queens. He had known Art Garfunkel since they were both children attending the same New York school. In 1957, they called themselves Tom and Jerry and recorded a song called "Hey! Schoolgirl" that became a top-forty hit. They had no follow-up material, so they both shrugged and went back to school.

During the next few years Paul sang occasionally with local groups, began and dropped out of law school, and went to England, where he sang in folk clubs, and developed a reputation. When he returned to America, he and Garfunkel teamed up again, signed to Columbia Records, and cut their first album, *Wednesday Morning 3 A.M.*

Quickly established by the success of "The Sound of Silence," the duo went on to produce one hit after another: "Homeward Bound," "The Dangling Conversation," "I am a Rock," "Mrs. Robinson," and "Bridge over Troubled Water," the last from the multimillion-selling album of the same name. After that song, the team split up, with Art Garfunkel going on to act in the film *Catch 22* and Paul Simon continuing to create beautiful music as a solo performer. Since he's been on his own, Simon has had such monster hits as "The Boxer," "Mother and Child Reunion," "Still Crazy after All These Years," and 1977's "Slip Sliding Away."

MARGO SMITH

It was Margo Smith's philosophy as well as her musical talent that led her to burst upon the country music world with four top-ten and two number-one singles in the space of three short years. Her philosophy is simple. The pretty, dark-haired former school teacher from Dayton, Ohio, says, "I believe very simply that you should never say you can't until you have tried. It is no sin to try and fail, but the real sorrow comes from never trying."

Margo's natural musical talents shone through in her classrooms, where she would often use country and folk songs. If she needed a certain type of song to illustrate a point, she would simply write one on the spot.

Before long her talents became known throughout Ohio. After several years and, following the suggestions of her friends, Margo began singing professionally. In 1975, 20th Century Records signed her to a recording contract; her first record, her own song called "There I Have Said It," zoomed to number five in the country charts. When 20th Century phased out its country division, Margo was tapped by Warner Brothers. Her first three records for them were top-ten country hits, and her fourth, 1978's "Don't Break the Heart that Loves You," was a country chart-topper, followed in almost no time by a second hit, "It Only Hurts for a Little While."

Today, Margo has attained some other lofty achievements: She has progressed from opening act to headliner; she is in demand on television's most popular country shows; and the Grand Ole Opry has given her a standing invitation to appear whenever she can.

"I am grateful for all the good things that have happened to me," says Margo, "but none of this would have happened if I hadn't tried. It all goes back to my bit of philosophy. If you want something, go after it. If you try and fail, it's no big deal."

1978 Discography: *Don't Break the Heart that Loves You*

PATTI SMITH

New wave rock-and-shock heroine Patti Smith faces what may be her most difficult artistic challenge in 1978: a hit single. "Because the Night," a collaboration with Bruce Springsteen, walloped charts and the airwaves, casting top-ten attention on the revolutionary lady whose 1978 album, *Easter,* was a top-twenty chart-climber as well.

Patti, a visionary artist who works in many areas, has been and is a poet, actress, playwright, activist, rock critic, filmmaker, artist, stand-up comic, and rock-and-roll star. During the late sixties and early seventies, with sidekick critic Lenny Kaye, she read poetry, published her writing in *Creem,* and then let music take over.

She felt rock and roll, an early love, had been in serious decline since 1970. Her hard-driving, minimalist music was one of the first expressions of punk philosophy, a reaction against what she considered the over-produced flabbiness of rock. In 1974, she and Lenny recorded her first single, "Hey, Joe." Late that year they formed a band and cut their performing teeth at a variety of East and West Coast small clubs. The underground buzzed with news of her howling energy. In New York City, Patti and her friends set down their roots at CBGB, the Soho club that was unofficial home to punk.

Patti's first album, *Horses,* was released to great critical acclaim in 1975. *Radio Ethiopia* was her next. In 1977, her career was slowed but by no means stopped by a fall from the stage in a Florida auditorium. Bravely, wearing a neck brace, Patti appeared at her old haunts. *Easter,* her 1978 album, is a powerful primitive/sophisticated experience, drawing together primitive chants, doo-wop, and aggressive rock and roll.

1978 Discography: *Easter*

SIR GEORG SOLTI

The highlights of Sir Georg Solti's remarkable life in music follow one another with astonishing rapidity. Every musical task he attempts he

Margo Smith

Patti Smith Courtesy Arista Records

Sir Georg Solti

Bruce Springsteen

The Statler Brothers Courtesy Mercury Records

Rod Stewart

277

Steely Dan

Barbra Streisand

Styx

Joan Sutherland

Donna Summer

handles with consummate skill and artistry, easily scaling one musical height after another.

Born October 21, 1912, in Budapest, Sir Georg studied with the top Hungarian composers: Zoltán Kodály, Ernst von Dohnanyi, and Béla Bartók. He was conductor of the Budapest Opera and assistant to Arturo Toscanini at the Salzburg Festival early in his career. Before the beginning of World War II, Sir Georg was forced to flee Hungary. He settled in Switzerland as a refugee and was unable to obtain a work permit to conduct. So he earned his living by drawing on his early training as a pianist, apearing in concerts and recitals. No ordinary pianist, he won, in 1942, first prize at the International Piano Competition in Geneva.

In 1946, he was invited to conduct a performance of Beethoven's *Fidelio* in Munich. The performance was a glorious success and led to Maestro Solti's appointment as musical director of the Bavarian State Opera. For the next six years he worked diligently with the company until he had returned it to its former glory.

Between 1952 and 1962, Sir Georg was artistic and musical director of the Frankfurt City Opera. In 1962, he became musical director of the Royal Opera House, Covent Garden, London, where he remained until 1971. When he left that position, he was knighted by Britain's Queen Elizabeth for his decade of service.

But perhaps Sir Georg's most spectacular contributions have been made as music director of the Chicago Symphony Orchestra. It was with the Chicago that he completed his masterful interpretations of the Mahler symphonies. With the Chicago he recorded Mahler's Symphony No. 8 ("Symphony of a Thousand"), which went on to win three Grammy awards. In 1975, his recording of Berlioz's *Symphonie Fantastique* won three Grammies; his recording of the nine Beethoven symphonies won a Grammy for Best Classical Album in 1976.

In 1978, he and the Chicago scooped up two more Grammies, one for the *Verdi Requiem* and one for his recording of Ravel's *Boléro.*

His long and varied career has been filled with honors. He has appeared as guest conductor with many of the world's leading orchestras and opera companies; he is the holder of honorary doctor of music degrees from Yale and DePaul universities in the United States and from Oxford University and the University of Leeds in England; he has won the coveted French Academy's Grand Prix du Disque eleven times, more than any other conductor. His historic recording of Wagner's Ring Cycle, featuring the Vienna Philharmonic and such renowned stars as Kirsten Flagstad, Birgit Nilsson, Dietrich Fischer-Dieskau, and Joan Sutherland, is perhaps his most celebrated recording achievement.

BRUCE SPRINGSTEEN

Springsteen's back, and the expected hysteria over his return materialized with a rush. Within four weeks of its release, his new album, *Darkness on the Edge of Town,* was a platinum-winner; his singles "Prove It All Night" and "Badlands" rocketed onto the pop charts, and he was greeted by the hungry adoration of fans in a bruising eighty-date tour of seventy cities. That he's glad to be back is obvious as he greets his audiences with the same fervor they have for him.

They've been waiting a long time for Bruce's blistering visions, those rocking fans. It was two years and nine months between *Born to Run*'s hopeful energy and this year's return of one of the early seventies' most promising artists. Prevented from touring and recording by legal difficulties with former manager Mike Appel, Springsteen's natural talents have been enhanced by the mystic aura created by absence and longing.

His first album, *Greetings from Asbury Park, NJ,* was met with the whispers, stares and knowing nudges of the rock media. Although he clearly showed a debt to Bob Dylan, his songs rang with a power and energy of imagination that separated him from every other Dylan-influenced singer/songwriter/guitarist.

His next album effort, *The Wild, the Innocent and the E-Street Shuffle* was the first record to display the talents of his tight, profes-

sional back-up group, the E-Street Band. With the release of that album, critical acclaim threatened to sweep him off his feet. He was hailed as the new messiah of rock and roll by none other than *Rolling Stone*'s Jon Landau, who said of him, "I have seen the future of rock 'n' roll, and it's called Bruce Springsteen."

A lesser personality would have folded under the weight of such responsibility. Bruce, however, recorded *Born to Run.* Released in late 1975, the album and title single lived up to his reputation and won him a gold record.

His latest album, with its urgent, sometimes poignant imagery and the desperate violence just beneath the surface, is a brilliant counterpoint to the discofied tone of 1978.
1978 Discography: *Darkness on the Edge of Town*

STATLER BROTHERS

Harold Reid—Vocals

Lew DeWitt—Vocals

Don Reid—Vocals

Phil Balsey—Vocals

Since 1955, when they sang together for the first time as a gospel group in Lynhurst Methodist Church in their hometown of Staunton, Virginia, Harold Reid, Lew DeWitt, Don Reid, and Phil Balsey—better known as the Statler Brothers—have been stopping shows with their sweet country harmonies and gentle humor. Harold recalls that everyone in the church loved the Statlers. "I never figured out," he adds laughingly, "whether the congregation thought we were great because we were great or because we were free."

Today, with years of chart-topping country singles, six consecutive awards from the Country Music Association for Vocal Group of the Year, 1977's award from the Academy of Country Music as Top Vocal Group of the Year, a million-selling album (*Best of the Statler Brothers*), 1978 top country singles in "Do You Know You Are My Sunshine" and "Who Am I to Say," and still another top-ten country album in 1978's *Entertainers...On and Off the Record*, there should be no doubt in Harold's mind that even the embryonic Statlers provided that early audience with something a little more substantial than a free ride.

Perhaps there was some doubt in their minds in those early days, because the group broke up in 1958. In 1960, they reformed as the Kingsmen, still primarily a gospel group, singing at churches, banquets, and on local television while continuing to hold down full-time jobs.

In 1964, they got their first break when they met Johnny Cash at a show in Roanoke, Virginia. Cash asked them to open a show for him and afterwards told them that he liked their act. "Well," says Harold, "I went home and called twice a week on the phone for four months. One night we finally tracked him down doing some television show and got to talk to him. We had to go to work for him to pay the telephone bill."

They were able to pay more than the telephone bill, as they toured with Cash for the next eight years. Since that time they have won Grammies for "Flowers on the Wall" and "The Class of '57" and have had huge country hits with "Bed of Rose's," "Do You Remember These?" "I'll Go to My Grave Loving You," "Thank God I've Got You," and "I Was There."
1978 Discography: *The Holy Bible* (reissue)
The Statler Brothers' Christmas Card
Entertainers ... On and Off the Record

STEELY DAN

Donald Fagen—Keyboards, vocals

Walter Becker—Bass, vocals

After five merely gold albums, Steely Dan, with *Aja*, their 1977 event, has achieved the mighty platinum, the million-seller. With telegraphic lyrics and vigorous, jazz-flavored rock, Steely Dan has achieved a high level of acclaim.

The core of the group, songwriters Donald Fagen and Walter Becker, first met in the late 1960s while attending New York's Bard College. They started writing music together and then tried to peddle their songs in New York City. When that yielded no results, they started a group, also notable for its lack of success. So they took jobs in 1970 as back-up musicians for Jay and the Americans.

Record producer Gary Katz met them in New York. Katz, who had just been hired by ABC Records in Los Angeles, talked his company into hiring Becker and Fagen as contract writers in 1972. After work, they rehearsed Steely Dan, a group they had put together with some fine musicians from the East. In June, 1972, *Can't Buy a Thrill,* their first album, provided America's ears with two tasty top-ten hits: "Do It Again" and "Reelin' in the Years." *Countdown to Ecstasy,* their 1973 album, was a bit less accessible than their first, but from their third, *Pretzel Logic,* with its advanced jazz textures, came the top-ten hit "Rikki Don't Lose that Number."

Group tensions, however, due to Becker's and Fagen's reluctance to tour and the other band member's need for the financial sustenance supplied by touring, led to the breakdown of the group, with band members scattering to more lucrative positions.

Other musicians were called in to continue breathing life into the musical creations of Fagen and Becker, but their next album, *Katy Lied,* was a disappointment. By 1976, however, *Royal Scam,* with its truckload of twenty-four musicians, showed Becker and Fagen back in their stride, and *Aja,* in its provocative innovation, goes even beyond.

ROD STEWART

His breakup with Britt Ekland makes headlines; he raises eyebrows with a raunchy promotional film for his single "Hot Legs"; does a randy semi-strip for television audiences on "Cher...Special." His makeup, even for a rock star, is bold. Instead of mellowing as he ages, Rod Stewart more and more is becoming rock's bad boy.

In spite of all the "hot Rod" antics, his career in 1978 seemed to be at a higher peak than ever. His 1977 album *Foot Loose and Fancy Free* sold more than a million copies and was given a platinum award at the beginning of the year; the single "You're in My Heart" became his third gold one. He won *Billboard's* Song of the Year Award for "Tonight's the Night," 1977's monster, and he drew sell-out crowds to his American concert tour at the end of 1977 with Air Supply.

Rod's been hard at work on his music since 1964, when he began his career. For the first few years he played with a number of different bands, including Long John Baldry's Hoochie Coochie Men; Steampacket, featuring Brian Auger and Julie Droscoll; and Jeff Beck's band.

In 1969, he was signed to Mercury Records as a solo artist and also teamed with Ron Wood, Kenny Jones, Ronnie Lane, and Ian McLagan in the group Faces. *The Rod Stewart Album* and *Gasoline Alley* were his first two solo LP's, but his first big hit was from his third album, *Every Picture Tells a Story.* That song, the haunting "Maggie May," still stands as one of the best of the seventies, and for some time both the album and the single dominated 1971's charts.

Between 1970 and 1975 Stewart also recorded and toured with Faces, but in 1975 the strain of a double career was beginning to tell. While his 1972 solo album *Never a Dull Moment,* with the smash single "You Wear it Well," went gold, his next two albums—*Smiler* and *Atlantic Crossing*—were not successful. So, in 1975, Stewart announced that his days as a member of Faces were over and that he was going to be a strictly solo act from then on. In 1976 came proof that he had made the right decision—the huge platinum-seller *A Night on the Town* with its equally huge single, "Tonight's the Night."

In 1978, there's been no let-up for the gravel-voiced singer. After his American tour he took a brief vacation, then was off to Paris to cut a new album, then off on a three-month tour of Great Britain. Stewart says he works so hard because he feels the hot breath of competition breathing down his neck at all times.

BARBRA STREISAND

If Barbra Streisand beams even more radiantly than usual in 1978, it's because her career has taken new leaps forward. Her 1977 smash single, the Grammy-winning "Evergreen," won her her first Grammy since 1965 for Best Pop Female Vocal Performance. *Billboard* voted her Easy Listening Artist of the Year, and *A Star Is Born* was voted Soundtrack of the Year. She recorded the theme for the much publicized Faye Dunaway vehicle *The Eyes of Laura Mars* (produced by husband Jon Peters), and her 1978 album, *Songbird,* produced the number-one easy listening title smash, and became her sixteenth gold LP. (Or perhaps her twenty-second. No one is exactly sure how many gold albums Barbra has gathered.)

The irrepressible lady who has been driven by a desire to be somebody special since early childhood has achieved that goal many times over. The formerly funny-looking kid who regularly haunted the offices of casting agents and was just as regularly turned away, never gave up her dream. She clung to it with determination, grit, and hard, hard, work, and eventually her extraordinary talent began making her dream come true.

The tangible results of that dream include her Oscar for *Funny Girl,* the Emmy she won for her television special, her gold records, her two command performances at the White House, and perhaps just as gratifying as her professional accolades, her two-time election to the International Best-Dressed List.

Barbra is proud that she did it all as she is, as an original. "I arrived here without having my nose fixed, my teeth capped, or my name changed, and that is very gratifying to me."
1978 Discography: *Songbird*

STYX

Dennis DeYoung–Keyboards	
John Panozzo–Drums	
Tommy Shaw–Guitars	
James Young–Guitar	
Chuck Panozzo–Bass	

Back on the South Side of Chicago, Styx had its beginnings as TW4. Like most fledgling bands, they found that it was easy to get audiences to respond to well-known songs, harder to get them to sit still for unfamiliar original material. The four neophytes kept trying, and in 1970 landed their first record contract with Wooden Nickel Records; they changed their name to Styx, a name that captured the passion and darkness of their hard-rock sound.

Four albums for Wooden Nickel were relegated to radio oblivion until 1972, when phones at radio station WLS in Chicago started ringing off the wall with requests for "Lady," a cut from their second album, *Styx II.* The program director began playing the song; it was officially re-released as a single, became a national hit, and the strength of that song thrust *Styx II* to gold status.

It was not immediate stardom for the band, however. So they went label shopping, signed with A & M, and soon produced *Equinox,* which was the first record they felt really expressed them. Shortly after that album was released, their lead guitarist left the group suddenly. After a frantic search for a replacement, Styx found Tommy Shaw, who added the electricity the group needed. Onstage guitar duels between Tommy and James Young brought fans to their feet with excitement. The band attracts a following in the United States and an even stronger one in Canada, where they are greeted with a near-hysterical fervor. *Equinox* was awarded a platinum disk in Canada, and *Crystal Ball,* their second A & M album, has been certified gold there.

It was 1977's *The Grand Illusion,* an enthusiastic set, that really put Styx in the top rank of rock-and-rollers. The album has sold more than 2 million copies, and "Come Sail Away," a single from *The Grand*

Illusion, became a top-ten pop hit early in the year. Today they stay on the road for most of the year, not just to stimulate airplay for their album, but because, as Dennis DeYoung remarks, "Music is meant to be performed live. Records cannot be a true substitute."
1978 Discography: *Pieces of Eight*

DONNA SUMMER

For Donna Summer 1978 was a year of reaching out beyond her image as disco sex queen into a new performing sophistication. She sailed into the year with her second gold single, "I Feel Love," her fifth gold LP, *Once Upon a Time,* and *Billboard's* award as Disco Artist of the Year. Her live shows at such varied venues as the Las Vegas Hilton and the Latin Casino in Cherry Hill, New Jersey, pulled SRO crowds to witness dynamic performances in which Donna sang, danced, and generally pulled out all musical stops.

She also triumphed in the movie *Thank God It's Friday,* a bit of musical summer fluff that was the source of her gold single "Last Dance." As Nicole Sims, the ambitious young singer determined to seize the spotlight, Donna revealed to fans a genuine acting and comedic talent. As she says of the part, "This role is an extension of me...she's got to sing." An intense promotional blitz preceded the movie, winning Donna two appearances on "The Merv Griffin Show" and an unprecedented shot as host-for-a-day on "American Bandstand," the first time Dick Clark has given up his spot to anyone.

Donna's ambitions have always extended beyond singing. "I always wanted to be an actress. I want to play lots of other parts and show my other colors." Donna's first success came when, at the age of eighteen, she left her native Boston to perform in the European company of *Hair.* She fell in love with Europe, and stayed on, singing whenever she could. Producers Giorgio Moroder and Pete Bellotte heard her singing in a local club in Munich and insisted that she cut three songs for them. All of them sold, and one, "Hostage," became a big European hit. Donna turned out one smash after another and became a major European star.

Her first big break in America came when Casablanca Records President Neil Bogart heard her single "Love to Love You, Baby." The song had not been as successful in Europe as Donna's other recordings, but when Bogart played it for friends at Los Angeles parties, the reaction was immediate. People were moved to dance and insisted on hearing it again and again. Acting on a hunch, Bogart asked Moroder to record a twenty-minute version of the song; when the final sixteen-minute, fifty-second "Love to Love You" was released, it quickly soared to gold and gave Donna an instant sex-queen label.

Although Donna is a sensationally sultry siren, her sexuality is not her only quality. She sings all kinds of songs, from light opera to church hymns. She's a composer, writing most of the songs she sings. She cowrote the title song for the film *The Deep,* is a devoted mother, and an inventor.
1978 Discography: *Donna Summer Live and More*

JOAN SUTHERLAND

Her liquid, superbly controlled, brilliantly pure soprano has been called "The voice of the century." Her appearances on television have introduced opera and her name to millions of households. With husband Richard Bonynge as her accompanist (Bonynge himself was honored by Queen Elizabeth II during 1977's Silver Jubilee Celebration for his service to the performing arts as director of two opera companies and as an internationally acclaimed conductor and musical scholar), in 1978 Joan Sutherland continues to divide her time between recording, singing with the world's leading opera companies, and giving solo recitals.

A native Australian, Joan Sutherland is the daughter of a fine contralto who sang semiprofessionally. Joan assumed that would be her destiny as well, and when she finished high school she took a secretarial course and studied voice at the Sydney Conservatory. In 1947, she made her professional debut in a concert performance of Purcell's *Dido and Aeneas.* In 1949, she won the *Sun* Aria Contest, sponsored by Australia's leading newspaper, and in 1950 she won first prize in the Mobil Quest, winning one thousand pounds and the title "Australia's Best Singer." She made her operatic debut a few months later in the premiere of Sir Eugene Goossens's opera *Judith.*

From that time on there was no thought in Miss Sutherland's mind of singing as an avocation. She knew the stage was where she belonged, and she traveled to London, where she enrolled in the Royal College of Music. There she met an old friend from the Sydney Conservatory, pianist Richard Bonynge, who became her accompanist, coach, advisor, and eventually her husband. It was Bonynge who persuaded Sutherland to try the bel canto roles of early nineteenth-century opera, those difficult hybrids that call for the power of a dramatic soprano and the flexibility of the coloratura. When she attempted her first such role, in the world premiere of Sir Michael Tippett's *Midsummer Marriage,* she was greeted with enthusiastic critical acclaim.

Her international reputation was secured at London's Covent Garden, when, in 1959, for the first time in thirty years, a new production of Donizetti's *Lucia di Lammermoor* was created for her. The dress rehearsal was attended by both Callas and Schwarzkopf; "After her first aria," reported Winthrop Sargeant in *The New Yorker,* "the members of the orchestra unexpectedly put down their instruments and applauded her, and after the Mad Scene even the chorus onstage shouted bravos." London critics went mad, and her triumph in *Lucia* began a demand for her performances around the world.

Her American debut in 1960 was a triumph; her La Scala debut in 1961 earned her a fifteen-minute ovation; her Metropolitan Opera debut in *Lucia* was one of the great historical debuts for that company. In 1978, two of her albums, *Il Trovatore* and *Operatic Duets* with Luciano Pavarotti, were top-charted classical winners.

T

JAMES TAYLOR

Both James Taylor and wife Carly Simon say they would like a quieter lifestyle, but with Carly beginning to discover the delights of touring and James continuing to turn out hit records, it's difficult to imagine how they will find their way out of the public pressure cooker.

James, who won the 1977 Grammy award for Best Pop Vocal Performance, Male, for his mellow single "Handy Man," has had unsettling experiences with the effects of a tidal wave of critical praise and public adulation. At the beginning of the 1970s, after several years of paying his musical dues, he cut his second album, *Sweet Baby James* which up and sold more than 3 million copies. (The first, *James Taylor,* had been praised by critics but largely ignored by the record-buying public.) Two superior songs, "Fire and Rain" and "Country Road," became massive hits; James was hailed as the new voice of the seventies. With a background that included stays in two mental hospitals and a bout with hard drugs, sensitive James shook in his shoes at the responsibilities such positive response engendered.

James reacted by keeping a low profile: doing guest shots on the albums of buddies Carole King and Joni Mitchell; "Steamroller Blues," one of James's songs, was a hit for Elvis Presley. In the first half of 1972, James stepped cautiously back into the limelight and won his first gold single with the gentle "You've Got a Friend," from the album *Mud Slide Slim and the Blue Horizon.* Two other albums, *One Man Dog* and *Walking Man,* followed, and James made his acting debut with Dennis Wilson in *Two Lane Blacktop.*

In 1972, James and Carly married, bringing a new joy and stability to his life. For the Chapel Hill, North Carolina, doctor's son, the marriage has meant new strengths; with the support of a strong mate has come a surer sense of himself.

James Taylor   Courtesy Columbia Records

Mel Tillis   Courtesy MCA Records

Lynn Goldsmith

Robin Trower   Courtesy Chrysalis Records

John Travolta

282

His music, in the recent albums *Gorilla, In the Pocket,* and *J. T.,* reflected a new gladness. The late 1977 single "Your Smiling Face" also contained this new sunniness. In 1978, James performed with Carly in several shows that bathed their fortunate audiences in a special radiance.

MEL TILLIS

When you hear Mel Tillis talk, the first thing you notice is his stutter, the stutter he developed after a bout with malaria as a very young child in Pahokee, Florida. That stutter made his life miserable for years, until, in the late 1950s, he decided he would just have to learn to live with it and treat it positively. Today, the stammer is undoubtedly one of the things that contributes to Mel's lovableness, and it's certainly useful to him as a comedic tool. For example, Mel will come onstage and say in his laconic drawl, "I wrote a talking part in 'Detroit City,' which was a stupid thing on my part. If I had to record it I'd still be in the studio."

Voted the Country Music Entertainer of the Year in 1976 by the Country Music Association, Mel Tellis is a consummate musical talent. He sings, tours, records, heads his own Sawgrass Music Publishing Company, and, over the years, has written nearly a thousand songs. Many of his songs he has recorded himself; others have become smashes for other artists, such as "Detroit City," a gold-winner for Bobby Bare and "Ruby, Don't Take Your Love to Town," a million-seller for Kenny Rogers and the First Edition. Because of these and hundreds of others, Mel became a member of the Songwriter's Hall of Fame in 1976.

In addition to logging in some 120,000 miles on a tour circuit that includes some two hundred annual bookings, Tillis spends a lot of time on television. At the end of 1977 he was part of Macy's Thanksgiving Parade and appeared as a gonger on "The Gong Show." He was also a guest on "The Donny and Marie Show." His two top-ten singles in 1978 were "What Did I Promise Her Last Night" and "I Believe in You."

JOHN TRAVOLTA

John Travolta's sexy swagger at the beginning of *Saturday Night Fever* revealed one side of him; his swift, vulnerable smile and the genuine cheeriness in his eyes reveal the other. It is this combination of animal sexuality and little-boy eagerness to please that has made John Travolta 1978's conquering hero: To millions of fans, he is The Man.

Born in Englewood, New Jersey, to a former star athlete and an actress, Travolta was bitten by the theater bug early, quitting high school so he could devote more of his time to acting. He was a natural. Briefly honed and polished in the demanding crucible of New York's famed Actors Studio, the training ground for such talents as Marlon Brando, Al Pacino, and Robert De Niro, Travolta learned quickly. As he told reporter Tom Burke in Burke's perceptive *Rolling Stone* interview, "I always did have this ability to observe people, watch them awhile, and very quickly absorb their...essence and then reproduce it."

That talent quickly became the most important thing in his life. His first stage role was in an Actors Studio production of *Who'll Save the Ploughboy.* He soon found himself in an off-Broadway production of *Rain,* the road company of *Grease,* and finally on Broadway in the Andrew Sisters' show *Over Here.*

He had just been offered a part in the Broadway show *The Ritz* for the then-astronomical sum of $750 a week when he was asked to audition for the Vinnie Barbarino role in "Welcome Back, Kotter." He was reluctant to leave his first important role for what seemed to him a distant possibility. Manager Bob LeMond advised him to try for it. His success as Vinnie was immediate, inspiring some ten thousand fan letters a week and making his name a household world. He was tapped for a role in Brian de Palma's film *Carrie,* and the lead in the

television special "The Boy in the Plastic Bubble." Actress Diana Hyland was his costar and the two feel deeply in love. His relationship with her was the first such closeness he had ever experienced. In addition to being his lover, she was his friend, helping him see the potential of the role he had been offered in *Saturday Night Fever.* In 1977, John was shattered when she died of cancer. Her memory remains precious to him, but he has thrown himself into his work, and slowly the scars are healing.

The release of *Saturday Night Fever* established him as a major film star. His performance in *Grease* was a delight, and he and Olivia Newton-John scored with the number-one platinum single "You're the One that I Want" and "Summer Nights" from the film's soundtrack. His own recording career includes two hit singles, "Let Her In" and "Slow Dancing," from the albums *John Travolta* and *Can't Let You Go.*
1978 Discography: *Grease* soundtrack

ROBIN TROWER

London-born Robin Trower's musical history dates back to 1959, when at age fourteen he bought his first guitar. His first heroes, like the first heroes of millions of other aspiring rock and rollers, were Elvis, Chuck Berry, and Jerry Lee Lewis. But, when he was nineteen, Robin first heard B. B. King, James Brown, Ray Charles, and Muddy Waters. Their R & B style was a revelation to him. "That's the music I've been trying to recreate in my own way ever since," Robin says.

In the early sixties Robin joined with an R & B group called the Paramounts, but after five less-than-successful singles the band fell apart. One of its members, however, Gary Brooker, had teamed with Keith Reid to write music. Brooker called on Trower to join with him and several other musicians in a group called Procol Harum, whose "Whiter Shade of Pale," that haunting blend of R & B and classical, became one of the biggest hits of the 1960s.

Robin stayed with Procol Harum until 1971, when tensions between his needs and the needs of the band could no longer be ignored. Robin had a vision he wanted to achieve and found he couldn't do it within the confines of the Procol Harum style. On his own, he briefly tried to form a new group, called Jude, but soon realized that he had to follow his own internal voices. He then formed the Robin Trower Band, and their first album, *Twice Removed from Yesterday,* was a success in America.

Trower's slow, expressive guitar style matured during the next few years, winning many fans of progressive, inventive rock and rhythm and blues. Albums like *Bridge of Sighs, For Earth Below,* and *Robin Trower Live* captured the sensual spirituality that is his unique style. For Robin the gold sales figure achieved by his 1977 album *In City Dreams* means that he has been able to achieve his dream of maintaining musical integrity while winning commercial acceptance. He says, "I think you're either born a musician or you're not. If you are, there's no other path. Ambitions are different, nowadays. The main ambition is to succeed, to make hit records and a lot of money, and be some sort of star. When we started, back in the Middle Ages, we never even thought of making a record. You got together to play. That was where you wanted to be. I don't think I've lost that attitude."
1978 Discography: *Caravan to Midnight*

CONWAY TWITTY

One of the hardest-working singers in the country-music field, an arena known for its hard-working performers, Conway Twitty has a reputation for being one of the nicest. His patience with overwrought fans is legendary, as is his kindness to old friends, his helpfulness to aspiring young performers, and his general good-hearted warmth.

Born Harold Jenkins in Mississippi, Twitty had heard country music greats all his life but had decided he couldn't compete with boyhood idols like Ernest Tubb and Hank Snow. In 1956, shortly after leaving the service, he heard Elvis Presley on a jukebox and was inspired to try rock and roll. After a short time, he won himself a record

Bonnie Tyler   Courtesy RCA Records and Tapes

Conway Twitty   Courtesy MCA Records

284

contract and came out with "It's Only Make Believe," the song that shot him to fame. It was then that he changed his name, taking his new one from the towns of Conway, Arkansas, and Twitty, Texas.

As a rockabilly singer he had some success, but after a few years his career went into decline. Having developed confidence that he could compete with the top music stars in any area, he returned to his first love, country music. He scored immediately with the hit "Hello, Darlin'," and his recordings have been at the top of the country charts ever since. With Loretta Lynn, he formed a dynamic musical duo, their shining songs together winning them each many fans. In 1978, he and Loretta performed throughout the South, selling out such venues as the Montgomery Civic Center in Alabama, the first time a country act has ever accomplished that feat. In April, the duo was invited to the White House, where they performed for Jimmy Carter and some two hundred guests connected with the music industry. "From Seven till Ten/You're the Reason Our Kids Are Ugly," was a top-ten country single for Loretta and Conway. Twitty's 1978 album and its title single, "Georgia Keeps Pulling on My Ring," both became top-ten country hits.

1978 Discography: *Georgia Keeps Pulling on My Ring*

BONNIE TYLER

"When people call you an 'overnight success' they think that somehow you got there without working," Bonnie Tyler says wryly. After eight years of slugging it out in local cabarets, at rugby socials, and in small clubs in her native Swansea, Wales, in 1978 Bonnie became an "overnight" success with her song "It's a Heartache," which reached number one in Australia, Norway, Sweden, Austria, and South Africa, and the top five in Great Britain, Germany, Holland, Belgium, Switzerland, Finland, Denmark, Israel, and the United States. In the States, the gold-winning song also reached the top ten on the country and easy-listening charts, and her album of the same name quickly won gold.

Bonnie always wanted fame. As a child, Bonnie recalls, "I used to hold the handle of the vacuum cleaner as a make-believe microphone and imagine I was on TV. My only early ambition was to appear on 'Top of the Pops.'" The petite, blue-eyed singer, whose gravel-edged voice is often compared to that of Rod Stewart, is finally the international Top of the Pops.

Bonnie started singing in clubs when she was seventeen, and, although she was happy and fulfilled singing there, she was goaded on when she watched other singers her age on television.

Her break came when she was spotted by a talent scout for songwriter Ronnie Scott. She recorded his "Lost in France," which, to her surprise, became a huge hit all over Europe. The next one, "More than a Lover," was also a hit. When her third song, "It's a Heartache," became a European hit, Warren Schatz of RCA Records in New York flew to Europe and signed Bonnie to the label. Despite her great global success, Bonnie is happy to live in Sewen, the tiny village outside Swansea where she was born, with her husband, Bobby Sullivan.

JOE WALSH

He forged his reputation as one of rock's blazing guitarists with the James Gang. Then, when the band got bigger and more successful (due, in part to such simmering Walsh beauties as "The Bomber," "Funk #49," "Tend My Garden," and "Walk Away"), Joe quit and headed for the mountains of Boulder, Colorado, where he tinkered with ham radios and built up a tremendous creative charge.

That pressure was released in 1972 with *Barnstorm*, an album

named after the trio of Walsh, drummer Joe Vitale, and bassist Kenny Passarelli. Then came the million-seller *The Smoker You Drink, the Player You Get*, with its smash songs "Rocky Mountain Way" and "Meadows." In 1975, Barnstorm parted ways amicably; Walsh produced Dan Fogelberg's *Souvenirs* and worked with Don Henley and Glenn Frey on a third solo album, *So What*, which was followed by his live album *You Can't Argue with a Sick Mind*.

But, as Walsh told reporter Jim Girard in 1977, "After three or four solo albums, I was just running out of strength. I hated to oversee the whole business end and sing every song and be exhausted after each set. For the longest time I was trying to negate all that and get my ass in a group." So, in 1976, the Eagles quietly announced that Joe Walsh had signed on as guitarist/writer/vocalist/keyboardist. His contributions to their gigantic 1977 hit *Hotel California* included the basic guitar idea for "Life in the Fast Lane," one of the star cuts from that album.

With his latest disk, *But Seriously, Folks*, selling half a million copies and sailing up to the top twenty of the pop charts in its first month of release, Joe now can enjoy the best of both possible worlds: the input of new ideas provided by a group and the ability to do just what he wants to do as a solo artist.

1978 Discography: *But Seriously, Folks*

WAR

Harold Brown—Drums

Charles Miller—Saxophone

Howard Scott—Lead guitar

B. B. Dickerson—Bass

Lonnie Jordan—Keyboards

Papa Dee Allen—Congas and percussion

Lee Oskar—Harmonica

This dynamic seven-man outfit began back in 1969 in Harold Brown's Long Beach, California, garage, when Harold, Charles Miller, Howard Scott, B. B. Dickerson, Lonnie Jordan, and Papa Dee Allen heard a bright musical future in their jamming. They gave themselves the name the Night Shift and quickly won a reputation as the best club and back-up band in L.A. Producer/manager Jerry Goldstein first went to see the band at a room called The Rag Doll Club. Because he had heard good things about them, he invited Eric Burdon and harmonica player Lee Oskar along. As usual, the Night Shift heated up the place with their steaming music. After the set, Lee Oskar hopped onstage and joined them in a nonstop jam.

Eric Burdon, who had recently left the Animals, knew they were dynamite. They changed the name of the band to War, and Burdon joined forces with them on their first smash single, "Spill the Wine," from their first LP, *Eric Burdon Declares War*.

During 1970, War toured England, knocking critics off their seats in London, where they played Ronnie Scott's jazz club with Jimi Hendrix along for the ride. In 1971, Burdon and War released *Black Man's Burdon* and began an extensive European tour. Burdon couldn't complete the tour because of exhaustion, but War went gamely on without him, scoring on their own.

In 1971, they released *War*, their first LP without Burdon. Their second album, *All Day Music*, contained the smash hits "All Day Music" and "Slippin' into Darkness," winning them a huge pop following. The second album sold more than a million copies, their first platinum. They followed this with a double-platinum-winner, *The World Is a Ghetto*. During the next few years the band scored with such singles as "The Cisco Kid," "Gypsy Man," "Me and Baby Brother," and the historic "Why Can't We Be Friends?" (from the platinum album of the same name), which had the honor of becoming cosmic rock and roll when it was beamed into outer space during the historic link-up of U.S. astronauts and Russian cosmonauts.

At the end of 1977, *Galaxy* became their sixth gold LP. Solo

Joe Walsh   Henry Diltz

War   Courtesy MCA Records

Grover Washington, Jr.   Bruce W Talamon

286

albums by individual members of the band were released throughout the year, and smash European and American tours left their audiences joyously glazed by the force of War's music.

GROVER WASHINGTON, JR.

He's won more awards in two years than some performers collect in a lifetime, yet to hear Grover tell it, you'd never know how big a star he is. "I hate being called a star. I'm a saxophone player," he says firmly.

His special musical gifts have won him the Golden Mike Award; in 1975 and 1976 *Record World* magazine named him Jazz Artist of the Year; *Ebony* gave him awards for Best Album, Best Alto Sax, and Best Tenor Sax in 1976; and also in 1976 he won the NAACP's respected Image Award as Recording Artist of the Year.

Grover's first professional job was at sixteen when he toured with the Four Clefs. He traveled with several other musical groups during the next few years. At Fort Dix, he strengthened his skills by playing in the army band. After his discharge, he settled in Philadelphia and kept right on playing with local musicians.

His reputation spread throughout the Northeast, and before long he was invited to record with John Hammond for CTI Records. He knocked out officials at CTI with his performance, and they quickly offered him a recording contract. Grover has been there ever since, turning out seven albums for the label. His fourth and fifth, *Mister Magic* and *Feels So Good,* were number-one hits on the jazz charts and soared high on pop and R & B charts as well. *A Secret Place* zoomed to the top spot in the jazz charts in one week and stayed there for many more. His most recent album, *Live at the Bijou,* was a number-one jazz LP and a top-ten soul LP, bobbing in and out of the top ten for months.

BOB WELCH

Bob Welch's story could have turned out dismally. After years of moving from one unsuccessful band to another, in 1971, when the guitarist/songwriter was down on his luck in Paris, he was tapped to join Fleetwood Mac as a replacement for Jeremy Spencer. He played with the group for four years, writing a good deal of Fleetwood's material. At the end of 1974, a chaotic year in which the group defended its name against the chicanery of a former manager, moved to Los Angeles, recorded a new album, and piled one tour on another, Welch realized that he was burned out. "I was emotionally fried," he explains. "I realized it would be better for both me and the band if I left."

History and the pages of the pop media tell us that Welch's departure was followed by Mick Fleetwood's meeting with Stevie Nicks and Lindsey Buckingham and the subsequent 1970s monsters *Fleetwood Mac* and *Rumours.* But what about poor Bob Welch? How did he feel about leaving Fleetwood Mac just as all those years of hard work were about to pay off so spectacularly? Welch, who had remained friendly with the band, was delighted by their success. And now, with his first solo album, *French Kiss*—a platinum pleasure containing a gold single, "Sentimental Lady"—it looks as though the Welch story will have a happy ending.

Of course, success was not immediate for him. For two years he worked with a hard-rock trio called Paris, but, after two albums, problems in the group became too great, and they called it quits. After the breakup Welch sat down and churned out twenty songs. He then presented the material to Capitol Records. "They agreed to do the record without knowing if it was gonna be Paris or Bob Welch or anything," he says. The result was *French Kiss,* an almost one-man record, with Bob covering every instrument but the drums. *French Kiss* has one cut, however, on which Bob has some pretty powerful back-up help. On "Sentimental Lady," a remake of his classic Fleetwood Mac song, Mick Fleetwood, Lindsey Buckingham, and Christine McVie provide drums, guitar, keyboards, and back-up vocals.

Fleetwood, who is now Welch's manager, certainly has a great interest in seeing Bob Welch's star rise successfully. If the success of *French Kiss* is any indication, it certainly will.

DOTTIE WEST

Sparkling, vivacious country star Dottie West is riding the crest of still another success wave in 1978, helped by the completely accidental recording she made with Kenny Rogers. Producer Larry Butler, who had long had the idea of recording Dottie and Kenny together, says, "Kenny was visiting the studio when we were recording, and when he heard 'Every Time Two Fools Collide,' he asked her if he could sing on the cut. It was completely unplanned...they walked out into the studio and re-cut the vocal. From the first note I knew we had hooked it."

The country winner led to the album of the same name, another country smash, and to a flood of demands for the two singers to appear together. The two cohosted the NBC-TV Special "The Largest Indoor Country Music Show," in April.

All of this duo excitement has not kept Dottie from winning in 1978 with a solo performance of "Come See Me and Come Lonely," continuing a prize-winning country career that began when she was majoring in music at Tennessee Tech. There she started out by playing nightclubs. After several years of learning the ropes, she cut her first record in 1959. In 1961, she won the B.M.I. Writer's Award for a song called "Is This Me?"

Her career began to gather momentum with hit songs like "Here Comes My Baby," but it wasn't until the early 1970s that she wrote the song which was to become her trademark, "Country Sunshine." Written for a Coca Cola commercial, (the commercial won the advertising industry's Cleo award), the song became a huge country hit and won her two Grammy nominations.

1978 Discography: *Every Time Two Fools Collide* (with Kenny Rogers)

DENIECE WILLIAMS

Singer/songwriter Deniece Williams soared to another impressive musical peak this year. Her duo with Johnny Mathis—the smooth, soulful "Too Much, Too Little, Too Late"—was an inspired pairing. The disk flashed to the top of the pop, soul, and easy-listening charts and earned Deniece and Johnny their first gold record as a duo. Capping that achievement was a sold-out command performance at the London Palladium for Prince Charles, the fairy-tale climax of an enchanted European tour.

Born in Gary, Indiana, Deniece always sang. She always took her talent for granted, however, never considering music as a career. Even after a month-and-a-half tour with Stevie Wonder and some concert dates with the Rolling Stones, Niecy was unsure that show business was what she wanted. But life on the road had made life at home seem rather uneventful—when Wonder's next invitation came, she accepted it gladly.

Since 1972, her career has been thriving. She toured for four years with Wonder as part of his back-up group, Wonderlove, and sang on every album he has recorded. Always in great demand as an extra voice, Deniece has appeared on recordings by such performers as Minnie Riperton, Roberta Flack, and Valerie Carter. During those years, Niecy discovered she could write songs as well as perform them, and her own compositions have been recorded by the Emotions, Stanley Turrentine, Merry Clayton, and Frankie Valli.

By 1976, she was ready to go out on her own, and she fortuitously met Maurice White, leader of Earth, Wind and Fire, who was looking for a new act to produce for Columbia. Their collaboration on *This Is Niecy* led to her first gold album, an impressive debut.

1978 Discography: *That's What Friends Are For* (with Johnny Mathis)

John Williams

Dottie West

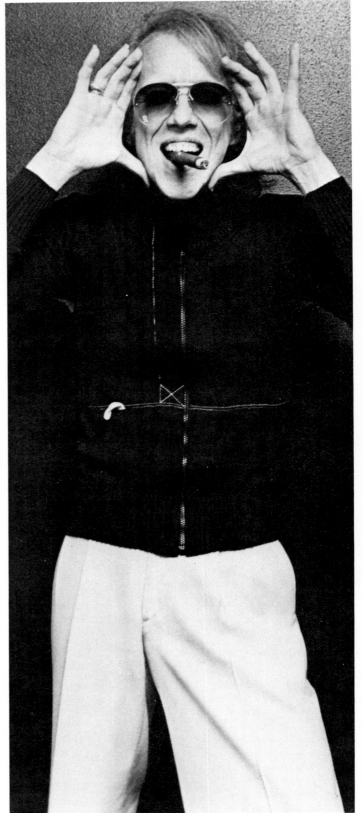

Bob Welch Olivier Ferrand

DON WILLIAMS

You would expect country titan Don Williams to leave 'em howling at the Wembley Festival, England's famous country music extravaganza. He's adored in England, where his albums dot the charts (in 1976 he had six albums on the British charts at the same time—as numbers one through four, fifteen, and nineteen) and achieve gold status.

But he chose a tougher challenge in 1978: to win the attention of ten thousand hard-core rock fans who had come to see headliner Eric Clapton perform. Does this mean that heart-of-country Williams is looking for a larger audience? Don has been pondering changes in his performances. He's talked about adding a keyboard player and has been considering more performances with Clapton, who thinks Williams is the greatest. At this year's Wembley Festival he appeared with a string section.

However, it's unlikely that Don will change the style that has seen him create so many country hits for the past eight years. As he put it to *Billboard*'s Pat Nelson, "If I'm saying something that holds an interest for someone mainly interested in rock 'n' roll but who appreciates what I do as well, then that's the way it'll have to be—without me changing gears."

The spare, straightforward style of "Amanda," "Come Early Morning," "Atta Way to Go," "The Ties that Bind," "Till the Rivers Run Dry," and some five hundred other songs is a reflection of the man himself. In a business dominated by the freaky, the outrageous, the superstar persona, Williams is refreshingly low-key, modest, and sober. He's a family man, a man who protects his wife and children from the glare of publicity, a private man who drawls, "I'm not a goody, goody guy. I don't fancy myself that way at all. I'm just not a big hanger-outer—never have been. I'd just rather be at home with my wife and sons."

Born in the small town of Floydada, Texas, Don first picked up a guitar when he was twelve. He fell in love with the instrument immediately, learned to play from his mother, and would rush home after school to pick out tunes he heard on the radio. Like so many other aspiring musicians, he played and sang with a succession of small groups during high school and his stint with the army.

In 1964, he and two other country singers formed the Pozo Seco Singers. With them he had a huge hit, "Time," still considered a classic.

Don Williams

When the group broke up in 1970, Don began writing country songs for others. Some of the stars who recorded his work include Charley Pride, Sonny James, Johnny Cash, and Lefty Frizzell. Urged by many producers to record his own songs, he began to turn out a string of hits. At the end of 1977 Williams scored again with "I'm Just a Country Boy," a number-one country smash, and in 1978 his "I've Got a Winner in You" became a top-ten country hit.
1978 Discography: *Expression*

JOHN WILLIAMS

Born in New York in 1932, John Williams studied at the University of California in Los Angeles and at the Juilliard School of Music in New York with Rosina Lhevinne, world-renowned mistress of the piano. His achievements as a composer and conductor have been glittering, including scores for more than forty top films, such as *The Cowboys, Jane Eyre, Goodbye, Mr. Chips, The Poseidon Adventure, Towering Inferno, Earthquake, Jaws,* and *Black Sunday.* He has also composed much music for television, but it wasn't until 1977, when his futuristic score for *Star Wars* trumpeted its triumphant message from movie screens across the land, that his name became a household word.

The score for *Star Wars* was by no means Williams's first winner. He twice received the American Television Academy's Emmy award for Best Musical Composition, and in 1976 he won the British Acad-

289

Deniece Wiliams

emy of Film and Television Arts Award for best original score. He has won the Academy Award three times, for *Fiddler on the Roof* in 1972, *Jaws* in 1976, and *Star Wars* in 1978. He also walked off with three Grammies for that brilliant score.

Perhaps the first serious American composer to bridge the chasm between classical and pop music, Williams's symphonic works have been performed by many major American orchestras. His First Symphony was premiered in 1966 by the Houston Symphony Orchestra, conducted by André Previn, and was performed again in London by the London Symphony Orchestra in July of 1972. He has just completed a violin concerto and has the distinction of seeing his recording of his themes from *Star Wars* and *Close Encounters* a number-one classical LP as well as a top pop seller.

Stevie Wonder

Aaron Rapoport

Warren Zevon

Paul McCartney

Courtesy Capitol Records

290

Courtesy Motown

WINGS WITH PAUL McCARTNEY

Paul McCartney–Bass, guitars, synthesizer, vocals

Linda McCartney–Synthesizers, organ, piano, vocals

Denny Laine–Guitars, bass, piano

Wings' last album was the gloriously successful *Wings Over America,* a bountiful two-record set that captured the excitement of their 1976 American tour. But that album was released at the end of 1976, and twenty-eight songs can give pleasure for only so long. At the beginning of 1978, Paul McCartney's fans were hungry for his music. They leaped on *London Town,* gobbling up a million copies instantly, sending it into the top twenty its first week on the charts. "With a Little Luck," the first single from the album, was a chart-topper, giving Paul a grand total of six number-one singles since the Beatles broke up, tying Elton John and the Bee Gees for the most number-one singles in the 1970s.

Paul himself, delighted by the birth of his first son, James Louis, in September 1977, is firmly established in a life of domestic bliss and tranquility. For him and for his wife Linda Eastman, family comes first. Their home on Scotland's Mull of Kintyre (celebrated in McCartney's 1978 song "The Mull of Kintyre," Britain's biggest-selling single of all time) is a retreat and a shelter, a place to enjoy each other, their three daughters, and their new son.

McCartney on his own was not always so personally and professionally successful. It was a struggle for him to establish himself during his first couple of years as a solo performer.

His first solo albums, *McCartney* and *Ram,* were not treated well by the critics, and his first stumbling efforts with Wings, the albums *Wild Life* and *Red Rose Speedway,* did not do well. But even in those disappointing disks Paul's musical and melodic gifts sparkled in a handful of smash singles such as "Uncle Albert/Admiral Halsey," "My Love," "Hi Hi Hi," "Live and Let Die."

The next three albums, however, *Band on the Run, Venus and Mars,* and *Wings at the Speed of Sound,* were authoritative and commanding. Paul had hit his stride, and singles like "Listen to What the Man Said," "Letting Go," and "Silly Love Songs," became instant classics.

Today, pure and simple enjoyment colors McCartney's personal and professional life. He enjoys his life in every way, even to the point of setting up a recording studio on a yacht and recording *London Town* on it while sailing to the Virgin Islands.

STEVIE WONDER

Blind from birth, his radiant upturned face has become a symbol of light and life. In the tradition of the blind poet, Stevie Wonder's musical genius continually captures the heart of life's meaning. His breathtaking sweep of five Grammies in 1977 was the third time he has received such a stunning critical accolade, leaving no doubt in anyone's mind that, at age twenty-eight, Stevie Wonder stands alone, a musical titan of unequalled gifts. At the end of 1977, his Grammy-encrusted 1976 album, the ebullient *Songs in the Key of Life,* was still winning awards. It was voted the American Music Award as 1977's Favorite Soul Album; Stevie won as the Favorite Male Vocalist; and he also won two *Billboard* awards, as Male Artist and Soul Artist of the Year.

Born Steveland Morris in Saginaw, Michigan, and raised in Detroit, at age ten Stevie came to the attention of Berry Gordy, Jr., head of Tamla-Motown Records. Gordy signed him immediately, and the intense youngster had his first number-one hit when he was twelve, with a single called "Fingertips, Pt. 2." During the 1960s and early 1970s, he produced such vital songs as "Uptight," "For Once in My

Life," "I Was Made to Love Her," "A Place in the Sun," "My Cherie Amour," "Signed, Sealed, Delivered," "Heaven Help Us All," "You Are the Sunshine of My Life," "Superstition," and "Super Woman."

Then, on the afternoon of August 6, 1973, Stevie was critically injured in a head-on collision with a logging truck. He lay in a coma, near death, while family, friends, and his fans prayed fervently that he would recover. Somehow, the amazing Wonder pulled through. In March 1974, as though to confirm his new lease on life, he won his first set of five Grammies, including one for Album of the Year for his 1973 LP *Innervisions.* His next album, *Fulfillingness' First Finale,* also won him five Grammys, including Album of the Year, Best R & B Vocal Performance, Male, for "Boogie on Reggae Woman," and Best R & B Song for "Living in the City."

In 1978, Stevie has been working on a new album. On April 11, his publishing and management companies gave a reception at Osko's in Los Angeles. The event began at eight; Stevie didn't appear until midnight and then took an hour to give out ninety platinum plaques to those musicians and management representatives who had been connected with *Songs in the Key of Life.* At 1:00 A.M. he gave a memorable, magical concert that all present agreed would have been worth waiting even longer to hear.

1978 Discography: *The Secret Life of Plants*

Z

WARREN ZEVON

From his earliest days, Warren Zevon intended to become a serious composer. The praise that he and his work have received from the media indicates that he has achieved a rare hybrid: serious rock and roll. Reviewers credit his work with humor, violence, and a sparkling, ironic wit; audiences go wild over his rambunctious onstage energy.

Born in Chicago thirty-two years ago, Warren spent his childhood moving from one western town to another. He began writing songs in the sixties; one of those early efforts, "She Quit Me," was included in the soundtrack of *Midnight Cowboy* and earned him a gold record. Commercials for Ernest and Julio Gallo followed, but Warren was too excitable for advertising. (He admits to having once rubbed a pot roast on his chest, as described in "Excitable Boy," but somehow makes it sound almost reasonable. "My wife had cooked it," he explains, "and I wanted to show my appreciation.")

After he and the advertising business had parted ways, he went on to tour with the Everly Brothers as their piano player and bandleader. When the Everlys broke up, he worked for a while playing piano and singing in the clubs of San Francisco; he then moved to Aspen, where he was appointed honorary coroner of Pitkin County, Colorado, in 1974.

While in Spain during 1975 he corresponded with old friend Jackson Browne, who persuaded Zevon to return to Los Angeles to cut his first album. *Warren Zevon* was produced by Browne and contained some songs that Linda Ronstadt was to record, such as "Hasten Down the Wind," "Carmelita," and "Poor Poor Pitiful Me." His album was an awesome debut, adored by the critics for its assurance and intelligence.

After a month's tour of the United States and Europe at the end of 1976, Warren vacationed in Spain and East Africa, turning out the songs which appear on his second album, *Excitable Boy.* This one aroused even more fervent adulation than the first. Critical gushes flowed for the songs, the instrumental work (featuring on most cuts members of Linda Ronstadt's band and on one song John McVie and Mick Fleetwood of Fleetwood Mac), and for the very presence of such Los Angeles cronies as Linda Ronstadt, Jackson Browne, John David Souther, Karla Bonoff, and Jennifer Warnes. Record buyers soon sent the disk to gold acclaim, and audiences across the country greeted him eagerly on his 1978 tour.

1978 Discography: *Excitable Boy.*

NEWCOMERS

MEAT LOAF

Meat Loaf–Lead vocals

Jim Steinman–Piano

Karla Da Vito–Vocals

At the end of 1977, an album called *Bat Out of Hell* came screaming out of Cleveland International/Epic Records. It was a dynamite charge led by 260 titanic pounds of ferocious rock and roll called Meat Loaf. Born in Dallas, Texas, into a family of southern gospel singers, Meat retains a wild-eyed revivalist intensity. He sings so hard that after a show he often collapses, gasping for breath, requiring oxygen to revive him. Meat earned his musical stripes pounding it out with several West Coast bands and was a lead singer on Ted Nugent's high-octane outing *Free-for-All.*

The incredible Meat Loaf met with writer/arranger/pianist Jim Steinman on the occasion of "The National Lampoon Show." After a year of working together, they were booked to perform at Carnegie Hall, where Steinman's hungrily powerful rock-and-roll constructions gave Meat some songs he could get his teeth into and snarl about. Karla Da Vito added her incandescent, waiflike presence to the mix; Todd Rundgren stepped in and produced their first album.

In 1978, their first album was certified gold; the band had a gold single with "Two Out of Three Ain't Bad"; appeared on "Saturday Night Live"; and performed to SRO crowds wherever they appeared.

PLAYER

Peter Beckett–Lead vocals, guitar

J. C. Crowley–Lead vocals, keyboards, guitar

Ronn Moss–Bass

John Friesen–Drums

Peter Beckett and J. C. Crowley were born worlds apart. Peter hails from Liverpool, England, and J. C. is a Texan. But when manager Mark Roswell introduced the two at a Hollywood party, they clicked. A few days later the two musicians got together and began to share their years of knowledge and experience (Peter gained his performing with a number of British and American groups, including Friends and Skyband; J.C., playing with a handful of local bands) and started to write together.

Their partnership was working smoothly when they were introduced to bass player Ronn Moss and drummer John Friesen. Ronn, a native of Los Angeles, and John, born in Idaho and raised in Los Angeles, had met when they were in high school. They played in some fledgling bands together and kept in touch when John became assistant musical producer and drummer for the Ice Follies, with whom he toured the world, producing his own successful Ice Follies extravaganza called "America on Ice."

There was an instant chemistry among the four, and that reaction exploded in their first smash single, "Baby Come Back," which was certified gold and became a number-one pop and top-ten soul disk.

"This Time I'm in It for Love," the second single from their debut album, *Player,* was also a top-ten 1978 winner.
1978 Discography: *Danger Zone*

VAN HALEN

Michael Anthony–Bass

Dave Lee Roth–Lead vocals

Alex Van Halen–Drums

Edward Van Halen–Guitar

"We come on like a supernova," says lead singer David Roth of his group, Van Halen. Indeed, with stratospheric rushes on guitar, a bass that vibrates the bones, the crisp, precise drums of Alex Van Halen, and David Roth's powerful wailing, the band's performances can be compared to a cosmic explosion. They are so impressive that it took Mo Ostin and Ted Templeman of Warner Brothers Records almost no time to decide to sign them. The two executives saw Van Halen perform at Los Angeles's Starwood one night and offered them a recording contract the next day.

"We always knew we'd be discovered," says Roth, "but when it happened it was right out of the movies."

The members of the group had been playing together since high school; in 1974 they formed Van Halen. They cut their teeth in small clubs, beer bars, backyard parties, and dance contests in the Los Angeles area, gathering a following with their white-hot rock-and-roll energy. Their first album, *Van Halen,* which captures their clean, spacious intensity, was released in February and was gold by May. In 1978, the group toured America, Europe, and Japan, meeting sensational response wherever they went.
1978 Discography: *Van Halen*

Meat Loaf   **Player**   Courtesy RSO Records   Courtesy Epic Records

Van Halen   Courtesy Warner Brothers Records

Musical Lifelines

NOVEMBER 1977

Born:

11/9   To Robert Kimball (author of books about the American Musical Theater) and Abigail Kuflik (music reporter) a son.

Married:

11/21   Mitch Weissman (Paul McCartney in *Beatlemania*) to Toni Bonavita in New York.

Died:

11/1   Clarence Fuhrman (82), pianist and band leader.

11/4   Greta Keller (70s), cabaret singer.

11/4   Adam Gilger (86), violinist, clarinetist, composer, conductor.

11/5   Guy Lombardo (75), world-renowned leader of the Royal Canadians, without whom New Year's Eve will never be the same.

11/5   John Merronne (77), pianist, composer, leader of bands in Philadelphia area during 1920s and 1930s.

11/8   Joel M. Friedman (52), president of W/E/A Corporation, founder of W/E/A, the distribution arm of Warner Brothers/Elektra/Atlantic Records.

11/9   Guido Roetter (64), Las Vegas-based pianist and composer.

11/11   Randolph P. Joyce (25), singer, composer, guitarist; a child singer on Roy Rogers's shows and in *The Sound of Music*; of leukemia.

11/11   Terry Shand, songwriter; wrote "You Don't Have to Be a Baby to Cry."

11/12   Lawrence E. Deutsch (57), president of Los Angeles Music Center Opera Association.

11/13   Donald Brown (32), member of Scottish folksinging duet Lomond Folk.

11/15   Richard Addinsell (73), British composer of film, television, and theatrical scores; wrote *Warsaw Concerto*.

11/15   Billy Taylor, Jr. (51), popular jazz bassist.

11/17   Fred W. McCall, Jr. (72), band professor and director at the University of Miami; music director for the Orange Bowl for more than thirty years.

11/17   Paul Hooreman (74), musical historian, composer, and lecturer; resided in Brussels.

11/18   Teddi King (48), New York-based jazz singer.

11/19   Sonny Criss (50), saxophonist; shot to death in Los Angeles.

11/19   Hazen H. Brown (68), pianist.

11/20   Lester Koenig (58), founder (in 1949) and owner of Good Time Jazz and Contemporary Records.

11/20   Walter (Gates) Grigatis (65), pianist, orchestra leader, and composer; did many rock 'n' roll and jazz arrangements, including "The Twist" and songs for Bobby Vinton, the Supremes, Gene Pitney.

11/21   Stephen A. Wolf (34), partner in Los Angeles-based concert promoters Wolf-Rismiller Concerts, Inc.; shot during a robbery attempt at his home.

11/24   Joseph Vetere (69), cellist and musical contractor for Philadelphia's Shubert Theatre.

11/25   Lucia Liverette, musicologist residing in Los Angeles.

11/27   Anthony S. (Tony) Mamarella (53), producer of "American Bandstand" for ten years; president and general manager of the Philadelphia-based Swan Records between 1960 and 1968.

11/30   Felix Giglio (56), violinist with NBC, musical contractor.

DECEMBER

Born:

12/21   To Frank Patterson (singer) and Elly O'Grady (concert pianist) a son, in Dublin.

Married:

Joan Manual Serrat (Catalan folksinger) to Candela Tiffon, in Pyrenees, Spain.

Died:

12/5 Ned Harvey (60), band leader at Concord Hotel, New York.

12/5 Rahsaan Roland Kirk (41), jazz musician, specialist on wind instruments; after giving a concert in Bloomington, Indiana. Kirk, blind since birth, was a master of the tenor sax, manzello, stritch, and flute, and would often play two simultaneously.

12/7 Dr. Peter Carl Goldmark (71), the man who developed the long-playing record and revolutionized the recording industry; killed in an auto accident in Westchester, New York.

12/7 Bill Boyd (67), country and western singer.

12/7 Albert (Al) Shanks (71), Toledo-based musician and nightclub owner.

12/14 Cato Mann (Mr. Cato) (90), big-band pioneer.

12/16 Thomas Schippers (47), conductor laureate of Cincinnati Symphony.

12/18 Cyril Ritchard (79), actor, singer, director; world renowned for his many musical and theatrical roles, especially Captain Hook in *Peter Pan.*

12/18 Sam Weiss (67), drummer, orchestra leader, and entertainer; played with bands on the Catskill, N.Y. hotel circuit and appeared on the Jack Benny Show.

12/22 Lotte Schone (86), Paris-based operatic soprano.

12/29 Marguerite Giroud Cummin (78), semiclassical singer.

12/31 Paul Ackerman (69), Editor emeritus of *Billboard* magazine, music editor for more than thirty years.

JANUARY 1978

Born:

1/11 To Gary Kurfirst (manager of Talking Heads) and wife, a son.

1/23 To Neil Bogart (president of Casablanca Records and Filmworks) and wife, a son.

Married:

Peter Green (founder and former leader of Fleetwood Mac) to Jane Samuel.

Died:

1/2 Paul F. Blunt, country and western singer and musician.

1/6 Dick Porter (46), lead singer of the Ink Spots.

1/6 Popsie Randolph (57), former road manager for Benny Goodman; later turned to photography and built up a major catalog of band-era photographs.

1/6 Alexander D. Richardson (81), Radio City Music Hall organist.

1/9 Charles Newman (76), lyricist for many Hollywood and Broadway scores, member of ASCAP since 1929.

1/10 Don Gillis (65), composer and former producer of NBC Symphony radio broadcasts under Toscanini.

1/10 Bob Harvey (64), pianist and orchestra leader who resided in Seattle.

1/11 Hal C. Davis (63), president of the American Federation of Musicians, Vice-President of the AFL-CIO in New York.

1/14 Larry Grayson (46), singer and production coordinator of Las Vegas nightspots.

1/14 Jack Jackson (71), Britain's first "modern" disk jockey; introduced American swing on the BBC in London.

1/15 Lewis E. Gensler (81), songwriter whose credits include "Love Is Just Around the Corner."

1/16 Jack Amlung (77), orchestra leader residing in Dallas.

1/17 James F. Godsey, country-music entertainer, residing in Raleigh, North Carolina.

1/18 LaVonne Satterfield (56), singer/songwriter.

1/21 Charles Peterson (62), big-band-era trumpeter.

1/23 Terry Kath (31), bass guitarist, songwriter, and singer with rock group Chicago®; accidentally shot himself in Los Angeles.

1/23 Vic Ames (51), one of the Ames Brothers singing group; in an auto accident in Nashville.

1/23 Colman (Connie) Hechter (42), publisher of "Insider," a Minneapolis area music magazine.

1/25 Nicklos Parillo (90), former marching band director.

1/26 Rudolph Ringwall (86), member of the Cleveland Orchestra for more than thirty years.

1/27 Lennington Heppe Shewell (68), theremin virtuoso.
1/27 Beulah Frazier (Wortham) (64), nightclub singer in Philadelphia area.
1/27 Fred Mazzari (66), cellist with Houston Symphony Orchestra.
1/27 John E. Thorne (45), bass player/vocalist.
1/28 Harold F. Ward (44), Chicago area nightclub singer.
1/29 Leo Russotto (81), first vocal director of Radio City Music Hall, pianist, and vocal coach.
1/30 Marie-Louise Damien (Damia) (88), chanteuse.
1/31 Gregory Herbert (30), saxophonist with Blood, Sweat and Tears; of an accidental drug overdose.

FEBRUARY

Married:

2/24 Ekaterina Novitskaya (Soviet violinist who defected to the West) to François Hervey, in Mons, Belgium.

Separated:

David Bowie (singer) and wife Angela.
Mick Jagger (lead singer of the Rolling Stones) and wife Bianca.

Died:

2/2 Gerry Camdon (29), Irish guitarist, in Dublin.
2/3 Sidney Edwards (66), cellist.
2/4 Alice H. Goodman (72), wife of Benny Goodman, sister of John Hammond.
2/6 Frances Wayne (50s), singer with the first Woody Herman Herd.
2/6 Collen Gray (Tex) Satterwhite (57), composer and trombonist, author of "The Moment of Truth."
2/15 Alex Bradford (51), gospel singer and composer; collaborated with Vinnette Carroll to write "Your Arms Too Short to Box with God."
2/16 Leo Diston (70), staffer at Chappell Music, New York.
2/18 Eleanor Morrison (48), opera press representative in New York.
2/18 Ivan Ballen (69), record producer/manufacturer and president of the Gotham Record Corporation.

2/19 Pankaj Mullick, Indian music director and musician.
2/23 George E. Novak (53), leader of Polka Kings Band in the 1940s and 1950s.
2/25 Gladys Mills (55), British popular pianist.
2/28 Loraine Elizabeth Wolf (75), Las Vegas-based singer.
Nat Brandwynne (67), Caesars Palace orchestra conductor.

MARCH

Married:

3/1 Elkie Brooks (pop singer) to Trevor Jordan (recording engineer) in Hertfordshire, England.
Steve Miller (singer, songwriter, guitarist) to Jenny Louise Turner, in Oregon.

Died:

3/4 Arthur E. Hall (77), composer, winner of several ASCAP awards.
3/5 Cesare Andrea Bixio (82), dean of Italian pop music; wrote over 2,000 tunes and 300 music tracks.
3/11 Claude François (39), popular French singer; accidentally electrocuted in Paris.
3/11 Ruth O'Neill (87), concert management executive.
3/12 Tolchard Evans (77), songwriter; authored more than 1,000 numbers including "Lady of Spain".
3/12 Mon Rivera (53), Puerto Rican musician and vocalist; played clarinet, guitar, and piano and recorded for Fania Records.
3/12 Sophia Vembo (66), Greek singer.
3/13 Ken Wright, composer and musician; arranged and played accordion with the NBC "National Barn Dance."
3/17 Malvina Reynolds (77), songwriter, singer, and entertainer; author of "Little Boxes" and "What Have They Done to the Rain."
3/21 Louis Cottrell, Jr. (67), Dixieland band leader and clarinetist.
3/23 Bill Kenny (63), last original member of the Ink Spots.
3/23 Paul Dowdy (36), conductor of the La Crosse, Wisconsin, Symphony Orchestra; killed in an auto accident.

3/28 Harold Johnson (60), trumpeter with Duke Ellington.

3/28 Elizabeth Keith Oxenaar (Lysbeth Hughs), sang and played harp in the Connecticut area.

3/31 Rick Evers, husband and manager of singer/songwriter Carole King; of an accidental drug overdose.

APRIL

Born:

4/28 To Carol Strauss (public relations vice-president for D.I.R. Broadcasting) and Michael Klenfner (executive vice-president at Atlantic Records) a daughter.

Married:

4/12 Aretha Franklin (soul singer) to Glynn Turman (actor) in Detroit, Michigan.

4/16 John McVie (bassist with Fleetwood Mac) to Julie Rubens, in West Hollywood, California.

4/20 Richard Shapp (opera singer) to Luminitza Coler, in Pennsylvania.

4/29 Bill Stevenson, (guitarist with Rudy Owens and City Lights) to Kathryn Ross, in Houston.

4/29 Denise Nettleton (member of Cherry Pink) to Jim Jacobs (coauthor of *Grease*), in Las Vegas.

Died:

4/1 Robert E. Smith (71), opera authority.

4/1 Payson Re, pianist and bandleader.

4/3 Ray Noble (71), British orchestra leader and songwriter; author of "Good Night Sweetheart."

4/3 Paul Johnson (38), Capitol Records national black-product promoter.

4/5 Carlo Tagliabue (80), singer with the Met and La Scala.

4/6 Nicolas Nabokov (75), Russian-born composer residing in New York.

4/6 Hilda Korins (Burke) (73), former singer with the Met.

4/8 Peter Igelhoff (73), German composer.

4/11 George Cory (55), songwriter; wrote the lyrics for "I Left My Heart in San Francisco"; an apparent suicide.

4/11 Ray McAuley (33), Canadian singer and band leader.

4/13 Gertrude Monk Taylor (87), pianist in the Philadelphia and New York areas.

4/17 Ethel Bartlett (82), pianist residing in Los Angeles.

4/21 Sandy Denny (31), singer and songwriter, founding member of the folk-rock group Fairport Convention; after a fall in London.

4/22 Will Geer (76), primarily known for his many acting roles but was greatly admired as a popularizer of American folk music in the 1920s and 1930s.

4/23 Joseph A. Haverbeck (80), former member of the Paul Whiteman Band, member of the Banjo Dusters.

4/25 Archie Levington (71), former vice-president at Motown, music publisher.

4/27 Edna Elizabeth Forman (61), music copyist for film and television.

4/27 Josef Marais (72), composer and performer with a folk duo.

4/28 Ben Gage (63), big-band singer in the 1940s. Aram Khachaturian (74), Russian composer, best known for "Sabre Dance."

MAY

Born:

5/2 To Jeff Gregerson (singer with Sunshade and Rain) and wife, a daughter.

5/17 To Colin Romoff (conductor/arranger) and wife, a son.
To Mel Teeples (singer with Sunshade and Rain) and wife, a son.

Married:

5/8 Donny Osmond (singer) to Debra Glenn, in Salt Lake City, Utah.

5/13 Sally Carr (cabaret and recording artist) to Chic Young in Glasgow.

5/14 Peter Graves (bandleader and session player) to Cheryl Lawrence, in Ft. Lauderdale, Florida.

Died:

5/1 Alan Bernstein (37), lyricist; wrote "After the Lovin."

5/2 Gretchen Hood (91), soprano residing in Bethesda, Maryland.

5/4 William A. Mathews, Jr. (85), musician with Ringling Brothers Barnum & Bailey Circus.

5/6   Jack H. Libofsky (Jackie Lee) (51), pianist and nightclub performer.

5/10   Boris Khaikin (73), Russian orchestra conductor.

5/14   Alexander Kipnis (87), Russian-born basso.

5/14   Silvia de Grass (48), member of Los Alegres Tres group in Puerto Rico.

5/14   William P. Lear (75), inventor, in addition to the Lear Jet and many other things, of the car radio and the 8-track stereo cartridge.

5/16   William Steinberg (78), former music director of the Pittsburgh and Boston symphony orchestras.

5/16   Frank Turney Gibson (69), Kansas City area musician and orchestra leader.

5/20   Beatrice Landeck Marks (74), author of 32 books and music educator.

5/29   Sally Westfall (64), big-band singer with Sammy Kaye; operated her own nightclub.

5/30   Albert John Tronti (53), director of the house orchestra at the Sahara Tahoe.

JUNE

Born:

6/24   To Jimmy Damon (singer) and wife, a daughter.

Married:

6/13   Sarah Vaughan (singer) to Waymon Reed (trumpeter with Count Basie) in Chicago.

6/18   Derek Shulman (musician with Gentle Giant) to Sharon Laufer, in Dallas.

Died:

6/1   Milton Garred (53), string bass jazz performer, music conductor for Brazil Academy of Music.

6/4   Barry Winton (75), violinist and former bandleader.

6/4   Clarence W. (Pete) Wollery, singer and music publisher.

6/9   Carroll Hardy (48), Buffalo, New York, jazz disk jockey.

6/12   Johnny Bond (62), western singer and songwriter; appeared on Gene Autry's radio show, made films with Roy Rogers, Autry, and Tex Ritter; wrote "Ten Little Bottles" and "Hot Rod Lincoln," among others.

6/14   Quinn Wilson (69), tubist, bassist, composer, arranger who spanned the era of Jelly Roll Morton to the beginning of rock and roll.

6/19   Mabel Wayne (80), songwriter and pianist, member of ASCAP; wrote "Ramona" and "In a Little Spanish Town."

6/26   Kenneth Deckow (64), musician with the Normandie Boys Trio.

6/27   Alexander J. Bigard, Jr. (80), jazz trumpeter residing in New Orleans.

JULY

Married:

7/6   Tammy Wynette (singer) to George Richey (record producer), in Florida.

Died:

7/3   Elektra Rozanska (79), opera singer residing in Pasadena, California.

7/4   Samuel H. Pottle (48), composer and musical director of "Sesame Street."

7/7   Paul Reif (68), composer for film, theatre, and serious works.

7/10   Michel Grisikoff (85), violinist, composer, and concertmaster.

7/10   Cal Clifford (74), jazz trumpeter residing in Hollywood.

7/10   Walker Smith (78), retired orchestra leader.

7/12   Leo Edwards (92), songwriter, charter member of ASCAP, producer of cabaret shows in New York.

7/16   Edis de Phillippe (61), founder and director of Israel National Opera.

7/23   J. Maloy Roach, songwriter who authored "One Little Candle," which was taken as the theme of the Christopher Society.

7/25   Henry (Hank) Newman (73), country and western singer of the 1930s.

7/27   Willem Van Otterloo (70), Dutch conductor, formerly with the Hague Philharmonic Orchestra; in a traffic accident.

7/30   Glen Goins (24), former lead guitarist and singer with Parliament/Funkadelic; was producing a new group, Quazar, and leading his own band, Mutiny; of Hodgkin's disease.

7/31   Enoch Light (71), leader of Enoch Light and the Light Brigade, a big-band of the 1930s and

1940s; founder of Command and Project 3 Records, high fidelity and stereophonic specialist companies.

7/31 Guenther Rennert (67), German opera director who had staged works at the Metropolitan, La Scala, Munich, Hamburg, and Glyndebourne.

AUGUST

Born:

8/1 To George Harrison (former Beatle) and Olivia Arras, a son, Dhani, in Windsor, England.

8/2 To Boz Scaggs (rock singer) and wife Carmella, a son, Austin William, in San Francisco.

8/7 To Wayne Cilento (dancer currently appearing on Broadway in *Dancin'*) and wife, a son, in New Rochelle, New York.

Married:

8/7 Garth Porter (keyboards player with Sherbet) to Mary Byrnes, in Sydney, Australia.

8/11 Charo (singer) to Kjell Raoten (television producer), in South Lake Tahoe, California.

8/19 Bonnie Ward (with Carnegie Hall Management) to Steven Simon (conductor of Westchester County Symphony), in New York.

Died:

8/1 Rudolph Kolisch (82), violinist and founder of a string quartet which performed the works of Schoenberg; faculty member at the New England Conservatory in Boston.

8/2 Carlos Chavez (79), prominent Mexican composer and conductor.

8/3 Ed Pratt (48), saxophonist with Ray Charles; of a heart attack, in Pomona, California.

8/5 Viola Claiss (87), leader of all-woman orchestra and theater organist; in West Palm Beach, Florida.

8/5 Queenie Smith (80), Broadway musical comedy star in the 1920s, appearing in many Broadway plays and such movies as *Show Boat, On Your Toes, My Sister Eileen,* and the more recent *Foul Play;* of cancer, in Burbank, California.

8/6 Gene Mann (72), manager of Greek Theatre; in Los Angeles.

8/7 Leslie Perrin (57), British publicist who worked with Tom Jones, the Rolling Stones, and Frank Sinatra, among others; in Surrey, England.

8/7 Eddie Calvert (56), trumpet player whose version of "O Mein Papa" in 1953 made him the first British instrumentalist to win a gold disk in America; of a heart attack, in Johannesburg, South Africa.

8/14 Giuseppe "Joe" Venuti (exact age unknown, mid-70s to early 80s), first and foremost jazz violinist; appeared in the bands of such figures as Paul Whiteman, Hoagy Carmichael, and the Dorsey Brothers, and backed such singers as Ethel Waters and Bing Crosby; of cancer, in Seattle.

8/14 Victor Sylvester (78), prominent British dance and band leader; of apparent heart attack, in Le Lavandou, France.

8/15 Irene Kral (46), singer; with husband formed duo Irene and Roy; in Encino, California.

8/17 Peppy De Albrew (late 70s), former dancer and night club owner; in New York.

8/18 Brian Patrick Crosby (18), grandson of the late Bing Crosby; of injuries sustained in motorcycle accident, in Los Angeles.

8/18 Doris Waters (74), British music hall star, famous as one half of sister act known as Gert & Daisy between early 1930s through World War II; in London.

8/18 Charles E. Virian (80), who as Charles Edwards was vaudeville and night club performer and songwriter; in Hollywood.

8/19 Matty King (72), self-taught dancer who appeared in the Broadway shows *Artists and Models* and *Broadway Nights;* in Florida.

8/20 Joseph Galkin, discoverer of the Tommy Tucker Orchestra, which he managed for 15 years, and discoverer of Otis Redding; of kidney failure, in Atlanta.

8/22 Sam H. Lazarov (78), violinist and leader of the Sam Lazarov Melody Makers, first band to broadcast on radio from the Memphis Peabody Hotel; after a long illness, in Memphis.

8/24 Louis Prima (67), bandleader and composer whose career included night clubs, concerts, television, radio, and motion pictures; with former wife Keely Smith formed highly successful duo; in coma since October 1975, following surgery for removal of brain tumor.

8/26 Robert Shaw (51), stage and screen star, novelist, playwright; appeared in such films as *From Russia with Love, The Sting, Jaws, Black Sunday,* and *The Deep* and was the author of *The Man in the Glass Booth.* He appeared in the title role of *Elmer Gantry* in a short-lived (one performance) Broadway musical version of the novel by Sinclair Lewis; of apparent heart attack in Tourmakeady, County Mayo, Ireland.

8/26 Helen King (72), president of the California Copyright Conference and founder of Songwriters Resources and Services; of cancer, in Los Angeles.

SEPTEMBER

Married:

George Harrison (former Beatle) to Olivia Arras, in England.

Died:

9/3 Joe Davis (81), music publisher, songwriter, and record manufacturer whose songs include "Sunset Serenade" and "Milkman's Matinee"; he also cowrote several songs with the late Fats Waller, some of which are currently included in the Broadway production of *Ain't Misbehavin';* of a heart attack, in New York City.

9/7 Keith Moon (31), drummer with the Who; in England.

9/9 Jack L. (Leonard) Warner (86), youngest and most bombastic of the legendary Warner Brothers, pioneers of the movie business; began his show business career singing illustrated song-slides while the reels were changed in his brother's first theater, The Bijou, in a storefront in New Castle, Pennsylvania. His company introduced talkies in 1926 with the part talkie, *Don Juan,* featuring John Barrymore, followed in 1927 by the phenomenally successful *The Jazz Singer.* After riding out the depression and providing years of patriotic films during and after World War II, surviving the tumultuous coming of television and its challenge to the film industry, Warner almost died in a car crash on the French Riviera in 1958. To the amazement of his doctors he survived and went on to create such successful musical films as *My Fair Lady* and *Camelot;* of pulmonary edema, in Los Angeles.

9/24 Ruth Etting (81), tempestuous night club singer, Broadway and film actress who was known for such songs as "Ten Cents a Dance," "It All Depends on You," "Love Me or Leave Me," "Mean to Me," and "Everybody Loves My Baby"; after a long illness, in Colorado Springs, Colorado.

9/28 Stanley Blinstrub (81), owner of Blinstrub's of Boston, once the largest club in the United States; in Newton, Massachusetts.

9/30 Edgar Bergen (75), beloved ventriloquist whose wooden creations Charlie McCarthy and Mortimer Snerd warmed the hearts and tickled the funnybones of American audiences for fifty-six years; of a heart attack, in Las Vegas.

OCTOBER

Married:

10/9 Kim Moon (former wife of Keith Moon) to Ian McLaglan (of Small Faces) in London.

Died:

10/6 Johnny O'Keefe (43), called the Elvis Presley of Australia; of a heart attack, in Australia.

10/9 Jacques Brel (49), Belgian songwriter who became famous in America through the hit musical "Jacques Brel Is Alive and Well and Living in Paris"; of cancer, in Paris.

10/16 Dan Dailey (62), singer and dancer in thirties and forties musicals, including the Broadway musicals *Babes in Arms* and *I Married an Angel;* starred in such films as *Mother Wore Tights, My Blue Heaven,* and *Pride of St. Louis;* of anemia, in Hollywood.

10/23 Mother Maybelle Carter (69), matriarch of the singing Carter Family; in Nashville.

The Melody Lingers On...

Louis Prima (1912-1978)

Keith Moon (1946-1978)

Edgar Bergen (1903-1978)

Ruth Etting (1897-1978)

Will Geer (1902-1978)

Dan Dailey (1916-1978)

Cyril Ritchard (1897-1977)

Robert Shaw (1927-1978)

301

Fan Club Directory

ABBA: Fan Club, c/o Polar International, Baldersgatan, 1/P.O. Falck S-100 41 Stockholm 26, Sweden

AEROSMITH: Fan Club, c/o The Wherehouse, 55 Pond Street, Waltham, MA 02154

BEACH BOYS: Fan Club, 10880 Wilshire Blvd., Suite 306, Los Angeles, CA 90024

BEE GEES: Fan Club, c/o Renee Schreiber, 2155 Baylis Avenue, Elmont, NY 11003

DEBBY BOONE: Fan Club, Chris Bujnovski, 526 Boeing Avenue, Greenfields, Reading, PA 19601

BOSTON: Fan Club, 1289 N. Crescent Heights Blvd., Suite 303, Los Angeles, CA 90046

PETER BROWN: International Fan Club, P.O. Box 55-7929, Ludlam Branch, Miami, FL 33155

JIMMY BUFFETT: c/o Front Line Management, Suite 307, 8380 Melrose Avenue, Los Angeles, CA 90069

CAPTAIN AND TENNILLE: 23815 Tiara Street, Woodland Hills, CA 91364

CARPENTERS: Fan Club, c/o Rosina Sullivan, P.O. Box 1084, Downey, CA 90240

JOHNNY CASH: House of Cash, P.O. Box 508, Hendersonville, TN 37075

SHAUN CASSIDY: Fan Club, P.O. Box 222, Beverly Hills, CA 90210

NATALIE COLE: Natalie's Fan Club, P.O. Box 181, Beverly Hills, CA 90213

BOOTSY COLLINS: Maggatropolis, c/o Sancctum, 109 Hollywood Avenue, Oxnard, CA 93030

COMMODORES: Fan Club, P.O. Box 784, Radio City Station, New York, NY 10019

CON FUNK SHUN: Fan Club, c/o Linda McCall, 161 Sandpiper Drive, Vallejo, CA 94590

BILLY "CRASH" CRADDOCK: Fan Club, President: Leola Butcher, P.O. Box 1585, Mt. Vernon, IL 62864

PABLO CRUISE: Fan Club, P.O. Box 779, Mill Valley, CA 94941

JOHN DENVER: P.O. Box 1587, Aspen, CO 81611

NEIL DIAMOND: Friends of Neil Diamond, P.O. Box 3357, Hollywood, CA 90028

EAGLES: c/o Front Line Management, Suite 307, 3830 Melrose Avenue, Los Angeles, CA 90069

EARTH, WIND & FIRE: c/o Kalimba Productions, 9615 Brighton Way, Beverly Hills, CA 90210

ELECTRIC LIGHT ORCHESTRA: c/o Jet Records, 44 Parkside, London SW19 5NB, England

ENGLAND DAN & JOHN FORD COLEY: Fan Club, c/o Janice Schaeffer, 310 N. Raynor, Joliet, IL 60435

DONNA FARGO: Fan Club, P.O. Box 15881, Nashville, TN 37215 Attn: Linda Culp

FLEETWOOD MAC: Fan Club, Box 35916, Los Angeles, CA 90036

FOGHAT: c/o Foghat Productions, P.O. Box 398, Port Jefferson, NY 11777

FOREIGNER: c/o E.S.P. Inc., Attn: Foreigner Fan Club, 1790 Broadway, Penthouse, New York, NY 10019

PETER FRAMPTON: Fan Club, P.O. Box 5400, Grand Central Station, New York, NY 10017

LEIF GARRETT: c/o The Scotti Brothers, 9229 Sunset Blvd., Los Angeles, CA 90069

CRYSTAL GAYLE: Fan Club, Jeff Davidson, P.O. Box 712, Oyster Bay, NY 11771

ANDY GIBB: Fan Club, Factors Etc., Inc., Geissler Park, Bear, DE 19701

HEART: Fan Club, P.O. Box 66524, Seattle, WA 98166

DAN HILL: c/o Finkelstein-Fiedler, 98 Queen Street E., Suite 2B, Toronto, Ont. M5C 1F6, Canada

ENGELBERT HUMPERDINCK: Yolanda Kletecka, President, The Engelettes International Fan Club, P.O. Box 223, Corona, NY 11368

ISLEY BROTHERS: c/o T-Neck Records, 1650 Broadway, Room 1401, New York, NY 10019

JEFFERSON STARSHIP: c/o Grunt Records, 2400 Fulton Street, San Francisco, CA 94118

WAYLON JENNINGS: P.O. Box 11848, Nashville, TN 37211

ELTON JOHN: Fan Club, 211 S. Beverly Drive, Suite 200, Beverly Hills, CA 90212

QUINCY JONES: Mellow Management, 6430 Sunset Blvd., Suite 1210, Los Angeles, CA 90028

JOURNEY: Fan Club, P.O. Box 404, San Francisco, CA

KANSAS: Fan Club, c/o Century Merchandising, 8899 Beverly Blvd., Suite 906, Los Angeles, CA 90048

KISS: Kiss Army, 7949 Deering, Canoga Park, CA 91304

L.T.D: Fan Club, 6367 West 6th Street, Los Angeles, CA 90048

LORETTA LYNN: Fan Club, P.O. Box 177, Wild Horse, CO 80862

BARRY MANILOW: Fan Club, c/o Kate Naughton, P.O. Box 967, Radio City Station, New York, NY 10019

MARSHALL TUCKER BAND: Marshall Tucker Band, 300 East Henry Street, Spartanburg, SC 29302

JOHNNY MATHIS: International Fan Club, P.O. Box 69278, Los Angeles, CA 90069

PAUL McCARTNEY & WINGS: Fun Club, P.O. Box 4UP, London W1A 4UP, England

STEVE MILLER: Fan Club, P.O. Box 25883, West Los Angeles, CA 90025

RONNIE MILSAP: Fan Club, P.O. Box 23109, Nashville, TN 37202

EDDIE MONEY: c/o Winterland Productions, 890 Tennessee Street, San Francisco, CA 94107

MOODY BLUES: Fan Club, c/o Threshhold Records, 53-55 High Street, Cobham, Surrey KT2 3DP, England

ANNE MURRAY: Fan Club, P.O. Box 1069, Radio City Station, New York, NY 10019

WILLIE NELSON: Fan Club, Route 6, Box 95-A, Austin, TX 78746

OLIVIA NEWTON-JOHN: United Fan Mail, P.O. Box 1432, Beverly Hills, CA 90210

TED NUGENT: Fan Club, c/o The Wherehouse, 55 Pond Street, Waltham, MA 02154

DONNY & MARIE OSMOND: Fan Club, Box 5000, Provo, UT 84601

PARLIAMENT: Maggatropolis, c/o Sancctum, 109 Hollywood Avenue, Oxnard, CA 93030

DOLLY PARTON: Dolly Parton Enterprises, 811-18th Avenue S., Nashville, TN 37203 Attn: Cassie

TEDDY PENDERGRASS: Teddy Bear Fan Club, 215 S. Broad Street, Suite 302, Philadelphia, PA 19107

QUEEN: International Fan Club, 40 South Audley Street, London W1, England

EDDIE RABBITT: c/o The Scotti Brothers, 9229 Sunset Blvd., Los Angeles, CA 90069

LOU RAWLS: P.O. Box 4475, N. Hollywood, CA 91607

HELEN REDDY: Fan Club, c/o Jim Keaton, 932 S. Buchanan Street, #2, Arlington, VA 22204

REO SPEEDWAGON: Fan Club, 6516 Post Oak Drive, West Bloomfield, MI 48033

MARTY ROBBINS: Fan Club, c/o Peggy Ann Munson, 3811 Wylly Avenue, Brunswick, GA 31520

KENNY ROGERS: Fan Club, 9744 Wilshire Blvd., Los Angeles, CA 90212

ROSE ROYCE: P.O. Box 7487, Burbank, CA 91510

DIANA ROSS: VIP, 9157 Sunset Blvd., Los Angeles, CA 90069 Attn: Larry Kleno

BOZ SCAGGS: c/o Front Line Management, Suite 307, 3830 Melrose Avenue, Los Angeles, CA 90069

SHA NA NA: Sha Na Na Fan Mail, Lexington Broadcasting Co., 800 Third Avenue, New York, NY 10022

FRANK SINATRA: Fan Club, c/o Solters & Roskin, 62 West 45th Street, New York, NY 10036

PATTI SMITH: Fan Club, c/o Nana Lee Berry, Box 673, Richland Center, WI 53581

STATLER BROTHERS: P.O. Box 2703, Staunton, VA 24401

BARBRA STREISAND: Fan Club, c/o CBS Records, 51 West 52nd Street, New York, NY 10019

STYX: Fan Club, P.O. Box 27091, Los Feliz Station, Los Angeles, CA 90027

MEL TILLIS: Fan Club, P.O. Box 12146, Nashville, TN 37212

JOHN TRAVOLTA: c/o CMC, 8899 Beverly Blvd., Suite 906, Los Angeles, CA 90048

CONWAY TWITTY: Fan Club, c/o Edith Ridge, Geff, IL 62842

JOE WALSH: c/o Front Line Management, Suite 307, 3830 Melrose Avenue, Los Angeles, CA 90069

DOTTIE WEST: Fan Club, Betty Lewis, President, P.O. Box 10547, Houston, TX 77018

DENIECE WILLIAMS: c/o Kalimba Productions, 9615 Brighton Way, Beverly Hills, CA 90210

DON WILLIAMS: Fan Club, c/o Pauline Cochran, 95 Pinehurst Drive, Hazelville, GA 30354

STEVIE WONDER: Stevie Wonder's Universal Family, P.O. Box 1091, Radio City Station, New York, NY 10019

VAN HALEN: Van Halen Merchandising & Fan Club, P.O. Box 2128, N. Hollywood, CA 91602

Music Publications

AMERICAN FIDDLERS NEWS
American Old Time Fiddlers Assn.
6141 Morrill Ave.
Lincoln, NB 68507

AMERICAN RECORD GUILD
ARG Publishing, Inc.
1 Windsor Pl.
Melville, NY 11746

AQUARIAN
#1 The Crescent
Montclair, NJ 07042

BEST OF POPULAR MUSIC
Heritage Music Press
501 E. 3rd St.
Dayton, OH 45401

BILLBOARD
Billboard Publications, Inc.
9000 Sunset Blvd.
Los Angeles, CA 90069

BING
International Crosby Circle
c/o Reg Bristo
7 Greenmeadow Close
Cwmbran, Gwent NP4 3NR
England

BLACK MUSIC
IPC Specialist & Professional
Press, Ltd.
Surrey House
1 Throwley Way
Sutton, Surrey SM1 4qQ
England

BLUEGRASS UNLIMITED
Bluegrass Unlimited Inc.
Box 111
Broad Run, VA 22014

BLUES & SOUL MUSIC REVIEW
Contempo International, Ltd.
42 Hanway St.
London W.1
England

BOOGIE
221 Venetian Ave.
Gulfport, MI 39501

BRASS BAND REVIEW
17 Wimbledon Close
The Downs
London S.W.20
England

CARIBBEAT
Quad Publications
159 W. 33rd St.
Room 1010
New York, NY 10001

CASH BOX
Cash Box Publishing Co., Inc.
6363 Sunset Blvd.
Suite 930
Los Angeles, CA 90028

CIRCUS MAGAZINE
115 East 57th St.
New York, NY 10022

CLAVIER
Instrumentalist Co.
1418 Lake St.
Evanston, IL 60204

CONCERT NEWS
118 No. 18th St.
St. Louis, MO 63103

CONTEMPORARY KEYBOARD
G.P.I. Corporation
Keyboard Players International
P.O. Box 615
Saratoga, CA 95070

COUNTRY MUSIC MAGAZINE
475 Park Ave. South
Suite 1102
New York, NY 10022

COUNTRY MUSIC PEOPLE
Country Music Press, Ltd.
Powerscroft Rd.
Footscray, Sidcup
Kent
England

COUNTRY SONG ROUNDUP
Charlton Publications, Inc.
Charlton Bldg.
Derby, CT 06418

COUNTRY STYLE
Country Style Publications Co., Inc.
11058 W. Addison St.
Franklin Park, IL 60103

CRAWDADDY
Crawdaddy Publishing Co., Inc.
72 Fifth Ave.
New York, NY 10011

CREATIVE WORLD
Stan Kenton's Creative World
1012 S. Robertson Blvd.
Box 35216
Los Angeles, CA 90035

CREEM
187 S. Woodward Ave.
Birmingham, MI 48011

CRESCENDO
Interlochen Arts Academy
National Music Camp
Interlochen, MI 49643

CRESCENDO INTERNATIONAL
Crescendo Publications, Ltd.
122 Wardour St.
London W.1
England

CUE
545 Madison Ave.
New York, NY 10022

DIFFERENT DRUMMER
BOAPW, Ltd.
Box 136
Rochester, NY 14601

DISC AND THAT
Pruit-Scott Publications
P.O. Box 228
Kingsbridge Station
Bronx, NY 10463

DISCO INTERNATIONAL
37 Foley St.
London W.1
England

DISCOTHEKIN MAGAZINE INC.
111 8th Ave.
New York, NY 10011

DISCO WORLD
6 Cottage Place
White Plains, NY

DOWN BEAT
Maher Publications, Inc.
222 W. Adams St.
Chicago, IL 60606

DRUM CORPS NEWS
Drum Corps News, Inc.
P.O. Box 146
Revere, MA 02151

ELVIS MONTHLY
Albert Hand Publications, Ltd.
41-43 Derby Rd.
Heanor
Derbyshire
England

ENGLISH DANCE AND SONG
English Folk Dance and Song
Society
Cecil Sharp House
2 Regents Park Rd.
London N.W.1 7AY
England

ENTERTAINMENT SPECTRUM
79 Thomas St.
Bloomfield, NJ 07003

FLAG; THE MUSIC SCENE
P.B. Enterprises
310 Evesham Rd.
Glendora, NJ 08029

FOCUS
739 South James Road
Columbus, OH 43227

GESTURE
Box 1079
Northland Center
Southfield, MI 48075

GILBERT AND SULLIVAN
JOURNAL
Sullivan Society
23 Burnside
Sawbridge, Herts CM21 OEP
England

GOOD NEWS
Gospel News Association
P.O. Box 1201
816 19th Ave.
South Nashville, TN 37202

GUITAR PLAYER
Guitar Players International
P.O. Box 615
Sarasota, CA 95070

GUITAR REVIEW
Society of the Classic Guitar
409 E. 50th St.
New York, NY 10022

HARMONIZER
Society for the Preservation and
Encouragement of Barber Shop
Singing in America, Inc.
6315 Third Ave.
Kenosha, WI 53141

HI-FI STEREO BUYERS GUIDE
Davis Publications, Inc.
229 Park Ave. South
New York, NY 10003

HIGH FIDELITY
ABC Leisure Magazine, Inc.
130 E. 59th St.
New York, NY 10022

HIT PARADER
Charlton Publications, Inc.
Charlton Bldg.
Derby, CT 06418

HOT NOTES
New York Jazz Museum
125 W. 55th St.
New York, NY 10019

JAZZ TIMES
British Jazz Society
10 Southfield Gardens
Twickenham
Middlesex
England

LIVING BLUES
Living Blues Publications
Box 11303
Chicago, IL 60611

MELODY MAKER
IPC Specialist and Professional
Press, Ltd.
Surrey House
1 Throwley Way
Sutton, Surrey SM1 4qQ
England

MODERN RECORDING
Cowan Publishing Corp.
14 Vanderventer Ave.
Port Washington, NY 11050

MUGWUMPS' INSTRUMENT
HERALD: The magazine of folk
instruments
12704 Barbara Rd.
Silver Spring, MD 20906

MULESKINNER NEWS
Carlton Haney Publications
Rt. 2, Box 304
Elon College, NC 27244

MUSIC: the AGO and RCCO
magazine
American Guild of Organists
630 Fifth Ave., Suite 2010
New York, NY 10020

MUSIC AND MUSICIANS
Hansom Books
Artillery Mansions
75 Victoria St.
London S.W.1H OHZ
England

MUSIC CITY NEWS
Music City News Publishing
Co., Inc.
Box 22975
1302 Division St.
Nashville, TN 37202

MUSIC EDUCATORS JOURNAL
(Institutional subscriptions only)
Music Educators National
Conference
Center for Educational
Associations
1902 Association Drive
Reston, VA 22090

MUSIC GIG
Gig Enterprises, Inc.
415 Lexington Ave.
New York, NY 10017

MUSIC JOURNAL
Music Journal, Inc.
20 Hampton Rd.
Southampton, NY 11968

MUSIC WEEK
Morgan Grampian, Ltd.
30 Calderwood St.
Woolwich, London S.E.18 6QH
England

MUSICAL OPINION
Musical Opinion, Ltd.
3-11 Spring Rd.
Bournemouth, Dorset BH1 4QA
England

MUSICAL PRODUCT NEWS &
MUSICAL ELECTRONICS
Sound Publishing Co., Inc.
156 E. 37th St.
New York, NY 10016

MUSICAL TIMES
Novello and Co., Ltd.
1-3 Upper James St.
London W.1R 4BP
England

MUSICIAN'S GUIDE
Musician's Guide Publications
739 Boylston St.
Boston, MA 02116

NEW MUSICAL EXPRESS
IPC Magazines, Ltd.
Third Floor
5-7 Carnaby St.
London W.1V 1PG
England

NEW RECORDS
H. Royer Smith Co.
2019 Walnut St.
Philadelphia, PA 19103

OKLAHOMA BLUEGRASS
GAZETTE
Oklahoma Bluegrass Club, Inc.
419 N. Beard
Shawnee, OK 74801

OLD TIME MUSIC
c/o Tony Russell, Ed.
33 Brunswick Gardens
London W.8 4AW
England

OPERA
Seymour Press, Ltd.
334 Brixton Rd.
London S.W.9
England

OPERA NEWS
Metropolitan Opera Guild, Inc.
1865 Broadway
New York, NY 10023

ORGANIST
Bill Worrall Productions
Box 4399
Downey, CA 90241

PERFORMANCE MAGAZINE
Suite 308
1216 Pennsylvania Ave.
Ft. Worth, TX

PIANO QUARTERLY
Piano Quarterly, Inc.
Box 815
Wilmington, VT 05363

PICKIN'
Universal Graphics Corp.
46 Ford Rd.
Denville, NJ 07834

POLYPHONY
PAIA Electronics, Inc.
1020 West Wilshire Blvd.
Oklahoma City, OK 73116

POP TOP
Little Face, Inc.
909 Beacon St.
Boston, MA 02215

POPULAR MUSIC & SOCIETY
Bowling Green State University
Department of Sociology
Bowling Green, OH 43403

R and B Magazine
Pea Vine Music Co.
18632 Nordhoff St.
Northridge, CA 91324

RADIO FREE JAZZ
Sabin's Discount Records
3212 Penn. Ave. S.E.
Washington, DC 20020

RECORD EXCHANGER
Vintage Records
Box 2144
Anaheim, CA 91804

RECORD MIRROR
Morgan-Grampian, Ltd.
40 Longacre
London WC2E 9JT
England

RECORD RESEARCH
65 Grand Ave.
Brooklyn, NY 11205

RECORD WORLD
Record World Publishing Co., Inc.
1700 Broadway
New York, NY 10019

ROCK
257 Park Ave. South
New York, NY 10010

ROCK AND SOUL SONGS
Charlton Publications, Inc.
Charlton Bldg.
Derby, CT 06418

ROCK AROUND THE WORLD
1108 Boylston St.
Boston, MA 02215

ROCK SCENE
Four Seasons Publications
Fairwood Road
Bethany, CT 06525

ROLLING STONE
Straight Arrow Publishers
745 Fifth Ave.
New York, NY 10022

SCENE
1314 Huron Road
Cleveland, OH 44115

SHOUT
Clive Richardson, Ed.
46 Slades Dr.
Chislehurst, Kent BR7 6JX
England

SING OUT
Sing Out, Inc.
270 Lafayette St.
New York, NY 10013

SINGING NEWS
2611 W. Cervantes
P.O. Box 5188
Pensacola, FL 32505

SONG HITS
Charlton Publications, Inc.
Charlton Blvd.
Derby, CT 06418

SOUL SOUNDS
1133 Broadway
Rm. 1625
New York, NY 10010

SOUNDS
40 Longacre
London W.C2E 9JT
England

STEREO REVIEW
Ziff-Davis Publishing Co.
1 Park Ave.
New York, NY 10016

SYMPHONY NEWS
American Symphony Orchestra
League
Symphony Hill, P.O. Box 669
Vienna, VA 22180

TIME BARRIER EXPRESS
Time Barrier Enterprises, Inc.
Box 1109
White Plains, NY 10602

VARIETY
154 W. 46th St.
New York, NY 10036

THE VILLAGE VOICE
80 University Place
New York, NY 10003

WHO PUT THE BOMP
P.O. Box 7112
Burbank, CA 91510

Record Companies

- ABC Records, 8255 Beverly Blvd., Los Angeles, CA 90048.
  - *Labels*
  - *Owns:* ABC, ABC–Audio-Treasury, ABC–Backbeat, ABC–Blue Thumb, ABC–Command, ABC–Dot, ABC–Duke, ABC–Dunhill, ABC–Hot Buttered Soul, ABC–Impulse, ABC–Paramount, ABC–Peacock, ABC–Songbird, ABC–Westminster, ABC–Westminster Grand Award.
  - *Distributes:* Anchor, Shelter, Hickory.
- A & M Records, Inc., 1416 N. La Brea Ave., Hollywood, CA 90028.
  - *Labels*
  - *Owns:* A & M, Horizon.
- AVI Records, 9220 Sunset Blvd., Los Angeles, CA 90069.
- Abkco Records, Inc., 1700 Broadway, New York, NY 10019.
- Accent Records, 6533 Hollywood Blvd., Hollywood, CA
  - *Owns:* Accent (distributed by GNP Crescendo), New Sound.
  - *Distributes:* In Sound.
- Anchor, see ABC.
- Angel, see Capitol.
- Apple, see Capitol.
- Archive, see Polydor.
- Ariola America, Inc., 8671 Wilshire Blvd., Beverly Hills, CA 90211.
  - *Labels*
  - *Owns:* Ariola.
- Arista Records, Inc., 6 W. 57 St., New York, NY 10019.
  - *Labels*
  - *Owns:* Arista, Savoy.
  - *Distributes:* Haven, Morning Sky, Buddah, Kama Sutra, Celebration, Desert Moon, Pi Kappa, Wynner.
- Asch, see Folkways, Stiff.
- Asylum, see Elektra/Asylum/Nonesuch.
- Atco, see Atlantic.

- Atlantic Recording Corp., 75 Rockefeller Plaza, New York, NY 10019.
  - *Labels*
  - *Owns:* Atco, Atlantic, Cotillion.
  - *Distributes:* Big Tree, Finnadar, Little David, Rolling Stones, Swan Song, Wing & a Prayer.
- Bang/Bullet Records, 2107 Faulkner Rd. NE, Atlanta, GA 30324.
  - *Labels*
  - *Owns:* Bang, Bullet, Shout, Solid Gold.
- Barnaby Records, 816 N. La Cienega Blvd., Los Angeles, CA 90069.
  - *Distributed by:* Janus.
- Bearsville Records, Inc., 75 E. 55th St., New York, NY 10022.
  - *Distributed by:* Warner Brothers.
- Beserkeley Records, 1199 Spruce St., Berkeley, CA 94707.
  - *Distributed by:* GRT.
- Big Tree Enterprises, Ltd., 75 Rockefeller Plaza, New York, NY 10019.
  - *Distributed by:* Atlantic.
- Biograph Records, Inc., 16 River St., Chatham, NY 12037.
  - *Labels*
  - *Owns:* Biograph, Center, Melodeon.
- Black Forum, see Motown.
- Bluebird (New York, NY), see RCA.
- Blue Candle, see TK Productions.
- Blue Horizon, see Sire.
- Blue Sky Records, Inc., 745 Fifth Ave., Suite 1803, New York, NY 10022.
  - *Distributed by:* CBS.
- Blues Time, see RCA.
- Broadsides, see Folkways.
- Brother Records, Inc., 3621 Sepulveda Blvd., Suite 3, Manhattan Beach, CA 90266.
  - *Distributed by:* Warner Brothers.
- Buddah/Kama Sutra Records, Inc., 810 Seventh Ave., New York, NY 10019.
  - *Labels*
  - *Owns:* Buddah, Kama Sutra.
- Bullet, see Bang/Bullet.

- Butterfly Records, 8833 Sunset Blvd., Los Angeles, CA 90069.
- CBS Records, 51 W. 52 St., New York, NY 10019.
  Labels
  Owns: CBS, Columbia, Epic, Columbia/Melodiya Odyssey, Portrait, ARC-Columbia.
  Distributes: Blue Sky, Caribou, Full Moon, Jet, Kirshner, Lifesong, Nemperor, Ode, Philadelphia Int'l, Playboy, Virgin, Tabu, T-Neck, Unlimited Gold.
- CBS Records, Int'l (division of CBS Inc.), 51 W. 52 St., New York, NY 10019.
- CTI, see Motown and Creed Taylor.
- Caedmon, 505 Eighth Ave., New York, NY 10018.
- Camden, see RCA.
- Capitol Records, Inc., 1750 N. Vine St., Hollywood, CA 90028.
  Labels
  Owns: Angel, Capitol, EMI, EMI America, Melodiya/Angel, Seraphim.
  Distributes: Apple, Ariola America, Harvest.
- Capricorn Records, Inc., 535 Cotton Ave., Macon, GA 31208.
  Distributed by: Polygram Distribution Corp.
- Cardinal, see Vanguard.
- Caribou Records, 8500 Melrose Ave., Los Angeles, CA 90069.
  Distributed by: CBS.
- Casablanca Record and Film Works, Inc., 8255 Sunset Blvd., Los Angeles, CA 90046.
  Labels
  Owns: Casablanca.
  Distributes: Chocolate City, Oasis, Millennium, Parachute.
  Distributed by: Polygram Distribution Corporation.
- Chimneyville, see Malaco and TK Productions.
- Chi-Sound, see United Artists.
- Chocolate City, see Casablanca.
- Chrysalis Records, Inc., 9255 Sunset Blvd., Suite 212, Los Angeles, CA 90069.
- Classic Jazz, see Music Minus One.
- CMH Records, Inc., P.O. Box 39439, Los Angeles, CA 90039.
- Columbia, see CBS.
- Columbia Special Products, 51 W 52 St., New York, NY 10019.
  Labels
  Owns: Collector's Series.
- Connoisseur Society, Inc., 390 West End Ave., New York, NY 10024.

- *Labels*
  Owns: Connoisseur.
- Coral, see MCA.
- Cotillion, see Atlantic.
- Cream Records, Inc., 8025 Melrose Ave., Los Angeles, CA 90046.
- Curtom Records, Inc., 5915 N. Lincoln Ave., Chicago, IL 60659.
  Labels
  Owns: Curtom, Gemigo.
  Distributed by: Warner Brothers.
- D G (Deutsche Grammophon), see Polydor.
- Dade, see TK Productions.
- Dark Horse, see Warner Brothers.
- Dash, see TK Productions.
- De-Lite Recording Sound Corp., 200 W. 57 St., New York, NY 10019.
  Labels
  Owns: De-Lite.
  Distributes: Gang, Vigor.
- Deutsche Grammophon, see Polydor.
- Dial, see Phonogram.
- Disc-Reet, 5831 Sunset Blvd., Hollywood, CA 90028
- Dixieland Jubilee, see GNP Crescendo.
- Drive, see TK Productions.
- ECM, See Warner Bros.
- EMI, see Capitol.
- EMI America, see Capitol.
- ESP-Disk, Ltd., 5 Riverside Dr., Krumville, NY 12447.
  Label
  Owns: ESP.
- Elektra/Asylum/Nonesuch Records, 962 N. La Cienega, Los Angeles, CA 90069.
  Labels
  Owns: Asylum, Elektra, Nonesuch, Slipped Disc.
- Epic, see CBS.
- Erato, see RCA.
- Everyman Classics, see Vanguard.
- Fantasy/Prestige/Milestone Records, 10 and Parker Sts., Berkeley, CA 94710.
  Labels
  Owns: Fantasy, Milestone, Prestige.
  Distributes: Stax.
- Finnadar, see Atlantic.
- Flying Dutchman Productions, Ltd., 1133 Ave. of the Americas, New York, NY 10012.
  Labels
  Owns: Flying Dutchman, Signature.

- Folkways Records, 43 W. 61 St., New York, NY 10023.
  - *Labels*
  - *Owns:* Asch, Broadsides, Folkways, RBF.
- Fontana, see Phonogram.
- Full Moon, see CBS.
- GNP Crescendo Records, 9165 Sunset Blvd., Los Angeles, CA 90069.
  - *Labels*
  - *Owns:* GNP Crescendo, Dixieland Jubilee, Largo.
  - *Distributes:* Accent.
- Gang, see De-Lite and Pickwick—PIP.
- Gateway Records, 17 E. 48 St., New York, NY 10017.
- Glades, see TK Productions.
- Gold Seal, see RCA.
- Gordy, see Motown.
- GRS Record Co., 1236 India St., Tampa, FL 33602.
  - *Labels*
  - *Owns:* GRS, Fareback, Headphones.
- GRT Records, 1226 16 Ave. S., Nashville, TN 37212.
  - *Labels*
  - *Owns:* Beserkeley, Janus, Ranwood.
- Grunt, see RCA.
- Happy Time, see Pickwick.
- Harvest, see Capitol.
- Hi, see Cream.
- Hickory, see ABC.
- Hilltop, see Pickwick.
- Historical Anthology of Music, see Vanguard.
- Inner City, see Music Minus One.
- Island Records, Inc., 7720 Sunset Blvd., Los Angeles, CA 90046.
  - *Labels*
  - *Owns:* Antilles, Island, Mango.
  - *Distributes:* Pacific Arts, True North.
  - *Distributed by:* Warner Brothers.
- Janus Records (division of GRT Records), 8776 Sunset Blvd., Los Angeles, CA 90069.
  - *Labels*
  - *Owns:* Janus, Shock.
  - *Distributes:* Barnaby, Happy Fox.
- Jet, see CBS.
- Juana, see TK Productions.
- Kama Sutra, see Buddah/Kama Sutra.
- Kayvette, see TK Productions.
- Kirshner Entertainment Corp., 1370 Ave. of the Americas, New York, NY 10019.
  - *Distributed by:* CBS.
- Kudu, see Motown and Creed Taylor.

- Laurie Records, 20 F. Robert Pitt Dr., Monsey, NY 10952.
- Limelight, see Phonogram.
- Little David Records Co., Inc., 8921 Sunset Blvd., Los Angeles, CA 90069.
  - *Distributed by:* Atlantic.
- London Records, Inc., 539 W. 25 St., New York, NY 10001.
  - *Labels*
  - *Owns:* London, Parrot, Phase 4, Richmond Opera Series, Deram.
  - *Distributes:* Argo, Buk, Das Alte, Threshold, Werk, L'Oiseau-Lyre, Telefunken.
- Lotta, see TK Productions.
- MCA Records, Inc., 100 Universal City Plaza, Universal City, CA 91608.
  - *Labels*
  - *Owns:* Coral, MCA.
  - *Distributes:* Goldhawke, Midsong, Tally.
- MGM, see Polydor.
- Malaco, Inc., 3023 W. Northside Dr., Jackson, MS 39213.
  - *Labels*
  - *Owns:* Chimneyville, Malaco.
  - *Distributed by:* TK Productions.
- Mango, see Island.
- Marlin, see TK Productions.
- Melodiya/Angel, see Capitol.
- Melodiya/Columbia, see CBS.
- Mercury, see Phonogram.
- Midland Int'l. Records, Inc., 1650 Broadway, New York, NY 10019.
  - *Distributed by:* MCA.
- Milestone, see Fantasy/Prestige/Milestone.
- Mr. Pickwick, see Pickwick.
- Monument Record Corp., 21 Music Square E., Nashville, TN 37203.
  - *Labels*
  - *Owns:* Monument, Sound Stage 7.
  - *Distributed by:* Phonogram.
- Morning Sky Records, 9128 Sunset Blvd., Los Angeles, CA 90069.
  - *Distributed by:* Arista.
- Motown Record Corp., 6255 Sunset Blvd., Hollywood, CA 90028.
  - *Labels*
  - *Owns:* Black Forum, Gordy, Hitsville, Motown, Mowest, Prodigal, Rare Earth, Soul, Tamla.
  - *Distributes:* Salvation.
- Mowest, see Motown.

- Music Minus One, 43 W. 61 St., New York, NY 10023.

  Labels

  Owns: Classic Jazz, Inner City, Music Minus One (MMO), Guitar World, Proscenium.
- Nemperor, see CBS.
- Nonesuch, see Elektra/Asylum/Nonesuch.
- Oasis (CA), see Casablanca.
- Ode Records, Inc., 1416 N. La Brea, Hollywood, CA 90028.

  Distributed by: CBS.
- Odyssey, see CBS.
- Oyster, see Polydor.
- Pablo Records, 451 N. Canon Dr., Beverly Hills, CA 90210.

  Distributed by: RCA.
- Paradise, see Warner Brothers.
- Phase 4, see London.
- Philadelphia Int'l. Records, 309 S. Broad St., Philadelphia, PA 19107.

  Labels

  Owns: Philadelphia Int'l., TSOP.

  Distributed by: CBS.
- Philips, see Phonogram.
- Phonogram, Inc./Mercury Records (subdivision of Polygram Corp.), 1 IBM Plaza, Chicago, IL 60611.

  Labels

  Owns: Fontana, Limelight, Mercury, Philips, Smash.

  Distributes: De-Lite, Dial, UK, Vertigo, Monument, Sound Stage 7.
- Pickwick Int'l. USA, 7500 Excelsior Blvd., Minneapolis, MN 55426.

  Labels

  Owns: Happy Time, Hilltop, Mr. Pickwick, Pickwick, Playhour, Showcase, Soul Parade.

  Distributes: Another Record Co.

  PIP Division:

  Owns: PIP.

  Distributes: Gang, Vigor.
- Playboy Records, Inc., 8560 Sunset Blvd., Los Angeles, CA 90069.

  Labels

  Owns: Playboy.

  Distributed by: CBS Records.
- Playhour, see Pickwick.
- Polydor, Inc., 810 Seventh Ave., New York, NY 10019.

  Labels

  Owns: Archive, DG (Deutsche Grammophon),

  MGM, Polydor, Polydor/Kolob, Verve.

  Distributes: Oyster, Spring.
- Prestige, see Fantasy/Prestige/Milestone.
- Private Stock Records, Ltd., 40 W. 57 St., New York, NY 10019.

  Labels

  Owns: Private Stock.
- Proscenium, see Music Minus One.
- RCA Records, 1133 Ave. of the Americas, New York, NY 10036.

  Labels

  Owns: Bluebird, Gold Seal, RCA, Red Seal, Sixth Avenue, Victrola.

  Distributes: Dream, Erato, Gold Mind, Grunt, Pablo, Soul Train, Rocket, Tattoo, Tom N' Jerry, Windsong, Salsoul.
- RSO Records and Tapes, Inc., 9200 Sunset Blvd., Los Angeles, CA 90069.

  Distributed by: Polygram Distr. Corp.
- Ranwood, see GRT.
- Rare Earth, see Motown.
- Red Seal, see RCA.
- Reprise, see Warner Brothers.
- Richmond Opera Series, see London.
- The Rocket Record Co., 211 S. Beverly Dr., Beverly Hills, CA 90212.

  Distributed by: RCA.
- Rolling Stones, see Atlantic.
- SPEBSQSA (Society for the Preservation and Encouragement of Barber Shop Quartet Singing in America, Inc.), 6315 Third Ave., Kenosha, WI 53141.
- Salsoul, see RCA.
- Salvation, see Motown and Creed Taylor (Partial catalog).
- Seraphim, see Capitol.
- Shelby Singleton Corp., 3106 Belmont Blvd., Nashville, TN 37212.

  Labels

  Owns: Midnight Sun, Plantation, SSS Int'l., Sun.
- Shield, see TK Productions.
- Shout, see Bang/Bullet.
- Showcase, see Pickwick.
- Silver Blue Records, 401 E. 74 St., New York, NY 10021.

  Distributed by: TK Productions.
- Sire Records, Inc., 165 W. 74 St., New York, NY 10023.

  Labels

  Owns: Blue Horizon, Sire.

Distributed by: Warner Brothers.
- Solid Gold, see Bang/Bullet.
- Soul, see Motown.
- Soul Parade, see Pickwick.
- Soul Train Records (division of Cornelius-Giffey Entertainment Co.), 9200 Sunset Blvd., Penthouse 15, Los Angeles, CA 90069.
    Distributed by: RCA.
- Sound Stage 7, see Monument.
- Spring, see Polydor.
- Stone Dogg, see TK Productions.
- Swan Song, see Atlantic.
- TK Productions, Inc., 495 SE 10 Court, Hialeah, FL 33010.
    Labels
    Owns: Alston, Blue Candle, Cat, Dade, Dash, Drive, Glades, Marlin, Stone Dogg, TK, Weird World.
    Distributes: Chimneyville, Juana, Kayvette, Lotta, Malaco, Shield, Silver Blue, Wicked, Wolf.
- T-Neck, see CBS.
- TSOP, see Philadelphia Int'l. and CBS.
- Tabu, see CBS.
- Tamla, see Motown.
- Tattoo Records, 9454 Wilshire Blvd., Suite 309, Beverly Hills, CA 90212.
    Distributed by: RCA.
- Creed Taylor, Inc., 1 Rockefeller Plaza, New York, NY 10020.
    Labels
    Owns: CTI, Kudu, Salvation, Three Brothers.
- Three Brothers, see Motown and Creed Taylor.
- Threshold, see London.
- 20th Century Records, 8544 Sunset Blvd., Los Angeles, CA 90069.
    Labels
    Owns: 20th Century.
    Distributes: Westbound.
- UK, see Phonogram.
- United Artists Records of America, 6920 Sunset Blvd., Los Angeles, CA 90028.
    Labels
    Owns: Blue Note, Liberty, United Artists.
    Distributes: Chi-Sound.
- Unlimited Gold, see CBS.
- Utopia, see RCA.
- Vanguard Recording Society, Inc., 71 W. 23 St., New York, NY 10010.
    Labels
    Owns: Bach Guild, Cardinal, Everyman Classics,

Historical Anthology of Music, Vanguard.
- Vertigo, see Phonogram.
- Victrola, see RCA.
- Vigor, see De-Lite and Pickwick—PIP.
- Virgin, see CBS.
- WEA Int'l., Inc., 75 Rockefeller Plaza, New York, NY 10019.
    Labels
    See Warner Brothers, Elektra, and Atlantic.
- Warner Brothers Records, Inc., 3300 Warner Blvd., Burbank, CA 91510.
    Labels
    Owns: Reprise, Warner Brothers.
    Distributes: Bearsville, Brother, Curtom, Dark Horse, Disc-Reet, ECM, Island, Paradise, Sire, Warner Curb, Warner Spector, Whitfield.
- Warner Curb, see Warner Brothers.
- Warner Spector, see Warner Brothers.
- Weird World, see TK Productions.
- Whitfield, see Warner Brothers.
- Windsong, see RCA.
- Wing & a Prayer, see Atlantic.
- Wolf, see TK Productions.

Index